ANNUAL EDITIONS

United States History

Volume 2—Through the Present Reconstruction

Twenty-First Edition

EDITOR

Robert James Maddox (Emeritus)
Pennsylvania State University
University Park

Robert James Maddox, distinguished historian and professor emeritus of American history at Pennsylvania State University, received a BS from Fairleigh Dickinson University in 1957, an MS from the University of Wisconsin in 1958, and a PhD from Rutgers in 1964. He has written, reviewed, and lectured extensively, and is widely respected for his interpretations of presidential character and policy.

Mc Graw Hill

Connect Learn Succeed™

ANNUAL EDITIONS: UNITED STATES HISTORY, VOLUME 2, TWENTY-FIRST EDITION

1 2 3 4 5 6 7 8 9 0 QDB/QDB 1 0 9 8 7 6 5 4 3 2 1 0

ISBN: 978–0–07–805074–9
MHID: 0–07–805074–X
ISSN: 0733–3560

Managing Editor: *Larry Loeppke*
Senior Developmental Editor: *Debra A. Henricks*
Senior Permissions Coordinator: *Shirley Lanners*
Marketing Specialist: *Alice Link*
Project Manager: *Robin A. Reed*
Design Coordinator: *Margarite Reynolds*
Cover Graphics: *Kristine Jubeck*
Buyer: *Laura Fuller*
Media Project Manager: *Sridevi Palani*

Compositor: Laserwords Private Limited
Cover Image: Library of Congress, Prints and Photographs Division [LC-USF34-9058-C (inset);
© H. Wiesenhofer/PhotoLink/Getty Images (background)

Library in Congress Cataloging-in-Publication Data
Main entry under title: United States History. Vol. 2: Reconstruction Through the Present. 21/e.
  1. United States—History—Periodicals. 2. United States—Historiography—Periodicals. 3. United States—Civilization—Periodicals. I. 1. Maddox, Robert James, *comp*. II. Title: United States History.
Vol. 2: Reconstruction Through the Present
658'.05

Editors/Academic Advisory Board

Members of the Academic Advisory Board are instrumental in the final selection of articles for each edition of ANNUAL EDITIONS. Their review of articles for content, level, and appropriateness provides critical direction to the editors and staff. We think that you will find their careful consideration well reflected in this volume.

ANNUAL EDITIONS: United States History, Volume 2
21st Edition

EDITOR

Robert James Maddox (Emeritus)
Pennsylvania State University
University Park

ACADEMIC ADVISORY BOARD MEMBERS

Preface

In publishing ANNUAL EDITIONS we recognize the enormous role played by the magazines, newspapers, and journals of the public press in providing current, first-rate educational information in a broad spectrum of interest areas. Many of these articles are appropriate for students, researchers, and professionals seeking accurate, current material to help bridge the gap between principles and theories and the real world. These articles, however, become more useful for study when those of lasting value are carefully collected, organized, indexed, and reproduced in a low-cost format, which provides easy and permanent access when the material is needed. That is the role played by ANNUAL EDITIONS.

This volume covers the 155 years between the end of the Civil War and the present. The United States at the start of the period was a very different world from the one we live in today. Revolutionary changes have taken place in virtually every area. Following the development of automobiles, people were able to travel in hours distances that would have previously taken days. Airplanes have put any place on the globe within reach. Radio, television, and computers have vastly changed the transmission of knowledge, earlier restricted to word of mouth or the printed page. Still, many of the problems we face today have echoes in the past: race relations, gender roles, domestic terrorism, and environmental problems to name just a few. At least one new epidemic—AIDS—has become a scourge just as smallpox once was. We can all profit from the study of history, not to get solutions for specific problems, but to discover in the past some guidelines for our own time.

The study of history has changed over the years. Someone once said that historians wrote about "chaps," meaning white males who enjoyed positions of power or influence. Older history books tended to concentrate on presidents, titans of industry or finance, and military leaders. Women usually were mentioned only in passing, and then primarily as the wives or lovers of important men. Minority groups were treated, if at all, as passive objects of social customs or legislation. Mention of sexual orientation was simply out of the question.

Now virtually everything that has happened is considered fit for study. Books and articles tell us about the lives of ordinary people, about groups previously ignored or mentioned only in passing, and about subjects considered too trivial or commonplace to warrant examination. History "from the bottom up," once considered innovative, has become commonplace. Welcome as these innovations are, they often are encumbered by two unfortunate tendencies: many are freighted down with incomprehensible prose, and many are produced to advance agendas the authors try to fob off as scholarship.

Traditional history is still being written. For better or worse, there *have* been men and women who have exercised great power or influence over the lives and deaths of others. They continue to fascinate. Presidents such as Woodrow Wilson and Franklin D. Roosevelt had to make decisions that affected enormous numbers of people at home and abroad. The Wright brothers opened a new era in human history with their invention of a practical airplane. And the relatively unknown Belva Lockwood, who never held elected office, caused quite a stir in her day.

Annual Editions: American History, Volume II, constitutes an effort to provide a balanced collection of articles that deal with great leaders and great decisions, as well as with ordinary people, at work, at leisure, and at war. Practically everyone who uses the volume will think of one or more articles he or she considers would have been preferable to the ones actually included. Some readers will wish more attention had been paid to one or another subject, others will regret the attention devoted to matters they regard as marginal. That is why we encourage teachers and students to let us know what they believe to be the strengths and weaknesses of this edition.

Annual Editions contains a number of features designed to make the volume "user friendly." These include a *Topic Guide* to help locate articles on specific individuals or subjects; and the *Table of Contents abstracts* that summarize each article with key concepts in boldface. The essays are organized into six units. Each unit is preceded by an overview that provides background for informed reading of the articles, briefly introduces each one, and presents *Key Points to Consider* questions. Please let us know if you have any suggestions for improving the format.

There will be a new edition of this volume in two years, with approximately half the readings being replaced by new ones. By completing and mailing the postpaid article rating form included in the back of the book, you will help us determine which articles should be retained and which should be dropped. You can also help to improve the next edition by recommending (or better yet, sending along a copy of) articles that you think should be included. A number of essays included in this edition have come to our attention in this way.

Robert James Maddox

Robert James Maddox
Editor

Contents

UNIT 1
Reconstruction and the Gilded Age

The concepts in bold italics are developed in the article. For further expansion, please refer to the Topic Guide.

UNIT 2
The Emergence of Modern America

UNIT 3
From Progressivism to the 1920s

The concepts in bold italics are developed in the article. For further expansion, please refer to the Topic Guide.

UNIT 4
From the Great Depression to World War II

The concepts in bold italics are developed in the article. For further expansion, please refer to the Topic Guide.

UNIT 5
From the Cold War to 2010

The concepts in bold italics are developed in the article. For further expansion, please refer to the Topic Guide.

UNIT 6
New Directions for American History

The concepts in bold italics are developed in the article. For further expansion, please refer to the Topic Guide.

The concepts in bold italics are developed in the article. For further expansion, please refer to the Topic Guide.

Correlation Guide

The *Annual Editions* series provides students with convenient, inexpensive access to current, carefully selected articles from the public press. **Annual Editions: United States History, Volume 2—Reconstruction through the Present, 21/e** is an easy-to-use reader that presents articles on important topics such as *culture, diplomacy, labor,* and many more. For more information on *Annual Editions* and other *McGraw-Hill Contemporary Learning Series* titles, visit www.mhhe.com/cls.

This convenient guide matches the units in **Annual Editions: United States History, Volume 2, 21/e** with the corresponding chapters in two of our best-selling McGraw-Hill History textbooks by Brinkley and Davidson et al.

Annual Editions: United States History, Volume 2, 21/e	The Unfinished Nation: A Concise History of the American People, Volume 2: From 1865, 6/e by Brinkley	Experience History: Interpreting America's Past, 7/e by Davidson et al.
Unit 1: Reconstruction and the Gilded Age	**Chapter 15:** Reconstruction and the New South	**Chapter 18:** The New South and the Trans-Mississippi West 1870–1914
Unit 2: The Emergence of Modern America	**Chapter 16:** The Conquest of the Far West **Chapter 17:** Industrial Supremacy **Chapter 18:** The Age of the City **Chapter 19:** From Crisis to Empire	**Chapter 19:** The New Industrial Order 1870–1914 **Chapter 20:** The Rise of an Urban Order 1870–1914 **Chapter 21:** The Political System under Strain at Home and Abroad 1877–1900
Unit 3: From Progressivism to the 1920s	**Chapter 20:** The Progressives **Chapter 21:** America and the Great War **Chapter 22:** The New Era	**Chapter 22:** The Progressive Era 1890–1920 **Chapter 23:** The United States and the Collapse of the Old World Order 1901–1920 **Chapter 24:** The New Era 1920–1929
Unit 4: From the Great Depression to World War II	**Chapter 23:** The Great Depression **Chapter 24:** The New Deal **Chapter 25:** The Global Crisis, 1921–1941 **Chapter 26:** America in a World at War	**Chapter 25:** The Great Depression and the New Deal 1929–1939 **Chapter 26:** America's Rise to Globalism 1927–1945
Unit 5: From the Cold War to 2010	**Chapter 27:** The Cold War **Chapter 28:** The Affluent Society **Chapter 29:** The Ordeal of Liberalism **Chapter 30:** The Crisis of Authority **Chapter 31:** From the "Age of Limits" to the Age of Reagan	**Chapter 27:** Cold War America 1945–1954 **Chapter 28:** The Suburban Era 1945–1963 **Chapter 29:** Civil Rights and Uncivil Liberties 1947–1969 **Chapter 30:** The Vietnam Era 1963–1975 **Chapter 31:** The Conservative Challenge 1976–1992 **Chapter 32:** Nation of Nations in a Global Community 1989–Present
Unit 6: New Directions for American History	**Chapter 32:** The Age of Globalization	**Chapter 32:** Nation of Nations in a Global Community 1989–Present

Topic Guide

This topic guide suggests how the selections in this book relate to the subjects covered in your course. You may want to use the topics listed on these pages to search the Web more easily.

On the following pages a number of websites have been gathered specifically for this book. They are arranged to reflect the units of this Annual Editions reader. You can link to these sites by going to www.mhhe.com/cls

All the articles that relate to each topic are listed below the bold-faced term.

African Americans
1. The American Civil War, Emancipation, and Reconstruction on the World Stage
2. How a War of Terror Kept Blacks Oppressed Long after the Civil War Ended
29. Crisis at Central High
32. King's Complex Legacy
41. Ending the Slavery Blame-Game

Baby boomers
44. Boomer Century

Bryan, William Jennings
19. Evolution on Trial

Bush, George W.
36. The Rove Presidency

Carnegie, Andrew
5. Gifts of the "Robber Barons"

Chief Joseph
3. The Nez Perce Flight for Justice

Clinton, Bill
35. The Tragedy of Bill Clinton

Cody, William
4. How the West Was Spun

Cold war
27. Dollar Diplomacy
28. Command Performance
30. Launch of a New World
34. Soft Power: Reagan the Dove

Culture
4. How the West Was Spun
9. Where the Other Half Lived
11. Joe Hill: 'I Never Died,' Said He
19. Evolution on Trial
20. Remember the Roaring '20s?
29. Crisis at Central High
30. Launch of a New World
31. Will the Left Ever Learn to Communicate across Generations?
32. King's Complex Legacy
33. The Spirit of '78, Stayin' Alive
40. Becoming Us
41. Ending the Slavery Blame-Game
42. The American Character
44. Boomer Century

Darrow, Clarence
19. Evolution on Trial

Depression, the great
21. 15 Minutes That Saved America
22. Lessons from the Great Crash

23. When America Sent Her Own Packing
24. Labor Strikes Back

Diplomacy
16. To Make the World Safe for Democracy
27. Dollar Diplomacy
34. Soft Power: Reagan the Dove
38. An Empire at Risk

Eisenhower, Dwight D.
26. Ike at D-Day

Environment
18. Between Heaven and Earth: Lindbergh: Technology and Environmentalism
43. Global Warming: Who Loses—and Who Wins?

Evolution
19. Evolution on Trial

Ford, Henry
15. The $5 Day

Government
1. The American Civil War, Emancipation, and Reconstruction on the World Stage
2. How a War of Terror Kept Blacks Oppressed Long after the Civil War Ended
6. Lockwood in '84
17. The Democrats' Deadlocked Ballot Brawl of 1924
21. 15 Minutes That Saved America
22. Lessons from the Great Crash
35. The Tragedy of Bill Clinton
36. The Rove Presidency
37. Good Health in America?
43. Global Warming: Who Loses—and Who Wins?

Hill, Joe
11. Joe Hill: "I Never Died," Said He

Immigrants
9. Where the Other Half Lived
23. When America Sent Her Own Packing
40. Becoming Us

King, Martin Luther, Jr.
32. King's Complex Legacy

Ku Klux Klan
2. How a War of Terror Kept Blacks Oppressed Long after the Civil War Ended

Labor
8. Utopia Derailed
14. A Day to Remember: March 25, 1911: Triangle Fire
15. The $5 Day
24. Labor Strikes Back

Internet References

The following Internet sites have been selected to support the articles found in this reader. These sites were available at the time of publication. However, because websites often change their structure and content, the information listed may no longer be available. We invite you to visit www.mhhe.com/cls for easy access to these sites.

AE: United States History, Volume 2

General Sources

American Historical Association
www.historians.org

This is the logical first visitation site for someone interested in virtually any topic in American history. All affiliated societies and publications are noted, and AHA links present material related to myriad fields of history and for students with different levels of education.

Harvard's John F. Kennedy School of Government
www.ksg.harvard.edu

Starting from this home page, click on a huge variety of links to information about American history, ranging from data about political parties to general debates of enduring issues.

History Net
www.thehistorynet.com

Supported by the National Historical Society, this frequently updated site provides information on a wide range of topics. The articles are of excellent quality, and the site has book reviews and even special interviews.

Library of Congress
www.loc.gov

Examine this website to learn about the extensive resource tools, library services/resources, exhibitions, and databases available through the Library of Congress in many different subfields that are related to American history.

Smithsonian Institution
www.si.edu

This site provides access to the enormous resources of the Smithsonian, which holds some 140 million artifacts and specimens in its trust for "the increase and diffusion of knowledge." Here you can learn about American social, cultural, economic, and political history from a variety of viewpoints.

The White House
www.whitehouse.gov

Visit the home page of the White House for direct access to information about commonly requested federal services, the White House Briefing Room, and the presidents and vice presidents. The "Virtual Library" allows you to search White House documents, listen to speeches, and view photos.

UNIT 1: Reconstruction and the Gilded Age

Anacostia Museum/Smithsonian Institution
www.si.edu/archives/historic/anacost.htm

This is the home page of the Center for African American History and Culture of the Smithsonian Institution. Explore its many avenues. This is expected to become a major repository of information.

American Memory
www.memory.loc.gov/ammem/ammemhome.html

American Memory is a gateway to rich primary source materials relating to the history and culture of the United States. The site offers more than 7 million digital items from more than 100 historical collections.

UNIT 2: The Emergence of Modern America

The Age of Imperialism
www.smplanet.com/imperialism/toc.html

During the late nineteenth and early twentieth centuries, the United States pursued an aggressive policy of expansionism, extending its political and economic influence around the globe. That pivotal era in the nation's history is the subject of this interactive site. Maps and photographs are provided.

William McKinley 1843–1901
www.cweb.loc.gov/rr/hispanic/1898/mckinley.html

Browse through this Library of Congress site for insight into the era of William McKinley, including discussion of the Spanish-American War.

American Diplomacy: Editor's Corner— Two if by Sea
www.unc.edu/depts/diplomat/AD_Issues/amdipl_15/edit_15.html

This essay provides a brief biography of Alfred Thayer Mahan and reviews his contributions to and influence on expansionism in American foreign policy.

Great Chicago Fire and the Web of Memory
www.chicagohs.org/fire

This site, created by the Academic Technologies unit of Northwestern University and the Chicago Historical Society, is interesting and well constructed. Besides discussing the Great Chicago Fire at length, the materials provide insight into the era in which the event took place.

UNIT 3: From Progressivism to the 1920s

International Channel
www.i-channel.com

Immigrants helped to create modern America. Visit this interesting site to experience "the memories, sounds, even tastes of Ellis Island. Hear immigrants describe in their own words their experiences upon entering the gateway to America."

World War I—Trenches on the Web
www.worldwar1.com

Mike Lawrence's interesting site supplies extensive resources about the Great War and is the appropriate place to begin exploration of this topic as regards the American experience in World War I. There are "virtual tours" on certain topics, such as "Life on the Homefront."

Internet References

World Wide Web Virtual Library
www.iisg.nl/~w3vl

This site focuses on labor and business history. As an index site, this is a good place to start exploring these two vast topics.

The Roaring 20's and the Great Depression
www.snowcrest.net/jmike/20sdep.html

An extensive anthology of web links to sites on the Roaring 20's and the Great Depression.

UNIT 4: From the Great Depression to World War II

Works Progress Administration/Folklore Project
www.lcweb2.loc.gov/ammem/wpaintro/wpalife.html

Open this home page of the Folklore Project of the Works Progress Administration (WPA) Federal Writers' Project to gain access to thousands of documents on the life histories of ordinary Americans from all walks of life during the Great Depression.

Hiroshima Archive
www.lclark.edu/~history/HIROSHIMA

The Hiroshima Archive was originally set up to join the on-line effort made by many people all over the world to commemorate the 50th anniversary of the atomic bombing. It is intended to serve as a research and educational guide to those who want to gain and expand their knowledge of the atomic bombing.

The Enola Gay
www.theenolagay.com/index.html

The official website of Brigadier General Paul W. Tibbets, Jr. (Ret.) offers a wealth of historical analysis and photographs of the events surrounding the use of atomic weapons on Japan in 1945.

UNIT 5: From the Cold War to 2010

Cold War
www.cnn.com/SPECIALS/cold.war

This site presents U.S. government policies during the Cold War. Navigate interactive maps, see rare archival footage online, learn more about the key players, read recently declassified documents and tour Cold War capitals through 3-D images.

The American Experience: Vietnam Online
www.pbs.org/wgbh/amex/vietnam

Vietnam Online was developed to accompany Vietnam: A Television History, the award-winning television series produced by WGBH Boston.

The Gallup Organization
www.gallup.com

Open this Gallup Organization home page to access an extensive archive of public opinion poll results and special reports on a huge variety of topics related to American society, politics, and government.

STAT-USA
www.stat-usa.gov/stat-usa.html

This site, a service of the Department of Commerce, contains daily economic news, frequently requested statistical releases, information on export and international trade, domestic economic news, and statistical series and databases.

U.S. Department of State
www.state.gov

View this site for an understanding of the workings of what has become a major U.S. executive-branch department. Links explain what exactly the department does, what services it provides, what it says about U.S. interests around the world, and much more.

UNIT 6: New Directions for American History

American Studies Web
www.georgetown.edu/crossroads/asw

This eclectic site provides links to a wealth of Internet resources for research in American studies, from agriculture and rural development, to history and government, to race and ethnicity.

National Center for Policy Analysis
www.public-policy.org/web.public-policy.org/index.php

Through this site, click onto links to read discussions of an array of topics that are of major interest in the study of American history, from regulatory policy and privatization to economy and income.

The National Network for Immigrant and Refugee Rights (NNIRR)
www.nnirr.org

The NNIRR serves as a forum to share information and analysis, to educate communities and the general public, and to develop and coordinate plans of action on important immigrant and refugee issues. Visit this site and its many links to explore these issues.

STANDARDS: An International Journal of Multicultural Studies
www.colorado.edu/journals/standards

This fascinating site provides access to the *Standards* archives and a seemingly infinite number of links to topics of interest in the study of cultural pluralism.

Supreme Court/Legal Information Institute
www.supct.law.cornell.edu/supct/index.html

Open this site for current and historical information about the Supreme Court. The archive contains many opinions issued since May 1990 as well as a collection of nearly 600 of the most historic decisions of the Court.

UNIT 1

Reconstruction and the Gilded Age

Unit Selections

Key Points to Consider

- Discuss "The American Civil War, Emancipation, and Reconstruction on the World Stage." How did these events influence people in other nations?

- Why did the U.S. government keep pushing the Nez Perce from one place to another? What alternatives did Chief Joseph and other leaders have?

- What practices did industrial leaders use that earned them the name "Robber Barons." What, if any, were their positive contributions?

- Discuss William "Buffalo Bill" Cody's Wild West shows. Aside from providing entertainment, how and why did these extravaganzas appeal to white Americans? What myths did they help propagate?

- Discuss events leading to the Wounded Knee Massacre?. Who were the "Ghost Dancers," and what were they trying to achieve?

Student Website
www.mhhe.com/cls

Internet References

Anacostia Museum/Smithsonian Institution
    www.si.edu/archives/historic/anacost.htm
American Memory
    www.memory.loc.gov/ammem/ammemhome.html

Abraham Lincoln had wanted to reunite the nation as quickly as possible after four years of war. During the last months of his life, he had instituted simple procedures through which Southern states could resume their positions within the union. Only a few high-ranking Confederate officials were prohibited from participating. Where did this leave the former slaves? Lincoln's version of reconstruction would result in the South being ruled by essentially the same people who had brought about secession. Those who became known as "Radical" or "Extreme" Republicans refused to abandon Freed People to their former masters. They wished to use the power of the federal government to ensure that blacks enjoyed full civil and legal rights. At first they thought they had an ally in Vice President Andrew Johnson, who assumed the presidency after Lincoln's assassination. When this proved untrue, a grueling struggle ensued that resulted in Johnson's impeachment and the Radicals in command of reconstruction. The South was divided into five military districts and federal troops were sent to protect the rights of Freed People. White Southerners used every means possible to keep blacks "in their place." As discussed in the article "How a War on Terror Kept Blacks Oppressed Long after the Civil War Ended," these methods included terrorist organizations such as the Ku Klux Klan and the Knights of the White Camellia. "The American Civil War, Emancipation, and Reconstruction" among other things, analyzes the ultimate failure of Radical Reconstruction.

Historians used to debate whether business leaders during the latter part of the nineteenth century should be regarded as "industrial statesmen" or "robber barons." Most of them were both. "Gifts of the 'Robber Barons'" examines two such individuals, Andrew Carnegie and Andrew Mellon. Without denying the shady business practices these men often employed, the author concludes that they, and others like them, did much to create a modern industrial society.

William "Buffalo Bill" Cody's Wild West shows provided plenty of excitement. There were shootouts, daring rescues, and cavalry charges, among other things. "How the West was Spun" points out that they also provided myths comforting to white Americans. They justified Indian removal in the name of progress and reassured whites that, however civilized they might be, they could "beat the braves and bullies of the world at their own game."

In 1884, at a time when women could not even vote, Belva Lockwood ran for the presidency on the Equal Rights Party ticket. She was regarded as a gadfly by some and resented

Library of Congress, Prints and Photographs Division [LC-USZ62-41756]

by others. Many women suffragists, for instance, regarded her candidacy as harmful to their cause because they incorrectly believed that the Republican Party provided the best hope for attaining the vote. "Lockwood in '84" shows that many of the planks in her platform that seemed radical at the time have since become standard practice.

The treatment of American Indians constitutes a sordid chapter in this nation's history. Time after time tribes were pushed off their ancestral lands, often with violence or the threat of violence. Frequently they were promised that if only they moved to this or that area they would be permitted to live in peace thereafter. Such promises usually lasted only until whites decided they wanted those lands, too. "The Nez Perce Flight for Justice" and "A Day to Remember: December 29, 1890" provide two examples of this experience.

The American Civil War, Emancipation, and Reconstruction on the World Stage

EDWARD L. AYERS

Americans demanded the world's attention during their Civil War and Reconstruction. Newspapers around the globe reported the latest news from the United States as one vast battle followed another, as the largest system of slavery in the world crashed into pieces, as American democracy expanded to include people who had been enslaved only a few years before.[1]

Both the North and the South appealed to the global audience. Abraham Lincoln argued that his nation's Civil War "embraces more than the fate of these United States. It presents to the whole family of man, the question, whether a constitutional republic, or a democracy . . . can, or cannot, maintain its territorial integrity." The struggle. Lincoln said, was for "a vast future," a struggle to give all men "a fair chance in the race of life."[2] Confederates claimed that they were also fighting for a cause of world-wide significance: self-determination. Playing down the centrality of slavery to their new nation, white Southerners built their case for independence on the right of free citizens to determine their political future.[3]

People in other nations could see that the massive struggle in the United States embodied conflicts that had been appearing in different forms throughout the world. Defining nationhood, deciding the future of slavery, reinventing warfare for an industrial age, reconstructing a former slave society—all these played out in the American Civil War.

By no means a major power, the United States was nevertheless woven into the life of the world. The young nation touched, directly and indirectly, India and Egypt, Hawaii and Japan, Russia and Canada, Mexico and Cuba, the Caribbean and Brazil, Britain and France. The country was still very much an experiment in 1860, a representative government stretched over an enormous space, held together by law rather than by memory, religion, or monarch. The American Civil War, played out on the brightly lit stage of a new country, would be a drama of world history. How that experiment fared in its great crisis—regardless of what happened—would eventually matter to people everywhere.

More obviously than most nations, the United States was the product of global history. Created from European ideas, involvement in Atlantic trade, African slavery, conquest of land from American Indians and European powers, and massive migration from Europe, the United States took shape as the world watched. Long before the Civil War, the United States embodied the possibilities and contradictions of modern western history.

Slavery was the first, most powerful, and most widespread kind of globalization in the first three centuries after Columbus. While colonies came and went, while economies boomed and crashed, slavery relentlessly grew—and nowhere more than in the United States. By the middle of the nineteenth century, the slave South had assumed a central role on the world stage. Cotton emerged as the great global commodity, driving factories in the most advanced economies of the world. The slaves of the South were worth more than all the railroads and factories of the North and South combined; slavery was good business and shrewd investment.

While most other slave societies in the hemisphere gradually moved toward freedom, the American South moved toward the permanence of slavery. Southerners and their Northern allies, eager to expand, led the United States in a war to seize large parts of Mexico and looked hungrily upon the Caribbean and Central America. Of all the slave powers—including the giants of Brazil and Cuba, which continued to import slaves legally long after the United States—only the South and its Confederacy fought a war to maintain bondage.[4]

Ideas of justice circulated in global intercourse just as commodities did and those ideas made the American South increasingly anomalous as a modern society built on slavery. Demands for universal freedom came into conflict with ancient traditions of subordination. European nations, frightened by revolt in Haiti and elsewhere and confident of their empires' ability to prosper without slavery, dismantled slavery in their colonies in the western hemisphere while Russia dismantled serfdom.

Black and white abolitionists in the American North, though a tiny despised minority, worked with British allies to fight the acceptance of slavery in the United States. A vision of the South as backward, cruel, and power-hungry gained credence in many places in the North and took political force in the Republican party. The global economy of commodities and ideology, demanding cotton while attacking slavery, put enormous and contradictory strains on the young American nation.[5]

Meanwhile, a new urge to define national identity flowed through the western world in the first half of the nineteenth century. That determination took quite different forms. While some people still spoke of the universal dreams of the French and American Revolutions, of inalienable attributes of humankind, others spoke of historical grievance, ethnic unity, and economic self-interest. Many longed for new nations built around bonds of heritage, imagined and real.[6]

White Southerners, while building their case for secession with the language of constitutions and rights, presented themselves as a people profoundly different from white Northerners. They sought sanction for secession in the recent histories of Italy, Poland, Mexico, and Greece, where rebels rose up against central powers to declare their suppressed nationhood, where native elites led a "natural, necessary protest and revolt" against a "crushing, killing union with another nationality and form of society."[7]

As the South threatened to secede, the Republicans, a regional party themselves, emphasized the importance of Union for its own sake, the necessity of maintaining the integrity of a nation created by legal compact. It fell to the United States, the Republicans said, to show that large democracies could survive internal struggles and play a role in world affairs alongside monarchies and aristocracies.[8]

Once it became clear that war would come, the North and the South seized upon the latest war-making strategies and technologies. From the outset, both sides innovated at a rapid pace and imported ideas from abroad. Railroads and telegraphs extended supply lines, sped troop reinforcements, and permitted the mobilization of vast armies. Observers from Europe and other nations watched carefully to see how the Americans would use these new possibilities. The results were mixed. Ironclad ships, hurriedly constructed, made a difference in some Southern ports and rivers, but were not seaworthy enough to play the role some had envisioned for them. Submarines and balloons proved disappointments, unable to deliver significant advantages. Military leaders, rather than being subordinated by anonymous machinery, as some expected, actually became more important than before, their decisions amplified by the size of their armies and the speed of communication and transport.[9]

The scale and drama of the Civil War that ravaged America for four years, across an area larger than the European continent, fascinated and appalled a jaded world. A proportion of the population equal to five million people today died and the South suffered casualties at a rate equal to those who would be decimated in Europe's mechanized wars of the twentieth century.

The size, innovation, and destructiveness of the American Civil War have led some, looking back, to describe it as the first total war, the first truly modern war. Despite new technologies and strategies, however, much of the Civil War remained old-fashioned. The armies in the American Civil War still moved vast distances on foot or with animals. The food soldiers ate and the medical care they received showed little advance over previous generations of armies. The military history of the Civil War grew incrementally from world history and offered incremental changes to what would follow. Although, late in the war, continuous campaigning and extensive earthen entrenchments foreshadowed World War I, Europeans did not grasp the deadly lesson of the American Civil War: combining the tactics of Napoleon with rapid-fire weapons and trenches would culminate in horrors unanticipated at Shiloh and Antietam.[10]

Diplomacy proved challenging for all sides in the American crisis. The fragile balance of power on the Continent and in the empires centered there limited the range of movement of even the most powerful nations. The Confederacy's diplomatic strategy depended on gaining recognition from Great Britain and France, using cotton as a sort of blackmail, but European manufacturers had stockpiled large supplies of cotton in anticipation of the American war. British cartoonists, sympathetic to the Confederacy, ridiculed Abraham Lincoln at every opportunity, portraying him as an inept bumpkin—until his assassination, when Lincoln suddenly became sainted. Overall, the North benefited from the inaction of the British and the French, who could have changed the outcome and consequences of the war by their involvement.[11]

Inside the United States, the change unleashed by the war was as profound as it was unexpected. Even those who hated slavery had not believed in 1861 that generations of captivity could be ended overnight and former slaves and former slaveholders left to live together. The role of slavery in sustaining the Confederacy through humbling victories over the Union created the conditions in which Abraham Lincoln felt driven and empowered to issue the Emancipation Proclamation. The Union, briefly and precariously balanced between despair and hope, between defeat and victory, was willing in 1862 to accept that bold decision as a strategy of war and to enlist volunteers from among black Americans.[12]

The nearly 200,000 African Americans who came into the war as soldiers and sailors for the Union transformed the struggle. The addition of those men, greater in number than all the forces at Gettysburg, allowed the Union to build its advantage in manpower without pushing reluctant Northern whites into the draft. The enlistment of African Americans in the struggle for their own freedom ennobled the Union cause and promised to set a new global standard for the empowerment of formerly enslaved people. The world paid admiring attention to the brave and disciplined black troops in blue uniforms.[13]

The destruction of American slavery, a growing system of bondage of nearly four million people in one of the world's most powerful economies and most dynamic nation-states, was a consequence of world importance. Nowhere else besides Haiti did slavery end so suddenly, so completely, and with so little compensation for former slaveholders.[14] Had the United States failed to end slavery in the 1860s the world would have felt the difference. An independent Confederate States of America would certainly have put its enslaved population to effective use in coal mines, steel mills, and railroad building, since industrial slavery had been employed before secession and became more common during wartime. Though such a Confederacy might have found itself stigmatized, its survival would have meant the evolution of slavery into a new world of industrialization. The triumph of a major autonomous state built around slavery would have set a devastating example for the rest of the world, an encouragement to forces of reaction. It would have marked the repudiation of much that was liberating in Western thought and practice over the preceding two hundred years.[15]

Driven by the exigencies of war, Northern ideals of color-blind freedom and justice, so often latent and suppressed, suddenly if briefly bloomed in the mid-1860s. The Radical Republicans sought to create a black male American freedom based on the same basis as white male American freedom: property, citizenship, dignity, and equality before the law. They launched a bold Reconstruction to make those ideals a reality, their effort far surpassing those of emancipation anywhere else in the world. The white South resisted with vicious vehemence, however, and the Republicans, always ambivalent about black autonomy and eager to maintain their partisan power, lost heart after a decade of bitter, violent, and costly struggle in Reconstruction. Northern Democrats, opposing Reconstruction from the outset, hastened and celebrated its passing.[16]

If former slaves had been permitted to sustain the enduring political power they tried to build, if they had gone before juries and judges with a chance of fair treatment, if they had been granted homesteads to serve as a first step toward economic freedom, then Reconstruction could be hailed as a turning point in world history equal to any revolution. Those things did not happen, however. The white South claimed the mantle of victim, of a people forced to endure an unjust and unnatural subordination. They won international sympathy for generations to follow in films such as *Birth of a Nation* (1915) and *Gone With the Wind* (1939), which viewed events through the eyes of sympathetic white Southerners. Reconstruction came to be seen around the world not as the culmination of freedom but as a mistake, a story of the dangers of unrealistic expectations and failed social engineering. Though former slaves in the American South quietly made more progress in landholding and general prosperity than former slaves elsewhere, the public failures of Reconstruction obscured the progress black Southerners wrenched from the postwar decades.[17]

When the South lost its global monopoly of cotton production during the Civil War, governments, agents, and merchants around the world responded quickly to take the South's place and to build an efficient global machinery to supply an ever-growing demand in the world market. As a result, generations of black and white sharecroppers would compete with Indian, Brazilian, and Egyptian counterparts in a glutted market in which hard work often brought impoverishment. The South adapted its economy after the war as well. By the 1880s, the South's rates of urban growth, manufacturing, and population movement kept pace with the North—a remarkable shift for only twenty years after losing slavery and the Civil War— but black Southerners were excluded from much of the new prosperity.[18]

As the Civil War generation aged, younger men looked with longing on possible territorial acquisitions in their own hemisphere and farther afield. They talked openly of proving themselves, as their fathers and grandfathers had, on the battlefield. Some welcomed the fight against the Spanish and the Filipinos in 1898 as a test of American manhood and nationalism. The generation that came of age in 1900 built monuments to the heroes of the Civil War but seldom paused to listen to their stories of war's horror and costs.

The destruction of slavery, a major moral accomplishment of the United States Army, of Abraham Lincoln, and of the enslaved people themselves, would be overshadowed by the injustice and poverty that followed in the rapidly changing South, a mockery of American claims of moral leadership in the world. Black Southerners would struggle, largely on their own, for the next one hundred years. Their status, bound in an ever-tightening segregation, would stand as a rebuke to the United States in world opinion. The postwar South and its new system of segregation, in fact, became an explicit model for South Africa. That country created apartheid as it, like the American South, developed a more urban and industrial economy based on racial subordination.

Americans read about foreign affairs on the same pages that carried news of Reconstruction in the South. Even as the Southern states struggled to write new constitutions. Secretary of State William Henry Seward purchased Alaska in 1867 as a step toward the possible purchase of British Columbia. President Grant considered annexation of Santo Domingo, partly as a base for black Southern emigration; he won the support of black abolitionist Frederick Douglass, who wanted to help the Santo Domingans, but was opposed by Radical Republican Senator Charles Sumner.

Americans paid close attention to Hawaii in these same years. Mark Twain visited the islands in 1866, and Samuel Armstrong—the white founder of Hampton Institute, where Booker T. Washington was educated—argued that Hawaiians and former slaves in the South needed similar discipline to become industrious. At the same time, Seward signed a treaty with China to help supply laborers to the American West, a treaty that laid the foundation for a large migration in the next few decades. In 1871, American forces intervened militarily in Korea, killing 250 Korean soldiers. The leaders of the Americans admitted they knew little about their opponents, but brought the same assumptions about race to the conflict that they brought to their dealings with all non-Europeans everywhere, Koreans—like Hawaiians, Chinese, American Indians, and African Americans—needed to be disciplined, taught, and controlled.

No master plan guided Americans in their dealings with other peoples. In all of these places, the interests of American businessmen, the distortions of racial ideology, and hopes for partisan political advantage at home jostled with one another. As a result, the consequences of these involvements were often unclear and sometimes took generations to play out. Nevertheless, they remind us that Americans paid close attention to what was happening elsewhere, whether in the Franco-Prussian War (1870–1871), where the evolution of warfare continued to become more mechanized and lethal, or the Paris Commune (1871), where some thought they saw the result of unbridled democracy in chaos and violence—and wondered if Reconstruction did not represent a similar path.

Some people around the world were surprised that the United States did not use its enormous armies after the Civil War to seize Mexico from the French, Canada from the English, or Cuba from the Spanish. Conflict among the great powers on the European Continent certainly opened an opportunity and the United States had expanded relentlessly and opportunistically throughout its history. Few Americans, though, had the stomach for new adventures in the wake of the Civil War. The fighting against the American Indians on the Plains proved warfare enough for most white Americans in the 1870s and 1880s.[19]

The United States focused its postwar energies instead on commerce. Consolidated under Northern control, the nation's economy proved more formidable than ever before. The United States, its economic might growing with each passing year, its railroad network and financial systems consolidated, its cities and towns booming, its population surging westward, its mines turning out massive amounts of coal and precious minerals, its farms remarkably productive, and its corporations adopting new means of expansion and administration, became a force throughout the world. American engineers oversaw projects in Asia, Africa, and Latin America. American investors bought stock in railroads, factories, and mines around the globe. American companies came to dominate the economies of nations in Latin America.[20]

Americans became famous as rich, energetic, and somewhat reckless players amid the complexity of the world. As the Civil War generation aged, younger men looked with longing on possible territorial acquisitions in their own hemisphere and farther afield. They talked openly of proving themselves, as their fathers and grandfathers had, on the battlefield. Some welcomed the fight against the Spanish and the Filipinos in 1898 as a test of American manhood and nationalism. The generation that came of age in 1900 built monuments to the heroes of the Civil War but seldom paused to listen to their stories of war's horror and costs.

The American Civil War has carried a different meaning for every generation of Americans. In the 1920s and 1930s leading historians in a largely isolationist United States considered the Civil War a terrible mistake, the product of a "blundering generation." After the triumph of World War II

and in the glow of the Cold War's end, leading historians interpreted the Civil War as a chapter in the relentless destruction of slavery and the spread of democracy by the forces of modernization over the forces of reaction. Recently, living through more confusing times, some historians have begun to question straightforward stories of the war, emphasizing its contradictory meanings, unfulfilled promises, and unintended outcomes.[21]

The story of the American Civil War changes as world history lurches in unanticipated directions and as people ask different questions of the past. Things that once seemed settled now seem less so. The massive ranks, fortified trenches, heavy machinery, and broadened targets of the American Civil War once seemed to mark a step toward the culmination of "total" war. But the wars of the twenty-first century, often fought without formal battles, are proving relentless and boundless, "total" in ways the disciplined armies of the Union and Confederacy never imagined.[22] Nations continue to come apart over ancient grievances and modern geopolitics, the example of the United States notwithstanding. Coerced labor did not end in the nineteenth century, but instead has mutated and adapted to changes in the global economy. "A fair chance in the race of life" has yet to arrive for much of the world.

The great American trial of war, emancipation, and reconstruction mattered to the world. It embodied struggles that would confront people on every continent and it accelerated the emergence of a new global power. The American crisis, it was true, might have altered the course of world history more dramatically, in ways both worse and better, than what actually transpired. The war could have brought forth a powerful and independent Confederacy based on slavery or it could have established with its Reconstruction a new global standard of justice for people who had been enslaved. As it was, the events of the 1860s and 1870s in the United States proved both powerful and contradictory in their meaning for world history.

Notes

1. For other portrayals of the Civil War in international context, see David M. Potter, "Civil War," in C. Vann Woodward, ed., *The Comparative Approach to American History* (New York: Basic Books, 1968), pp. 135–451; Carl N. Degler, *One Among Many: The Civil War in Comparative Perspective*, 29th Annual Robert Fortenbaugh Memorial Lecture (Gettysburg, PA: Gettysburg College, 1990); Robert E. May, ed., *The Union, the Confederacy, and the Atlantic Rim* (West Lafayette, IN: Purdue University Press, 1995); Peter Kolchin, *A Sphinx on the American Land: The Nineteenth-Century South in Comparative Perspective* (Baton Rouge: Louisiana State University Press, 2003). My view of the workings of world history has been influenced by C. A. Bayly, *The Birth of the Modern World, 1780–1914: Global Connections and Comparisons* (Malden, MA: Blackwell, 2004). Bayly emphasizes that "in the nineteenth century, nation-states and contending territorial empires took on sharper lineaments and became more antagonistic to each other at the very same time as the similarities, connections, and linkages between them proliferated" (p. 2). By showing the "complex

interaction between political organization, political ideas, and economic activity," Bayly avoids the teleologital models of modernization, nationalism, and liberalism that have dominated our understanding of the American Civil War.

2. Lincoln quoted in James M. McPherson, *Abraham Lincoln and the Second American Revolution,* reprint (New York: Oxford University Press: 1992, 1991), p. 28.

3. The seminal work is Drew Gilpin Faust, *The Creation of Confederate Nationalism: Ideology and Identity in the Civil War South* (Baton Rouge: Louisiana State University Press, 1988). For an excellent synthesis of the large literature on this topic, see Anne S. Rubin, *A Shattered Nation: The Rise and Fall of the Confederacy, 1861–1868* (Chapel Hill: University of North Carolina Press, 2005).

4. For a useful overview, see Robert W. Fogel, *Without Consent or Contract: The Rise and Fall of American Slavery* (New York: W. W. Norton, 1989).

5. David Brion Davis, *Slavery and Human Progress* (New York: Oxford University Press, 1984); Davis, *The Problem of Slavery in the Age of Revolution, 1770–1823* (Ithaca, NY: Cornell University Press, 1975); and Davis, *Inhuman Bondage: The Rise and Fall of Slavery in the New World* (Oxford University Press, 2006).

6. For helpful overviews of the global situation, see Steven Hahn, "Class and State in Postemancipation Societies: Southern Planters in Comparative Perspective," *American Historical Review* 95 (February 1990): 75–98, and Hahn, *A Nation Under Our Feet: Black Political Struggles in the Rural South From Slavery to the Great Migration* (Cambridge, MA: Belknap Press of Harvard University Press, 2003).

7. Quoted in Faust, *Creation of Confederate Nationalism,* p. 13.

8. There is a large literature on this subject, not surprisingly. A useful recent treatment is Susan-Mary Grant, *North Over South: Northern Nationalism and American Identity in the Antebellum Era* (Lawrence: University of Kansas Press, 2000). Peter Kolchin also offers penetrating comments on nationalism in *A Sphinx on the American Land,* pp. 89–92.

9. Brian Holden Reid, *The American Civil War and the Wars of the Industrial Revolution* (London: Cassell, 1999), pp. 211–13; John E. Clark Jr., *Railroads in the Civil War: The Impact of Management on Victory and Defeat* (Baton Rouge: Louisiana State University Press, 2001); Robert G. Angevine, *The Railroad and the State: War, Politics, and Technology in Nineteenth-Century America* (Stanford, CA: Stanford University Press, 2004).

10. For a range of interesting essays on this subject, see Stig Forster and Jorg Nagler, eds., *On the Road to Total War: The American Civil War and the German Wars of Unification, 1861–1871* (Washington, DC: The German Historical Institute, 1997).

11. See D. P. Crook, *The North, the South, and the Powers, 1861–1865* (New York: Wiley, 1974); R. J. M. Blackett, *Divided Hearts: Britain and the American Civil War* (Baton Rouge: Louisiana State University Press, 2001); James M. McPherson, *Crossroads of Freedom: Antietam* (Oxford: Oxford University Press, 2002); Robert E. May, ed., *The Union, the Confederacy, and the Atlantic Rim;* and Charles M. Hubbard, *The Burden of Confederate Diplomacy* (Knoxville: University of Tennessee Press, 1998).

12. See Allen C. Guelzo, *Lincoln's Emancipation Proclamation: The End of Slavery in America* (New York: Simon and Schuster. 2004).

13. See Joseph T. Glatthaar, *Forged in Battle: The Civil War Alliance of Black Soldiers and White Officers* (New York: Free Press, 1990).

14. See Leon Litwack, *Been in the Storm So Long: The Aftermath of Slavery,* 1st Vintage ed. (New York: Vintage, 1980, 1979) and the major documentary collection edited by Ira Berlin, Leslie S. Rowland, and their colleagues, sampled in *Free At Last: A Documentary History of Slavery, Freedom, and the Civil War* (New York: The New Press, 1992).

15. See Davis, *Slavery and Human Progress,* for a sweeping perspective on this issue.

16. The classic history is Eric Foner, *Reconstruction: America's Unfinished Revolution, 1863–1877* (New York: Harper and Row, 1988), I have offered some thoughts on Reconstruction's legacy in "Exporting Reconstruction" in *What Caused the Civil War? Reflections on the South and Southern History* (New York: W. W. Norton, 2005).

17. On the legacy of Reconstruction, see David W. Blight, *Race and Reunion The Civil War in American Memory* (Cambridge, MA: Belknap Press of Harvard University Press, 2001).

18. For a fascinating essay on the South's loss of the cotton monopoly, see Sven Beckert, "Emancipation and Empire: Reconstructing the Worldwide Web of Cotton Production in the Age of the American Civil War," *American Historical Review* 109 (December 2004): 1405–38. On South Africa: John W. Cell, *The Highest Stage of White Supremacy: The Origins of Segregation in South Africa and the American South* (Cambridge: Cambridge University Press, 1982) and George M. Fredrickson, *White Supremacy: A Comparative Study in American and South African History* (New York: Oxford University Press, 1981).

19. See the discussion in the essays by Robert E. May and James M. McPherson in May, ed., *The Union, the Confederacy, and the Atlantic Rim.*

20. For the larger context, see Eric J. Hobsbawm, *The Age of Empire, 1875–1914* (New York: Pantheon, 1987) and Bayly, *Birth of the Modern World.*

21. I have described this literature and offered some thoughts on it in the essay "Worrying About the Civil War" in my *What Caused the Civil War?*

22. Reid, *American Civil War,* p. 213.

Bibliography

Surprisingly, no one book covers the themes of this essay. To understand this era of American history in global context, we need to piece together accounts from a variety of books and articles. For recent over views of different components of these years, see Jay Sexton, "Towards a Synthesis of Foreign Relations in the Civil War Era, 1848–1877," *American Nineteenth-Century History* 5 (Fall 2004): 50–75, and Amy Kaplan, *The Anarchy of Empire in the Making of U.S. Culture* (Cambridge, MA; Harvard University Press, 2002).

Robert E. May, in the introduction to the book he edited, *The Union, the Confederacy, and the Atlantic Rim* (West Lafayette, IN: Purdue University Press, 1995), provides a useful summary of the larger context of the war. Though it is older, the perspective of D. P. Crook, *The North, the South, and the Powers, 1861–1865* (New York: Wiley, 1974) brings a welcome worldliness to the discussion. On the crucial debate in Britain, see Howard Jones, *Union in*

Peril: The Crisis Over British Intervention in the Civil War (Chapel Hill: University of North Carolina Press, 1992) and R. J. M. Blackett, *Divided Hearts: Britain and the American Civil War* (Baton Rouge: Louisiana State University Press, 2001).

James M. McPherson offers characteristically insightful, and hopeful, analysis in several places. Perhaps the single best focused portrayal of the interplay between events in the United States and in the Atlantic World is in his *Crossroads of Freedom: Antietam* (Oxford: Oxford University Press, 2002). McPherson's essay, " 'The Whole Family of Man': Lincoln and the Last Best Hope Abroad," in May, ed., *The Union, the Confederacy, and the Atlantic Rim,* makes the fullest case for the larger significance of the war in encouraging liberal movements and belief around the world.

Peter Kolchin's, *A Sphinx on the American Land: The Nineteenth-Century South in Comparative Perspective* (Baton Rouge: Louisiana State University Press, 2003), offers an elegant and up-to-date survey that puts the conflict in the larger context of emancipation movements. A useful overview appears in Steven Hahn, "Class and State in Postemancipation Societies: Southern Planters in Comparative Perspective," *American Historical Review* 95 (February 1990): 75–98.

Another pioneering work is Drew Gilpin Faust, *The Creation of Confederate Nationalism: Ideology and Identity in the Civil War South* (Baton Rouge: Louisiana State University Press, 1988). Faust changed historians' perspective on nationalism in the South, which had been considered largely fraudulent before her account. Building on Faust are two recent books that offer fresh interpretations: Anne S. Rubin, *A Shattered Nation: The Rise and Fall of the Confederacy, 1861–1868* (Chapel Hill: University of North Carolina Press, 2005) and Susan-Mary Crant, *North Over South: Northern Nationalism and American Identity in the Antebellum Era* (Lawrence: University of Kansas Press, 2000).

On the much-debated issue of the relative modernity and totality of the Civil War, see Stig Förster and Jörg Nagler, eds., *On the Road to Total War: The American Civil War and the German Wars of Unification, 1861–1871* (Washington, DC: The German Historical Institute, 1997); the essays by Stanley L. Engerman and J. Matthew Gallman, Farl J. Hess, Michael Fellman, and Richard Current are especially helpful. Brian Holden Reid, in *The American Civil War and the Wars of the Industrial Revolution* (London: Cassell, 1999), offers a concise but insightful portrayal of the war in larger military context.

For a powerful representation of the role of slavery in this history, David Brion Davis's works are all helpful. His most recent account synthesizes a vast literature in an accessible way: *Inhuman Bondage: The Rise and Fall of Slavery in the New World* (Oxford University Press, 2006).

Excellent examples of what might be thought of as the new global history appear in Sven Beckert, "Emancipation and Empire: Reconstructing the Worldwide Web of Cotton Production in the Age of the American Civil War," *American Historical Review* 109 (December 2004): 1405–38; and Gordon H. Chang, "Whose 'Barbarism'? whose 'Treachery'? Race and Civilization in the Unknown United States-Korea War of 1871," *Journal of American History* 89 (March 2003): 1331–65.

EDWARD L. AYERS is Dean of the College of Art and Sciences at the University of Virginia, where he is also the Hugh P. Kelly Professor of History. He has published extensively on nineteenth-century Southern history, his most recent publication being *In the Presence of Mine Enemies: War in the Heart of America, 1859–1863* (2003), which received the Bancroft Prize. An earlier book, *The Promise of the New South* (1992), was a finalist for both the Pulitzer Prize and the National Book Award. In addition, Ayers has created and directs a prize-winning Internet archive, "Valley of the Shadow: Two Communities in the American Civil War," containing original sources related to two towns at either end of the Shenandoah Valley, one in Virginia and the other in Pennsylvania.

How a War of Terror Kept Blacks Oppressed Long after the Civil War Ended

A massacre in Hamburg, S.C., epitomized the violence that eviscerated Reconstruction.

STEPHEN BUDIANSKY

In the spring of 1876, Martin Witherspoon Gary, South Carolina planter, lawyer and ex-Confederate general, took out a small notebook, wrote "Plan of Campaign" at the top of a page and jotted down in a hurried hand a few ideas for the upcoming election:

- 1st, Determine if necessary to kill every White Radical in this county
- 2nd, Every mulatto Radical leader
- 3rd, Every negro leader—make no individual threats but let this be known as a fixed settled thing
- 4th, We must send speakers to all of their political meetings, who must denounce the rascality of these leaders face to face. The moral effects of this denunciation will be of great effect
- 5th, Thorough military organization in order to intimidate the negro
- 6th, Every white man must be at the polls by five o clock in the morning of the day of election, and must go prepared to remain there until the votes are counted
- 7th, Make no threats—gently in manner, strongly in deed
- 8th, There is no use in arguments for the negro

From 1865 to 1877, more than 3,000 freedmen and their white Republican allies would be murdered across the South. The truth would be buried for decades in myths and cover stories that blamed the victims, hid the political purpose of the violence and wildly exaggerated the supposed wrongs committed against the white Southerners by the "carpetbag" governments.

But the simple fact was that this was a war of terror, led by ex-Confederates who were determined to reverse the verdict of Appomattox. Terror had overthrown Alabama's Reconstruction

government in 1874, Mississippi's in 1875. Now in the spring of 1876 it was South Carolina's turn.

General Gary was an impatient man that spring. Two years earlier he had bought a fine plantation house in Edgefield County, a place that shared a reputation for rich soils and violence. It was regarded as one of the state's most violent counties, with many cases of "murder or manslaughter, growing out of personal quarrels," a local judge noted. The place was so violent that jokes had grown up about it. You could tell a high-toned Edgefield gentleman, it was said, because he was the one with four huge navy-sized revolvers stuck in his belt. A mad dog needed to be shot on a street over in Augusta, Ga., just across the Savannah River; a policeman called out to the crowd that had gathered, "Is there a man from Edgefield here?"

Upon his arrival there, Gary called together 137 local planters for a "tax union meeting."

The men took out a notice in the *Edgefield Advertiser* declaring themselves "ready to strike for white supremacy," and announcing that they were drawing up lists of blacks to whom land would not be rented as punishment for their political activity.

Gary had always been unruly. At Appomattox he refused to surrender and galloped off the field instead. He then led 200 men of his brigade to escort President Jefferson Davis and his cabinet from Greensboro, N.C., to his mother's house in Cokesbury, S.C. "Volatile" was the word that friends and foes alike used to describe him. He had a head as bald as a billiard ball, a hard stare and a long beak of a nose; his nickname was "The Bald Eagle."

Now in the spring of 1876 he was again spoiling for action and impatient with those who would compromise or surrender. He stormed over the refusal of the state's Democrats to endorse a "straight out" ticket of uncompromising white conservatives in the upcoming elections; there was even talk of the Democrats throwing in the towel altogether and supporting the moderate Republican incumbent governor.

Other prominent Edgefield men shared Gary's violent impatience. There was Matthew C. Butler, another lawyer and ex-Confederate general, who the previous year had led 1,000 armed white men to hunt down a local black militia captain—who had got away in the end. And there were the Tillman brothers, George and Ben. Ben Tillman was not yet 30 but this last of 11 children, whose father had died when he was 2, was well on his way to becoming one of the largest landowners in the county between what he had inherited and what he had bought, some 2,000 acres of land. He had been old enough to fight the last year of the Civil War but before he could enlist was incapacitated by a rumor, which an army surgeon then cut out from behind his left eye. He managed to survive the ordeal but lost the eye.

Ben Tillman had since joined the Sweetwater Sabre Club, 45 young white men from Edgefield and Aiken counties. The men bought themselves uniforms, sabers and army pistols, and many had improved carbines and Winchester rifles. A large majority had shotguns. There was agreement among the members of the club that nothing was so useful as a shotgun to mow down a bunch of men at short range. In the event of trouble, they had a system of couriers who could spread the alarm and get everyone assembled on two hours' notice. They would meet at the little Sweetwater Baptist Church, about eight miles north of the predominantly black town of Hamburg.

Hamburg had been practically a ghost town at the end of the Civil War. It lay on low land frequently flooded by the Savannah River, its former prosperity as a market town long since bypassed by the railroads. But the place offered the freedmen who moved there strength in numbers and safety in remoteness. Edgefield County's population was 60 percent African American, but Hamburg's was soon 75 percent; within a few years its population swelled to 1,100 as the town became home to hundreds of black families who had broken free of the life of contracted farm workers, a life scarcely distinguishable from slavery. Among their numbers were schoolteachers, railroad employees, blacksmiths; a successful cotton broker, a printer, a clerk of the court; shoemakers, painters, carpenters and a constable. Hamburg became a small but significant center of African-American political autonomy, electing a black mayor, town councilmen, county commissioners, state legislators and forming a state National Guard company. One of their own, Prince Rivers, a former sergeant in the U.S. Colored Troops who fought for the Union, was appointed as the local trial justice, or magistrate.

One day during that spring of compromise that so incensed Martin Witherspoon Gary, the Bald Eagle had got his neighbors together and told them that "one ounce of fear was worth a pound of persuasion." He told them, and they agreed, that they should "seize the first opportunity that the negroes might offer them to provoke a riot and teach the negroes a lesson." As Ben Tillman later recalled, "Nothing but bloodshed and a good deal of it could answer the purpose of redeeming the state." The idea was to set about "terrorizing the negroes at the first opportunity," and "having the whites demonstrate their superiority by killing as many of them as was justifiable."

The idea was to terrorize the blacks and have the whites demonstrate their superiority by killing as many of them as was justifiable.

Hamburg was the place for it if any place was. Nothing could be easier than to provoke trouble there, since young white rowdies were doing it all the time. Edgefield men had to drive through Hamburg to cross the bridge to Augusta, and they were often causing trouble, razzing the black town constable, galloping their horses down the sidewalks, ignoring the posted sign that said to dip water out only with a clean vessel and sticking their faces right into the public town well to take a drink. They would shoot off their guns and whoop and curse the "radicals" outside the house of Samuel J. Lee, the black county commissioner who had been in the state legislature and even served as speaker of the house a few years earlier.

The town marshal, Jim Cook, would sometimes arrest the white troublemakers, hauling them in and fining them $5. One particularly cocky local white youth who lived on a plantation just a couple of miles out of town, Thomas J. Butler, often went around talking about the main street through Hamburg as "my road" or "my fathers street." There had been plenty of bad blood already.

In July 1876, Tommy Butler was 22. On the 4th of July he and his brother-in-law Henry Getzen were in a buggy driving through Hamburg, coming from Augusta. There would later be some dispute about whether the two men had sat in their buggy on the street in Hamburg for a half-hour watching things first and had then circled around the block, or whether they had come just that minute from Augusta when they were heading down Market Street. And there was plenty of dispute about whether the men of Company A of the 18th Regiment of the South Carolina National Guard, who were parading to celebrate the Fourth, were taking up the entire 150-foot-wide street or just a third of it and whether the two men could have gone around if they so chose. But there is no dispute that they did not so choose and instead whipped their horse into a trot as they came right down the middle of the road.

There were a few hundred townsfolk at the parade; they had gathered at 3 P.M. to listen to a reading of the Declaration of Independence, and then at 4:30 the militia company had put on its show of marching and drill.

The black militiamen parading with rifles and bayonets and the white men in the buggy came to a halt facing each other.

"Mr. Getzen, I do not know for what reason you treat me in this manner," said Dock Adams, the captain of the company, a resident of Hamburg and a boss carpenter by trade.

"What?" Getzen replied.

Author Stephen Budiansky on the Terror after Appomattox

Stephen Budiansky discusses his newest book, The Bloody Shirt: Terror after Appomattox, *which exposes the extent to which violence and calculated techniques of terror—not unfamiliar to us in the 21st century—overthrew Reconstruction and effectively closed the door to black suffrage and civil rights for nearly another century.*

Where did your book title come from? Southerners used the phrase "waving the bloody shirt" to imply that by calling attention to somebody who had been a victim of Southerners, Northerners were simply trying to stir up old enmities and to say "look how terrible Southerners still are." Because of this—that it was all got up for partisan purposes—they could claim therefore there must be no truth to it.

But the terror was largely in the open? On the one hand there's a huge coverup constantly going on, and you see white terrorist leaders and even whole communities telling the most outrageous lies to deny these murders even took place, or to suggest that they were just Northern press fabrications. But on the other hand there's a glorification of the violence as a manly virtue and an expression of racial superiority. The white papers in Mississippi and Louisiana during the 1874 and 1875 elections are just full of blood-curdling threats—"carry the election peaceably if we can, forcibly if we must." In the same breath they would justify the violence by blaming their own victims: Yes, we did shoot these black political leaders and lynch this county commissioner, but that just goes to show how far "decent men" have been pushed—what happens when you try to make white men submit to rule by "our own slaves."

Little was done to disguise their fundamental belief in white supremacy? I was struck while researching how open the race issue was. In the 150 years since, I think historians who tended to apologize for the actions of white Southerners glossed over the degree to which race was the issue. They point to corruption in the Reconstruction governments and carpetbaggers. But go back and read the papers at the time, the issue, open and shut, was race. The white Democrat appeals in the South during the period were completely on racial grounds. You see over and over the statement, "This is a white man's government for white men only." Democratic candidates would proudly proclaim "I am for white supremacy."

Prevailing popular opinion seems, even today, to be that Reconstruction was an experiment doomed to failure. Despite new scholarship over the last half-century, there remains an impression, in popular culture and even in some textbooks, that it was over-reaching. Conservative whites back then called it "a frightful experiment," and that same tone persists in a lot of popular interpretations. This impression was deliberately created by Southern white Democrats at the time, that you were taking "ignorant" Negroes and putting them into the state legislature and that it was impossible that such an experiment, motivated by vindictiveness on the part of Northern radicals wanting to punish the defeated South, can succeed. Part of why this came to be the accepted view by mainstream historians was

the rising tide of nationalism and scientific racism in the late 19th century. Even Northern historians started to say that blacks were inherently inferior; that therefore it was impossible that they could take on the responsibilities of governing; and that therefore the whites who had claimed to believe in racial equality during this period were at best naive and at worst hypocritical and corrupt.

You write about some extremely dedicated and idealistic Northern whites who went South after the war. There were people clearly idealistically motivated, seeking to build a new society based on equality regardless of color. Most so-called carpetbaggers were people who decided to settle in the South, not to plunder and go back North. They were determined to make a life there. Not only were they idealistic, fighting against terrible odds with great courage in the face of often violent social ostracism, but they were convinced they were going to succeed—not because they were foolish or naive but because what they were doing was so obviously right, in the great tradition of American liberty and freedom. And they were backed by the federal government, the army and three Constitutional amendments. It's a bugaboo of history that we think what did happen was inevitable.

Why didn't they prevail? I argue that the consummate cause for the collapse of Reconstruction was very calculated terrorist violence on the part of conservative white Southerners who knew exactly what they were doing. The new 1868 state constitutions had to provide for equal voting rights regardless of race. Across the South about three-quarters of the delegates elected to these state conventions were Republicans and of them close to half were native white Southerners. In no state of the South were a majority of the delegates Northern whites. Only in South Carolina were native blacks a majority. The point being there was a substantial number of white Southerners willing to support Reconstruction. It was only under constant violence and social ostracism that the Southern Republicans were defeated. It took extraordinary courage for Southern whites to support the Republican program when it was much easier to just throw in the towel and start voting Democratic. It wasn't overreaching—Reconstruction was overthrown by the adroit use of military force in a form that we would recognize today unquestionably as terrorism.

How did relatively small numbers succeed against federal troops? Few federal officers understood how to fight against terrorists, and there was institutional reluctance to be playing what the army officers themselves looked down on as being mere constabulary duty. Southerners effectively exploited the apprehensions of the public at large about the use of military force. They would deliberately provoke incidents to cause a military reaction. This is classic terrorism. And so the initial act of killing a minor black politician would be forgotten. What would be exploited for all its worth was: "Look, they've sent the federal bayonets to crush us here."

Seems like familiar tactics. The tactics and situations facing the army during Reconstruction precisely anticipate modern insurgency and counterinsurgency wars.

(continued)

By 1876 Southern blacks must have felt completely abandoned. After participating in the writing of constitutions, holding office, making economic progress, and then suddenly they're effectively stripped of their vote and their protection, they did feel abandoned. They were shown what's possible, only to have it taken away.

What compelled you to write about the Reconstruction era? The parallels to today are just so striking. As a writer and a historian, it fills me with a sense of outrage, not only that these things happened on American soil and the perpetrators got away with it, but also that history for so long has covered their tracks.

"Aiming to drive through my company."

"Well, this is the rut I always travel."

"That may be true, but if ever you had a company out here I should not have treated you in this kind of a manner. I would have gone around and shown some respect to you."

"Well, this is the rut I always travel, and I don't intend to get out of it for no damn niggers."

There was more cursing from Tommy Butler. He later solemnly averred he had been "very mild and peaceful" during the confrontation, to which a member of the militia company said if that was the case, "It is the first time that he ever was."

After several minutes Adams ordered his company to "open order" and let the buggy drive through. Some of the men in the ranks grumbled that they would rather stand there all day and all night than move aside, and more words were exchanged. Adams tried to silence them. Butler and Getzen reached for their pistols and threatened to shoot anyone who stuck a bayonet in their horse. Then it started to rain, and Adams was able to convince the company to head back toward its drill room in the Sibley Building. Marshal Jim Cook showed up and shouted at the white men that he would arrest them if they ever came through town again, but by then they were several hundred yards down the road and weren't about to stop or turn back.

The next morning Tommy Butler, his father, Robert, and Henry Getzen showed up at Trial Justice Prince Rivers' office on Market Street to swear out a complaint against Dock Adams for obstructing the road. Rivers immediately summoned Adams for a hearing. Since Adams didn't have a lawyer Rivers allowed him to cross-examine Getzen. Things got so heated that Rivers found Adams in contempt for the language he used and ordered the hearing postponed until Saturday, July 8, at 4 P.M., to give everyone a chance to cool off.

At 3 o'clock on that very hot Saturday afternoon, a buggy pulled up to the door of Prince Rivers' magistrate's office on Market Street. In the buggy sat General Matthew C. Butler (no relation to Tommy Butler). He called to William Nelson, Rivers' constable who was sitting at his desk inside the open door with his feet propped up on the door frame.

"Where is Rivers?"

"Mr. Rivers is at his house, I reckon," replied the constable, "but he will be here directly."

In the street more buggies pulled up along with some men on horses. Getzen, the Butlers and several other men were armed. Tommy Butler had a shotgun, and Getzen had a carbine.

"I have come here as counsel to these people," the general barked. "Go and tell him to come here to me."

Nelson kept his same attitude and replied, "I am not Mr. Rivers' office boy; I am a constable, and I am here 'tending to my business. He told me that he would be here at 4 o'clock, and he won't come any quicker by my going after him."

"Do you know who you are talking to?"

"I am talking to General Butler, I believe."

"You God-damned son of a bitch, you want to have a hole put through you before you can move. God damn you sitting down there with your feet cocked up."

"Well, general, I am not dead," Nelson replied, "but if you are going to kill me, why just kill me, and that is all you can do."

When Rivers arrived, he called the court into session and sent Nelson to fetch Dock Adams and the other officers of the militia company who had been summoned to give their testimony about the incident.

Meanwhile, the street was filling up with armed white men. There were about 100 men on horseback, carrying pistols, 16-shooter rifles and shotguns. The road heading down into town from above was screened by a bluff, so there had not been much warning they were coming.

Nelson went back to tell Rivers he thought there was going to be trouble. "I reckon not," Rivers replied, but Nelson said, "We better get away from this office." Meanwhile Adams and the militia officers had sent word that they were not about to show up at Rivers' court because they were certain an ambush was being prepared. General Butler announced that he and his men were not going to leave town until the black militia company turned over all their guns to him personally. And that was when the Hamburg townspeople knew they really had a war on their hands.

From the top of the Sibley Building, Adams, Nelson and 36 other militia company members who had taken refuge there watched as the streets filled up with more white rifle club men. Horsemen were positioned on the streets that ran to the north and east of the square the building occupied. To the south, General Butler was pointing to the stone abutment of the railroad bridge along the river's edge, about 75 yards away. Men filed down and took up position behind it.

An order rang out: "All men having carbines or rifles step five paces to the front."

It was almost dark when the first shot from down by the river flashed brightly against the black water behind. A bullet tore through the metal gutter on the roof right by Nelson's side.

For a half-hour the firing continued. The men inside the building had only about three rounds apiece and waited to fire back. When they did, they fired one shot right into the head of McKie Meriwether, a 25-year-old member of the Sweetwater

Sabre Club who was down along the riverbank firing up at the building with the others, and he pitched over dead.

A voice in the street below said, "Go to Augusta and get a keg of powder and we'll blow the damned building up." Another said, "Bring a cannon with you."

It was dark now and the full moon had not yet risen. The militiamen began slipping out the back of the building to save themselves as they could. A half-hour later the air was rent by the bass report of a cannon, the rippling rain of shrapnel against the brick face of the building and the splintering of the solid mahogany roof beams within. They fired a couple more times until the rifle club men realized there was no longer any return fire coming from the building.

Then came the sound of axes and hatchets throughout the block as the rifle club men broke down doors and smashed floorboards, searching for the hidden militiamen. Voices echoed around the square. "There is some damned nigger in this yard." "There goes one of the God-damned sons of bitches!"

William Nelson and Moses Parks had jumped over the fence into the next lot and were hiding in the shadows behind Davis Lepfeld's store on the northwest corner of the block. A voice shouted, "Who is there?" Parks made a run for it, trying to leap over the high fence on the north side of the block. There was a scramble of feet, shouting and gunshots, and as Parks fell to the ground someone cried, "God damn him, I got him." Nelson crawled back on all fours into the yard of the house and crouched against the brick privy for a while. But the moon had come up and he heard a bunch of men nearby; he pulled a board up and crawled right into the sink of the privy itself.

Over by a peach tree near the railroad trestle, another militiaman heard a second man spring over the fence a little farther down the street and voices shouting at him to halt. Amid the confused sounds of shouting and running footsteps on the street came the crack of pistol shots and then the single boom of a shotgun. Another man lay dead and the hiding militiaman recognized Tommy Butler's voice. He saw Butler looking down at the body and expressing great satisfaction that they had got Jim Cook. The town marshal was not a member of the militia company but must have known he was the most marked man in town and had holed up with the militiamen for protection and then tried to make a break for it. Butler rifled through the dead man's pockets for the $5 he had once been fined by the marshal, and not finding any money he lifted a nice looking watch off the corpse. Then the men cut out Cook's tongue and placed it in his hand and someone said, "Keep that till morning, and let them see what we have done."

"He'll chief no more in Hamburg," said another, "but in hell." By about 11 P.M. the rifle club men had rounded up 27

They cut out the marshal's tongue and said: Let them see what we have done. . . . He'll chief no more in Hamburg, but in hell.

---

militiamen and marched them down Market Street just between the last house and the South Carolina Railroad. They were surrounded by a ring of men with guns, pistols, axes, hatchets and grubbing hoes.

Ben Tillman and his squad had been in on the shooting of Cook on the street north of the Sibley Building. Two of McKie Meriwether's cousins were in his company, and they said it was a damned poor piece of work to have lost one of their best men and have only two dead Negroes to show for it. So they made their way up to where the prisoners were being held. It was now 2 A.M. Henry Getzen, who lived close enough to Hamburg to know some of the men, was delegated the task of designating the "meanest characters" among them.

One of the prisoners was Allan Attaway, a county commissioner and a lieutenant of the militia. When he saw Getzen approach he called out to him. "Mr. Getzen, do what you can for me."

"God damn you, I will do what I can for you directly," Getzen replied. "I know you."

Several rifle club men then grabbed Attaway and marched him across the railroad tracks down to a field. "Turn around you yellow son of a bitch," a voice yelled. There was the sound of gunshots, and then the white men returned, without Attaway.

Getzen called out other men: David Phillips, Pompey Curry, Albert Myniart, Hampton Stephens. Each was marched off across the railroad and each time the sound of shooting came back across the night. Pompey Curry managed to break away and run when his name was called. He was shot in the leg below the knee and fell to the ground, playing dead until he managed to crawl away and hide in the bushes when the men went back for their next prisoner.

When it was over, Ben Tillman pronounced himself "more than satisfied" with his "strenuous day's work," and when he and the boys reached Henry Getzen's place as the first streaks of red dawn appeared in the sky, they stopped and ate some watermelons before continuing on their way home.

Tillman would later allow that probably the killing of prisoners would not have happened but for the loss of "young Meriwether," but all was for the best as it turned out, since "the purpose of our visit to Hamburg was to strike terror, and the next morning when the negroes who had fled to the swamp returned to the town, the ghastly sight which met them of seven dead negroes lying stark and stiff certainly had its effect." They had been "offered up as a sacrifice," said Tillman, "to the fanatical teachings and fiendish hate of those who sought to substitute the rule of the African for that of the Caucasians of South Carolina."

What the black people of Hamburg most remembered were the words they heard over and over from the white men as they were shooting and killing and cavorting through the night.

"By God, we've killed a sufficient number to prevent nigger rule any longer."

"We've put a quietus on nigger rule for all time to come."

By God, we'll carry South Carolina; about the time we kill four or five hundred more, we will scare the rest.

"By God, we'll carry South Carolina; about the time we kill four or five hundred more, we will scare the rest."

"This is the beginning of the redemption of South Carolina."

A few weeks later the Democrats reconvened to nominate Confederate cavalry hero Wade Hampton as its standard-bearer for governor. "The Rubicon Passed at Hamburg—The Straight-Out Policy The True One" declared the *Aiken Courier-Journal.*

Hampton's political campaign became a series of military triumphs that autumn as columns of 1,000 or more armed white men marched across the state, breaking up Republican political meetings or shooting the occasional black militiaman or politician who still dared to defy them. Ben Tillman made sure to be on hand the day that fall when the Sweetwater Sabre Club got hold of Simon Coker, a black state senator they did not much care for. They marched him out to a field, made him kneel and shot him dead. Then one of the boys put his pistol up to the dead man's head and shot once more, remarking as he did that he remembered what a mistake they had made in Hamburg with Pompey Curry: "Captain, I did not want any more witnesses to come to life again."

And Ben Tillman, with his pistol, was at his post bright and early on Election Day at a small poll in Edgefield County. When the vote was counted at the end of the day it was 211 to 2 for the Democrats, which was not surprising since he had not let any black men vote at all. General Gary had done the same thing at Edgefield Court-House, where even U.S. troops had not been able to do much more than clear a path about 4 feet wide to the ballot box between the armed white men. When the vote was counted for all of Edgefield County, the Democrats had won 5,500 to 3,000, which was impressive not only because the Democrats' vote had exceeded by 3,000 the number of white voters in the county but also because the total vote had exceeded by 2,000 the entire number of the county's voting-age men. Hampton claimed to have carried the state by 1,000 votes, even though black registered voters outnumbered whites 3-to-2.

On June 1, 1877, the new governor dismissed Prince Rivers as trial justice of Hamburg. A few days later the legislature, now firmly in Democratic hands thanks to the expulsion of 22 duly elected Republican members, repealed the charter of the town of Hamburg.

And so ended "Negro rule" in Hamburg.

As seen in *American History* (April 2008), pp. 30, 32–37; original to *The Bloody Shirt: Terror After Appomattox* by Stephen Budiansky (Viking Penguin, 2008). Copyright © 2008 by Stephen Budiansky. Reprinted by permission of Viking Penguin, a division of Penguin Group (USA) Inc.

The Nez Perce Flight for Justice

W. DAVID EDMUNDS

The charismatic Indian leader Chief Joseph stood on the bank of the Snake River, looking across the water to Idaho and beyond to his people's new home, the Nez Perce reservation in the Clearwater Valley. With him were several hundred men, women, and children, many on horses, dragging their belongings behind them on travois. These Northern Plateau Indians, who called themselves Nee-Me-Poo (The People) or Iceyeeye Niim Mama'yac (The Children of the Coyote), were deeply unhappy about being turned out of the Wallowa Valley of northeastern Oregon, where their people had lived for centuries. But federal officials had given Chief Joseph and his people an ultimatum only six months earlier, forcing them to join other Nez Perce who had signed a treaty more than a decade before and moved to the reservation.

Until 1877 the Nez Perce had prided themselves on their friendship with Americans, beginning when they welcomed the Lewis and Clark Expedition in September 1805. In the decades that followed, as the young republic pushed west, increasing numbers of settlers trespassed on their lands. Even so, the Nez Perce had patiently avoided any open conflict.

In 1877 Chief Joseph was 37 years old, strikingly handsome, married, and the father of several children, all of whom, except one daughter, Kapap Ponmi, or "Brook Song," had died in infancy. He was a skilled negotiator but had little left to work with. Worried about his people's future, Joseph distrusted the U.S. officials but believed he had little choice and reluctantly agreed to relocate his people.

Swollen with late spring snowmelt, the Snake River moved fast, its strong currents largely hidden below its rippled surface. When the Nez Perce started to cross, things went wrong almost immediately. Several of their livestock were torn away down river and lost to sight. Joseph directed the rescue effort, which scattered the people all along the bank. In the midst of this confusion, some frontier ne'er-do-wells took advantage of the situation to raid the Nez Perce's stock of fine Appaloosas. Hours later, the now exhausted and angry Nez Perce had gathered up their animals and set up camp just south of the reservation. They dug up camas bulbs for food and brooded about their forced expulsion.

Tensions had long simmered between white incomers and the Indians already pressed onto the reservation. On June 13 a few young warriors from Chief White Bird's village killed four settlers whom they believed had mistreated their kinsmen. When news reached Joseph, he counseled caution, but fearing reprisal, the new arrivals withdrew to White Bird Canyon, near present-day Grangeville, Idaho. On June 18 scouts reported the approach of a large party of U.S. troops and local volunteers commanded by Capt. David Perry.

Joseph sent out a negotiating party under a white flag, but the volunteers fired upon them, setting off the Battle of White Bird Canyon. Although outnumbered two to one and poorly armed, the Nez Perce inflicted a devastating defeat on Perry's party, killing 34 soldiers before the army retreated. Meanwhile, Nez Perce war parties raided neighboring ranches, killing 14 civilians.

White Bird Canyon thrust Joseph onto the horns of a dilemma. The U.S. Army still reeled from its defeat at the Little Big Horn and the death of George Armstrong Custer the year before. Joseph understood that federal officials would act decisively to suppress any acts of resistance. He still preferred to negotiate, or at least to retreat back to the Wallowa Valley and mount a defense among familiar surroundings. But the other chiefs believed that while negotiations were no longer possible, the U.S. army at least would never pursue them over the mountains into Montana. The Nez Perce fled into the rugged country between the Salmon, Snake, and Clearwater rivers.

Gen. Oliver Howard, commander of the Department of the Columbia, turned his attention to Chief Looking Glass's village. While Looking Glass had not taken part at White Bird Canyon, Howard, mistakenly believing that he was actively recruiting for the "hostiles," ordered Capt. Stephen Whipple and two companies of cavalry to arrest him. While Howard and the rest of his command pursued Joseph into the mountains, Whipple attacked Looking Glass's village on July 1, killing mostly women and children. The chief and most of his people escaped, although losing many of their horses.

Whipple's attack drove Looking Glass, a skilled military leader well versed in the mountain trails leading into Montana, into Joseph's camp, along with all his followers, increasing the "hostile" ranks to approximately 300 warriors and 500 women and children. Looking Glass added his voice to those urging a retreat to Montana, and Joseph reluctantly agreed.

While Looking Glass, White Bird, and other war chiefs directed the defense, Joseph focused his efforts upon the formidable task of ensuring that the refugees had food and adequate transportation. The route across Idaho passed through a challenging topography of towering mountains and canyons blocked by deadfalls, and made use of narrow trails that would tax the endurance even of seasoned warriors. Most of the refugees were tribal elders, women, and children, many riding horses, but some walking along the steeper trails, gasping for air at the higher altitudes. Some women and children led horses dragging travois or packed with hides for small tepees or other shelters, while others searched for roots and berries. Hunting parties scoured the route for game and slaughtered stray livestock but were hard-pressed to fill their cooking pots.

In late July, Joseph led the Nez Perce over the treacherous Lolo Pass in the Bitterroot Mountains, then around a barricade U.S. soldiers had built across the trail and into the Bitterroot Valley. Footsore and short of provisions, but well ahead of their pursuers, they stopped along the Big Hole River near modern Wisdom, Montana, in early August to hunt and rest their mounts.

None realized that Col. John Gibbon and about 175 troopers from Fort Shaw in western Montana had approached. Shortly before dawn on August 9, 1877, Gibbon's men opened fire on the sleeping Indians. The warriors rallied, forced the soldiers to retreat, and captured a mountain howitzer. When night fell, Joseph led the way south and up the Big Hole Valley. The Nez Perce escaped at a cost of 30 warriors killed, along with at least 60 women and children. The U.S. forces' casualties totaled 29 dead and 40 wounded.

Shortly before dawn, Gibbon's men opened fire on the sleeping Indians.

The hard-beset band crossed Bannock Pass into Idaho, then turned eastward along the Lemhi Valley. Howard followed, but on August 20, while Joseph hurried the main party toward Wyoming, Nez Perce scouts captured or scattered so many of Howard's horses at the Camas Meadows that the general postponed his pursuit until he could recapture or recoup his livestock. By late August the weary Nez Perce had crossed through what is now Yellowstone Park and descended Clark's Fork of the Yellowstone. In September they eluded Col. Samuel Sturgis and the remnants of the 7th Cavalry until they were overtaken by, and threw back, Sturgis's force at Canyon Creek on September 13. By mid-September the Nez Perce had spent three months fleeing and fighting off pursuers across 1,000 miles of steep mountains, rocky trails, and raging rivers.

On September 17 Sturgis turned his troopers back, but Joseph and what remained of the Nez Perce trekked on. Leaving the Missouri, they skirmished with a wagon train and a small party of volunteers from Fort Benton, then stopped on September 25 on the northern fringe of the Bear Paw Mountains to catch their breath and rest their exhausted horses. Scouts reported that both Howard's and Sturgis's commands lay far behind. Only 40 miles separated them from Canada, but the weather had turned cold and blustery. While some did not want to stop, Looking Glass assured them that they had several days to rest, hunt, and restock their larders, before heading north.

Again the chiefs underestimated their enemies. Howard had telegraphed Col. Nelson Miles at Fort Keogh in southeastern Montana, prompting Miles and 400 troopers to ride northwest, guided by Lakota and Cheyenne scouts. Undetected, on the morning of September 30 they swept in on the Bear Paw encampment. When the first shots rang out, Joseph and his daughter were outside the camp tending their horses. Galloping back, Joseph rallied a party of warriors who repulsed two cavalry charges. When a third foray penetrated the village, he led a counterattack that again drove the troops to retreat, but meanwhile the Lakota and Cheyenne had scattered or captured many of the Nez Perce horses. The surviving Nez Perce took refuge on a ridge overlooking the encampment. The battle continued throughout the day. As night fell, a blizzard swept in from the northwest.

Still not contemplating surrender, Joseph and the other chiefs argued over the next move. Realizing the hopelessness of their situation, Joseph stated his willingness to negotiate a settlement, but not an unconditional capitulation. White Bird feared that they would hang should they surrender. Looking Glass, who believed that Sitting Bull would send assistance from Canada, took a sniper's bullet on October 3 and died.

Two days later, Howard arrived with reinforcements at the battlefield. After conferring, Miles and Howard sent a messenger to Joseph guaranteeing him that if the Nez Perce surrendered they could return to Idaho; if not, the assault would be renewed. For Joseph the choice was clear. Burdened with women, children, and tribal elders, he could not escape to Canada. On the afternoon of October 5 he rode forward, reluctantly met with Miles and Howard, and delivered his famous speech: "I am tired. My heart is sick and sad. From where the sun now stands, I will fight no more forever." Chief Joseph and about 400 of his followers surrendered. Another 300 Nez Perce led by White Bird slipped through the American lines and eventually joined the Sioux in Canada under Sitting Bull.

While Miles was sincere in his promises, federal officials refused to honor them. Joseph and his people were shipped first to Kansas, then south to Indian Territory. After Joseph journeyed to Washington and repeatedly pled for their return to the Northwest, in 1884 they were finally placed on the Colville Reservation in Washington, where Chief Joseph died in 1904. Yet the epic of undaunted resolution struck a responsive chord, even among their enemies. Howard and Miles united in praising their bravery, military ability, and perseverance. Journalists lionized Chief Joseph, and for many readers the handsome, eloquent chieftain and his people emerged as the embodiment of the "noble red man's" justifiable resistance to heavy-handed U.S. Indian policy. Regardless of stereotypes, their flight and resistance remain remarkable epics of American history, while today the modern Nez Perce people play a viable part in the American nation.

How the West Was Spun

Buffalo Bill Cody heralded the closing of the frontier by reassuring Americans that they would never be too civilized to beat the braves and bullies of the world at their own game.

STEPHEN G. HYSLOP

When fabled bison hunter William "Buffalo Bill" Cody first staged his Wild West show in 1883, he needed more than heroic cowboys, villainous Indians, teeming horses and roaming buffalo to transform it from a circus into a sensation. He needed star power. And there was one man who guaranteed to provide it: the Sioux chief widely blamed for the uprising that overwhelmed George Armstrong Custer's 7th Cavalry at the Battle of Little Bighorn only a decade earlier. "I am going to try hard to get old Sitting Bull," Cody said. "If we can manage to get him our ever lasting fortune is made."

It took two years, but Cody finally got his man. In June 1885, Sitting Bull joined the Wild West show for a signing bonus of $125 and $50 a week—20 times more than Indians who served as policemen on reservations earned. Buffalo Bill reckoned his new star would prove to be an irresistible draw. With the Indian wars drawing to a close, and most Plains Indians confined to reservations, Buffalo Bill set the stage for a final conquest of the frontier. Since accompanying an army patrol as a scout shortly after the Battle of Little Bighorn and scalping the Cheyenne warrior Yellow Hair, he was known as the man who took "the first scalp for Custer." As the man who now controlled Sitting Bull, he symbolically declared victory in the war for the West and signaled a new era of cooperation with the enemy. Cody excluded the chief from acts in which other Indians made sham attacks on settlers and then got their comeuppance from heroic cowboys. All Sitting Bull had to do was don a war costume, ride a horse into the arena and brave an audience that sometimes jeered and hissed.

Sitting Bull's mere presence reinforced the reassuring message underlying Cody's Wild West extravaganza, as well as the Western films and novels it inspired, that Americans are generous conquerors who attack only when provoked. At the same time, Cody's vision of the West spoke to the fiercely competitive spirit of an American nation born in blood and defined by conflict on the frontier, where what mattered most was not whether you were right or wrong but whether you prevailed. The lesson of his Wild West was that sharpshooting American cowboys like Buffalo Bill could be as wild as the Indians they fought and match them blow for blow. The real frontier might be vanishing, but by preserving this wild domain imaginatively and reenacting the struggle for supremacy there, he gave millions of Americans the feeling they were up to any challenge.

Buffalo Bill's Wild West depended on Cody's ability to draw shrewdly on his frontier experiences to make himself a commanding figure. He earned his nickname, he claimed, by killing 4,280 buffalo during an 18-month stint for the Kansas Pacific Railroad in the late 1860s. Indiscriminate hunting was encouraged by the army as part of a campaign to wipe out buffalo herds that gave subsistence to free-roaming Plains Indians. The Indians did not take well to having this food supply annihilated. Cody told of being chased once by 30 Indians on horseback. Cavalry guarding the tracks came to his aid, and together they killed eight "redskins," he said, expressing sympathy only for a horse one of the warriors was riding, killed by a shot from his trusty rifle Lucretia: "He was a noble animal, and ought to have been engaged in better business."

Later in life Cody mused that Indians deserved better. But his early exploits on the Plains and his autobiographical account of those feats, designed to portray him as a classic frontier enforcer, came first. His crowning claim involved the rescue of a white woman from the clutches of Indians. In July 1869, he was serving as a scout for the 5th Cavalry when it surprised hostile Cheyennes in an encampment at Summit Springs, Colorado Territory, where one white woman held captive was killed in the ensuing battle and one rescued. Official records give credit for locating the camp to Pawnee scouts—who volunteered to serve the army against their traditional tribal foes—and make no mention of Buffalo Bill. But Cody boasted of killing Cheyenne Chief Tall Bull during the engagement after creeping to a spot where he could "easily drop him from the saddle" without hitting his horse, a "gallant steed" he then captured and named Tall Bull in honor of the chief.

This fabricated tale demonstrated Cody's knack for translating the grim realities of Indian fighting into rousing adventure stories in which he symbolically appropriated the totemic power of defeated warriors by claiming their scalp, horse or captives, much as Indians did in battle. But he took care to distinguish his bravery from the bravado of warriors who refused to fight fair and targeted women and children. Left unmentioned in his account of the Battle of Summit Springs—which, like the Battle of Little Bighorn, he incorporated as an act in his Wild West show—was that women and children were among the more than 70 Cheyennes killed or captured.

After returning with the cavalry from Summit Springs to Fort Sedgwick in Colorado, Buffalo Bill met Edward Judson, who was looking for Western heroes to celebrate in the dime novels he wrote under the name Ned Buntline. His fiction did so much to create and inflate the reputation of Buffalo Bill that actors were soon playing him on stage. "I was curious to see how I would look when represented by some one else," Cody recalled, so while visiting New York in 1872 he attended a performance of *Buffalo Bill: The King of the Border Men* and was called on stage. He soon realized that he could succeed in the limelight simply by being himself, or by impersonating the heroic character contrived by Buntline.

"I'm not an actor—I'm a star," he told an interviewer soon after making the transition from frontier scout to itinerant showman. Crucial to his ascent to stardom was his awareness that he needed to become something more than a stereotypical Indian fighter or "scourge of the red man." He never renounced that role and continued to bank on it throughout his career, but his genius as an entertainer lay in softening his own image—and that of the Wild West—just enough to reassure Americans that the conquest he dramatized was a good clean fight that had redeeming social value without robbing this struggle for supremacy of its visceral appeal.

Buffalo Bill's first appearance on stage in Chicago gave little hint of the bright future that awaited him in show business. He and other ornery frontiersmen blasted away at Indians ludicrously impersonated by white extras in a murky plot concocted by Buntline. One reviewer called the acting "execrable" and concluded that such "scalping, blood and thunder, is not likely to be vouchsafed to a city a second time, even Chicago." Nonetheless, the show proved commercially successful, and Buffalo Bill made $6,000 over the winter, substantially improving his take in seasons to come by forming his own troupe called the Buffalo Bill Combination.

For several years, he combined acting with summer stints as a scout or guide, honing his skills as an entertainer by conducting wealthy dudes from the East and European nobility on hunting expeditions and diverting them with shows of skill that sometimes involved Indians hired for the occasion. Buffalo Bill enjoyed "trotting in the first class, with the very first men of the land," and came away convinced that a Wild West spectacle involving real cowboys and Indians could appeal to all classes and become, as it was later billed, "America's National Entertainment."

Other showmen of the era tried to mine that same vein by mounting Wild West themed circuses in which sharpshooters and bronco-busters demonstrated their skills. But when Buffalo Bill launched his Wild West show in 1883, he set his aim higher. He wanted an epic production with theatrical flair that defined the West and drew viewers into it. After a lackluster first season, marred by his drunken escapades with a fellow sharpshooter and business associate named Doc Carver, he teamed with Nate Salsbury, a shrewd theater manager, and hired director Steele MacKaye to make the production more than a series of stunts by creating a show within the show called *The Drama of Civilization.* First staged in the winter of 1886 in New York's Madison Square Garden, where it was viewed by more than a million people, the pageant was set against painted backdrops and included four acts that purported to represent the historical evolution of the West from "The Primeval Forest," occupied only by wild Indians, to "The Prairie," where civilization appeared with the arrival of wagon trains, setting the stage for further progress in the form of "The Cattle Ranch" and "The Mining Camp."

Buffalo Bill wanted a high-toned epic production with theatrical flair and elaborate staging that defined the West and drew viewers into it.

The elaborate staging fulfilled Buffalo Bill's stated goal of offering "high toned" entertainment, but the acts themselves suggested that the coming of the white man had done little to tame the Wild West. The climactic mining camp episode included a duel between gunfighters and an attack on the Deadwood Stagecoach by bandits, playing much the same role as that performed by marauding Indians in other performances. In the grand finale, the mining camp was blown away by a cyclone, suggesting that if wild men did not defeat those trying to civilize the West, wild nature surely would.

At heart the Wild West extravaganza was less about the triumph of civilization than ceaseless struggle in which "barbarism and civilization have their hands on each other's throat," as one observer put it. Cody could not afford to become so high toned that he robbed the show of the smoke and thunder that many came to see, and he surely welcomed notices like that from a reviewer who promised the public that "Buffalo Bill's 'Wild West' is wild enough to suit the most devoted admirer of western adventure and prowess." At the same time, Cody promoted the show as family entertainment, suitable for women and children. By hiring Annie Oakley, whom Sitting Bull nicknamed "Little Sure Shot," Cody graced his cast with a deadly shot who was so demure and disarming that spectators who might otherwise have been scared away by gunplay were as eager to attend as those for whom fancy shooting was the main draw.

European blue bloods also found the show enchanting. In 1887 Buffalo Bill and an entourage of 100 whites, 97 Indians, 180 horses, 18 buffalo, 10 elk, 5 Texan steers, 4 donkeys and 2 deer traveled to England to help celebrate the Jubilee Year of Queen Victoria. In addition to staging twice-a-day shows during a five-month stay in London for crowds that averaged around 30,000, the Wild West troupe gave a command performance for the queen in which the Prince of Wales and the kings of Belgium, Greece, Saxony and Denmark rode around the arena in a stagecoach with Buffalo Bill fending off marauding Indians from the driver's seat. In the process, Buffalo Bill's pop interpretation of the American frontier was validated as high culture and for the next five years the Wild West toured the major capitals of Europe.

Despite his warm reception throughout Europe, when Buffalo Bill brought the show home in 1893 he was shunned as too commercial by the organizers of the Columbian Exposition in Chicago, a grandiose celebration of civilization in America that featured 65,000 exhibits in an array of gleaming Beaux Arts buildings dubbed the White City. Undeterred, Buffalo Bill camped out across the street and drew an audience that summer of more than 3 million people, including a group of historians who took a break one afternoon from a conference at the exposition to see the Wild West show and later that evening heard their colleague Frederick Jackson Turner deliver his landmark essay "The Significance of the Frontier in American History."

Turner portrayed the settling of the West as a largely peaceful process, in which the availability of "free land" on the frontier served as a safety valve, releasing social tensions by providing fresh opportunities for Americans who might otherwise have been stifled in their ambitions for a better life. But Cody, for all the historical distortions in his show, hit on a fundamental truth that eluded the erudite Turner: There was no free land. Everything that American settlers claimed, from the landing at Jamestown to the closing of the frontier in 1890, was Indian country, wrested from tribal groups at great cost. Buffalo Bill's Wild West remains with us to this day because he recognized that fierce competition and strife had as much to do with the making of America as the dream of liberty and justice for all.

Ultimately, it was Indians who lent an air of authenticity to Buffalo Bill's Wild West. He could not hire Indians without the government's permission and faced scrutiny and criticism from officials who argued that his show displayed Indians as bloodthirsty warriors while the government was trying to convert them to a peaceful, productive existence. But he was keenly aware of their importance to the production and tried to ensure they were well treated. Luther Standing Bear, a Sioux who served as chief of the Indian performers on one European tour, expressed gratitude for the support Buffalo Bill showed when he complained that Indians were being served inferior food. "My Indians are the principal feature of this show," he recalled Buffalo Bill telling the dining steward, "and they are the one people I will not allow to be misused or neglected."

Black Elk, whose dictated reminiscences to poet John Neihardt were published in 1932 under the title *Black Elk Speaks,* shared Luther Standing Bear's appreciation for the way he and other performers were treated by Buffalo Bill, or Pahuska (Long Hair). When Black Elk wearied of life on tour and said he was "sick to go home," Buffalo Bill was sympathetic: "He gave me a ticket and ninety dollars. Then he gave me a big dinner. Pahuska had a strong heart."

But Black Elk's memories of the show itself were more ambivalent. "I liked the part of the show we made," he said, "but not the part the Wasichus [whites] made." Like other Sioux hired by Buffalo Bill, he enjoyed commemorating their proud old days as mounted warriors but seemingly recognized that their role was defined and diminished by what whites made of it. Describing the command performance of Buffalo Bill's Wild West for Queen Victoria, he recalled that she spoke to Indian performers after they danced and sang for her and told them something to this effect: "All over the world I have seen all kinds of people; but today I have seen the best-looking people I know. If you belonged to me, I would not let them take you around in a show like this." Whether or not she spoke such words, Black Elk evidently felt that "a show like this" did not do his people great honor.

The show relegated Indians to the vanishing world of war bonnets and scalp dances— the only Indian culture many whites recognized.

The willingness of proud warriors who once resisted American authority to join Cody's show demonstrated that they were capable of adapting to the modern world. Yet the conventions of the Wild West relegated them to the past, a vanishing world of tepees, war bonnets and scalp dances that was the only Indian culture many whites recognized. One chief who toured with Cody, Iron Tail, was said to be a model for the Indian Head nickel, with a bonneted warrior on one side and a buffalo on the other—icons that became cherished as distinctively American only when the way of life they represented was on the verge of extinction.

Sitting Bull, whose appearance in the show prompted many other Sioux to join the traveling troupe, epitomized the wide gulf between the myth perpetuated by Buffalo Bill's Wild West and the harsh reality Indians faced with the closing of the frontier. By all accounts he got on well with Cody. But he hated the hustle and bustle of Eastern cities and only stayed with the show for four months. In the years that followed, government officials grew concerned about the emergence of the Ghost Dance, a messianic religious movement on the reservations that promised Indians who joined in the ritualistic dance eternal life in a bountiful world of their own, where they would be reunited with their lost loved ones and ancestors. Reports in late 1889 that Sioux who joined this movement were wearing "ghost shirts," which they believed would protect them from bullets, increased fears among authorities that the movement would turn violent. When Sitting Bull began encouraging the Ghost Dancers, Maj. Gen. Nelson Miles called upon Buffalo Bill to find him and bring him in, hoping that the chief would yield peacefully to a man he knew and trusted.

Cody headed west to Bismarck, N.D., in December 1890 and reportedly filled two wagons with gifts before setting off in his showman's outfit to track down Sitting Bull on the Standing Rock Reservation. The escapade is clouded in legend and it remains unclear whether or not Cody was serious about trying to arrest Sitting Bull. In any case he got waylaid by two scouts working for the Indian agent James McLaughlin, who wanted credit for corraling Sitting Bull himself. This was no longer Cody's show, and it would play out as a reminder of the grim realities that underlay his rousing performances.

On December 15, McLaughlin sent Indian police to arrest Sitting Bull. A struggle ensued, and shots were fired. Sitting Bull was killed instantly. His son, six of his supporters and six policemen also died. Two weeks later, fighting erupted at nearby Wounded Knee Creek on the Pine Ridge Reservation between a band of Sioux caught up in the Ghost Dance movement and troops of Custer's old regiment, the 7th Cavalry, after soldiers grappled with a deaf young Indian who refused to hand over his gun. When the shooting stopped, 25 soldiers and about 150 Sioux, many of them women and children, lay dead. In the words of Charles Eastman, a mixed-blood Sioux physician who searched among the victims for survivors, Wounded Knee exposed the lurking "savagery of civilization."

The massacre marked the tragic end of the real Indian wars.

Gifts of the "Robber Barons"

JAMES NUECHTERLEIN

Even those who consider American history one long triumphal march tend to pass quickly over the decades of industrial expansion and consolidation between the Civil War and the early years of the 20th century. Industrialization was a necessary prelude to mass prosperity; but in America, as elsewhere, it often made for a dispiriting spectacle—pollution, urban blight, glaring material inequalities, ethnic and class conflict, moral dislocation.

To observers at the time, modern America's coining of age often seemed like an unraveling of the social fabric. Because so much had changed so quickly, precise explanations were hard to come by, but the responsibility for what had gone wrong settled quickly on those who had most obviously benefited. If, broadly speaking, industrialization was the problem, the men who ran the system—and who often got enormously rich doing so—had to be made to answer for its shortcomings.

Thus was born the notion of the "robber barons," and it has had a long historical shelf life. Until well into the second half of the 20th century, historians of post-Civil War industrial capitalism echoed contemporary observers both in their emphasis on the system's costs and in their indictment of those in charge.

In recent decades, a measure of economic sophistication has crept into accounts of the era, and the tendency to dwell on personal or institutional villainy has abated. For all its unlovely aspects, the period was one of dynamic economic growth, and those at the top must have been doing at least some things right. They may have gained disproportionately from economic progress, but most workers found their own real wages on the upswing. Industrial development was not the zero-stun game that progressive historians imagined it to be, nor is the concept of "robber barons" an adequate rubric to summarize either the men or the age to which it refers.

Evidence for this view abounds in two outstanding new biographies—David Nasaw's *Andrew Carnegie*[1] and David Cannadine's *Mellon: An American Life.*[2] Nasaw teaches at the Graduate Center of the City University of New York, Cannadine at the Institute of Historical Research, University of London. Neither author ignores or minimizes the flaws in his subject's behavior. But by offering portraits in the round, both resist historical reductionism. Readers may not come away admiring Andrew Carnegie or Andrew Mellon, but they will know better than simply to relegate them to historical pigeonholes.

That is particularly the case with Carnegie, a force of nature and, as Nasaw makes clear, a figure of fascinating complexity. In his business operations, he was sometimes a robber baron, sometimes an enlightened industrial statesman. More significantly, his life was about much more than business, and in his various non-business ventures he fit into no consistent analytical category. As a man, he was devious, deceptive, egomaniacal, and occasionally ruthless; he was also kindly, generous, dutiful, and possessed of an encompassing curiosity that suggested broad human sympathies. He defies convenient summing-up.

Carnegie's career was the American Dream personified. He was born in 1835 in Dunfermline, Scotland, to a poor, none-too-industrious weaver and his ambitious and resourceful wife. The family emigrated to America in 1848, settling near relatives and friends just outside Pittsburgh. Andrew, who had next to no formal education, went immediately to work as a bobbin boy in a cotton mill. Dissatisfied with the physical drudgery, he became a telegraph messenger, taught himself Morse code, and soon became the private telegraph operator and chief assistant to Thomas A. Scott, head of the Pennsylvania Railroad in the Pittsburgh region.

Bright, energetic, and personable—his inveterately optimistic and positive disposition attracted people to him all his life—Carnegie rose quickly in the railroad and considerably augmented his income with investments on the side, especially in oil.

After leaving the company at age thirty, he continued to work with Scott and the railroad's president, J. Edgar Thomson, in a number of joint ventures, contracting with the Pennsylvania and other railways to supply raw materials and grade crossings, and manufacture rails, bridges, and rolling stock of all varieties. He was already a rich man when he expanded from iron to steel in the early 1870's. By the time he retired in 1901, his share of the proceeds from the sale of Carnegie Steel to J.P. Morgan came to almost $120 billion in today's currency, making him the richest man in America, quite possibly the world.

Carnegie considered himself a businessman of probity and integrity and, by the standards of the day, he was. Attacks on his character genuinely baffled and appalled him. Nonetheless, as Nasaw notes, over the course of his career he engaged in activities that included sweetheart deals with corporate cronies, profiting from inside information, the floating of overvalued bonds, stock speculation, and involvement in pools to set minimum prices and allocate market shares. Carnegie operated in an intensely competitive and lightly regulated business environment. Although he acted decently enough by the lights of the day, those lights appear somewhat dim in retrospect.

The greatest blemish on Carnegie's reputation was the notorious lockout and strike at the Homestead steel works near Pittsburgh in July 1892. Carnegie considered himself a friend of the working man—he referred proudly to his family's involvement in the radical Chartist movement in Britain in the 1830's and 40's—but the theoretical rights of workers gave way when they came in conflict with his companies' profit margins. His operating partner Henry Clay Frick attempted to break the Homestead strike by bringing in Pinkerton men, but workers were there to block them. Violence broke out, and by the time order was restored there were dead and wounded on both sides. For the rest of his life, Carnegie, who was vacationing in Scotland at the time of the strike, disavowed responsibility for Homestead, but Nasaw shows that he had prior knowledge of Frick's intentions—they kept in contact by cable—and cites instances of earlier labor conflicts in which Carnegie employed similar tactics.

Still, Carnegie's image as an industrialist of generally enlightened opinions was not without substance. A member of the GOP's progressive wing—he had first been drawn to the party for its antislavery sentiments—he favored establishment of the Interstate Commerce Commission, backed Theodore Roosevelt on railroad regulation, and spoke in favor of a government commission to regulate prices. He defended the progressive income tax and proposed stiff levies on inherited fortunes. He was even known to speak favorably, if vaguely, of a possible socialist future. In foreign policy he was a fervent anti-imperialist, a strong internationalist, and a near fanatical advocate of world peace.

When he was just thirty-three, Carnegie determined that he would no longer preoccupy himself with material gain. "The amassing of wealth," he wrote in a personal memo, "is one of the worst species of idolatry." He began to work only three or four hours a day, spending the rest of his time at intellectual pursuits, philanthropy, and leisure. Much of his effort was devoted to self-education. More than anything else, Carnegie wanted recognition as a man of letters, and to a considerable degree he attained it. He moved in distinguished literary circles in America and Britain (Matthew Arnold and Samuel Clemens were among his close associates), published in fashionable journals of ideas, and wrote the best-selling *Triumphant Democracy* (1886), which, as its title suggests, was an extended celebration of the achievements wrought by America's political and economic institutions.

For Carnegie, America's moral and material progress showed it to be in conformity with the scientific imperatives of Herbert Spencer's Social Darwinism, under whose influence he himself had converted from "theology and the supernatural" to "the truth of evolution." Evolutionary progress was not, to be sure, without its conundrums. "In particular," he wrote, "I don't at all understand the mysterious law of evolution, according to which the higher forms of life live upon the lower, rising through slaughter and extinction. That is profoundly, tragically obscure and perplexing." Still, the evolutionary consolation by which he overcame all doubts remained: "All is well, since all grows better."

Evolutionary theory provided, among other things, an argument for the social utility of millionaires like himself. Beginning in the 1880's, Carnegie elaborated that argument in a series of articles, later gathered into a book, that created the catchphrase with which his name is enduringly associated: the Gospel of Wealth. The simplest defense for great wealth was that it was a necessary byproduct of modern development. Earlier societies were restricted to the household or workshop method of manufacture and provided goods of uneven quality at high prices. Modern industrial society might generate greater inequalities of income, but it also produced dependable products at prices so low that now the poor could enjoy a style of material life available in the past only to the rich. Complex industrial society required as its leaders men with a special talent for organization and management; such men were relatively rare, and so could command a high level of compensation.

As Carnegie saw it, the emergence of the millionaire class resulted from the workings of immutable economic laws that societies ignored at their peril. Those in doubt about this "beneficent necessity," he explained, need only look about them: desperately poor nations like India, China, and Japan had few if any millionaires; as one went up the economic scale, from Russia to Germany to England, the incidence of millionaires proportionately increased. But none of these societies produced anything like America's abundant supply of the very rich, and in America—here, for Carnegie, was the clincher—the income of the many far surpassed that achieved anywhere else. The wealth gap was not a problem to be solved; it was an essential element in a system that worked to the good of all.

Another boon offered to society by millionaires was the proper use of the riches they accumulated that exceeded their personal needs. "The duty of the man of wealth," Carnegie said, is "to consider all surplus revenues which come to him simply as trust funds, which he is called upon to administer . . . in the manner which, in his judgment, is best calculated to produce the most beneficial results for the community."

That duty followed from the fact that, while the wealthy surely earned their riches, wealth itself came ultimately from the community. It was only the growth in the size and needs of the population that created the context in which business leaders could exercise their superior talents. In that sense, Carnegie noted, "the *community* created the millionaire's wealth."

Not all of his fellow millionaires, Carnegie conceded, did what duty required. Some left their fortunes not to the community but to their children, a practice Carnegie condemned as both self-regarding and, in the end, no favor to the children, for whom unearned wealth often turned out to be more blight than blessing. (Thus his support for steep inheritance taxes. Carnegie himself did not marry until he was past fifty, and he had only one child, a daughter.) Others earned Carnegie's rebuke by leaving their estates to be administered, often badly, by lesser men after their deaths. "It is well to remember," Carnegie warned, "that it requires the exercise of not less ability than that which acquired it to use wealth so as to be really beneficial to the community." Then there were those who gave their money away in their lifetimes but did so unwisely. Better to toss money into the sea, Carnegie thought, than to spend it "to encourage the slothful, the drunken, the unworthy." It was philanthropy that was needed, not heedless charity.

Whatever one thinks of his rationale, Carnegie was indeed serious about his philanthropic responsibilities. He did not quite succeed in his intention of giving away all of his money before his death in 1919, but he did disburse vast amounts and left the remainder (minus relatively modest bequests to his wife and various employees and friends) in a charitable trust.

His giving was diverse and sometimes idiosyncratic: it included, inter alia, thousands of community library buildings and endowments in America and Britain, thousands more organs for churches (to introduce parishioners to classical music), pensions for college professors, free tuition for students in Scottish universities, a scientific research institution in the nation's capital, a peace endowment, and a library, music hall, art gallery, and natural-history museum in Pittsburgh.

Carnegie's philanthropy was not motivated—as was the case with so many of his fellow millionaires—by guilt, religious convictions, or a desire to affect public opinion. He felt no pangs of conscience concerning his wealth, harbored no Calvinist or other theological beliefs, and settled on giving away his money long before he became a prominent target of public criticism. He surrendered his fortune because he thought it the right thing to do.

Carnegie had hoped that his retirement would be committed primarily to philanthropic activities. As it turned out, however, philanthropy became subordinate to the cause that consumed his final decades: world peace. He took a major role in opposing Britain's Boer War in South Africa and America's war with Spain and subsequent conflict with rebel forces in the Philippines. But his broader target was war itself, which he considered a moral anachronism among nations in the same way dueling had once been among individuals. The progress of civilization had eliminated the latter evil; that same progress, in combination with the increasing economic interdependence of nations, would do away with the former.

In this case, of course, what Nasaw terms his subject's "almost intolerable self-confidence" failed him. In his incessant, imperious, often condescending badgering of political leaders in Washington, London, and Berlin, he finally made himself "slightly ridiculous." Teddy Roosevelt bore more or less patiently with Carnegie's importunities in public, but referred to him privately as the leader of a "male shrieking sisterhood."

The outbreak of war in 1914 shattered, at least in the short run, Carnegie's naive faith that the ultimate result of the various policies he urged—bilateral arbitration treaties, international disarmament conferences, a permanent world court, a league of peace with enforceable powers—would be the cessation of armed conflict among nations. But if the Great War shook his pacifist dreams, it did not entirely destroy them. One of his last public acts was to write to Woodrow Wilson congratulating the President on his decision in 1917 to enlist America in what both of them believed would be the war to end war.

David Cannadine's biography of Andrew Mellon suffers in comparison with Nasaw's masterful work, but that has to do more with the book's subject than with its author. The historian Burton J. Hendrick, who wrote biographies of both Carnegie and Mellon (the latter was never published) and was thus uniquely positioned to offer a comparative judgment, concluded succinctly that "Mr. Mellon lacks the personal qualities that made Mr. Carnegie so attractive a subject, nor, in other ways, was he so great a man." Mellon's career was less interesting than Carnegie's, his mind less lively and original, his personality less compelling, his impact less memorable. Still, as Cannadine notes, his range of experience in business, politics, art collecting, and philanthropy has no equivalent among those commonly classed as robber barons, and it is well past time that he received full-scale treatment.

Cannadine concedes that he began his research prejudiced against his subject. At the outset, he says, he found Mellon "an unsympathetic person with unappealing politics." Mellon is best known to history as Secretary of the Treasury in the 1920's in the conservative administrations of Warren Harding, Calvin Coolidge, and Herbert Hoover. Cannadine, who is English (though he has studied and taught in the U.S.), admits that had he been an American during that period he would have voted against the Presidents whom Mellon served and thereafter in favor of Franklin D. Roosevelt. Nonetheless, he assures us that he has tried to remain evenhanded in his judgments, and he does scrupulously attempt to provide a comprehensive account of his subject that might satisfy both admirers and detractors. It does not, however, take a terribly perspicacious reader to conclude that the author's final estimation differs little from the one with which he began.

Mellon's career had none of the rags-to-riches romance of Carnegie's. He was born into comfortable circumstances in Pittsburgh in 1855; his father Thomas, whose Ulster Scots family had come to America in 1818 when he was five years old, had prospered as a lawyer, judge, businessman, and banker. Andrew inherited his father's aptitude for business, and already by 1882 had assumed control of T. Mellon and Sons Bank. Through the bank he gradually acquired interests in a broad range of enterprises: real estate, utilities, transportation, coal, steel, chemicals, oil, aluminum. By the turn of the century T. Mellon and Sons had become Mellon National Bank, and its head was now a very rich and powerful industrial financier.

Wealth and power did not translate into fame. Of the great industrialists of the age, Mellon was, until his entry into national politics in the 1920's, the least known. He was associated with no one major business, worked behind the scenes, and avoided publicity. He had none of Carnegie's flair and no desire for his notoriety. (The two men, twenty years apart in age, knew each other but were never close. In his dealings in steel, Mellon carefully avoided competition with Carnegie.) From childhood Mellon had been, even among his several siblings, a shy loner, remote and self-sufficient. He achieved his success through intellect and shrewd judgment, not force of personality.

Mellon's only experience in the public spotlight prior to the 1920's had been embarrassing and personally disastrous. He delayed marriage until 1901 when he was forty-six. He had met Nora McMullen on a cruise three years earlier, when she was nineteen, and had, for the first and only time in his life, fallen immediately and hopelessly in love. The two were utterly mismatched, their marriage a failure from the start. (Cannadine compares the union to that of Prince Charles and Diana Spencer.) Within a few years Nora had entered into a flagrant affair, and by 1912 the marriage was over, its dissolution marked by ugly, protracted, and widely publicized divorce proceedings that titillated the public and left the Mellons' two young children, Ailsa and Paul, with psychological scars that never entirely healed.

After the divorce, Mellon turned his attention not just to work but to the avocation of art collecting, which he had taken up in the late 1890's. Over the years, making his purchases through the prominent art dealers Roland Knoedler and Joseph Duveen, he built a magnificent personal collection. His greatest coup came in 1930–31, when he secretly purchased 21 of the finest paintings from the Hermitage collection in the Soviet Union for some $7 million, an acquisition—Cannadine calls it "the sale of the century"—made possible by Stalin's need for cash in his efforts to modernize the Soviet economy.

By 1920, Mellon was sixty-five and thinking about retirement. He was instead about to enter on a new career in national politics. Long active behind the scenes in the Republican party, he was particularly involved in the 1920 presidential campaign, pleased with the conservative turn in the party and nation that resulted in the nomination and landslide election of Warren Harding. His generous contributions and success at money-raising brought him to the attention of party leaders, and his name was put forward by conservatives to join Harding's cabinet as Secretary of the Treasury, in part to offset the presumed progressive influence of the incoming Secretary of Commerce, Herbert Hoover.

Mellon would serve under three Presidents, from 1921 to 1932. His major policies included reductions in interest rates and the national debt, cuts in taxes and government spending, and settlement of the huge debt that the European allies had incurred with the U.S. to finance their war efforts. On all these matters he achieved, over time, considerable success, and with the return of national prosperity he became a highly regarded figure. Mellon was hailed as "the greatest Secretary of the Treasury since Alexander Hamilton" and was even mentioned as a possible presidential candidate in 1928. This, of course, was before the stock-market crash of 1929 and the onset of the Great Depression, when praise turned to condemnation.

Examining Mellon's stewardship through the prism of the Depression, historians have more often than not been highly critical of his policies, even those prior to 1929. Cannadine, though a liberal in his politics and often disdainful of his subject's views, concludes that Mellon's tenure in the cabinet deserves "a more sympathetic appraisal than it has generally received." He defends in particular Mellon's tax policies, which have frequently been dismissed as special favors for the rich.

In cutting rates at the top, in fact, Mellon wanted to induce the wealthy to pay more in taxes, not less. The high wartime federal rates had prompted the wealthy to concentrate their investments in state and municipal bonds, which were tax-exempt. Mellon rightly supposed that lower income taxes would redirect investment from bonds, where returns were low, to taxable industrial stocks whose generally higher returns would offset the tax bite. Mellon, Cannadine notes, consistently held to the principle that payment of federal taxes should be proportionate to income. His reduction in top rates meant that the rich paid more than they had before, while his elimination of taxes for the first several thousand dollars of income meant that most Americans paid nothing.

Nor, Cannadine thinks, could Mellon have done much either to prevent the crash or to restore the economy in its aftermath. The government's monetary and fiscal tools were inadequate to both tasks. All in all, he concludes, "most of what happened in America between 1929 and 1932 would probably have happened regardless of who had been running the Treasury."

Where Cannadine *is* critical of Mellon concerns his practice, despite public denials, of continuing to look after his personal business interests while in office. There is no evidence of corrupt dealings, but there were times when Mellon urged policies that had favorable implications for companies he was involved in, like Gulf Oil and Alcoa. As Cannadine puts it, Mellon "simply never understood or accepted the notion of conflict of interest." Nor was this the first time that Mellon had cut ethical corners. Like Carnegie, Mellon thought of himself as a businessman of probity and honor, and by prevailing standards, he mostly was. On occasion, though, he indulged in practices that were similar to Carnegie's and that similarly would not pass muster today.

The triumph of Franklin Roosevelt and the New Deal turned Mellon's world upside down. As Cannadine writes, the new President considered Mellon "the embodiment of everything in the pro-business Republican world before 1932 that [he] loathed and was determined to destroy." Immediately upon assuming office in 1933, the administration ordered the Bureau of Internal Revenue to audit Mellon's income-tax returns during his last years in office. When the investigation found nothing amiss (the bureau's agents in fact recommended that Mellon be granted a refund for 1931) the administration, in an action Cannadine calls "wholly without precedent," turned the matter over to the Justice Department for criminal prosecution.

In May 1934, a grand jury unanimously refused to indict Mellon for knowingly filing a false return. But, instead of dropping the matter, the administration turned to a civil suit before the federal Board of Tax Appeals. Cannadine's careful analysis shows that Mellon had not, knowingly or unknowingly, violated the law. He died of bronchial pneumonia on August 26, 1937, some three months before the tax board announced its decision vindicating him.

What adds peculiar irony to this unsavory episode is that while the administration was proceeding in its political vendetta against Mellon, it was also negotiating with him about an extraordinary philanthropic gift he intended for the nation. For many years, Mellon had been planning to deed his art collection to "the people of the United States" and to build a gallery in the nation's capital in which that collection might be housed. In December 1936, after the tax board had concluded its hearings in his case, he made a formal offer to the President. Whatever his personal feelings toward Mellon, Roosevelt accepted the offer in a cordial meeting that proceeded as if the tax case did not exist.

Thus was born the National Gallery of Art, a philanthropic contribution that, in Cannadine's estimation, is without "precedent or parallel in the nation's history." The final worth of the gift, including the art, the building, and a substantial endowment, came to some $60 million in 1936 dollars. Mellon's gesture was self-effacing as well as generous: in an effort to encourage other patrons to make their own gifts of art to expand the collection, he stipulated that his name not appear on the building. Mellon's philanthropy, Cannadine makes clear, was as straightforward in motivation as Carnegie's had been: he felt no guilt for his fortune, was only nominally religious, and had always been disdainful of public opinion.

Cannadine devotes the final pages of his book to weighing Mellon's life in the balance. Though he attempts to do his subject justice, his own expressed support for the New Deal makes it difficult for him fully to comprehend Mellon's conservative political and social views, about which he offers frequent denigrating comments. Mellon should have been more critical of the social order in which he grew up, Cannadine suggests, and more sympathetic toward a Roosevelt who, he says again and again, was only striving to preserve capitalism. Thus he characterizes Mellon's antipathy to the New Deal as "imprudent, unimaginative, chilling." That anachronistic criticism, one feels sure, would utterly have baffled Andrew Mellon.

Cannadine is even harder on Mellon's personality than on his politics. He consistently places the overwhelming burden of blame on Mellon for his troubled relations with his wife and children, a judgment that appears to discount evidence of ambiguities and mutual misunderstandings that Cannadine himself presents. His sweeping condemnations of Mellon—"one of the most famously cold, taciturn, and repressed men of his generation"; "a hollow man, with no interior life"—seem imposed and gratuitous, unwarranted extrapolations from a life that, in the author's own account, sounds more complicated than the conclusions he puts forward about it.

None of this is to belittle Cannadine's achievement in writing an absorbing, intelligent, well-researched biography. But David Nasaw's approach seems preferable to me. While describing and analyzing Andrew Carnegie in brilliant detail, and offering occasional critical comments along the way, Nasaw does not attempt to characterize him. He says to his readers, in effect: here is a fascinating and multifaceted man, make of him what you will. Nasaw's own political views are decidedly liberal—as I discovered by stumbling across an op-ed piece he recently wrote—but they do not intrude on his narrative.

Carnegie and Mellon were very different creatures, but both of their lives bring into question the stereotype of the robber baron. Two men do not an era make, of course, but other recent biographical studies of industrial titans—Ron Chernow on John D. Rockefeller and Jean Strouse on J.P. Morgan, for example—point in the same direction.

In one key respect, however, the accounts of Nasaw and Cannadine do not support the efforts of an earlier generation of revisionists. In the 1950's, for instance, Allan Nevins defended John D. Rockefeller in part by arguing that he brought necessary order out of the chaos of the oil industry in the immediate post-Civil War period. Similar cases have been made for leaders in other industries. In this view, early industrial competition—cut-throat and frequently corrupt—had led to an untrustworthy boom-and-bust economy that undermined national prosperity. Against the backdrop of a reigning laissez-faire philosophy that precluded effective government intervention, the great industrial oligopolists supplied a measure of rough-and-ready economic stability that preceded the more formal controls on industry provided by Progressive and New Deal reforms.

Neither Cannadine nor Nasaw tries to make this case. Cannadine does not raise the issue, and Nasaw says quite explicitly that "the source materials I have uncovered do not support the telling of a heroic narrative of an industrialist who brought sanity and rationality to an immature capitalism plagued by runaway competition, ruthless speculation, and insider corruption." ("Nor," he immediately adds, "do they support the recitation of another muckraking exposé of Gilded Age criminality.")

Ultimately, the most persuasive way to rebut the robber-baron school of thought is to step back from its emphasis on the actions and intentions of particular individuals. Critics have presupposed that during this era the rich became rich at the expense of the general population. But (as I noted at the outset) this supposition flies in the face of the evidence of rising real wages. Indeed, as Milton Friedman once observed: "There is probably no other period in history, in this or any other country, in which the ordinary man had as large an increase in his standard of living as in the period between the Civil War and the First World War, when unrestrained individualism was most rugged." If Friedman is correct—or even anywhere near correct—the robber barons stand rehabilitated.

More precisely, they may be somewhat beside the point. Friedman did not mean to suggest that, but for specific men, the greatest economic boom in human history would not have occurred. Carnegie and Mellon were players—not interchangeable, of course, but also not indispensable—in an epic economic story whose outcome they only incidentally determined. Just as they were neither creators nor despoilers of general economic abundance, so too were they neither heroes nor villains in the roles they played. Like the rest of us, Carnegie and Mellon were made of mixed stuff, and were morally accountable as individuals, not as members of a class.

In that perspective we can appreciate the biographies of David Nasaw and David Cannadine without worrying whether they help to make or unmake a thesis. The stories they tell are not without larger significance; but the best stories, and the people who inhabit them, have never been reducible to neat moral and ideological categories.

Notes

1. Penguin, 878 pp., $35.00.
2. Knopf, 779 pp., $35.00.

JAMES NUECHTERLEIN, a former professor of American studies and political thought at Valparaiso University, is a senior fellow of the Institute on Religion and Public Life.

Lockwood in '84

In 1884, a woman couldn't vote for the president of the United States, but that didn't stop activist lawyer Belva Lockwood from conducting a full-scale campaign for the office. She was the first woman ever to do so, and she tried again for the presidency in 1888. It's time we recognized her name.

JILL NORGREN

In 1884, Washington, D.C., attorney Belva Lockwood, candidate of the Equal Rights Party, became the first woman to run a full campaign for the presidency of the United States. She had no illusion that a woman could be elected, but there were policy issues on which she wished to speak, and, truth be told, she welcomed the notoriety. When challenged as to whether a woman was eligible to become president, she said that there was "not a thing in the Constitution" to prohibit it. She did not hesitate to confront the male establishment that barred women from voting and from professional advancement. With the spunk born of a lifelong refusal to be a passive victim of discrimination, Lockwood told a campaign reporter, "I cannot vote, but I can be voted for." Her bid for the presidency startled the country and infuriated other suffrage leaders, many of whom mistakenly clung to the idea that the Republican Party would soon sponsor a constitutional amendment in support of woman suffrage.

In the last quarter of the 19th century, Lockwood commanded attention, and not just from the columnists and satirists whom she led a merry chase. Today she is virtually unknown, lost in the shadows of the iconic suffrage leaders Elizabeth Cady Stanton and Susan B. Anthony. That's an injustice, for Belva Lockwood was a model of courageous activism and an admirable symbol of a woman's movement that increasingly invested its energies in party politics.

Lockwood was born Belva Ann Bennett in the Niagara County town of Royalton, New York, on October 24, 1830, the second daughter, and second of five children, of Lewis J. Bennett, a farmer, and Hannah Green Bennett. Belva was educated in rural schoolhouses, where she herself began to teach at the age of 14. In her first profession she found her first cause. As a female instructor, she received less than half the salary paid to the young men. The Bennetts' teenage daughter thought this treatment "odious, an indignity not to be tamely borne." She complained to the wife of a local minister, who counseled her that such was the way of the world. But bright, opinionated, ambitious Belva Bennett would not accept that world.

From her avid reading of history, Belva imagined for herself a life different from that of her mother and her aunts—the life, in fact, of a great man. She asked her father's permission to continue her education, but he said no. She then did what she was expected to do: On November 8, 1848, she married Uriah McNall, a promising young farmer. She threw herself into running their small farm and sawmill, wrote poetry and essays, and determined not to let marriage be the end of her individuality. She wanted to chart her own course, and tragedy gave her an opportunity to do so. In April 1853, when she was 22 and her daughter, Lura, three, Uriah McNall died.

The young widow had a second chance to go out into the world. She resumed her teaching and her education. In September 1854, she left Lura with her mother and traveled 60 miles east to study at the Genesee Wesleyan Seminary in Lima. The seminary shared a building with the newly coeducational Genesee College, which offered a more rigorous program. Belva transferred to the college (becoming its third woman student), where she took courses in science and politics. She graduated with a bachelor's degree (with honors) on June 27, 1857, and soon found a position teaching high school in the prosperous Erie Canal town of Lockport. Four years later, she took over a small school in the south-central New York town of Owego. In 1866, Belva McNall traveled to Washington and began to reinvent herself as an urban professional. She was neither flamboyant nor eccentric. Indeed, had she been a man, it would have been apparent that her life was following a conventional 19th-century course: Talented chap walks off the farm, educates himself, seeks opportunities, and makes a name. But because Belva strove to be that ambitious son of ordinary people who rises in the world on the basis of his wits and his work, she was thought a radical.

In Washington, Belva taught school and worked as a leasing agent, renting halls to lodges and organizations. She tutored herself in the workings of government and the art of lobbying by making frequent visits to Congress. In 1868 she married Ezekiel Lockwood, an elderly dentist and lay preacher who shared her reformist views. We do not know precisely when she fell in love with the law. In antebellum America the profession belonged to men, who passed on their skill by training their sons and nephews and neighbors' boys. After the Civil War a handful of women, Lockwood among them, set out to change all that. She believed from her reading of the lives of great men that "in almost every instance law has been the stepping-stone to greatness." She attended the law program of Washington's National University, graduated in 1872 (but only after she lobbied for the diploma male administrators had been pressured to withhold), and was admitted to the bar of the District of Columbia in 1873 (again, only after a struggle against sex discrimination). When the Supreme Court of the United States refused to admit her to its bar in 1876, she single-handedly lobbied Congress until, in 1879, it passed, reluctantly, "An act to relieve the legal disabilities of women." On March 3, 1879, Lockwood became the first woman admitted to the high Court bar, and, in 1880, the first woman lawyer to argue a case before the Court.

From her earliest years in Washington, Lockwood coveted a government position. She applied to be a consul officer in Ghent during the administration of Andrew Johnson, but her application was never acknowledged. In later years, she sought government posts—for women in general and for herself in particular—from other presidents. Without success. When Grover Cleveland passed over Lockwood and appointed as minister to Turkey a man thought to be a womanizer, she wrote to compliment the president on his choice: "The only danger is, that he will attempt to suppress polygamy in that country by marrying all of the women himself." A year later, in 1886, in another communication to Cleveland, she laid claim to the position of district recorder of deeds and let the president know in no uncertain terms that she had a "lien" on the job. She did not give up: In 1911 she had her name included on a list sent to President William Howard Taft of women attorneys who could fill the Supreme Court vacancy caused by the death of Justice John Marshall Harlan.

What persuaded Lockwood that she should run for the highest office in the land? Certainly, she seized the opportunity to shake a fist at conservatives who would hold women back. And she was displeased with the enthusiasm for the Republican Party shown by suffrage leaders Susan B. Anthony and Elizabeth Cady Stanton. More than that, however, campaigning would provide an opportunity for her to speak her mind, to travel, and to establish herself on the paid lecture circuit. She was not the first woman to run for president. In 1872, New York City newspaper publisher Victoria Woodhull had declared herself a presidential candidate, against Ulysses Grant and Horace Greeley. But Woodhull, cast as Mrs. Satan by the influential cartoonist Thomas Nast, had to abandon her campaign barely a month after its start: Her radical "free love" views were too much baggage for the nascent women's movement to bear, and financial misfortune forced her to suspend publication of *Woodhull & Claflin's Weekly* at the very moment she most needed a public platform.

Years later, Lockwood—and the California women who drafted her—spoke of the circumstances surrounding her August 1884 nomination, their accounts colored by ego and age. Lockwood received the nod from Marietta Stow, a San Francisco reformer who spoke for the newly formed California-based Equal Rights Party, and from Stow's colleague, attorney Clara Foltz. Foltz later insisted that Lockwood's nomination amounted to nothing more than a lighthearted joke on her and Stow's part. But Stow's biographer, Sherilyn Bennion, has made a strong case that the nomination was, in fact, part of a serious political strategy devised by Stow to deflect attention from the rebuff given suffrage leaders that year at the Republican and Democratic conventions, and to demonstrate that "the fair sex" could create its own terms of engagement in American party politics. Women were becoming stump speakers, participants in political clubs, candidates for local office, and, in a handful of places, voters. (By 1884 the Wyoming, Utah and Washington Territories had fully enfranchised women, who in 14 states were permitted to vote in elections dealing with schools.) Marietta Stow began the Equal Rights Party because she had long been interested in matters of public policy and because readers of her newspaper, *The Women's Herald of Industry,* had expressed an interest in a "new, clean, uncorruptible party."

In July 1884 Stow urged Abigail Scott Duniway, an Oregon rights activist and newspaper editor, to accept the Equal Rights Party's nomination. But Duniway declined, believing, as Bennion writes, that "flaunting the names of women for official positions" would weaken the case for equal rights and provide "unscrupulous opponents with new pretexts and excuses for lying about them." Undiscouraged, Stow continued her search for a candidate. In August, she hit her mark.

Belva Lockwood, *Women's Herald* reader, had already begun to think of herself as a standard-bearer. On August 10 she wrote to Stow in San Francisco and asked rhetorically, and perhaps disingenuously, "Why not nominate women for important places? Is not Victoria Empress of India? Have we not among our country-women persons of as much talent and ability? Is not history full of precedents of women rulers?" The Republicans, she commented, claimed to be the party of progress yet had "little else but insult for women when [we] appear before its conventions." (She had been among those rebuffed that summer by the Republicans.) She was exasperated with the party of Lincoln and maddened by Stanton and Anthony's continuing faith in major-party politics: "It is quite time that we had our own party, our own platform, and our own nominees. We shall never have equal rights until we take them, nor respect until we command it."

Stow had her candidate! She called a party convention on August 23, read Lockwood's letter to the small group, and proposed her as the party's nominee for president of the United States, along with Clemence S. Lozier, a New York City physician, as the vice presidential nominee. Acclamation followed, and letters were sent to the two women. The dispatch to Lockwood read as follows: "Madam: We have the honor to inform you that you were nominated, at the Woman's National Equal-Rights Convention, for President of the United States. We await your letter of acceptance with breathless interest."

Lockwood later said that the letter took her "utterly by surprise," and she kept it secret for several days. On September 3, she wrote to accept the nomination for "Chief Magistrate of the United States" from the only party that "really and truly represent the interests of our whole people North, South, East, and West. . . . With your unanimous and cordial support . . . we shall not only be able to carry the election, but to guide the Ship of State safely into port." Lockwood went on to outline a dozen platform points, and her promptness in formulating policy signaled that she (and the party) intended to be taken seriously about matters of political substance.

Forecasters in '84 were predicting another close presidential race. Four years earlier, James Garfield had defeated Winfield Hancock by just 40,000 votes (out of nine million cast), and people were again watching the critical states of New York and Indiana. The nearly even division of registered voters between the two major parties caused Democratic candidate Grover Cleveland and Republican candidate James G. Blaine to shy away from innovative platforms. Instead, the two men spent much of their time trading taunts and insults. That left the business of serious reform to the minor parties and their candidates: Benjamin Butler (National Greenback/Anti-Monopoly), John St. John (Prohibition), and Samuel Clarke Pomeroy (American Prohibition). Butler, St. John, and Pomeroy variously supported workers' rights, the abolition of child and prison labor, a graduated income tax, senatorial term limits, direct election of the president, and, of course, prohibition of the manufacture, sale, and consumption of alcohol. Lockwood joined this group of nothing-to-lose candidates, who intended to promote the public discussion of issues about which Blaine and Cleveland dared not speak.

The design of Lockwood's platform reflected her practical savvy. The platform, she said, should "take up every one of the issues of the day" but be "so brief that the newspapers would publish it and the people read it." (She understood the art of the sound bite.) Her "grand platform of principles" expressed bold positions and comfortable compromise. She promised to promote and maintain equal political privileges for "every class of our citizens irrespective of sex, color or nationality" in order to make America "in truth what it has so long been in name, 'the land of the free and home of the brave." She pledged herself to the fair distribution of public offices to women as well as men, "with a scrupulous regard to civil service reform after the women are duly installed in office." She opposed the "wholesale monopoly of the judiciary" by men and said that, if elected, she would appoint a reasonable number of women as district attorneys, marshals, and federal judges, including a "competent woman to any vacancy that might occur on the United States Supreme Bench."

Lockwood's views extended well beyond women's issues. She adopted a moderate position on the contentious question of tariffs. In her statement of September 3, she placed the Equal Rights Party in the political camp that wanted to "protect and foster American industries," in sympathy with the working men and women of the country who were organized against free trade. But in the official platform statement reprinted on campaign literature, her position was modified so that the party

might be identified as middle-of-the-road, supporting neither high tariffs nor free trade. Lockwood urged the extension of commercial relations with foreign countries and advocated the establishment of a "high Court of Arbitration" to which commercial and political differences could be referred. She supported citizenship for Native Americans and the allotment of tribal land. As was to be expected from an attorney who earned a substantial part of her livelihood doing pension claims work, she adopted a safe position on Civil War veterans' pensions: She argued that tariff revenues should be applied to benefits for former soldiers and their dependents; at the same time, she urged the abolition of the Pension Office, "with its complicated and technical machinery," and recommended that it be replaced with a board of three commissioners. She vowed full sympathy with temperance advocates and, in a position unique to the platform of the Equal Rights Party, called for the reform of family law: "If elected, I shall recommend in my Inaugural speech, a uniform system of laws as far as practicable for all of the States, and especially for marriage, divorce, and the limitation of contracts, and such a regulation of the laws of descent and distribution of estates as will make the wife equal with the husband in authority and right, and an equal partner in the common business."

Lockwood's position paper of September 3 was revised into the platform statement that appeared below her portrait on campaign flyers. The new version expanded on certain points, adopted some sharper rhetoric, and added several planks, including a commitment that the remaining public lands of the nation would go to the "honest yeomanry," not the railroads. Lockwood stuck to her radical positions of support for women's suffrage and the reform of domestic law, but, in a stunning retreat, her earlier promises of an equitable allotment of public positions by sex and any mention of the need for women in the judiciary were absent from the platform.

Armed with candidate and platform, the leaders and supporters of the Equal Rights Party waited to see what would happen. A great deal depended on the posture adopted by the press. Fortunately for Lockwood and the party, many of the daily newspapers controlled by men, and a number of weeklies owned by women, took an interest in the newest contender in the election of '84. A day after she accepted the nomination, *The Washington Evening Star* made her candidacy front-page news and reprinted the entire text of her acceptance letter and platform of September 3. The candidate told a *Star* reporter that she would not necessarily receive the endorsement of activist women. Indeed, leaders of the nation's two top woman suffrage associations had endorsed Blaine, and Frances Willard had united temperance women with the Prohibition Party. "You must remember," Lockwood said, "that the women are divided up into as many factions and parties as the men."

On September 5, an editorial in the *Star* praised Lockwood's letter of acceptance: "In all soberness, it can be said [it] is the best of the lot. It is short, sharp, and decisive. . . . It is evident that Mrs. Lockwood, if elected, will have a policy [that] commends itself to all people of common sense." Editor Crosby Noyes rued the letter's late appearance: Had it existed sooner, "the other candidates might have had the benefit of perusing it and framing their several epistles in accord with its pith and candor." Newspaper reporting elsewhere was similarly respectful.

Abigail Duniway's warning that women candidates would meet with "unpleasant prominence" and be held up "to ridicule and scorn" proved correct, but Lockwood actually encountered no greater mockery than the men in the election. She had to endure silly lies about hairpieces and sham allegations that she was divorced, but Cleveland was taunted with cries of "Ma, Ma Where's My Pa" (a reference to his out-of-wedlock child). Cartoonists for *Frank Leslie's Illustrated* and *Puck,* mass-circulation papers, made fun of all the candidates, including Lockwood. This was a rite of passage and badge of acceptance. *Leslie's* also ran an article on Lockwood's campaign and contemplated the entrance of women into party politics with earnest good wishes: "Woman in politics. Why not?. . . . Twenty years ago woman's suffrage was a mere opinion. Today, it is another matter."

After establishing campaign headquarters at her Washington home on F Street, Lockwood wrote to friends and acquaintances in a dozen states asking that they arrange ratification meetings and get up ballots containing the names of electors (as required by the Constitution) pledged to her candidacy. This letter to a male friend in Philadelphia was a typical appeal: "That an opportunity may not be lost for the dissemination of Equal Rights principles, cannot, and will not the Equal Rights Party of Philadelphia hold a ratification meeting for the nominee, put in nomination a Presidential Elector, and get up an Equal Rights ticket? Not that we shall succeed in the election, but we can demonstrate that a woman may under the Constitution, not only be nominated but elected. Think of it."

Closer to home, party supporters organized a ratification meeting in mid-September at Wilson's Station, Maryland. (They bypassed the District to make the point that, under federal law, neither men nor women could vote in the nation's capital.) Lockwood delivered her first speech as a candidate at this gathering of about 75 supporters and journalists, and two Lockwood-for-president electors were chosen. She did not disclose at the rally that Clemence Lozier had declined the nomination for vice president—and not until September 29 did Marietta Stow decide to run in the second spot and complete the ticket.

Throughout September the national press spread the story of the Equal Rights Party and its candidate, and letters poured in to the house on F Street. They contained "earnest inquiries" about the platform, nasty bits of character assassination, and, from one male admirer, the following poem, which so amused Lockwood that she gave it to a reporter for publication:

O, Belva Ann!

Fair Belva Ann!

I know that thou art not a man;

But I shall vote,

Pull off my coat,

And work for thee, fair Belva Ann.

For I have read

What thou hast said,

And long I've thought upon thy plan.

Oh no, there's none

Beneath the sun

Who'd rule like thee, my Belva Ann!

The letters also brought invitations to speak in cities across the East and the Midwest. In late September, Lockwood prepared to go on the stump, her expenses covered by sponsors. Many of the lectures she gave were paid appearances; indeed, she claimed to be the only candidate whose speeches the public paid to hear. She was a widowed middle-class woman (her second husband, who was more than 30 years her senior, had died in 1877), and her livelihood depended on the earnings of her legal practice. So the time she devoted to politics had to pay. When the election was over, she told reporters that she had a satisfaction denied the other candidates: She had come out of the campaign with her expenses paid and "$125 ahead."

Lockwood took to the field in October. She made at least one full circuit in October, beginning in Baltimore, Philadelphia, and New York. Mid-month she delivered speeches in Louisville and in Cleveland, where she appeared at the Opera House before 500 people. In a loud and nasal voice, she attacked the high-tariff position of the Republicans on the grounds that it would injure American commerce, But she also assailed the free-trade policy of the Democrats, arguing that they were "willing to risk our manufacturing interests in the face of the starving hordes of pauper labor in other countries." She applauded the good that capital had done and said that "capital and labor did not, by nature, antagonize, and should not by custom."

If the people who came to hear Lockwood expected nothing but women's rights talk, they were disappointed. She and her party colleagues believed that the Equal Rights Party should not run a single-issue campaign. Of course, the platform introduced "feminist" ideas. But it also allowed Lockwood to address many other issues that preoccupied Americans. So she directed only a small part of her talk to describing how women had helped to make the country "blossom as a rose." She intended her candidacy to make history in the largest sense—by demonstrating that the Constitution did not bar women from running in elections or serving in federal elective office.

People who saw her for the first time said that her campaign photographs did not do her justice: The lady candidate had fine blue eyes, an aquiline nose, and a firm mouth, and she favored fashionable clothes. The cartoonists naturally focused on her sex, and the public had its own fun by creating dozens of Belva Lockwood Clubs, in which men meaning to disparage Lockwood paraded on city streets wearing Mother Hubbard dresses, a new cut of female clothing with an unconstructed design that freed movement and was considered improper to wear out of doors.

On November 3, the day before the election, Lockwood returned from a campaign tour of the Northwest. She had stayed "at the best hotels; had the best sleeping berths." Her last stop was Flint, Michigan, and she told a Washington reporter that 1,000 people had attended her (paid) talk there, a larger number than Ohio congressman Frank Hurd drew the following night. When asked on November 4 where she would await the election news, she replied that her house would be open throughout the evening, "the gas will be lighted," and reporters were welcome to visit. The historic first campaign by a woman for the presidency of the United States had ended, though in politics, of course, nothing is ever over.

When the ballots were tallied, Cleveland was declared the winner, with an Electoral College vote of 219 to 182. In the popular vote, he squeaked by with a margin of 23,000.

I n 1884 the United States had yet to adopt the "Australian" ballot, which has the names of all candidates for office printed on a single form. The system then in effect, dating from the beginning of the Republic, required that each political party in a state issue ballots that contained the names of that party's slate and the electors pledged to them. A supporter cast his vote by depositing the ballot of his chosen party in a box. Some states required that voters sign the back of their ballot, but the overall allocation of ballots was not controlled by polling place officials, and stuffing the box was not impossible. It was also possible for officials in charge of the ballot boxes to discount or destroy ballots. And that, Lockwood claimed, is precisely what happened.

In a petition sent to Congress in January 1885, she wrote that she had run a campaign, gotten up electoral tickets in several states, and received votes in at least nine of the states, only to determine that "a large vote in Pennsylvania [was] not counted, simply dumped into the waste basket as false votes." In addition, she charged that many of the votes cast for her—totalling at least 4,711—in eight other states ("New Hampshire, 379 popular votes; New York, 1,336; Michigan, 374; Illinois, 1008; Iowa, 562; Maryland, 318; California, 734 and the entire Electoral vote of the State of Indiana") had been "fraudulently and illegally counted for the alleged majority candidate."

She asked that the members of Congress "refuse to receive the Electoral returns of the State of New York, or count them for the alleged majority candidate, for had the 1,336 votes which were polled in said state for your petitioner been counted for her, and not for the one Grover Cleveland, he would not have been awarded a majority of all the votes cast at said election in said state." (Cleveland's margin of votes in New York was 1,149). Lockwood also petitioned Congress for the electoral vote of Indiana, saying that at the last moment the electors there had switched their votes from Cleveland to her. In fact, they had not; it was all a prank by the good ol' boys of Indiana, but either she did not know this or, in the spirit of political theater, she played along with the mischief and used it to her advantage.

The electoral votes of New York (36) and Indiana (15) had been pivotal in the 1880 presidential race. With her petition and credible evidence, Lockwood—perhaps working behind the scenes with congressional Republicans—hoped to derail Cleveland's victory and keep him from becoming the first Democratic

president since James Buchanan in 1856. She failed when the legislators ignored her petition, which had been referred to their Committee on Woman Suffrage. On February 11, Congress certified the election of New York governor Grover Cleveland as the 22nd president of the United States.

S ubsequent interviews suggest that Lockwood was satisfied with the campaign, if not with the vote counting. The U.S. Constitution had betrayed women in the matter of suffrage, but it did not, as she said, prohibit women's speech and women's candidacies. As a celebration of the First Amendment, Lockwood's campaign was a great success. It served the interests of women (though it angered Susan B. Anthony), the candidate, and the country. Lockwood ran as an acknowledged contender and was allowed to speak her mind. American democracy was tested, and its performance did not disappoint her.

After the election, while maintaining her law practice, Lockwood embarked on the life of travel that she had long sought— and that she continued until her early eighties. Not unlike 21st-century politicians, she capitalized on the campaign by increasing her presence on the national lecture circuit; she even made at least one product endorsement (for a health tonic). She had long worked as a pension claims attorney, and, while traveling as a lecturer, she used the publicity surrounding her appearances to attract clients who needed help with applications and appeals. In 1888, the Equal Rights Party again nominated her as its presidential candidate. She ran a more modest campaign the second time around, but she still offered a broad domestic and foreign policy platform and argued that "equality of rights and privileges is but simple justice."

Lockwood always spoke proudly of her campaigns, which were important but not singular events in a life that would last 87 years. She was a woman of many talents and interests. Blocked from political office or a high-level government position because of her sex, she sought new realms after the campaigns of 1884 and 1888 where she might raise questions of public policy and advance the rights of women. Representing the Philadelphia-based Universal Peace Union, she increased her work on behalf of international peace and arbitration at meetings in the United States and Europe. She participated in an often-interlocking network of women's clubs and professional organizations. And she maintained a high profile in the women's suffrage movement, which struggled throughout the 1890s and the first two decades of the 20th century to create a winning strategy. In the spring of 1919, the House of Representatives and the Senate acted favorably on legislation to amend the Constitution to give women the right to vote; the proposed Nineteenth Amendment went out to the states in a ratification process that would not be completed until August 1920. But Belva Lockwood never got the right to vote. She died in May 1917.

Lockwood remains the only woman to have campaigned for the presidency right up to Election Day. (In 1964, Senator Margaret Chase Smith of Maine entered several Republican primaries and received 27 delegate votes; in 1972, Representative Shirley Chisholm of New York ran in a number of Democratic primaries and won 151 delegates.) In 1914 Lockwood, then 84 years old, was asked whether a woman would one day be president. The former candidate answered with levelheaded prescience and the merest echo of her former thunder: "I look to see women in the United States senate and the house of representatives. If [a woman] demonstrates that she is fitted to be president she will some day occupy the White House. It will be entirely on her own merits, however. No movement can place her there simply because she is a woman. It will come if she proves herself mentally fit for the position."

JILL NORGREN, a former Wilson Center fellow, is professor of government and legal studies at John Jay College and the University Graduate Center, City University of New York. She is writing the first full biography of Belva Lockwood, to be published in 2003. Copyright © 2002 by Jill Norgren.

A Day to Remember: December 29, 1890

CHARLES PHILLIPS

The intermittent war between the United States and the Plains Indians that stretched across some three decades after the Civil War came to an end on December 29, 1890, at the Pine Ridge Reservation in South Dakota. The events leading up to its final act—the Wounded Knee Massacre—had been building since the late 1880s, when the son of a Paiute shaman named Wovoka had first introduced a series of new beliefs and practices to the Indian reservations of the West.

Fundamentally peaceful, Wovoka's movement envisioned the coming of a new world populated solely by Indians living on the Great Plains where buffalo were again plentiful. Generation upon generation of Indians slain in combat would be reborn into this new world, and all—the living and the formerly dead—would live in bliss, peace and plenty. U.S. Indian authorities claimed that in the hands of the defeated and embittered leaders of the Teton Sioux—men like Short Bull, Kicking Bear and eventually Sitting Bull himself—Wovoka's peaceful religion had taken on the militant overtones of a millennial uprising. Wovoka had created a ceremony called the Ghost Dance to invoke the spirits of the dead and facilitate their resurrection. The Sioux apostles of the Ghost Dance purportedly preached that it would bring about a day of deliverance—a day when they were strong enough again to wage all-out war against the whites. They had fashioned "ghost shirts," which they claimed white bullets could not penetrate. In any case, Ghost Dancing had quickly become the rage of the Western reservations such as Pine Ridge and Rosebud.

"Indians are dancing in the snow and are wild and crazy," an anxious Pine Ridge Reservation agent, Daniel F. Royer, telegraphed Washington in November 1890. "We need protection and we need it now. The leaders should be arrested and confined at some military post until the matter is quieted, and this should be done at once."

The Indian Bureau in Washington quickly branded the Ghost Dancers "fomenters of disturbances" and ordered the Army to arrest them. On November 20, cavalry and infantry reinforcements arrived at the Pine Ridge and Rosebud reservations, but their arrival did not intimidate the Sioux followers of Short Bull and Kicking Bear. Quite the contrary, it seemed to galvanize their resolve. A former Indian agent, Dr. Valentine McGillycuddy, advised Washington to call off the troops: "I should let the dance continue. The coming of the troops has frightened the Indians. If the Seventh-Day Adventists prepare their ascension robes for the second coming of the savior, the United States Army is not put in motion to prevent them. Why should the Indians not have the same privilege? If the troops remain, trouble is sure to come."

About 3,000 Indians had assembled on a plateau at the northwest corner of Pine Ridge in a nearly impregnable area that came to be called the Stronghold. Brigadier General John R. Brooke, commander of the Pine Ridge area, quickly dispatched emissaries to talk with the "hostiles." Brooke's commanding officer, hard-nosed Civil War veteran and Indian fighter Maj. Gen. Nelson A. Miles, did not approve of such parleys. He saw in them evidence of indecision, and, furthermore, believed the Indians would interpret talk as a sign of weakness. Miles decided to prosecute the campaign against the Ghost Dancers personally and transferred his headquarters to Rapid City, S.D.

While Miles was preparing this move, Sitting Bull—the most influential of all Sioux leaders—began actively celebrating the Ghost Dance and its doctrine at the Standing Rock Reservation that straddled the North and South Dakota border. The agent in charge there, James McLaughlin, weighed his options. He did not want to repeat the hysterical mistake of his colleague at Pine Ridge by telegraphing for soldiers. He decided instead to use reservation policemen—Indians—to effect the quiet arrest and removal of the old chief.

Unfortunately, General Miles would not accept it. For Miles, the arrest of Sitting Bull would be a momentous act in a great drama. It should not be left to Indians, and it should not be done secretively; if anything, it called for showmanship. Miles contacted the greatest showman the West had ever known: William "Buffalo Bill" Cody. As everybody in the country probably knew—Buffalo Bill had seen to that himself—he and Sitting Bull were friends, or, at least, Sitting Bull held Cody in high regard. Sitting Bull, after all, had been a star attraction in Buffalo Bill's Wild West Show. If any white man could convince Sitting Bull to step down, it would be Buffalo Bill.

Agent McLaughlin was aghast at the notion of carting in the likes of Buffalo Bill Cody to carry out what should be done quietly and without publicity. He was convinced that Buffalo Bill's presence would only inflame tempers and transform the proceedings into a circus or something worse. Accordingly, when Cody arrived at Standing Rock on November 27, McLaughlin saw to it that the celebrity was glad-handed and subtly shanghaied by the commanding officer of nearby Fort

Yates, Lt. Col. William F. Drum. Drum entertained Cody all night at the officers' club while McLaughlin worked feverishly behind Miles' back to have the showman's authority rescinded. It was a desperate plan, and McLaughlin had missed one crucial fact: The man capable of drinking Buffalo Bill Cody under the table had yet to be born. Come morning, Cody was bright eyed and ready to set out for Sitting Bull's camp. McLaughlin hastily arranged for additional delays—just long enough for the arrival of orders canceling Cody's mission. The old entertainer seethed but boarded the next train back to Chicago. He had not set eyes on Sitting Bull.

But the situation at Pine Ridge Reservation was heating up. Word reached McLaughlin that Short Bull and Kicking Bear had formally invited Sitting Bull to leave Standing Rock and join them and their people at the Stronghold on the reservation. The time had come to act. McLaughlin dispatched 43 reservation policemen on December 15 to arrest Sitting Bull before he set out for Pine Ridge. Officers surrounded the old chief's cabin as Lieutenant Bull Head, Sergeant Red Tomahawk and Sergeant Shave Head entered it.

The chief awoke from slumber, and, seeing the men, asked, "What do you want here?"

"You are my prisoner," said Bull Head. "You must go to the agency."

Sitting Bull asked for a moment to put his clothes, on. By the time the reservation police officers emerged with their prisoner, a crowd had gathered. A warrior named Catch-the-Bear called out, "Let us protect our chief!" and he leveled his rifle at Bull Head. He fired, hitting him in the side. The wounded policeman spun around with the force of the impact. His own weapon discharged, perhaps accidentally, perhaps intentionally. A round hit Sitting Bull, point blank, in the chest. Then policeman Red Tomahawk stepped into the fray and shot Sitting Bull in the back of the head.

McLaughlin had hoped to avoid a circus. As the reservation police officers scuffled with Sitting Bull's followers, the slain chief's horse—which Buffalo Bill had presented to him back when he was part of the Wild West Show—was apparently stimulated by the familiar noise of a crowd, and performed his repertoire of circus tricks.

Miles had not intended that Sitting Bull be killed, but it had happened, and the general accepted it as he would any casualty in the fog of war. Just now he had yet another Ghost Dancer to arrest, and that's where he focused his attention. Chief Big Foot was leader of the Miniconjou Sioux, who lived on the Cheyenne River. Unknown to Miles, Big Foot had recently renounced the Ghost Dance religion, convinced that it offered nothing more than desperation and futility. Miles was also unaware that Chief Red Cloud, a Pine Ridge leader friendly to white authorities, had asked Big Foot to visit the reservation and use his influence to persuade the Stronghold party to surrender. All Miles knew—or thought he knew—was that Big Foot was on his way to the Stronghold, and it was up to the Army to prevent him from joining Short Bull, Kicking Bear and the others. Miles dispatched troops across the prairies and badlands to intercept any and all Miniconjous, especially Big Foot.

On December 28, 1890, a squadron of the 7th Cavalry located the chief and about 350 Miniconjous camped near a stream called Wounded Knee Creek. Big Foot was in his wagon, huddled against the bitter winter. He was feverish, sick with pneumonia. During the night of the 28th, additional soldiers moved into the area, so that by daybreak on the 29th, 500 soldiers, all under the command of Colonel James W. Forsyth, surrounded Big Foot's camp. Four Hotchkiss guns, small cannons capable of rapid fire, were aimed at the camp from the hills around it. The mission was to disarm the Indians and march them to the railroad, where a waiting train would remove them from the "zone of military operations."

As the Indians set up their tepees on the night of the 28th, they saw the Hotchkiss guns on the ridge above them. "That evening I noticed that they were erecting cannons up [there]," one of the Indians recalled, "also hauling up quite a lot of ammunition." The guns were ominously trained on the Indian camp. A bugle call woke up the Indians the next morning. The sky was clear and very blue as the soldiers entered the camp. Surrounded by bluecoats on horses, the Indians were ordered to assemble front and center. The soldiers demanded their weapons. Outraged, medicine man Yellow Bird began dancing, urging his people to don their sacred shirts. "The bullets will not hurt you," he told them. Next, Black Coyote, whom another Miniconjou called "a crazy man, a young man of very bad influence and in fact a nobody," raised his Winchester above his head as the troopers approached him to collect it. He began shouting that he had paid much money for the rifle, that it belonged to him and that nobody was going to take it. The soldiers, annoyed, crowded in on him and then began spinning him around and generally roughing him up.

A shot rang out. Instantly, troopers began firing indiscriminately at the Indians. "There were only about a hundred warriors," Black Elk reported. "And there were nearly five hundred soldiers." The warriors rushed to where they had piled their guns and knives. Hand-to-hand fights broke out, and some of the Indians started to run. Then the Indians heard the "awful roar" of the Hotchkiss guns. Shells rained down, almost a round a second, mowing down men, women and children—each shell carrying a two-pound charge, each exploding into thousands of fragments. The smoke was thick as fog; the Indians were running blind. Louise Weasel Bear said, "We tried to run, but they shot us like we were buffalo." Yellow Bird's son, just 4 years old at the time, saw his father shot through the head: "My father ran and fell down and the blood came out of his mouth." Those who fled the camp were chased down by soldiers. Rough Feathers' wife remembered: "I saw some of the other Indians running up the coulee so I ran with them, but the soldiers kept shooting at us and the bullets flew all around us. My father, my grandfather, my older brother and my younger brother were all killed. My son who was two years old was shot in the mouth that later caused his death." Black Elk added: "Dead and wounded women and children and little babies were scattered all along there where they had been trying to run away. The soldiers had followed them along the gulch, as they ran, and murdered them in there." In one of the gulches, "two little boys" who had found guns were lying in ambush, and "they had been killing soldiers all by themselves."

An hour later the guns stopped. The place was silent. Trails of blood trickled along the ground heading out of camp toward the gulches. Hundreds of Indians lay dead or dying on the frosted earth alongside a score of soldiers, hit mostly by the fire of their own Hotchkisses. Clouds filled the sky, and soon a heavy snow began to fall. Three days later, New Year's Day 1891, after the blizzard had passed, a burial party was sent to pull the frozen Indians from beneath the blanket of snow and dump them in a long ditch, "piled one upon another like so much cordwood, until the pit was full." Many of the corpses were naked because soldiers had stripped the ghost shirts from the dead to take home as souvenirs.

General Miles scrambled to distance himself from what public outrage there was over the massacre at Wounded Knee. He relieved Forsyth of command and convened a court of inquiry, which exonerated the colonel. Miles protested, but his immediate superior, General John M. Schofield, together with Secretary of War Redfield Proctor, eventually reinstated Forsyth's command.

In the meantime, the massacre at Wounded Knee caused "hostile" and "friendly" Sioux factions to unite. Even though Chief Red Cloud protested and repudiated his people's participation, on December 30, Sioux under Kicking Bear attacked the 7th Cavalry near the Pine Ridge Agency along White Clay Creek. At first it looked like it might be another Custer debacle, but black troopers of the 9th Cavalry rode to the rescue and drove off the Indians.

General Miles acted quickly to assemble a force of 8,000 troops, deploying them to surround the Sioux, who had returned to the Stronghold. This time Miles was careful, acting slowly and deliberately to contract the ring—almost gently—around the Indians. As he did this, he urged them to surrender, and he pledged good treatment. Whether anyone believed Miles or not, it had become clear that what the Ghost Dance foretold was a hope forlorn. The Sioux laid down their arms on January 15, 1891, bringing decades of war to an end. While lives were lost on both sides at White Clay Creek and in other skirmishes here and there, the massacre at Wounded Knee is generally considered to be the last major engagement of the Indian wars.

From *American History,* by Charles Phillips, December 2005, pp. 16, 18, 20, 68. Copyright © 2005 by Weider History Group. Reprinted by permission.

Utopia Derailed

How the 1894 Pullman strike ended one magnate's vision of a working-class paradise.

ARTHUR MELVILLE PEARSON

Whatever 19th-century railcar magnate George Pullman took with him to the grave is likely to remain a mystery. Fearful that Labor-movement extremists would desecrate his corpse, Pullman left instructions that his lead-lined casket be covered in tar paper and asphalt, and laid in a massive vault of concrete reinforced with steel rails in Chicago's Graceland Cemetery. Over this tomb stands a towering Corinthian column with the name "Pullman" carved in its base. Fortunately, the historical record beneath the other monument bearing his name, the town of Pullman, is far more accessible. In what is today Chicago's far South Side, archaeologists are unearthing the remnants of a model community. Built to be "beautiful and harmonious," it was intended to be a place where, in the words of its founder, "strikes and other troubles that periodically convulse the world of labor would not need to be feared."

"This site affords opportunities to study the daily life of workers as well as class distinctions in this richly textured 19th-century planned community," says Jane Eva Baxter, associate professor and chair of DePaul University's anthropology department. It is also important to the present-day residents of Pullman, many of whom are intimately acquainted with the town's history and worked to save the neighborhood from demolition in the 1960s. "It provides a chance to examine a rare instance of a working-class community of today rising up to save itself from the wrecking ball," she says.

Pullman was designed with 900 "worker cottages" made of solid brick, more than 95 percent of which are still occupied today. In the center of town was a grand complex of commercial and industrial buildings, anchored by a corporate administration building topped with an iconic wood-framed clock tower. The town was also artfully laced with parks and gardens.

The *London Times* was not alone in hailing Pullman as "the most perfect town in the world," at least until a nationwide economic depression compelled the town's founder to lay off one-third of his workforce and slash the wages of the remainder by an average of 30 percent—without reducing rents. Unable to afford their beautiful homes, not to mention food and other necessities, workers walked off the job in the summer of 1894. Their appeal to the fledgling American Railway Union, led by

Eugene V. Debs, resulted in the union calling on its members to stop handling any trains that included Pullman cars. As Pullman all but monopolized passenger railcar operations, train traffic virtually came to a halt across the country.

Refusing to negotiate any kind of settlement, Pullman won the battle but lost the war. The strike petered out after a few months, due in no small part to aggressive intervention by the federal government. Public opinion, however, had turned against Pullman for his hard-line stance on his workers. A federal strike commission likewise laid much of the blame at Pullman's doorstep, and the Illinois Supreme Court ordered him to sell off the residential sections of his town, his self-proclaimed "greatest work." George Pullman died of a heart attack on October 19, 1897. His factory continued producing railroad cars until the mid-1960s, after which it was occupied by a succession of industrial interests.

In 1998, a few years before DePaul launched an anthropology program with an emphasis on historical archaeology in Chicago, a homeless man had heeded the voices in his head that told him to set fire to the Pullman administration building. Although the clock tower was destroyed in the ensuing blaze, many of the original administration building's 125-year-old masonry walls survived. Before reconstruction of the building began, site superintendent Mike Wagenbach wanted to make sure the effort would not destroy the sites subsurface historical record. In 2004, DePaul visiting professor Bill Middleton took 16 students to Pullman to conduct targeted excavations at what is now the Pullman State Historic Site.

Middleton and his students found very little in the areas that would be impacted by the reconstruction, which allowed the work to proceed. The following summer, Baxter began working at the site. Laboring in the shadow of the recovering administration building, her 22 students spent five weeks learning to survey, map, excavate, record, process, and document a number of compelling finds. These included portions of the underground tunnel through which power from an immense Corliss steam engine—the most powerful in the world at the time—was distributed to the manufacturing buildings and steam heat was channeled to public buildings and select residences.

Pullman has proved to be a gold mine for industrial archaeology. The one-of-a-kind Corliss, standing 40 feet tall and weighing 700 tons, was a big hit at Philadelphia's 1876 Centennial Exhibition, for which it was initially constructed. Housed in a glass-fronted building in Pullman, it was just as big an attraction there until it was cut up for scrap when the company was electrified in 1910, about the same time it made the transition from manufacturing wooden railcars to those made of steel.

Baxter is equally interested in the sociology of the workplace. "It seems obvious, but it's often overlooked in industrial archaeology. People actually worked in factories," she says. In 1892, Pullman employed more than 6,000 workers; about one-quarter were American born, and the rest came from nearly 30 different countries. "What was that like?" Baxter challenges her students to consider.

On this front, too, Pullman does not disappoint. Outside two of the remaining factory door openings of the administration building's north assembly shop wing, which survived the fire, the DePaul students found food refuse and fragments of ceramic cups and plates. Baxter surmises that lunch breaks were informal affairs, much as workers today might step outside for a smoke. Even more telling are the differences between two separate break areas. In one, unmarked 19th-century whiteware and cuts of meat (evidenced by the animal bones) are of a distinctly cheaper quality than that found in the other, suggesting that workers may have socialized according to class.

Even within a town that claimed to promote Utopian ideals, there were significant distinctions among Pullman workers. Beyond ethnic and religious differences, highly skilled craftsmen, including woodcarvers, cabinetmakers, blacksmiths, brass finishers, millwrights, and patternmakers, earned top dollar while unskilled laborers earned, in many instances, less than half that. And where an employee lived in Pullman ultimately came down to what he or she could afford to pay in rent. High-wage earners tended to live in the largest, fanciest, and most expensive residences clustered around the town center. Low-wage earners lived in houses and multifamily dwellings, which, moving away from the town center block by block, grew steadily smaller, more plain, and less expensive to rent. The overall effect was a hierarchy of housing that roughly paralleled worker wages.

Regardless of their place in the town's pecking order, workers would have passed by the largest and most ornate home in Pullman every day. Occupied by company manager H. H. Sessions, it was directly across the street from the main factory gate. According to an 1886 map, it was the only residence with a carriage house. A 1909 fire insurance map refers to the detached structure as a garage. Aside from one exceptionally poor-quality photograph, no other documentary evidence or living-memory exists of the two-story garage, though the house still stands.

Excavating the site—for many years an informal parking area for a succession of restaurants that operated in what locals still refer to as the Sessions House—students discovered the previously undocumented limestone foundation of the carriage house. Measuring about 30 feet long by 20 feet wide, it bore a cutout large enough to receive power and steam from the Corliss engine, indicating that the building was heated. Befitting the buildings function, students found numerous horse-and-carriage-related artifacts, such as bits of horse tack and related finery. They also unearthed household items and remains of plumbing, suggesting a caretaker was in residence.

The most intriguing discovery, however, came before the students even started digging. Atop the site were heaps of displaced soil, which Baxter learned had come from the home of Kris Thomsen, two doors away. Like many Pullmanites, Thomsen can recite the history of his house chapter and verse, from the impeccably restored gem that it is today, to its central role as a speakeasy during Prohibition, to its original function as the home and office of John McClean, the company physician. In preparation to install footings for a new back porch, outside what used to be the recovery room/dispensary, Thomsen's contractors excavated several buckets of soil and got rid of them where they thought no one would notice.

Fortunately, Baxter noticed and had her students sift through the dirt. In addition to an intact glass medicine vial, they found a cornucopia of personal items, including thimbles, glass marbles, hairpins, dish fragments, and even a small-caliber bullet casing. Most curious of all was what Baxter described as a disproportionately high concentration of buttons; primarily shell buttons common in the late 19th and early 20th centuries.

Company records reveal that McClean treated 4,155 injured factory workers over a 10-year period beginning in 1884—an average of more than one a day. The majority of injuries were serious enough to result in the loss of at least two days of work. "In your typical 19th-century industrial accident," Baxter points out, "your arm or hand is caught up in a belt or some piece of heavy machinery and it's not pretty." McClean, a former Civil War battlefield surgeon, would have known what to do, but first he would have had to cut the clothing off the injured limb. The cloth, disposed of with other household trash in the large backyard, would have rotted away over time, but the buttons remained as reminders of the danger inherent even in so advanced a manufacturing setting as Pullman.

On a bright, unseasonably mild Sunday in late July, Baxter scheduled a public archaeology day as part of the 2008 field school. The event was particularly meaningful to the present-day residents of Pullman, including those who rose up in the 1960s when a local chamber of commerce recommended demolishing the entire 19th-century town for real-estate development. "That really got everyone in an uproar," remembers George Ryan, who has lived in Pullman every one of his 88 years. "We had this big rally, people were standing up, yelling. We loved our community. For us, there was no better place to go." Pullman was and is still a largely working-class community, but over the years residents have obtained city, state, and national historic landmark status and helped preserve several key public buildings.

Twenty-five people showed up for the public archaeology day to carry on the legacy of community activism. Each volunteer was assigned to one of several student-led teams excavating the foundations of walls of the well-documented Arcade Building, one of the nation's first indoor malls. In its heyday, the three-story structure housed dozens of shops, along with a post office, the Pullman Bank, a 1,000-seat theater, and an 8,000-volume library.

Among the amateur archaeologists was Andy Bullen, who lives in one of Pullman's original "executive" houses with his wife, Linda. He developed and maintains the Pullman Virtual Museum (www.pullman-museum.org), an online digital catalogue of images from several of the region's archives. "To see the size of the foundation stones gives you this gut sense of the scale and mass of the building that you can't really get from pictures," he says. "To stand on the sidewalk where the federal soldiers stood before the strike of 1894—personally, it gives me this sense of belonging, of being part of the great chain of continuity."

As part of the 2008 field school, Baxter also had her students excavate a couple of present-day backyards, finding the remains of a previously undocumented root cellar and a smattering of personal items, including doll parts and china sherds that hint at the lives of 19th-century Pullman workers and their families.

But after two seasons, Baxter feels she's just scratched the surface. "The story of Pullman is not a simple one. It's not just the autocratic patriarch versus his unhappy workers. It's much more complex than that, much more subtle. But I need to investigate more."

Pullman residents can't wait for her return. "With more archaeology, more study and information," says Arlene Echols, who loved every minute the students spent excavating the backyard of her worker's cottage, "we'll all be better stewards of our historic homes, better stewards of our present community."

ARTHUR MELVILLE PEARSON is a freelance writer in Chicago.

UNIT 2

The Emergence of Modern America

Unit Selections

Key Points to Consider

- Discuss the kinds of conditions Jacob Riis found in the slums. What combination of factors made it difficult for individuals to escape this environment?

- How did Teddy Roosevelt's experiences in Cuba impress him with the need to protect the environment?

- Who was Joe Hill? Why did he become a legend to a large number of American workers?

- Discuss the Triangle Waist fire? Why did it cause such outrage? Did anything positive come out of the disaster?

Student Website
www.mhhe.com/cls

Internet References

The Age of Imperialism
www.smplanet.com/imperialism/toc.html
William McKinley 1843–1901
www.lcweb.loc.gov/rr/hispanic/1898/mckinley.html
American Diplomacy: Editor's Corner—If Two By Sea
www.unc.edu/depts/diplomat/AD_Issues/amdipl_15/edit_15.html
Great Chicago Fire and the Web of Memory
www.chicagohs.org/fire/

The United States underwent enormous changes during the 1880s and 1890s. Millions of people continued to live on family farms or in small towns. Millions of others flocked to the cities in search of a better life. It was a period of huge immigration, most of which landed in the poorer parts of cities. Most of these people came from Southern and Eastern Europe, and became known as the "new" immigration (previous waves had come from Ireland and Germany). Because their dress, their languages, and their customs differed so markedly from native born Americans, they were seen by many as inferior peoples. One of the essays in this section, "Where the Other Half Lived," shows the incredible poverty and crowded conditions some of these people had to endure.

Small and medium-sized businesses continued to exist, but corporations on a scale previously unheard of came to dominate the marketplace. Though the gross national product increased dramatically, the gap between rich and poor steadily widened. Corporate leaders, on the one hand, amassed unprecedented fortunes on which they paid no income taxes. Urban working families, on the other hand, often lived in unhealthy squalor even though all their members—including young children—worked in some shop or factory. Depressions, one beginning in 1873 and another in 1893, threw more people out of work than ever before. "A Brief History of Fear" tells how one financial panic was prevented from turning into a crash by the actions of banker J. Pierpont Morgan. Farmers had to sell what they produced in markets that fluctuated widely, but had to purchase equipment and other necessities at prices often fixed by the large companies. They also had to contend with the monopolistic practices of railroads, which charged "all the traffic would bear" for shipping and storing farm products. Minority groups, such as Indians and blacks, continued to suffer socially and economically through good times as well as bad.

Working conditions during this period often were abominable, and laborers usually had no choice but take whatever wages were offered. Indeed, for most companies labor was just another cost of doing business. It should be purchased as cheaply as possible and exploited to the utmost without regard for human consequences. Workers' efforts to create unions to give them some protection were vigorously fought, often with violence. "Joe Hill: 'I Never Died,' Said He" describes the life and times of Joe Hillstrom, better known as "Joe Hill," a legendary labor organizer and agitator. He became a martyr in the eyes of many workingmen after his execution for a murder he may not have committed.

Library of Congress Prints & Photographs Division [LC-USZ62-34985]

"A Day to Remember: March 25, 1911," provides another glimpse of the miserable conditions under which people had to work. In 1909 employees of the Triangle Waist Company had joined in a strike led by the Women's Trade Union League, calling for better pay, shorter hours, and improvement of miserable working conditions. They gained little from the strike, and the company management continued to impose the most degrading working conditions. A fire at Triangle in 1911 cost the lives of 146 women and brought to public attention the squalid and dangerous circumstances that existed there and in other sweatshops. Blocked exits and leaky fire hoses caused many unnecessary deaths.

Theodore Roosevelt often is remembered as a blustery figure charging around in Cuba with his "Rough Riders," or as the "trust-busting" president. His most enduring legacy, however, was his devotion to protecting the environment. "TR's Wild Side" traces his interest in saving wildlife to his experiences during the Spanish-American War.

The Wright Brothers are best known for successfully completing the first powered, manned flight at Kitty Hawk, North Carolina in 1903. That flight, however, covered only 872 feet and lasted 59 seconds. It was not until 1905 that they developed an airplane that could be "flown reliably over significant distances under the pilot's complete control." Crouch discusses the significance of this achievement.

Where the Other Half Lived

The photographs of Jacob Riis confronted New Yorkers with the misery of Mulberry Bend—and helped to tear it down.

VERLYN KLINKENBORG

A block below Canal Street in lower Manhattan, just a few hundred yards from City Hall, there is a small urban oasis called Columbus Park. Early on a spring morning, the sun rises over an irregular threshold of rooftops to the east of the park—a southern spur of Chinatown—and picks out details on the courthouses and state office buildings looming over the west side of the park. Carved eagles stare impassively into the sunlight. Incised over a doorway on the Criminal Courts Building is a strangely senseless quotation from Justinian. "Justice is the firm and continuous desire to render to every man his due," it says, as though justice were mainly a matter of desire.

Beneath the sun's level rays high overhead, Columbus Park seems almost hollow somehow, and since it is open ground—open playground, to be accurate—it exposes the local topography. The land slopes downward from Bayard Street to Park Street, and downward from Mulberry to Baxter. At the north end of the park, temporary fencing surrounds an ornate shelter, the sole remnant of the park's original construction in 1897, now given over to pigeons. Plane trees lean inward around the perimeter of the asphalt ball field, where a tidy squadron of middle-aged and elderly Asian women stretches in unison, some clinging to the chain-link fence for balance. One man wields a tai chi sword to the sound of Chinese flutes from a boom box. A gull spirals down out of the sky, screeching the whole way. All around I can hear what this city calls early morning silence, an equidistant rumble that seems to begin a few blocks away.

I watch all of this, the tai chi, the stretching, the old men who have come to sit in the cool spring sunshine, the reinforced police vans delivering suspects to the court buildings just beyond it all, and as I watch I try to remember that Columbus Park was once Mulberry Bend. Mulberry Street still crooks to the southeast here, but the Bend proper is long gone. It was the most infamous slum in 19th-century New York, an immeasurable quantity of suffering compacted into 2.76 acres. On a bright April morning, it's hard to believe the Bend ever existed. But then such misery always inspires disbelief.

The Bend was ultimately torn down and a park built on its site in 1897 after unrelenting pressure from Jacob Riis, the Danish-born journalist and social reformer. In *How the Other Half Lives,* an early landmark in reforming literature whose title became a catchphrase, Riis provides some numbers for Mulberry Bend, which he obtained from the city's Registrar of Vital Statistics. In 1888, he wrote, 5,650 people lived on Baxter and Mulberry streets between Park and Bayard. If Riis means strictly the buildings within the Bend, as he almost certainly does, then the population density there was 2,047 persons per acre, nearly all of them recent immigrants.

By itself, that's an almost meaningless figure. But think of it this way: In Manhattan today, 1,537,195 persons live on 14,720 acres, a density of slightly more than 104 per acre. (In 1890, the average density within the built-up areas of Manhattan was about 115 per acre.) If Manhattan were peopled as thickly today as the Bend was in 1888, it would have more than 30 million inhabitants, an incomprehensible figure, the equivalent of nearly the whole of California jammed onto a single island. To put it another way, if the people who live in Manhattan today were packed as tightly as the immigrants in Mulberry Bend were, they could all live in Central Park with room to spare. But these are suppositions, imaginary numbers. The truly astonishing figure, of course, is 5,650 persons—actual human beings, every one of them—living in Mulberry Bend, among the highest population density ever recorded anywhere.

Now consider a final set of numbers: According to Riis and the city statistician, the death rate of children under five in Mulberry Bend was 140 per 1,000, roughly 1 out of 7. This is likely to be an underestimate. (Citywide, the number was just under 100 per 1,000 and falling fast.) Today, Mulberry Bend would rank between Lesotho and Tanzania in under-five mortality and worse than Haiti, Eritrea, Congo, and Bangladesh. Last year, the under-five mortality rate for the United States was 8 per 1,000, or 1 out of 125.

Numbers, even numbers as striking as these, do not do a good job of conveying horror. But when the horror is literally fleshed out, it begins to make an impression, as it did on Riis himself. After coming to America in 1870, at age 21, and enduring a vagrant existence for a few years, he found work at the *New York Tribune* as a police reporter and was sent to the office at 303 Mulberry Street, a few blocks north of the Bend and across from police headquarters. Night after night, Riis visited the Bend, sometimes in police company, often not, and he reported what he saw—especially the extreme overcrowding—to the Board of Health. "It did not make much of an impression," Riis wrote in *The Making of an American.* "These things rarely do, put in mere words."

So Riis put them in pictures. With a flashgun and a hand-held camera, invented just a few years earlier, Riis began to take photographs of what he found in the Bend. "From them," he wrote, "there was no appeal." They made misery demonstrable in a way that nothing else had. No political or economic or cultural theory could justify the crowding his photographs document. There was no explaining away the sense of oppression and confinement they reveal. In picture after picture you see not only the poverty and the congestion of the Bend—the stale sweatshops and beer dives and five-cent lodging houses—but the emotional and psychological consequences of people living on top of each other.

Since the mid-20th century, Riis has been considered one of the founders of documentary photography. Over the years, his photographs of Mulberry Bend and other New York slums have become a part of the city's conscience. But his approach to photography was flatly utilitarian. "I had use for it," Riis wrote of the camera, "and beyond that I never went." Printing technology at the time meant that in books and articles his pictures had to be redrawn as wood engravings, considerably reducing their impact. The actual photographs were seen only in lantern slides accompanying his lectures. What mattered was not aesthetics but what the pictures showed. Riis had a similar use for words and statistics. They were merely tools to persuade New Yorkers to witness what was right in front of their eyes.

In one of his many articles on tenement housing, Riis printed a map of the Bend drawn from overhead, a silhouette showing the proportion of open space to buildings. Looking at that map is like looking at an old-fashioned diagram of a cell, a hieroglyphic of dark and light. It's hard to know what to call the spaces depicted by the white areas on Riis's map. *Yard* is too pastoral and *air shaft* too hygienic. Riis calls them "courts" and "alleys," but even those words are too generous. What the white spaces really portray are outdoor places where only a single layer of humans could live, many of them homeless children who clustered in external stairwells and on basement steps. In the tenements of the Bend—three, four, and five stories each—families and solitary lodgers, who paid five cents apiece for floor space, crowded together in airless cubicles. "In a room not thirteen feet either way," Riis wrote of one midnight encounter, "slept twelve men and women, two or three in bunks set in a sort of alcove, the rest on the floor."

For reformers, Riis included, the trouble with the Bend wasn't merely the profits it returned to slumlords and city politicians, nor was it just the high rents that forced tenants to sublet floor space to strangers. The problem was also how to portray the Bend in a way that conveyed its contagious force, the absence of basic sanitation, of clean water and fresh air, the presence of disease, corruption, and crime, the enervation and despair. It was, for Riis, the problem of representing an unrepresentable level of defilement. The power of his silhouette map, for instance, is flawed by its white margins, which falsely imply that conditions improved across the street, when, in fact, the entire Sixth Ward was cramped and impoverished. Even the grimmest of Riis's photographs show only a few people, at most, in the back alleys and basement dives. Powerful as they are, these pictures fail to convey the simple tonnage of human flesh in those dead-end blocks.

But the problem of Mulberry Bend was also how to interpret it. On a bright spring morning in the 1880s or early 1890s, a New Yorker—curiosity aroused, perhaps, by one of Riis's articles—might have strolled over to Mulberry or Baxter Street to see for himself. What he found there would depend on his frame of mind. It might have been, as photographs suggest, a bustling streetfront crowded with people going rather shabbily about the ordinary sorts of business, much as they might in other neighborhoods. Such a New Yorker—disinclined to push through to the dark inner rooms a few flights up or to the dismal courts and alleys behind or to the dank beer dives below—might conclude that perhaps Riis had exaggerated and that perhaps all there was to see here was a people, immigrants nearly all of them, who were insufficiently virtuous or cleanly or hardworking or American. It would be possible for such a person to blame Mulberry Bend on the very people who were its victims. But when the tenements were condemned and their inhabitants moved into decent housing, particularly in Harlem, they blended imperceptibly into the fabric of the city.

Riis has been faulted for his glib descriptive use of racial and ethnic stereotypes, a convention of his time that sounds raw and coarse to us now. In his defense, he came to understand that the power of a place like Mulberry Bend was enough to corrupt its residents, no matter who they were, as it had the Irish, and then the Italians who were their successors in the Bend. No iniquity within the Bend was as great, to Riis, as the political and financial iniquity that sustained the tenements there.

But the tragedy of Mulberry Bend isn't only that it came to exist and, once in existence, to be tolerated. It was also that when the city finally tore down the Bend and at last built the park that Calvert Vaux had designed for the site, a kind of forgetfulness descended. A New Yorker coming to the newly built Mulberry Bend Park in 1897, or to its renaming in 1911, or merely to watch the sun rise on a bright spring morning in 2001, might never know that there had been such a place as the Bend. The park that stands in its place is some kind of redemption, but without memory no redemption is ever complete. And without action of the kind that Riis undertook, justice remains only a matter of desire.

TR's Wild Side

As a Rough Rider in the Spanish-American War, Theodore Roosevelt's attention to nature and love of animals were much in evidence, characteristics that would later help form his strong conservationist platform as president.

DOUGLAS BRINKLEY

On June 3, 1898, 39 days into the Spanish-American War, Theodore Roosevelt and his Rough Riders arrived in Florida by train, assigned to the U.S. transport *Yucatan.* But the departure date from Tampa Bay for Cuba kept changing. Just a month earlier, the 39-year-old Teddy had quit his job as assistant secretary of the Navy, taken command of the 1,250-man 1st Volunteer Cavalry Regiment along with Leonard Wood, and began a mobilization to dislodge the Spanish from Cuba.

Roosevelt worried that if the ship didn't leave soon, his men's livers weren't going to withstand all the booze they were consuming. The first day was incredibly humid, with a hot, glassy atmosphere and scant wind. Anxious for war, Teddy was unperturbed by the omnipresent swarms of chiggers and sandflies. To kill time he studied Florida's botany, learning to distinguish lignum-vitae (holywood) trees from blue beech and ironwood at a glance.

The very word *wild* had a smelling-salt-like effect on Theodore Roosevelt. As a Harvard undergraduate he had studied nature from a scientific perspective, full of rigor and objectivity. To Roosevelt wilderness hunting and bird-watching were the ideal bootcamps for a military career. By studying how grizzly bears tracked their prey, he developed warrior skills. First-rate soldiers were best made in America, he believed, by learning to live in the wild. If a soldier understood how to read a meadowlark call or crow squawk, then his chances of battlefield survival were enhanced. An alertness to all things wild was, in Roosevelt's eyes, a prerequisite for excelling in modern society. Success would fall upon the individual who could outfox a blizzard or survive a heat wave.

Roosevelt possessed in spades the qualities that Harvard naturalist Edward O. Wilson has called "biophilia": the desire to affiliate with other forms of life, the same impulse that lifts the heart at a sudden vision of a glorious valley, a red-rock canyon, or a loon scooting across a mud bog at dusk. Wilson suggests that, at heart, humans *want* to be touched by nature in their daily lives. His hypothesis offers a key to understanding why Roosevelt as president would add over 234 million acres to the public domain between 1901 and 1909. He responded both scientifically and emotively to wilderness. The shopworn academic debate over whether Roosevelt was a preservationist or a conservationist is really moot. He was both, and a passionate hunter to boot, too many sided and paradoxical to be pigeonholed. Even within the crucible of the Spanish-American War, Roosevelt managed to acquire exotic pets and to write about the Cuban environment, actions that provide valuable insight into Roosevelt's developing conservationist attitudes.

While waiting to ship out, he studied the waterfowl along the wharf front and marshy inlets: ibis, herons, and double-crested cormorants, among scores of others. Beneath his cavalry boots on the Tampa beaches were sunrise tellin, wide-mouthed purpura, ground coral, bay mud, and tiny pebbles mixed with barnacles and periwinkles. Writing to his friend Henry Cabot Lodge, he turned quasi geobiologist, evoking Florida's semitropical sun, palm trees, shark-infested shallows, and sandy beaches much like those on the French Riviera. The Gulf of Mexico, the ninth-largest body of water in the world, interested Roosevelt to no end.

Spending those days in Tampa Bay, various conservation historians believe, later influenced Roosevelt's creation of federal bird sanctuaries along Florida's coasts. What Roosevelt learned from being stationed on the Gulf Coast was that the market hunters were having a bad effect on Florida's ecosystem, including the Everglades, Indian River, Lake Okeechobee, and the Ten Thousand

Islands. The previous year, his friend the New York-based ornithologist Frank M. Chapman had warned him that tricolor herons and snowy egrets were being slaughtered for their feathers. Now huge mounds were heaped around the Tampa harbor, bird carcasses piled 20 or 30 yards high to rot in the sun. If the slaughter wasn't stopped, the crowded, beautiful roosts of Florida would vanish and their inhabitants would go the way of the passenger pigeon, the ivory-billed woodpecker, and the Labrador duck.

Even as he shaped his regiment for combat, Roosevelt retained his fascination with animals, an aspect that distinguishes his war memoir *The Rough Riders* from all other accounts of the 1898 Cuban campaign. And in his 1913 autobiography Roosevelt presented his theory about the role of pets in sustaining morale. Compared with his accounts of military tactics and the toll of yellow fever, such passages can seem frivolous, but they do offer a valuable perspective on Roosevelt as a war leader and as a person.

Largely due to Roosevelt, the 1st Volunteer Cavalry Regiment took three animal mascots with them, all the way from basic training in San Antonio through their port stay in Tampa Bay. For starters, there was a young mountain lion, Josephine, given by trooper Charles Green of Arizona. Roosevelt spent as much time around the cougar cub as he could. Although he wrote in *The Rough Riders* that Josephine had an "infernal temper," he adored everything about her: her sand-colored coat, dark rounded ears, white muzzle, and piercing blue eyes, which turned brown as she matured. Eventually Josephine would weigh at least 90 pounds and be able to pull down a 750-pound elk with her powerful jaws. The *New York Times* reported that she "rejoiced" when her name was uttered and was beloved by all the men. But one time she got loose, climbed into bed with a soldier, and began playfully chewing on his toes. Roosevelt later chuckled in *The Rough Riders* that "he fled into the darkness with yells, much more unnerved than he would have been by the arrival of any number of Spaniards."

Another steadfast comrade from the wild was a New Mexican golden eagle nicknamed "Teddy" in Colonel Roosevelt's honor. Roosevelt loved to watch these raptors swooping down to pluck a snake or other prey, and he even learned the art of falconry, wearing leather gloves and calling his namesake back to camp after it had gone hunting. "The eagle was let loose and not only walked at will up and down the company streets, but also at times flew wherever he wished," Roosevelt recalled.

Josephine and Teddy had to be left behind in Tampa, but a "jolly dog" named Cuba and owned by Cpl. Cade C. Jackson of Troop A from Flagstaff, Arizona, did accompany the Rough Riders. Having dirty gray, poodle-like fur

and the personality of a Yorkie, the little dog could be easily scooped up with the swipe of a hand. (One story, in fact, claims that Jackson had stolen Cuba just so from a railcar.) Frisky as a dog could be, Cuba accompanied the regiment "through all the vicissitudes of the campaign." Aboard the *Yucatan,* Roosevelt asked a Pawnee friend to draw Cuba—who ran "everywhere round the ship, and now and then howls when the band plays"—for his daughter Ethel. Perhaps because Roosevelt was so comfortable with the trio of animals—knowing how to feed the eagle mice and to scratch Josephine behind the ears—the mascots added a compelling dimension to the press coverage of the Rough Riders. But even if TR did use the mascots to play to the cameras, they were part and parcel of his lifelong need to be associated with animals.

Frisky as a dog could be, Cuba accompanied the regiment "through all the vicissitudes of the campaign."

When the *Yucatan* finally set sail on June 13, Roosevelt was nearly giddy with joy at escaping Tampa. As the 49 vessels in the convoy steamed south in three columns, he noted that the Florida Keys area was "a sapphire sea, wind-rippled, under an almost cloudless sky." When he first caught sight of the shoreline of Santiago Bay, waves beating in diagonals, he wrote to his sister Corinne that "All day we have steamed close to the Cuban Coast, high barren looking mountains rising abruptly from the shore, and at a distance looking much like those of Montana. We are well within the tropics, and at night the Southern Cross shows low above the Horizon; it seems strange to see it in the same sky with the Dipper."

At both San Antonio and Tampa Bay, his two horses Rain-in-the-Face and Texas practically never left his side. With Vitagraph motion picture technicians filming the Rough Riders wading ashore, a trooper was ordered to bring his steeds safely onto the beach. Alas, a huge wave broke over Rain-in-the-Face. Unable to burst free from his harness, he inhaled seawater and drowned. For the only time during the war Roosevelt went berserk, "snorting like a bull," as Albert Smith of Vitagraph recalled, "split[ting] the air with one blasphemy after another." As the other horses were brought ashore, Roosevelt kept shouting "Stop that god-damned animal torture!" every time saltwater got in a mare's face.

On June 23 the Rough Riders debarked at the fishing village of Siboney about seven miles west of Daiquiri, behind Gen. Henry Ware Lawton's 2nd Division and Gen. William Shafter's 5th Corps. The soldiers took ashore blanket rolls, pup tents, mess kits, and weaponry, but no one thought to give them any insect repellent. There was no wind, and they felt on fire. The tangled jungles and chaparral of Cuba, particularly in early summer, were breeding grounds for flies that now swarmed the camps. Cuba also boasted 100 varieties of ants, including strange stinging ones that seemed to come from a different world. Unafraid of the soldiers, little crouching chameleons with coffin-shaped heads changed color from bright green to dark brown, depending on the foliage they rested on. "Here there are lots of funny little lizards that run about in the dusty roads very fast," Roosevelt wrote to his daughter Ethel, "and then stand still with their heads up."

Roosevelt's letters crackle with the kind of martial detail also found in Stephen Crane's 1895 Civil War novel *The Red Badge of Courage*. Yet they're also crowded with natural history, with observations about the "jungle-lined banks," "great open woods of palms," "mango trees," "vultures wheeling overhead by hundreds," and even a whole command "so weakened and shattered as to be ripe for dying like rotten sheep." There was a strange confluence in Cuba between Roosevelt and the genius loci, as he constantly sought to conjure up nature as a way to increase his personal power.

Both in Roosevelt's correspondence and his war memoir, the land crab is everywhere, its predatory omnipresence almost the central metaphor of his Cuban campaign. Carcinologists had noted that the local species, *Gecarcinus lateralis,* commonly known as the blackback, Bermuda, or red land crab, leaves the tropical forests each spring to mate in the sea. It made for an eerie spectacle all along Cuba's northern coast as these misshapen creatures, many with only one giant claw, crawled out of the forests across roads and beaches to reach the water. Swollen with eggs, the female red land crabs nevertheless made their journey to incubate in the Caribbean Sea, traveling five to six miles a day over every obstacle imaginable. Roosevelt noted that they avoided the sun's glare, often struggling to shade just like wounded soldiers. While basically land creatures, these burrowing red crabs—their abalone-like shells thick with gaudy dark rainbow swirls—still had gills, so they needed to stay cool and moist. "The woods are full of land crabs, some of which are almost as big as rabbits," Roosevelt wrote to Corinne. "When things grew quiet they slowly gathered in gruesome rings around the fallen."

For the first time as an adult, Roosevelt was in the tropics. The very density of vegetation he encountered was daunting, the white herons often standing out against the greenery like tombstones. He now knew how Charles Darwin must have felt in the Galápagos and Tahiti. Cuba's red land crabs were his tortoises or finches; everything about them spoke of evolution. Unlike the stone crabs of

Maine, these red crabs weren't particularly good-tasting. Still, with supplies sparse, the soldiers smashed them with rocks, discarded the shells, and mixed the meat into their hardtack, calling the dish "deviled crab." Although the crabs were not dangerous, many Rough Riders were jarred awake at night by their formidable pincers. And they were persistent—a buddy would shake them scurrying away from the bedroll, only to find them back a short while later.

After they stormed Santiago, many of his troops lay wounded in ditches.

In *The Rough Riders,* Roosevelt vividly described the timeworn, brush-covered flats in the island village of Daiquiri on which the regiment camped one evening, on one side the jungle, on the other a stagnant malarial pool fringed with palm trees. After they stormed Santiago, many of his troops, a third of whom had served in the Civil War, lay wounded in ditches while flies buzzed around them. Sometimes after an American died, villagers would strip the corpse of all its equipment. Humans could be scavengers, too. Roosevelt turned to avian and crustacean imagery to convey the horrors of death. "No man was allowed to drop out to help the wounded," he lamented. "It was hard to leave them there in the jungle, where they might not be found again until the vultures and the land-crabs came, but war is a grim game and there was no choice."

Ever since Roosevelt had discovered Darwin's writings as a boy growing up in New York City, analyzing species and subspecies characteristics became a daily habit. In his 1895 essay on "Social Evolution," published in the North American Review, he offered a parable about when the dictates of natural selection superseded love of wildlife. "Even the most enthusiastic naturalist," he wrote, "if attacked by a man-eating shark, would be much more interested in evading or repelling the attack than in determining the specific relations of the shark." By this criterion, Roosevelt was a dual success in Cuba. He not only thwarted the Spanish sharks but managed to make detailed diary notes regarding vultures and crabs, which he planned to use in his memoir of the war.

What he would call his "crowded hour" occurred on July 1, 1898, when, on horseback, he led the Rough Riders (plus elements of the 9th and 10th Regiments of regulars, African American "buffalo soldiers," and other units) up Kettle Hill near San Juan Hill in the battle of San Juan Heights. Once the escarpment was captured, Roosevelt, now on foot, killed a Spaniard with a pistol that had been recovered from the sunken Maine.

Roosevelt later said that the charge surpassed all the other highlights of his life. Somewhat creepily, it was reported, Roosevelt had beamed through the blood, mutilation, horror, and death, always flashing a wide grin as he blazed into the enemy. Whether he was ordering up artillery support, helping men cope with the prostrating heat, finding canned tomatoes to fuel the troops, encouraging Cuban insurgentes, or miraculously procuring a huge bag of beans, he was always on top of the situation, doing whatever was humanly possible to help his men avoid both yellow fever and unnecessary enemy fire. There was no arguing about it: Colonel Roosevelt had distinguished himself at Las Guasimas, San Juan, and Santiago (although the journalists did inflate his heroics to make better copy).

By the Fourth of July, Roosevelt had become a home-front legend, the most beloved hero produced in what the soon-to¬be secretary of state John Hay called "a splendid little war." With the fall of San Juan Heights and the Spanish fleet destroyed, Santiago itself soon surrendered. The war was practically over. The stirring exploits of Colonel Roosevelt were published all over the United States, turning him overnight into the kind of epic leader he had always dreamed of being.

But the hardships Roosevelt had suffered were real. Supplies like eggs, meat, sugar, and jerky were nonexistent. Hardtack biscuits—the soldiers' staple—had bred hideous little worms. Just to stay alive, the Rough Riders began frying mangoes. Worse still, the 100°F heat caused serious dehydration. Then there was the ghastly toll from tropical diseases. Diarrhea and dysentery struck the outfit. Fatigue became the norm. So many Rough Riders were dying from yellow fever and malaria that Roosevelt eventually asked the War Department to bring the regiment home to the Maine coast. On August 14 the Rough Riders, following a brief stopover in Miami, arrived at Montauk Point at the tip of Long Island (not Maine) and were placed in quarantine for six weeks.

In hard, good health, taut and fit, his face tanned, and his hair crew-cut, Roosevelt was living out his boyhood fantasy of being a war hero. He had endured the vicissitudes of combat with commendable grit, and now it was all glory. Something in the American wilderness experience, Roosevelt believed, including his long stints of hunting in the Badlands and Bighorns in the 1880s, had given him an edge over the Spaniards. The same with the Rough Riders, who hailed from the Southwest—Arizona, New Mexico, Oklahoma, and Indian Territory. Not a single Rough Rider got cold feet or shrank back.

Roosevelt believed that the American fighting spirit would only continue as long as outdoorsmen didn't get lazy and rest on their laurels. Slowly he was developing an underlying doctrine that he would call "the strenuous life." The majestic open spaces of western America, such as the Red River Valley, the Guadalupe Mountains, the Black Mesa, the Sangre de Cristo Range, the Prescott Valley, and the Big Chino Wash, had hardened his men into the kind of self-reliance Emerson had invoked in his writings. Wouldn't Rough Riders make terrific forest rangers? Didn't the wildlife protection movement need no-nonsense men in uniform to stop poaching in federal parks? "In all the world there could be no better material for soldiers than that offered by these grim hunters of the mountains, these wild rough riders of the plains," enthused Roosevelt.

While the Rough Riders recuperated under yellow-fever watch at Montauk, New York's Republican Party was urging Roosevelt to run for governor that fall. As he contemplated his political future, everybody clamoring to shake his hand, he found respite watching the pervasive raccoons and white-tailed deer of Montauk. There was even Nantucket juneberry along the sandplains to study. One hundred years later, to honor the Rough Riders' residence at Camp Wikoff in 1898, Montauk named a 1,157-acre wilderness area Roosevelt County Park.

In August the *New York Times* ran a feature story about Josephine, reporting that the colonel might raise the big cat at Oyster Bay. But his wife, Edith, put a stop to that plan, and Josephine was carted off to tour the West as a circus attraction. Unfortunately, she got loose or was stolen in Chicago and was never seen again.

The eventual fate of Teddy the golden eagle was just as disappointing. Quite sensibly, Roosevelt had given him to the Central Park Zoo, where he became a popular tourist attraction, but he was killed by two bald eagles put into his cage to keep him company. The body of the regiment's mascot was shipped to Frank Chapman at the American Museum of Natural History to be stuffed.

Cuba the dog's story, at least, had a happy ending. Discharged from quarantine, Corporal Jackson headed back to his home in Flagstaff and gave the celebrity terrier to Sam Black, a former Arizona Territory Ranger, with whose family he lived for 16 years in the lap of luxury. When Cuba died of natural causes, he was given a proper military funeral.

On August 20, 1898, Colonel Roosevelt was allowed to leave quarantine to return to his Oyster Bay home at Sagamore Hill for five days. By the time he got there, a groundswell of support had arisen for his gubernatorial candidacy. All around Oyster Bay, he was greeted with shouts of "Teddy!" (which he hated) and "Welcome, Colonel!" (which he loved). "I would rather have led this regiment," Roosevelt wrote a friend, "than be Governor of New York three times."

Cleverly, Roosevelt had kept diaries in Cuba, jotting down exact dialogue and stream-of-consciousness impressions. His editor at Charles Scribner's Sons, Robert Bridges, worried that if Roosevelt ran for governor the war memoir they'd been discussing would have to be put on hold. "Not at all," Roosevelt assured him. "You shall have the various chapters in the time promised."

Once back at Camp Wikoff, Roosevelt wandered Montauk Point, care taking his golden eagle and taking little Cuba on walks. Roosevelt seemed like a changed man, disconcertingly calm, studying the undercarriage of wigeon ducks as they flew overhead. Sometimes, particularly when reporters were around, he rode his horse up and down the beach. By having "driven the Spaniard from the New World," Roosevelt could relax—the burden of family cowardice and the shadow of his father's hiring of a surrogate for his Civil War service had passed away forever. With nothing more to prove, he could excel as a powerful politician, soapbox expansionist, true-blue reformer, naturalist, and conservationist.

On September 13 a bugle called, and the surviving Rough Riders dutifully fell into formation. In front of them was a card table with a blanket draped over a bulky object. The 1st Volunteer Cavalry had a parting gift for their humane and courageous colonel. Eventually the blanket was lifted to reveal an 1895 bronze sculpture by Frederic Remington, *Bronco Buster*. (A *cowboy* was the western term for a cattle driver, while a *bronco buster* broke wild horses to the saddle.) Tears welled up in Roosevelt's eyes, his voice choked, and he stroked the steed's mane as if it were real. "I would have been most deeply touched if the officers had given me this testimonial, but coming from you, my men, I appreciate it tenfold," Roosevelt said. The Rough Riders had found the best gift possible. It summed up Theodore Roosevelt well: a fearless cowboy, stirrup flying free, determined to tame a wild stallion by putting the spurs to it, a quirt in his right hand, and the reins gripped in the other. A Remington cast of the *Bronco Buster* now sits prominently in the White House Oval Office for President Barack Obama to appreciate.

The 42-year-old Roosevelt took more than just a Remington bronze to the White House in September 1901; his wilderness values and philosophy came with him, along with his saddle bag. Besides continuing to collect myriad White House pets, Roosevelt used his executive power to save such national heirlooms as the Grand Canyon, Crater Lake, Devils Tower, Mesa Verde, and the Dry Tortugas. On July 1, 1908, to help commemorate his "crowded hour" of battle at Santiago, President Roosevelt created 45 new national forests scattered throughout 11 western states. He also initiated many innovative protocols for range management, wildfire control, land planning, recreation, hydrology, and soil science throughout the American West. It was exactly a decade since his moment of military glory. His "crowded hour" 10 years later put much of the Rocky Mountains and the Pacific Northwest beyond the lumberman's ax. Adding to the conservationist theme, TR hired as forest rangers men who had served with him in combat. These ex-Rough Riders now protected wild America from ruin under the banner of Rooseveltian conservationism.

What particularly worried President Roosevelt at the dawn of the 20th century was that citizens of New York, Philadelphia, and Boston could not understand the splendor of the American West. "To lose the chance to see frigate birds soaring in circles above the storm," Roosevelt wrote, "or a file of pelicans winging their way homeward across the crimson afterglow of the sunset, or a myriad of terns flashing in the bright light of midday as they hover in the shifting maze above the beach—why the loss is like the loss of a gallery of masterpieces of the artists of old time."

As seen in *American Heritage*, Fall 2009, pp. 29–35. Adapted by the author from *The Wilderness Warrior: Theodore Roosevelt and the Crusade for America* (HarperCollins, 2009). Copyright © 2009 by Douglas Brinkley. Reprinted by permission of HarperCollins Publishers.

Joe Hill: 'I Never Died,' Said He

During the first years of the 20th century, Joe Hill moved like a phantom 'Johnny Laborseed' through the far-flung corners of the United States, everywhere planting working class solidarity through his songs, speeches— and even his death—to foster the growth of a burgeoning labor movement.

BEN LEFEBVRE

At one point in the early 20th century, 49 of the 50 United States had in their possession some of the ashes of one man. Inside envelopes sent to union halls around the country were the remains of Joe Hillstrom, popularly known as Joe Hill, a drifter, songwriter and, for some members of the organized labor movement, a martyr. His story is not as well known as it once was, but his ghost still walked the land vividly enough in 1925 that Alfred Hayes was able to compose a poem commemorating it:

From San Diego up to Maine

In every mine and mill,

Where workers strike and organize,

Says he, "You'll find Joe Hill."

Hill's life had all the elements of classic American myth: back roads wandering, music, ideals and confrontations with the law. It also proves the point that for individuals to become legends, the way they die is just as important as the way they live.

Joe Hill stepped onto Ellis Island in October 1902. Born Joel Emmanuel Hägglund in Gävle, Sweden, in 1879, he sailed with his brother to America after the deaths of their parents—their father, a railway conductor, died from injuries suffered in a workplace accident, and their mother died 15 years later from illness. Far from finding the sidewalks paved with gold, Hill had to take whatever odd job he could find just to survive, at one point even cleaning bar spittoons in the roughest parts of New York City for a few pennies a day. Tired of city life, he abandoned the slums and hit the road, armed only with the English he had learned at the Gävle YMCA and on the streets of New York.

The labor pool he entered—before organized unions had any influence—was a turbulent one. Just finding a job was in itself an enormous task. "Employment sharks" would sell supposed job opportunities to unemployed men, who would then travel great distances only to find that the job did not exist; other "sharks," working in cahoots with the employer, would sell jobs that were only good for a few days before they were resold to someone else. In addition, the working conditions in those jobs were more often than not abominable. Management during the early 20th century exploited child labor and immigrant workers to the hilt. This was the era in which 146 workers died in New York's Triangle Shirtwaist Company fire; 362 West Virginia coal miners perished in the Monongah mine disaster; and Pittsburgh steel workers endured 12-hour shifts, six days a week. Workers who asked for higher wages or safer conditions were fired, beaten or, in some cases, killed. Faced with these horrific conditions, Hill gradually became a labor activist.

Gathering information to chronicle Hill's life between 1902 and his arrest in Utah in 1914 is difficult, because so much of it is scattered all over the map. The tall man with blue eyes and dark hair was reportedly sighted in Philadelphia, the Dakotas and Hawaii. In 1905 he sent a Christmas card from Cleveland to his sisters in Sweden, and in 1906 he sent a letter to the Gävle newspaper describing his experience in the Great San Francisco Earthquake. Reports and personal letters, many contradictory, depict a sort of "Johnny Laborseed" traveling through the country doing odd jobs, assisting strikes and furthering the union cause. In 1910 he joined the Industrial Workers of the World's San Pedro chapter while working on the California waterfront.

The IWW, still in existence, is a radical offshoot of the American Federation of Labor. The split represented the difference between reform and revolution. Whereas the AFL fought for "A fair day's wage for a fair day's work," the IWW, or Wobblies, as they are known, have flown a banner reading "Abolition of the wage system" since the group's inception in 1905. The Marxist group strives to organize the workers of the world into "one big union," arguing that separate unions are too easily manipulated by the managerial establishment. Though the group eschews violence, it does advocate "direct action," including industrial sabotage, as a means to persuade management to see things from labor's point of view. The IWW claimed about 100,000 members during its golden age before World War I, but wielded influence disproportionate to its size. During the opening decades of the 20th century, it directed or took part in at least 150 strikes.

Hill was dedicated to the cause and participated in his fair share of organizing before and after becoming formally affiliated with the IWW. Louis Morean, a Wobbly in British Columbia striking against the Canadian Northern Railroad in 1912, wrote of a typical Joe Hill sighting in a letter: "Joe Hill made his appearance at our strike camp at Yale a week or 10 days after the strike. I didn't know Joe before but quite a few fellow workers knew him and [he] was very popular. Joe wrote [his song] 'Where the Fraser River Flows' the first few days he was in our strike camp. It became very popular with everybody."

Morean also brought up what was another of Hill's trademarks: his ability to move in and out of camps almost without a trace. After a raid by strikebreakers broke up the union's activities, Morean wrote: "One thing puzzled us. We had not seen Joe Hill either during or after the raid."

Hill was also reported to be participating in some of the union's more extreme activities. He is believed to have joined a group of several hundred Wobblies and Mexican rebels who temporarily seized control of Tijuana, Mexico, in January 1911. The group attempted to overthrow dictator Porfirio Díaz and establish "industrial freedom" in that country, but was forced to retreat when government troops beat them back. Wobbly participants in the event recalled Hill being there, but Hill himself later denied it. That was part of the mystery of Hill's life—he had an uncanny ability to be simultaneously everywhere and nowhere within the labor movement.

Hill's songwriting was part of the reason behind that mystery. Regardless of which strikes Hill did or did not attend, his songs put him there in spirit. He was musically inclined since childhood, and during his time in the IWW he composed tunes and lyrics while on the road and while in prison. He wrote songs in Malgren's Hall, the San Pedro local's meeting place, composing the tunes on the piano, violin, banjo or guitar. His fellow Wobblies bought the sheet music for such songs as "Mr. Block," "It's a Long Way Down to the Breadline" and "Rebel Girl" for a few cents apiece. When the IWW collected his work and published it as part of their Little Red Songbook, a collection of labor songs subtitled Songs to Fan the Flames of Discontent, Hill's fame grew among the Wobblies and helped energize the movement.

"Songs became a distinguishing element of IWW–supported strikes," wrote Gibbs M. Smith, author of the biography Joe Hill. "Strike songs infused heterogeneous groups of workers with a sense of unity and solidarity," Smith continued. "They were great morale builders and, as such, important tools." A number of Hill's songs rank among the group's best. His understanding of the common laborer's plight and the satiric criticism of management in his lyrics endeared him to the rank and file. Wobblies sang his songs in picket fines and during mass meetings and demonstrations; the songs echoed in the "hobo jungles"—makeshift encampments where drifters could find respite from their search for work.

Though his songs were popular with the rank and file, he still had to justify them to some of his union brethren. Some officials considered music a frivolous waste of time that distracted workers from a more serious education. "Now I am well aware of the fact that there are lots of prominent rebels who argued that satire and songs are out of place in a labor organization," Hill wrote in a letter to the editor of Solidarity, an IWW newspaper. "A pamphlet, no matter how good, is never read more than once, but a song is learned by heart and repeated over and over; and I maintain that if a person can put a few cold, common sense facts into a song, and dress them in a cloak of humor to take the dryness off them, he will succeed in reaching a great number of workers who are too unintelligent or too indifferent to read a pamphlet or an editorial on economic science."

Hill wrote one of his most famous songs in support of the 35,000 workers striking against the Illinois Central Railroad. Protesting the introduction of nonunion workers to break the strike, Hill composed "Casey Jones—The Union Scab." Workers took up the song's refrain after it was published in a bulletin issued to the strikers. Sung to the tune of "Casey Jones," it dealt with the fate of a hapless strikebreaker after his untimely demise:

> The angels got together, and they said it wasn't fair,
> For Casey Jones to go around a-scabbing everywhere.
> The Angel Union No. 23, they sure were there,
> And they promptly fired Casey down the Golden Stair.

Another of Hill's songs, "The Preacher and the Slave," is considered one of the best protest songs ever written in America. Folk musicians still perform it today, singing it to the tune of "In the Sweet Bye and Bye." Hill's lyrics satirize religious leaders who asked hard-up laborers to endure destitution today for promised riches in the afterlife. Its opening verse and chorus set the tone:

> Long-haired preachers come out ev'ry night
> Try to tell you what's wrong and what's right;
> But when asked, how about something to eat?
> They will answer with voices so sweet:
> You will eat bye and bye
> In the glorious land above the sky;
> Work and pray, live on hay,
> You'll get pie in the sky when you die.

Hill's final chorus, however, extols the virtues of concentrating on the here and now, instead of depending on the powers that be:

> You will eat bye and bye
> When you've learned how to cook and to fry.
> Chop some wood, it'll do you good,
> And you'll eat in the sweet bye and bye.

Little did Hill know that his life would be dependent on those powers that be in the very near future.

Shortly before 10 P.M. on January 10, 1914, John G. Morrison and his son Arling were closing their grocery store in Salt Lake City when they were violently interrupted. According to Morrison's youngest son, Merlin, the only eyewitness, two masked men entered the store brandishing guns, shouting, "We have got you now!" Arling pulled out a gun his father kept in the store and shot one of the assailants. The two masked men returned fire, killing Arling and John. They then escaped into the night, one of them clutching his chest as he ran.

The police deigned the murders a revenge case. John Morrison had been a police officer in the city at one time, and lived in fear of retribution from the men he had arrested during his five-year stint. That, along with the fact that no money had been taken from the till, made robbery an unlikely motive. The police started searching for suspects right away, and eventually found three or four likely perpetrators.

Unfortunately for Hill, he was one of a number of people who had suffered gunshot wounds that night. Hill had stopped in Utah while en route to Chicago, and had taken odd jobs to earn money for the remainder of the trip. Unemployed due to illness, he eventually found lodging with the Eseliuses, a Swedish family he knew in Salt Lake City. On the night of January 10, 1914, Hill left the family's home between 6 P.M. and 9 P.M. He did not return until around 1 the next morning. Neither Hill nor his accusers were ever able to satisfactorily account for his actions before midnight.

What is known is that Hill, his shirt and undershirt soaked with blood, visited the office of Dr. Frank McHugh at about 11:30 P.M. He had been shot, he said, in a quarrel with a friend, something to do with the friend's wife. The bullet had gone cleanly through Hill's chest and only grazed his left lung—no permanent damage had been done. The doctor patched him up, took him to the Eselius house and eventually took his story to the police. On January 13, the police arrested Hill for the murders of John and Arling Morrison. He was formally arraigned 15 days later.

The trial, which began on June 17, 1914, and lasted more than a year, was by all accounts a shambles. Neither side could, or would, give concrete descriptions of what had happened on the night of the 10th. Moreover, it became quickly evident that conservative Utah did not like Hill or the IWW. This was fine by the union—they did not like Utah either. Mormon church leaders had voiced strong anti-union sentiments throughout the IWW's attempts to organize Utah's workers.

Once Hill's membership in the IWW became apparent, the bad blood spilled into the courtroom. The court not only allowed the prosecution's dependency on circumstantial evidence to make its case, but also defended the ploy. Merlin Morrison could not positively identify Hill as the masked gunman until he was goaded to do so by state attorneys. The prosecution never established a past connection between Hill and Morrison, nor supplied any substantial motive for the killing.

Hill did not help his own case, either. Though stubbornly insisting that Utah was determined to "fix" the case against him, Hill refused to give a concrete alibi for the night of the 10th. Worse, he declined to clarify the circumstances under which he had received his gunshot wound, only saying that any explanation would sully a certain lady's honor. He disastrously acted as his own attorney during the preliminary trial, conducting amateurish questioning when he bothered to question the witnesses at all. His erratic behavior eventually turned the jury against him. When he stood up in the courtroom and attempted to fire his state-appointed attorneys, instructing them to "get out of that door," his case was as good as lost in the eyes of most Utahans. The evidence may not have been enough to find him guilty in a court of law, but it did not need to be. He was found guilty in the court of public opinion long before the judge's gavel fell.

On June 27, 1915, after brief deliberations, the jury decided against Hill. The judge sentenced him to death. His lawyers filed an appeal on July 3, 1915, which the Utah State Supreme Court denied.

When Wobblies heard that the man who wrote "The Preacher and the Slave" and "Mr. Block" was facing execution, thousands of letters poured into Utah from around America. The IWW mobilized, sending representatives to Salt Lake City to protest his conviction. They did this peaceably, if loudly, but fights still broke out between them and residents who did not like unions. Outside interests got into the act, too. Concerned about the court's obvious bias against Hill, the Episcopal bishop of the Salt Lake City diocese requested that Hill's sentence be commuted, as did a member of the Utah State House of Representatives. W.A.F. Ekengren, the Swedish minister to the United States, became personally involved in the case. Workers in Boulder City, Australia, threatened to boycott American-made goods if Hill was executed.

Then, on September 30, Utah Governor William Spry received a telegram:

> Respectfully ask if it would not be possible to postpone execution of Joseph Hillstrom, who I understand is a Swedish subject, until the Swedish minister has an opportunity to present his view of the case fully to your Excellency.
>
> —Woodrow Wilson

This kind of heavy political pressure could not be ignored. It did win Hill a reprieve, but it was short-lived. Utahans found it absurd that the president of the United States would lend a hand to a person they believed to be the embodiment of anarchism, and the court once again refused to reconsider the case. On October 18, Hill was brought into the courtroom and again sentenced to die. The press reported that when Hill tried to make a statement in the courtroom after the sentencing, officials silenced him. "The judge didn't want to hear what I had to say," Hill was quoted as saying while being escorted out, "and I don't blame him."

Hill's next month was taken up with waiting in the death house, giving interviews and writing letters. "One thing this jail has made out of me is a good correspondent," he wrote in one of his epistles. His surviving letters from that time show not only a man dealing with the issues of appearing a court case, but also one adept at turning his case into a rallying cry for "the cause." At times he seems to consciously contribute to the making of his own myth, describing himself as a "rebel true blue" and ready to die as such. At other times, Hill seems genuinely weary: ". . . all this notoriety stuff is making me dizzy in the head," he wrote to a friend. "I am afraid I am getting more glory than I really am entitled to." His last letter to "Big" Bill Haywood, leader of the IWW in Chicago, asks that his body be hauled out of the state: "I don't want to be caught dead in Utah," he wrote. That letter contained a phrase that still reverberates throughout labor unions today: "Don't waste any time mourning—organize!" He also wrote his last will and testament, published in the *Salt Lake Herald-Republican*:

My Will is easy to decide

For there is nothing to divide

My kin don't need to fuss and mourn

"Moss does not cling to a rolling stone."

My body? Oh! If I could choose

I would to ashes it reduce

And let the merry breezes blow

My dust to where some flowers grow.

Perhaps some fading flower then

Would come to life and bloom again.

On November 19, 1915, Hill was taken to the execution grounds. Wearing a dark blue suit of coarse material, he was sat down on a chair and blindfolded. A doctor used a stethoscope to search for his heart's exact position and placed a heart-shaped paper target over the spot. Five soldiers lined up, one of whom had a blank cartridge in his rifle. Deputy Shettler began the sequence of commands, calling out, "Ready . . . aim . . ."

"Fire," Hill called from his chair. "Go on and fire."

Shettler went on to command, "Fire," and the five rifles cracked. With that, Joe Hill—man, émigré, idealist, union activist, poet and, perhaps, even murderer—was dead. Four blackened circles on the target began to turn crimson, and the white paper heart turned red.

By the time of Hill's two funerals, the myth-making process had already begun. The *Salt Lake Herald-Republican* reported that the several thousand people who came to see Hill's body at a Salt Lake City funeral home included "newspaper boys, workingmen with their lunch boxes beneath their arms, business and professional men and women, people who were well dressed and poorly clad. The expressions of opinion were as varied as the appearance of the visitors."

More than 90 years later, they still are. Joe Hill was considered a militant labor agitator by some and a hero of enlightenment by others, but his life in many ways is overshadowed by his death. Clouding the issue are the scores of "eyewitness" testaments to his character that surfaced after his death, all of uncertain credibility. Some claimed he had the soul of a poet and would never take another's life; others said he was the Robin Hood sort, one who would not mind killing another human being if it furthered the cause of the workingman. The unions idolized Hill; the newspapers mostly vilified him. His family in Sweden collected and destroyed most records of him after he was executed, not wanting to be associated with the incident. Whether Hill was guilty of murder or not, he clearly did not receive a fair trial, one that might have credibly determined the truth.

When the IWW brought Hill's body back to the union's home base in Chicago, an estimated 30,000 people jammed the streets to catch a glimpse of his funeral procession. By midmorning, 5,000 people filled the West Side Auditorium to capacity to attend his funeral. The audience sang Hill's songs and listened to speeches; they celebrated the man they considered a martyr, and badmouthed Utah. His body was later cremated, his ashes placed in envelopes and sent to IWW locals in every state but Utah. Years later, his last wishes would be honored, when the IWW collected his ashes and scattered them to the wind. Hill's story, embedded with elements of classic American mythology, still stirs the imagination of some. The sentiment is probably best captured in Alfred Hayes' 1925 poem:

I dreamed I saw Joe Hill last night,

Alive as you or me.

Says I, "But Joe, you're ten years dead."

"I never died," said he.

From *American History*, by Ben Lefebvre, December 2005, pp. 57–62. Copyright © 2005 by Weider History Group. Reprinted by permission.

"A Machine of Practical Utility"

While lauded for their 1903 flight, the Wright brothers were not convinced of their airplane's reliability to sustain long, controlled flights until October 1905.

Tom D. Crouch

On the morning of October 5, 1905, Amos Stauffer and a field hand were cutting corn when the distinctive clatter and pop of an engine and propellers drifted over from the neighboring pasture. The Wright boys, Stauffer knew, were at it again. Glancing up, he saw the flying machine rise above the heads of the dozen or so spectators gathered along the fence separating the two fields. The machine drifted toward the crowd, then sank back to earth in a gentle arc. The first flight of the day was over in less than 40 seconds.

By the time Stauffer and his helper had worked their way up to the fence line, the airplane was back in the air and had already completed four or five elliptical sweeps around the field, flying just above the level of the treetops to the north and west. "The durned thing was still going around," Stauffer recalled later. "I thought it would never stop." It finally landed 40 minutes after takeoff, having flown some 24 miles and circled the field 29 times.

The 1905 Wright Flyer was the final link in an evolutionary chain of seven experimental aircraft.

Farmer Stauffer had been watching the goings-on in that Ohio cow pasture for two years, but he had never seen anything like this. Neither had anyone else. The 1905 Wright Flyer was the final link in an evolutionary chain of seven experimental aircraft: one kite (1899); three piloted gliders (1900, 1901, 1902); and three powered airplanes (1903, 1904, 1905). Each machine was a distillation of the lessons learned and the experience gained with its predecessors. The flight of October 5, 1905, was proof that the Wrights had achieved their goal of developing an aircraft that could be flown reliably over significant distances under the pilot's complete control. Six years of trial and error, discouragement and hope, disappointment and exhilaration, risk to life and limb, and brilliant engineering effort had ended in triumph.

Over a century later, the basic question remains. Why Wilbur and Orville? When the brothers began their aeronautical research in the spring of 1899, they seemed unlikely candidates to achieve the age-old dream of navigating the air. They were not college-educated men. Wilbur, 31, and Orville, 28, were living in their father's house while operating a neighborhood bicycle sales and repair shop, where they had just begun to build cycles, one at a time.

Yet these two apparently ordinary small businessmen were intuitive engineers, possessed of unusual talents, insights, and skills that perfectly suited them to the problem at hand. They had an instinctive grasp of the process of innovation—and a rare ability to imagine a machine that had yet to be built and to visualize how it would function. They could move from the abstract to the concrete with relative ease, as in the fall of 1901, when they designed a pair of wind-tunnel balances as mechanical analogues of the algebraic equations they had to apply to calculate the performance of the aircraft they were designing.

The passion that the brothers brought to solving difficult technical problems was another essential key to their success. It was what got them up in the morning and kept them going when the difficulties seemed impossibly daunting. "Isn't it astounding," Orville wrote to a friend in 1903, "that all of these secrets have been preserved for so many years just so that we could discover them!!"

Their first taste of success came on the morning of December 17, 1903, with four powered and controlled flights made on the sand flats south of Kitty Hawk, North Carolina. Although they had flown, the Wrights realized that their best flight of the day, 872 feet in 59 seconds, would not sound impressive to a world that had waited millennia for a flying machine.

Determined to solve the remaining problems, they transferred operations to a borrowed cow pasture eight miles east of their home in Dayton, where they flew for the next two years with scarcely anyone noticing. Without the steady winds and the long, sandy slopes of the Outer Banks, however, progress was slow. Finally learning to catapult themselves to flying speed, they began to stretch their time in the air, improve the design of their aircraft, and build their piloting skills.

As their flights grew ever longer in September and October 1905, local citizens and area journalists finally realized that something extraordinary was taking place in the sky over Torrence Huffman's pasture. Satisfied, the Wrights decided to stop flying altogether, worried that public demonstrations would reveal too much of their technology to potential rivals. They did not fly again until the spring of 1908, by which time they had a valid patent and contracts in hand for the sale of their machine. That August Wilbur stunned Europeans with his first public flights at the Hunaudières racetrack near Le Mans, France. A month later Orville demonstrated their machine to U.S. Army authorities at Fort Myer, Virginia.

Doubts about the Wright claims that had circulated during the years they had spent on the ground were immediately swept away. Wilbur and Orville Wright emerged as two of the first heroes of the new century. They were the inventors of the airplane in a much truer sense than Alexander Graham Bell can be said to have invented the telephone or Thomas Edison the motion picture.

TOM D. CROUCH, author of *The Bishop's Boys: A Life of Wilbur and Orville Wright* (W. W. Norton 1990), is senior curator of the Division of Aeronautics at the Smithsonian's National Air and Space Museum.

A Brief History of Fear

A century before the crisis of '07, there was the Great Panic of '07. What does history tell us? Fear is fanned by uncertainty, dubious values, confounding innovations, and the lack of a towering leader. Sound familiar?

JERRY USEEM

If there's any reliable guide to market panics, it would be George Washington. Atop his granite pedestal, with its commanding view of the intersection of Broad and Wall streets, he has witnessed more than a century of financial mayhem. Being cast in bronze, he can't convey the lessons of history so directly. But chief among them is: Panics are precisely the moment you need someone of his stature (roughly 12 feet).

To be clear: A panic is not a crash but the critical point at which fear (or the awful apprehension of something) can produce horror (a "sickening realization," to borrow Devendra Varma's distinction). The outcome, as Washington would know, hinges on the will of a few to accept—if only to avoid collective ruin—the still scarier role of leader.

There's a good body of evidence to support that conclusion. Andrew Jackson rid the nation of a central bank in 1836, which helped produce the Panic of 1837. An unforeseen effect of his policies—a host of barely regulated banks flooding the nation with paper money—produced bad results as well as some innovations: Reserve requirements could be met, for instance, by adding a layer of gold coins over a much bigger pile of tenpenny (or subprime) nails. No wonder banks chose Jacksonian $20 bills as our national ATM currency.

In 1857, panic got a technological boost. The failure of Ohio Life Insurance & Trust Co. would once have taken days or weeks to reach Wall Street. But the telegraph carried the contagion directly to the stock exchange and the economy at large. The incomplete nature of the news made it all the more alarming—the first time, but not the last, that technology fanned uncertainty.

If the Panic of 1873 has one timeless lesson, it's the physical inability of everyone to escape from trouble at the same moment. Jay Cooke, the railroad financier, had been stiffed by international lenders, and his bank (which then fronted the intersection of Wall and Broad) was suspending payments. *The New York Times* described the scene: "The brokers stood perfectly thunderstruck for a moment." Then they "surged out of the Exchange, tumbling pell-mell over each other in the general confusion, and reached their respective offices in race-horse

time. . . . The news of the panic spread in every direction downtown, and hundreds of people who had been carrying stocks in expectation of a rise, rushed into the offices of their brokers and left orders that their holdings should be immediately sold out. . . . Some of the men who were ruined swore, some of them wept." Forget about an orderly repricing of risk.

Which brings us to the Great Panic of '07, the drama—and trauma—that changed everything. It showed that you did need a man behind the curtain who could operate the levers in the Emerald City. Only he didn't have to be so small.

The directors of the Knickerbocker Trust thought they were being secretive when they met in a private dining room to discuss whether they should open their doors the next day, given its president's connection to a speculative copper scheme. They weren't secretive enough. According to Wall Street lore, they carelessly left the door ajar, and their conversation floated to the ears of a bystander and then, it seemed, to all 18,000 of its depositors. Soon they were lining up at Knickerbocker's palatial new headquarters at 34th Street and Fifth Avenue. For several days Knickerbocker tried to buy time (one trick was for tellers to count and recount the cash very slowly). On Sunday, with the bank closed, attention shifted to a private library a few blocks away, where a flock of reporters waited outside to find out what exactly J.P. Morgan was thinking.

Though semiretired, Morgan was the closest thing America had to a central banker. In recent years he had become acutely concerned about liquidity—that is, the lack of a lender of last resort should the nation's banking system hit another scare. Among the sources of uncertainty were so-called trust companies like Knickerbocker, which operated like commercial banks but, like hedge funds, fell outside regulatory purview.

Inside his library that Sunday night, Morgan was organizing an emergency-response team of six bankers, including the young secretary of Morgan-affiliated Bankers Trust, Benjamin Strong. As Jean Strouse recounts in her biography, *Morgan*, Strong was assigned to examine the books of troubled trusts to determine which were worth saving. Knickerbocker, they determined, was not, and it closed its doors. Depositors then turned on the next-weakest, the Trust Co. of America (TCA). Its ornate tower—finished earlier that year—was just doors from Morgan's office.

In TCA's offices, Ben Strong pored feverishly over its books. Shortly after 1 A.M., he walked the 30 paces to the corner, where he made a presentation to Morgan, who wordlessly waved away details to press the question, "Are they solvent?" Strong answered in the affirmative. Morgan turned to the heavies assembled around him: "This is the place to stop the trouble, then." As TCA employees trudged into Morgan's offices with sacks of securities and collateral, $3 million of U.S. currency was being sent to TCA's offices. Salvation had arrived.

The aftermath in Washington was more of an aftershock. "Something has got to be done," announced Senator Nelson W. Aldrich. "We may not always have Pierpont Morgan with us to meet a banking crisis." Indeed, the next panic would hit in 1914, a year after Morgan's death. But by that time the U.S. had a Federal Reserve—and the foresight to close the stock exchange at the outbreak of war.

Before it became known as the Great Crash, it was, for a few days, the Panic of 1929. Weeks of volatility accelerated into a free fall on Black Thursday. Once again a rescue effort was organized by private bankers at the corner, who made conspicuous buys of blue-chip stocks, but its effects were short lived. What followed was the even more devastating Black Tuesday, again exacerbated by the imperfections of technology (as would happen once more in 1987 when programmed stop orders triggered an automatic selloff). The stock ticker, which could print only 268 characters per minute, fell several hours behind. Old quotes left an information vacuum that gave the cycle of uncertainty another vigorous turn. (Groucho Marx fell into such a depression that an understudy had to take his place for several shows in Broadway's *Animal Crackers*.) Without a strong response from the Fed—whose chief voice, Benjamin Strong, had died the previous year—the market plunged into a chasm that would soon widen into the Great Depression.

Today the intersection of Wall and Broad looks in many ways as it did 100 years ago. Washington still holds his pose, while "Integrity," a giant work by the same sculptor, J.Q.A. Ward, still protects the works of man from its perch atop the stock exchange. But the House of Morgan is now Downtown Living by Philippe Starck. Fronting the former Trust Co. of America is an oversized sign in Tiffany blue announcing the jeweler's imminent arrival at *The Heart of Wall Street*. Cranes are busily converting the former Chase headquarters into condos. The rapid conversion of the area into an upscale neighborhood mirrors the intermingling of real estate and securities. But it also underscores the kind of destabilizing forces that are the preconditions for crises: a nebulous concern about income disparities, assets obtained with easy credit, the use of novel financial instruments that seep into the mainstream, and above all, the lack of what Henry James called the "imagination of disaster."

If history holds one lesson, it's that we never learn from it, at least not enough. As for what the future holds—well, let's not speculate. The market has a way of punishing those who do.

From *Fortune*, September 3, 2007, pp. 84, 86. Copyright © 2007 by Fortune Magazine. Reprinted by permission of Time, Inc. via Pars International Corp.

A Day to Remember: March 25, 1911
Triangle Fire

CHARLES PHILLIPS

At the end of the work day on March 25, 1911, Isidore Abramowitz, a cutter at the Triangle Waist Company located on the corner of Greene Street and Washington Place in the heart of Manhattan's Garment District, had already pulled his coat and hat down from their peg when he noticed flames billowing from the scrap bin near his cutting table. It was about 4:40 P.M., and within minutes the fire swept through the factory and killed more than 140 of the 500 people who worked there. The conflagration, for some 90 years considered the deadliest disaster in New York City history, would usher in an era of reform with implications far beyond those of mere workplace safety.

The Jewish and Italian immigrants working at Triangle, most of them young women, produced the fashionable shirtwaists—women's blouses loosely based on a man's fitted shirt—popularized by commercial artist Charles Dana Gibson, whose famous "Gibson Girl" had become the sophisticated icon of the times. Beginning in late 1909, these workers participated in a major strike led by the Women's Trade Union League demanding a shorter working day and a livable wage. The garment workers had also protested the deplorable working conditions and dangerous practices of the industry's sweatshops. A large proportion of these firetraps, like Triangle, were located in Manhattan's crowded Lower East Side.

The factory workers had support not only from the left wing of the American labor movement but also among the city's wealthy progressives. Such socially prominent women as Anne Morgan (banker J.P Morgan's daughter) and Alva Belmont (tycoon William H. Vanderbilt's ex-wife, who married banker Oliver Hazard Perry Belmont) ensured tremendous publicity for the strikers, and they helped stage a huge rally at Carnegie Hall on January 2, 1910. But they met with adamantine resistance from factory owners, led by Triangle partners Max Blanck and Isaac Harris, who hired thugs from Max Schlansky's private detective agency to break up the strike. The owners in general enjoyed the backing of Tammany Hall boss Charles E Murphy, which meant not only that the New York police were hostile to the workers but that strikebreakers were also available from the street gangs employed as muscle by Murphy's political machine.

When the strike ended, although the owners had agreed to some minor concessions and the radical newspaper *The Call*

declared the strike a victory, little had truly changed, and everyone on the Lower East Side knew it. Certainly the workers at Triangle still put in long hours for penurious wages, without breaks, in an airless factory located on the top three floors of a hazardous 10 story firetrap. Scraps from the pattern cutters piled up in open bins and spilled over at the workers' feet, where the higher paid cutters, often men, dropped the ashes or even tossed the smoldering butts of the cheap cigars they smoked.

Because Blanck and Harris feared pilfering by their employees, access to the exits was limited, despite the city's fire regulations. At closing, workers were herded to the side of the building facing Greene Street, where partitions had been set up to funnel one worker at a time toward the stairway or the two freight elevators before they could leave the building for the day. This allowed company officials to inspect each exiting employee and his or her belongings for stolen tools, fabric or shirtwaists. The stairway and passenger elevators on the opposite side of the building, facing Washington Place, were reserved for management and the public. The only other egress was a narrow and flimsy fire escape on the back side of the building, opposite Washington Place, that corrupt city officials in 1900 had allowed Blanck and Harris to substitute for the third stair way legally required by the city. Access to it was partially blocked by large worktables.

These arrangements all led the disaster when the fire broke out as the result—the fire marshal later ruled—of a match or a smoldering cigarette or cigar tossed into Abramowitz's scrap bin. The loosely heaped scraps of sheer cotton fabric and crumpled tissue paper flared quickly, and the fire was blazing within seconds. Accounts of the chaos that erupted vary greatly, but apparently Abramowitz reached up, grabbed one of the three red fire pails on the ledge above his coat rack, and dumped it on the flames. Other cutters snatched pails and tried in vain to douse the exponentially spreading blaze. Despite their efforts, the fabric-laden old structure, ironically called the Asch Building, began to burn quickly and fiercely.

Factory manager Samuel Bernstein directed his employees to break out the fire hoses, only to find them completely useless. Some claimed the uninspected hoses had rotted through, while others asserted that either the water tanks on the roof were empty or the flow of water from them was somehow blocked.

Having lost precious minutes in fruitless attempts to control the blaze, the workers looked for the means of escape.

A few rushed to the solitary, poorly constructed and inadequately maintained fire escape, which descended from the 10th floor to the 2nd, stopping above a small courtyard. Some of the young women who used it fell from one landing to the next; one of the male employees fell from the 8th floor to the ground. Others madly rushed toward the inward-opening doors on the Washington Place side, preventing them from being opened. (Some later claimed these doors were locked.) As more and more workers piled up at the doors, those at the front were nearly crushed. Only with great effort did Louis Brown, a young shipping clerk, bully his way through the pressed bodies and muscle them away from the exit so that he could open the doors. On the opposite side of the building, panicked workers who tried to exit the 8th floor on the Greene Street side were slowed by the funneling partitions, and found the stairway and elevators already jammed with workers fleeing from the 9th and 10th floors.

Afterward, there was much confusion and a lot of debate about which floor the Washington Place passenger elevators visited and when. The elevator operators—Joseph Zito and Gaspar Mortillo—certainly risked their lives by returning to burning floors to carry their co-workers to safety. They probably visited the 8th floor first, saving a lot of lives even as the panic there set in. Then they headed up to the 10th floor, the executive floor. Zito later guessed that they went to 10 twice, dropping off the first group only to find the floor empty on the next trip up.

All 70 workers on the 10th floor managed to escape, as did Blanck (and the two daughters he'd brought to work with him) and Harris, who showed a good deal of bravery in his efforts to save many of his 10th-floor employees. They all got out either by the early elevator trips, by way of the staircases or by ascending to the roof. New York University law students in a taller, adjacent building lowered ladders to the roof of the Asch Building, and the workers inched their way up them to safety.

Of all the Triangle employees, the 260 who worked on the 9th floor suffered the worst fate. According to some accounts, the alert and the fire reached them at the same time. The Greene Street exit was quickly jammed, and the doors to the Washington Place stairwell were found to be locked. Since the elevator car itself was packed with 10th-floor employees, some clambered down the greasy cables of the freight elevator.

Elevator operator Zito peered up the elevator shaft as those left behind faced grim choices. "The screams from above were getting worse," he later reported. "I looked up and saw the whole shaft getting red with fire. . . . They kept coming down from the flaming floors above. Some of their clothing was burning as they fell. I could see streaks of fire coming down like flaming rockets."

Others on the 9th floor wedged their way into the Greene Street staircase and climbed up to the roof. Still others ran to the fire escape, which proved incapable of supporting the weight of so many. With an ear-rending rip, it separated from the wall, disintegrating in a mass of twisted iron and falling bodies. In complete desperation, some 9th-floor workers fled to the window ledges. The firemen's ladders would not reach beyond the 6th floor, so the firefighters deployed a safety net about 100 feet below, and they exhorted the victims to jump. Some of the young women, in terror, held hands and jumped in pairs. But the weight of so many jumpers split the net, and young men and women tore through it to their deaths.

An ambulance driver bumped his vehicle over the curb onto the sidewalk, hoping against hope that jumpers might break their fall by landing on his roof. Deliverymen pulled a tarpaulin from a wagon and stretched it out. The first body to hit it ripped it from their hands. "The first ten [to hit] shocked me," wrote reporter William Gunn Shepherd before he looked up and saw all the others raining down.

Fifteen minutes after the fire started, the firemen—even then New York's finest, the pride of the city—were within moments of bringing the fire on the 8th floor under control. But the 9th was hopeless. On the 9th, the fire took over the entire floor. Later, burned bodies were found piled up in a heap in the loft. A second scorched cluster was discovered pressed up against the Greene Street exit, where they had been caught by the blaze before they could get out. At the time, the crowds watching could see groups of girls trapped in burning window frames, refusing to jump. When they could hold out no longer, they came tumbling through the windows in burning clumps.

Then it was over. The last person fell at about 4:57 P.M., and there was nothing left to do but deal with the dead—146 broken bodies. During the next few days, streams of survivors and relatives filed through the temporary morgue on 26th Street to identify the dead. Eventually, all but six were given names.

Even before the bodies stopped falling, veteran newsman Herbert Bayard Swope had interrupted District Attorney Charles Seymour Whitman's regular Saturday news briefing at his apartment in the Iroquois Hotel to announce the disaster. Whitman immediately rushed to the scene and began looking for somebody to blame. Since he couldn't go after the city itself, he got a grand jury to charge Blanck and Harris with negligent homicide for locking the doors to the back stairway. Defended in a celebrated trial by famed Tammany mouthpiece Max D. Steuer, himself a former garment worker, the "Shirtwaist Kings" were acquitted, much to the outrage of progressives everywhere.

But watching the fire that day was a young woman named Frances Perkins. Perkins happened to be enjoying tea with a friend who lived on the north side of Washington Square. She heard the fire engines and arrived just in time to see the bodies begin to fall. Already a rising star in the progressive firmament, she never forgot what she saw, and she never let it go. Through her efforts, and the efforts of others like her, the horrible images of the Triangle fire brought an anguished outcry for laws to compel heedless, greedy, cost-cutting manufacturers to provide for the safety of employees.

The pre-fire strikes, coupled with the Triangle disaster and its aftermath, unified union organizers, college students, socialist writers, progressive millionaires and immigrant shop workers. Tammany Hall boss Murphy quickly sensed that a transformation of the Democratic Party could take advantage of this new progressive coalition at the ballot box. As a result, he fully supported the New York Factory Investigating Commission, formed three months after the fire, to inspect factories throughout the state. The "Tammany Twins," Alfred E. Smith and Robert F. Wagner, who were the driving force behind the investigation, backed Perkins as she sat on the commission and took the lead in shaping its findings. The commission's report, compiled during $2\frac{1}{2}$ years of research, brought dramatic changes to existing laws and introduced many new ones.

Smith, of course, went on to become governor of New York and the Democratic nominee for the presidency in 1924 and 1928. When Franklin Delano Roosevelt followed in his footsteps and actually won election to the office in 1932, he brought Perkins with him into his New Deal, as the first female Cabinet member (secretary of labor), and Wagner as an adviser who drafted some of the most important progressive legislation in the country's history. In many ways, it is fair to say that the modern American welfare state of the 20th century's middle decades rose from the ashes of the Triangle fire.

From *American History,* by Charles Phillips, April 2006, pp. 16, 18, 70. Copyright © 2006 by Weider History Group. Reprinted by permission.

UNIT 3

From Progressivism to the 1920s

Unit Selections

Key Points to Consider

- How was the $5 day received by workers? What were Henry Ford's motives for offering it? What were the unanticipated consequences?

- What were Woodrow Wilson's goals with regard to world peace during and after the Great War? Why did he fail to achieve them?

- Charles Lindbergh's solo flight to Paris was a triumph of technology as well as personal courage. How did he view things differently in his later years?

- Why did the question of evolution stir up so much controversy during the Scopes trial? Why does it continue to be so controversial?

Student Website
www.mhhe.com/cls

Internet References

International Channel
  www.i-channel.com
World War I—Trenches on the Web
  www.worldwar1.com
World Wide Web Virtual Library
  www.iisg.nl/~w3vl
The Roaring 20's and the Great Depression
  www.snowcrest.net/jmike/20sdep.html

Reform movements in the United States have most often developed in the face of economic dislocation. The Populist crusade in the 1890s and the New Deal in the 1930s are typical. Progressivism was an exception. It developed during a period of relative prosperity. Yet more and more people became dissatisfied with existing conditions. Individuals who became known as "muckrakers" published books and articles that revealed the seamier side of American life. One focused on the terrible working conditions in the meat packing industry, another on corruption and cronyism in the Senate, still another on the "bossism" and "machine politics" he found in a number of cities. The popularity of muckraking in newspapers, journals, and books showed that many segments of the public were receptive to such exposures. The Progressive movement generally was led by white, educated, middle or upper-middle class men and women. They were not radicals, though their opponents often called them that, and they had no wish to destroy the capitalist system. Instead they wanted to reform it to eliminate corruption, to make it function more efficiently, and to provide what we would call a "safety net" for the less fortunate. The reforms they proposed were modest ones such as replacing political appointees with trained experts, having senators elected directly by the people, and conducting referenda on important issues. The movement arose on local levels, then percolated upward to state governments, then into the national arena.

Teddy Roosevelt as president had responded to progressive sentiment through actions such as his "trust busting." He did not seek a third term in 1908, and anointed William Howard Taft as the Republican candidate for the presidency. Taft won the election but managed to alienate both progressives and conservatives during his tenure in office. By 1912, progressivism ran strongly enough that the Democrat Party nominated Woodrow Wilson, who had compiled an impressive record as a reform governor in the state of New Jersey. Roosevelt, now counting himself a full-blown progressive, bolted the Republican Party when Taft was re-nominated and formed the Progressive or "Bull Moose" party. Roosevelt was still popular, but he managed only to split Republican support with the result that Woodrow Wilson won the election with just 42 percent of the popular vote.

The Ford Motor Company shocked the industrial world in January 1914, when it announced that it would double its workers' minimum wage to five dollars per day. Partly this was to encourage loyalty at a time when assembly line production was causing a great deal of absenteeism. The author of "The $5 Day" argues that Ford also wanted genuinely to share the wealth of this enormously profitable company. The new policy worked in the short-run as workers were reluctant to do without the higher wage. In the long-run, especially after the onset of the Great Depression, it had the unforeseen effect of encouraging labor unions, which Ford fought with everything at his disposal.

What we call "World War I" (contemporaries called it "The Great War") broke out in the summer of 1914. President Woodrow Wilson called upon the American people to remain neutral "in thought and deed" toward the warring powers. By April 1917, however, after Germany had resorted to "unrestricted submarine warfare" against neutral shipping, he asked Congress for a declaration of war. "To Make the World Safe for Democracy" describes Wilson's efforts to create a lasting peace at the war's end. He failed to get the kind of peace settlement he envisioned, and also failed to get his proposed League of Nations treaty past the Senate. Twenty years later another world war erupted.

The 1920s was a decade of great ferment. After a brief postwar recession, the economy became extremely prosperous although

not everyone shared in it. Interest in sports grew enormously, and stars such as Babe Ruth, Jack Dempsey, and Red Grange became household names. Prohibition, the "noble experiment," promised to rid the nation of the curse of what was referred to as "Demon Rum." Unfortunately, despite huge expenditures of time and money devoted to enforcing prohibition laws, the experiment failed to produce the results predicted. Bootlegging and homemade beverages made a mockery of what was supposed to be a dry era. Some have argued that the consumption of alcohol actually increased during the period. There can be no question that prohibition contributed to the rise of organized crime. "The Democrats' Deadlocked Ballot Brawl of 1924" describes how deeply the debate over prohibition affected politics. Although there were numerous other factors, the struggle between "wets" and "drys" almost tore the Democrat Party apart.

"Evolution on Trial" discusses the highly publicized Scopes trial of 1925 in Dayton, Tennessee. The teaching of evolution in public schools was a hot-button issue in many areas because it appeared to undermine the teachings of fundamentalist Christianity. Interest in the case was stimulated by the clash of opposing lawyers William Jennings Bryan and Clarence Darrow. Former presidential candidate Bryan argued for a literal interpretation of the bible, including the proposition that the earth was created in seven days. Darrow's cross-examination of Bryan proved devastating to the latter's claims. The author of this essay points out that 80 years later many residents of Dayton still refuse to accept Charles Darwin's theory about the common ancestry of humans and primates.

Charles Lindbergh's highly publicized solo flight across the Atlantic in 1927 made him the most popular man in the world. Boyishly handsome and modest, he represented the ideal American hero. His flight also seemed to epitomize the veritable explosion of technological advances of the time. "Between Heaven and Earth" tells of Lindbergh's achievements, but also points out that in later life he began to question the unregulated impact of technology on the environment.

"Remember the Roaring '20s?" analyzes the era, and draws parallels between this boom period and the more recent "bubble" that eventually burst in 2008. The great task facing businessmen during the '20s, the author argues, "was replacing the work ethic with a consumer ethic."

The $5 Day

By doubling his workers' salaries, Henry Ford solved his turnover problem—and also unwittingly set the stage for industrial unionism.

ROBERT H. CASEY

The word spread quickly on January 5, 1914. By 2 A.M. men were gathering outside the employment office of the huge Ford Motor Company plant in Highland Park, Michigan, ignoring the raw weather. Less than 12 hours earlier, the company's two top executives, Henry Ford and James Couzens, had called reporters into the latter's office to announce the company's plan to more than double its minimum wage to $5 for an eight-hour workday. Ten thousand job seekers rushed to the plant at the corner of Woodward Avenue and Manchester Street north of Detroit. The long-term results of this decision, for Detroit and the nation, would be profound and largely unanticipated.

What prompted Ford to adopt such a radical policy? Certainly it represented, at least in part, an effort to deal with his workers' response to the recently developed assembly line, which required little skill but whose mind-numbing repetition and relentless pace resulted in very high worker turnover. Ford hoped better pay would offset these difficulties; but in part his plan was an effort literally to share the wealth. In 1913 Ford Motor Company's net income was $27 million, and its seven stockholders split $11.2 million in dividends. Both Ford and Couzens believed that their employees deserved a bigger share.

The new policy began to unfold early in January 1914, when Ford convened a meeting to discuss production and wages for the coming year. Sources disagree over exactly who attended, but all agree that it concluded with a discussion about a substantial wage raise. Some of those present, including Ford, said Ford pushed the $5 a day idea. Others, including Couzens, claimed that it was Couzens. What's not disputed is that Ford and Couzens, who held nearly 70 percent of the company stock between them, met with their fellow stockholder Horace Rackham on January 5 and agreed on the new policy. Later that day Ford and Couzens held the news conference that brought the 10,000 job seekers to the plant.

The new policy solved Ford's turnover problem, made his employees the richest factory workers in the country, and elevated Ford to a folk hero. But those were only the short-term consequences. More important, the five-dollar day redefined the relationship between compensation and skill. Throughout history, workers had increased the price they demanded for their labor by increasing their skill levels. The master craftsman always made more money than the journeyman. Conversely, employers had reduced their labor costs by reducing the skill required to do their work. Thus, mechanizing the textile industry, by reducing the skill level required to spin yarn or weave cloth, reduced the value of spinners' and weavers' labor. But Ford was offering to pay his unskilled workers more, even as he told them he didn't want them to think, only to follow orders.

Other industrialists denounced Ford's new wage policies, but many, in and out of the automobile industry, eventually found it profitable to adopt his mass production and assembly line methods. Inevitably they found it necessary to pay his high wages as well. Rising factory wages made northern industrial cities magnets for foreign immigrants and rural Americans, accelerating existing migration trends. In Detroit, industries that could not pay automobile industry wages left the city, solidifying its status as a one-industry town.

Ford also unwittingly set the stage for industrial unionism. When the Great Depression hit, his and other assembly-line-based companies could no longer pay the prevailing level of wages, making plants fertile ground for union organizers as well as highly vulnerable to labor stoppages. Ford fought the unions with every means possible, legal and illegal, but even he was eventually forced to accept a contract with the United Auto Workers.

But the reversal of the wage/skill relationship turned out not to be permanent. By the 1980s American mass production enterprises found themselves competing with Japanese manufacturers who had learned that actively engaging workers and seeking their ideas improved not only morale but productivity and product quality. Increasingly sophisticated manufacturing technology also required more than manual dexterity and obedience. At the same time competition from lower-cost overseas producers, such as the Chinese, was reducing the number of American manufacturing jobs. By the end of the 20th century what remained of the American manufacturing base paid well, but was open only to those with higher skills. The high wage/low skill era had lasted less than a century.

ROBERT H. CASEY, author most recently of *The Model T: A Centennial History* (Johns Hopkins University 2009), is the John and Horace Dodge Curator of Transportation at The Henry Ford in Dearborn, Michigan.

To Make the World Safe for Democracy

World War I marked the first time that U.S. soldiers would sail east to decide a major European war.

JOHN LUKACS

Late on April 2, 1917, President Woodrow Wilson, flanked by a small cavalry escort, drove to the Capitol to address Congress to urge a declaration of war against Germany. He was tired. His speech contained no memorable phrases, save perhaps one: "The world must be made safe for democracy." A few eloquent words were uttered by the opponents of the declaration of war. They were not many; only 50 out of the 435 congressmen and six of the 96 senators stood against it. The Senate voted for war two days later, the House two days after that, on Good Friday.

This was nothing like Fort Sumter or Pearl Harbor. Two months before April 2, Germany had resumed unrestricted submarine warfare, which moved public opinion—and Wilson—toward war. Leading up to this time, the president had often been of two minds. But during the second half of March he convinced himself that he had no choice. April 1917 was a culminating point in the advance of American determination to oppose Germany by war, if it must. And America's subsequent entry into the war would prove one of the most important turning points in U.S. history.

For centuries, European soldiers had crossed the Atlantic from east to west; for the first time American soldiers would sail the other way.

For long centuries, even during the 19th century, European soldiers had crossed the Atlantic from east to west to protect their nations' interests in the Americas. Now, for the first time, two million American soldiers would sail the other way to decide a great European war. A central pillar of the American identity had been its distinctive New World character, independent and distinct from the Old. Now this would change, with the New World becoming involved in the destinies of the Old.

None of this was clear in 1917. Unlike in 1941, the vast economy of the United States was still unprepared for war. The mass of the two million American soldiers did not get to France until a year or more after the declaration of war. They went into combat with the German army after the French and the British, exhausted as they were, halted the last great German drive against Paris in June and July 1918. Still, the American presence in France decided the war.

American troops did not stay long in Europe. For a moment President Wilson seemed to be the leader of the entire world, but he did not have his way either in Paris or, a few months later, with the majority of the American people. They repudiated his version of a League of Nations; indeed, Americans rejected the entire episode of their involvement with Europe. For generations millions of immigrants had been flooding into the United States from the Old World; but a few years after 1917, a series of immigration acts, passed by great majorities in Congress and supported by American public sentiment, put an end to this nearly unrestricted mass movement of peoples. Ten years after 1917 many, if not most, Americans had come to regard the war of 1917–18 as a mistake.

But that too did not last. It was impossible to isolate America. By 1918 the principal financial center of the world had become New York, not London; the almighty dollar replaced the once sovereign pound sterling. In the 1920s European art masterpieces were routinely passing to America, bought by wealthy collectors. The United States was becoming a repository of much that was best in Old World civilization—and the Atlantic was no longer an estranging sea. Twenty years after 1918, Americans were riveted by the horrifying prospect of another world war, which the nation would eventually fight across both of the greatest oceans, bringing down despotic enemies on both sides of the globe. By 1945 the United States had become the strongest and most prosperous country in the world. But so she had been in 1918. Only now an American military presence stayed abroad.

Franklin Roosevelt took up many of Wilson's ideas. The United Nations was meant to be another, grander version of

Wilson's League of Nations. Lonely and ill, Wilson had died in February 1924, only 13 days after Vladimir Lenin. But his ideal of national self-determination prevails even now, long after the idea of a proletarian world revolution has disappeared. For a long time many people, including communists as well as anti-communists, believed that the most significant events in 1917 were the Russian Revolution and Russia's withdrawal from the First World War. But it was, in fact, America's entry into the war that was the defining moment.

JOHN LUKACS, winner of the 1994 Pulitzer Prize for *The End of the Twentieth Century and the End of the Modern Age* (Houghton Mifflin Harcourt), is professor of history emeritus at Chestnut Hill College.

From *American Heritage,* Winter 2010, pp. 73–74. Copyright © 2010 by American Heritage Publishing Co. Reprinted by permission.

The Democrats' Deadlocked Ballot Brawl of 1924

PETER CARLSON

Those TV yappers are in a tizzy about the upcoming Democratic convention. They keep jibber-jabbering about how neither Clinton nor Obama will have enough delegates to win the presidential nomination and they'll need to woo the high-powered superdelegates. They keep yakking about a *deadlocked convention!* Or, better yet, a *brokered convention!*

These young whippersnappers don't know doodley about a deadlocked convention. Most of them weren't even *born* the last time a convention fight went beyond the first ballot, which was in 1952.

Back in my day, Democrats had *real* conventions with *real* nomination fights that went on for dozens of ballots. It took 46 ballots to nominate Woodrow Wilson in 1912, and 44 ballots to nominate James Cox in 1920. Jeez, it took four ballots to nominate Franklin D. Roosevelt in 1932—and he was *FDR,* for crying out loud!

In those days, people weren't in such a damn hurry. They liked to vote for their state's "favorite son" candidate for a few ballots just to show some local pride. In 1932, FDR's campaign manager asked Sam Rayburn, who was the campaign manager for John Nance Garner of Texas, if he could get the Texas delegation to vote for FDR after the first ballot.

"Hell, no," Rayburn said, "we've got a lot of people up here who've never been to a convention before, and they've got to vote for Garner a few times."

But you didn't come all the way out here to the old folks' home to hear me beat my gums about the good old days. You want to hear about the greatest deadlocked convention of them all, don't you? That would be 1924, when the battle went on for 103 ballots and even governors were getting into fistfights on the convention floor.

Give me a minute to put my teeth in and I'll tell you all about it.

It was the Roaring Twenties, the days of hot jazz and bathtub gin, and the Democrats met in Madison Square Garden, which was packed to the rafters with New York characters, described in *The Washington Post* as "Tammany shouters, Yiddish chanters, vaudeville performers, Sagwa Indians, hula dancers, street cleaners, firemen, policemen, movie actors and actresses, bootleggers . . ." Plus 1,098 delegates and 15 presidential candidates.

To win, a candidate needed the votes of two-thirds of the delegates and, as the convention opened on June 24, nobody was even close. But the obvious front-runners were Al Smith, the governor of New York, and William McAdoo, a California lawyer who had been Woodrow Wilson's Treasury secretary and was Wilson's son-in-law.

Smith and McAdoo represented the two sides of America's cultural divide—what today's TV yappers would call the red states and blue states. Smith's backers tended to be Northern, urban, Catholic and "wet," meaning anti-Prohibition. McAdoo's supporters tended to be Southern or Western, rural, Protestant and dry.

Just to make things more interesting, a lot of McAdoo's rooters were members of the Ku Klux Klan, which was then at the height of its power. The Klan hated Catholics and Smith was a Catholic. (Needless to say, there were exactly zero black delegates.)

It wasn't going to be easy uniting these factions, but the party bosses tried. They managed to finesse the Prohibition issue with a compromise that called for the enforcement of all laws but avoided mentioning the hated law against hooch. They tried to finesse the Klan issue in the same way, writing a platform that denounced violent secret societies but neglected to actually mention the Klan.

That didn't work. The anti-Klan folks balked, demanding a resolution that named the Klan. This sparked an anti-Klan demonstration on the floor that led to fistfights as pro- and anti-Klan delegates fought for possession of various state banners. Believe it or not, the governors of Kentucky and Colorado got into fistfights trying to keep their state banners out of the hands of anti-Klan delegates.

Governors throwing punches—now, that's the kind of convention high jinks you just don't see anymore!

Ultimately, the anti-Klan resolution that *did*n't mention the Klan beat the anti-Klan resolution that did mention the Klan by exactly one vote.

And then this seething, angry crowd settled down to try to pick a presidential candidate. First came 15 windy nominating speeches, followed by 15 windy seconding speeches. This torrent of oratory produced only two words that anybody still remembers: FDR calling Smith the "happy warrior."

When FDR ended his speech, the crowd went nuts. Smith's Tammany machine had packed the galleries with thousands of hacks armed with drums, tubas, trumpets and a bunch of ear-piercing electric fire sirens that were so loud that people scooted out of the hall with their fingers in their ears.

"It sounded," *The Washington Post* reported, "like 10,000 voodoo doctors in a tropical jungle beating 10,000 tom-toms made of resonant washtubs."

The hacks in the galleries weren't so friendly to McAdoo. Anytime a speaker uttered his name, the hacks chanted, "Oil! Oil!"—a snide reference to the fact that McAdoo had received two mysterious payments from an oil baron implicated in the Teapot Dome scandal. It was as if Obama delegates greeted any mention of Hillary by hollering, "Whitewater! Whitewater!"

Anyway, after all this folderol, they finally called the roll for the first ballot and, needless to say, nobody got the 732 votes needed to win. McAdoo led with 431, followed by Smith with 241, and 13 other guys, mostly favorite sons with delusions of grandeur, each with fewer than 60 votes.

What happens when you get no winner? Those TV yappers probably don't know but the answer's simple: You vote again. That first day, which was June 30, they took 15 roll-call votes and *still* nobody was anywhere near victory. The next day, they came back and took 15 more roll-call votes and still nobody won.

This was the first convention broadcast on radio, and all over America people listened to the endless roll calls, each of them beginning with an Alabama delegate drawling, *"Al-a-ba-ma casts twen-ty of-ah votes* fo-ah *Os-cah Dub-ya Unnn-der-wood!"* Soon, everybody in America was mimicking that drawl, saying, *"Os-cah Dub-ya Unnn-der-wood!"*

The voting was weird, even for Democrats: On the 20th ballot, the Missouri delegation switched all 36 votes from McAdoo to John W. Davis, the favorite son from West Virginia, which got everybody all excited, but on the 39th ballot, they all switched back to McAdoo.

On Wednesday, the third day of voting, William Jennings Bryan asked the chairman for permission to explain his vote for McAdoo. Bryan was the grand old man of the Democratic Party, which had nominated him for president three times. He was the "Great Commoner" who'd delivered the legendary "Cross of Gold" speech at the 1896 convention. But when he started orating for McAdoo, he was drowned out by angry boos from the gallery and chants of "Oil! Oil!"

"His voice, which had competed in the past with foghorns and tornadoes, sounded like the hum of a gnat," *The Post* reported. "For the first time, Bill Bryan's larynx had met its master."

Listening on the radio, Americans were shocked to hear the rabble of evil New York shouting down a good Christian gentleman like Bryan.

On and on the voting went—50 ballots, 60 ballots, 70 ballots. The convention was supposed to be over but it still hadn't nominated a candidate, so it went into extra innings, like a tied baseball game. Some delegates gave up and left, others wired home for more money. The McAdoo people complained that rural delegates couldn't afford New York prices and urged the party to pay their hotel bills, which caused the Smith people to accuse the McAdoo people of trying to bribe the delegates by paying their hotel bills.

"This convention," wrote H.L. Mencken, the most famous reporter of the age, is "almost as vain and idiotic as a golf tournament or a disarmament conference."

But still it continued, day after day—80 ballots, 90 ballots, 100 ballots. Finally, both Smith and McAdoo gave up and released their delegates and on July 9, after 16 days and 103 ballots, the Democrats nominated John W. Davis of West Virginia for president.

The band played "Glory, Glory Hallelujah" and the delegates limped home, weary and bleary, their self-loathing exceeded only by their loathing of the other Democrats.

In the November election, Davis was creamed by Calvin "Silent Cal" Coolidge, a laid-back dude who didn't let the duties of his office interfere with his afternoon nap.

W hat? Speak up, young fella, I don't hear too good. Those Tammany fire sirens ruined my ears.

Fun? You wanna know if the 1924 convention was fun? Well, it was fun for the first 20 or 30 ballots, but after 50 or 60 it got a tad tedious, and by the 80th or 90th even the driest of the dry delegates longed to take a swan dive into a bottle of bootleg bourbon.

People said the 1924 convention was so ugly it would kill the Democratic Party. It didn't, but it did kill the romance of the deadlocked convention. After 1924, Democrats hated deadlocks even more than they hated rival Democrats.

At the 1932 convention, the party leaders started to panic after three ballots and McAdoo got up and urged the convention to avoid "another disastrous contest like that of 1924." FDR's people offered the vice presidency to anybody who controlled enough votes to break the deadlock. John Nance Garner took the deal, delivered the Texas delegation and ended up vice president, a job he later reportedly described as "not worth a bucket of warm spit."

The last time a convention went more than one ballot was 1952, when the Democrats took three ballots to nominate Adlai Stevenson, who was trounced by Dwight Eisenhower.

These days, both parties confine their brawling to the primaries and by the time the convention rolls around they're cooing and kissing like newlyweds. Now, conventions are just long infomercials for the candidates. They're so dull they make you pine for a deadlock.

Maybe that's why the TV yappers are jabbering about a deadlocked Democratic convention. Now that Clinton has won Ohio and Texas, they say, it's possible that neither she nor Obama may have enough delegates to win, so the nomination will be decided by the 796 superdelegates, the people we used to call the party bosses.

Well, I think they're full of baloney, but I hope they're right.

A little deadlock livens things up, and the prospect of floor fights, fistfights and backroom wheeling and dealing quickens the blood.

Two ballots, five ballots, 10 ballots—that would give an old geezer a reason to go on living. But, please, not 103 ballots. Take it from me, young fella, that's a little too much of a good thing.

Between Heaven and Earth
Lindbergh: Technology and Environmentalism

Glen Jeansonne and David Luhrssen describe how the pioneer aviator Charles Lindbergh was increasingly disturbed by the tension between technology and its impact on the environment. In his later career, in the 1960s, Lindbergh became a spokesman for the embryonic environmental movement as they describe here.

GLEN JEANSONNE AND DAVID LUHRSSEN

The fervour greeting Charles A. Lindbergh on his arrival in Paris on May 21st, 1927, was not unlike the excitement surrounding the first landing on the moon, four decades later. As the first person to pilot an aeroplane solo across the Atlantic, Lindbergh symbolized the triumph of technology over geography and the human spirit over the barrier of space.

Technology was initially Lindbergh's muse. He embraced it like most Americans of his day and became the embodiment of the country's boyish, can-do image, yet he himself soon became ambivalent about it. Crediting his flight to rapid advances in the 'scientific researches that have been in progress for countless centuries', he was uncomfortable that those advances enabled the world to participate in his triumph through radio and radiographs, flashing across the ocean at speeds faster than his plane could travel. The mass media made him the world's most famous person, but he was never entirely comfortable with fame, willing to use it in the cause of American neutrality in the Second World War, yet shrinking from its grip on his private life. He blamed the kidnapping and murder of his two-year-old son in 1932 on the excessive attention of the media.

Lindbergh's ambivalence about technology increased with the years. By the 1960s the man who was once an icon for progress—defined as humanity's conquest of the earth through technology—had become a tireless advocate of nature and aboriginal peoples against the encroachment of civilization. Perhaps Lindbergh had always carried within himself visions contrary to the onward march of science. Late in life he claimed his ambivalence towards technology had begun in childhood: 'Instinctively I was drawn to the farm, intellectually to the laboratory'. He also claimed in his memoir that misty spectres had followed him on his transatlantic flight years before, writing:

> My visions are easily explained away through reason, but the longer I live, the more limited I believe rationality to be. I have found that the irrational gives man insight he cannot otherwise attain.

Born on February 4th, 1902, Lindbergh spent much of his youth roaming his family's sprawling homestead on the Mississippi River. The family wealth gave Lindbergh first-hand experience of the latest technological advances and their impact on twentieth century life. The Lindbergh's first car with its hand crank was soon replaced by a model with a self-starting engine; machinery supplanted manual farm labour. The social transformation caused by steam turbines, automobiles, electricity and telephones 'confirmed my growing desire to become an engineer and take part in the world's unprecedented progress', as he recalled. Though eloquent and intellectually curious, Lindbergh never enjoyed school and was too much of an individual to conform readily to any curriculum. Bored with his studies, he was expelled in 1922 from the engineering course at the University of Wisconsin for poor grades. He had been thinking of dropping out anyway. Lindbergh wanted to learn how to fly.

The Wright Brothers built and flew the first successful aeroplane less than two years after Lindbergh's birth. Within a short time their rickety invention became a potent weapon. The acceleration of aircraft design spurred by the First World War also raised hopes that the new technology would bring together a world it had helped destroy. With safer, more dependable aircraft, the dream of commercial aviation was becoming reality. Lindbergh became a 'barnstormer' who entertained paying customers with aerial feats such as wing-walking and flying suspended from the belly of a plane. Envious of the more powerful aircraft being built for the army, Lindbergh enlisted as a reserve officer in 1925 while earning a living by delivering airmail.

Inspired by the much-publicized transpolar flights and other aeronautical adventures, his dreams soon turned to the flight, nonstop from New York to Paris, that would earn him such acclaim. It was a daring journey under the best conditions, given the fragility and limited range of contemporary aircraft. Unruffled by danger, accustomed to altitude and solitude, Lindbergh decided to fly the Atlantic alone.

His plane, *The Spirit of St Louis,* was a feat of engineering, a single-engine monoplane designed to his specifications. Soon after landing in Paris, the young aviator was dubbed 'Lucky Lindy' by the media despite his insistence that the flight represented a triumph for American engineering rather than a trial with fate. Lindbergh found the adulation uncomfortable. He was more concerned with extolling his US-made earth-inductor compass and air-cooled engine than his own act of derring-do. After Lindbergh had completed a whirlwind tour of European capitals, President Calvin Coolidge ordered him home, promoted him to colonel and decorated him in a ceremony listened to by millions on the radio.

In 1929 Lindbergh married Anne Morrow, a shy, intellectually-sophisticated ambassador's daughter, and pushed her to become an independent woman, an early, if perhaps inadvertent, feminist. Anne Lindbergh became a skilled aviator and one of the best-selling female authors of her time, an inspiration to women across America. The Lindberghs were a model modern couple, at the cutting edge of technological developments. Together they pioneered the use of aerial photography as an aid to archaeologists, focusing on Central American sites. When they flew to East Asia in 1931 scouting for US-Chinese air routes, Anne served as co-pilot, navigator and radio operator. The mission was part of Lindbergh's campaign on behalf of commercial aviation. As adviser to Pan American and TWA, he helped choose flight plans and locations for terminals, and became the poster boy for the dawning age of air travel. His flights over several continents sharpened his impression of the Earth's beauty. As early as the 1950s, he was dismayed by the changes visible from the air, the scars on the land, the pollution. Following the kidnap and tragic murder of their first son, the Lindbergh's aversion to publicity and fear that kidnappers might strike at their other children compelled them to leave the United States in 1935. After a sojourn in the United Kingdom where they lived quietly in the Kent countryside in a house rented from the writer Vita Sackville-West, the family moved in 1938 to a remote island off the coast of Brittany. Here Lindbergh worked with a French physician and Nobel Prize winner, Alexis Carrel, with whom he had begun collaborating years before at the Rockefeller Institute, New York. While at the institute, Lindbergh and Carrel perfected the perfusion pump, an apparatus that permitted an organ to live outside the body, making organ transplants feasible.

Lindbergh regretted that aviation, which symbolized the advance of civilization, might lead instead to its destruction.

In 1936 Lindbergh was invited to Germany at the request of the US military attache in Berlin, Major Truman Smith, who asked him to report on German air power. Following this visit Lindbergh was an honoured guest in Nazi Germany on several other occasions. Profoundly impressed, he pronounced the Luftwaffe as Europe's most powerful air force, though he was concerned about the uses to which it might be put. While his widely-reported remarks may have buttressed the mood of appeasement in Britain and France, Lindbergh took little pleasure from his observations. He regretted that aviation, which symbolized the advance of civilization, might lead instead to its destruction. As political storm clouds gathered over Europe, he began to wonder whether the technology that caused Western civilization to rise would lead to its fall. Lindbergh had first addressed the issue during his first visit to Germany at a lunch in his honour.

After returning home in April 1939, Lindbergh became an advocate of American neutrality, an isolationist adhering to the tradition that the US should stay aloof from foreign wars. Lindbergh was a charter member of the executive committee of America First when the organization was founded in September 1940. America First was an umbrella organization for a disparate group of people who opposed American involvement in the war and Roosevelt's efforts to assist Great Britain. It included liberals, conservatives and socialists, but also attracted a loud contingent of anti-semites and German sympathizers. Lindbergh's visits to Germany and his acceptance of a medal from Luftwaffe commander Hermann Goering tainted his reputation. The rancour between Roosevelt and Lindbergh became noisy after the president hinted publicly that Lindbergh harboured treasonous thoughts. In the aftermath, Lindbergh resigned his military commission. Following Japan's attack on Pearl Harbor (December 7th, 1941), America First disbanded. Lindbergh became a test pilot for military aircraft manufacturers and flew combat missions in the Pacific. Although he was still lionized by the military, the public had become wary of their former hero. The 1942 movie *Keeper of the Flame,* directed by George Cukor, starring Spencer Tracy and Katherine Hepburn, concerned a distinguished American traitor modelled in part on Lindbergh in the minds of many Americans.

Postwar, the cooling of passions enabled Lindbergh's rehabilitation as a national hero. He worked quietly as an advisor to the Strategic Air Command, troubled by the atomic bomb and the growth of weapons technology but fearful of the Soviet Union and the threat of a totalitarian victory in the arms race. He won a Pulitzer Prize for his 1953 bestseller *The Spirit of St Louis,* an account of his transatlantic flight, was appointed an Air Force brigadier general by Dwight D. Eisenhower, invited to the White House under John F. Kennedy, and honoured by Lyndon B. Johnson for his support of the pioneering work of Robert Goddard, the father of rocketry, on the technology that put man on the Moon. At Lindbergh's recommendation, Goddard was financed during the 1930s by the Guggenheim Foundation at a time when rocketry was often dismissed as science fiction.

During his final years in the 1960s and 70s Lindbergh's thoughts were focused more on the earth than the sky. Stripped of his status as an American idol, Lindbergh enjoyed the privacy he had long sought and was able to pursue his interests outside the public spotlight. As early as the 1930s the Lindberghs had flown to India, ostensibly on behalf of civil aviation but also in search of yogis and mystics. They spent many hours with Alexis Carrel at that time discussing subjects 'beyond conventionally-accepted fields of science'. Lindbergh became fascinated with the Chinese philosophy of Taoism, which emphasized harmony with nature. Perhaps these interests, considered exotic before the 1960s thrust them toward the mainstream, prepared Lindbergh for the final campaign of his career.

I felt revolted by some of the values I had held in the past, and on the martial and material development of science.

'I felt revolted by some of the values I had held in the past, and on the martial and material development of science,' Lindbergh wrote near the end of his life about his postwar reflections. 'I considered renouncing my profession and living far away from modern technology, some place where I could be in touch with nature and the earth'.

By the 1960s he cautiously emerged from seclusion as a champion of the rising environmental movement. Echoing Rachel Carson's *Silent Spring* (1962) and Paul Ehrlich's *The Population Bomb* (1968), books which influenced the rising counterculture, Lindbergh promoted clean air and water and measures curbing pesticides and development. In an article for the *Readers Digest* called 'Is Civilization Progress?' in 1964 he declared: 'Where civilization is most advanced, few birds exist. I realized that if I would have to chose, I would rather have birds than air planes.' During this last period of his life Lindbergh focused on East Asia and the South Pacific. His interest in the latter region was sparked through his association with British cultural anthropologist Tom Harrisson, who had lived among natives in the New Hebrides and Borneo.

The one-time champion of aviation tried to ban US landing rights for the supersonic airliner Concorde, and succeeded in blocking construction of an airbase on the Indian Ocean island of Aldabra, the breeding ground for the giant land tortoise. His name gained him the ear of government and corporate officers who might have ignored the pleas of lesser-known ecological activists.

In 1968 he gave his first public speech since America First, convincing the Alaska legislature to preserve wolves against extinction. He also adopted the cause of the great whales, persuading the Archer Daniels Midland corporation to reduce harpooning. He became an adviser to the Nixon administration, which proved remarkably eager to extend government regulation of the environment. As a member along with Prince Charles and Prince Bernhard of the Netherlands of the World Wildlife Federation's Committee of 100, Lindbergh lobbied heads of state on behalf of endangered species and habitats. He was especially persuasive with Philippines President Ferdinand Marcos, who he met in 1969 and who established a preserve for the tamarau, a wild buffalo, at his behest. Flying incognito to foreign destinations, Lindbergh was not content simply to remain in the conclaves of the powerful. For example, he embarked on a helicopter trip through the Philippine island of Mindoro to build community support for wildlife conservation. In 1970 Lindbergh became a leader of the Private Association for National Minorities (PANAMIN), a Filipino advocacy group championing tribal peoples against the encroachment of farmers and loggers.

Unlike many celebrity foreigners with a cause to push in the media, Lindbergh largely shunned publicity, lived for months with the tribes he supported and nearly came to blows with unsympathetic local authorities. He was photographed in a peasant's conical hat, brandishing an assault rifle in 1970.

In his final adventure, in 1972, Lindbergh joined an expedition to establish contact with a tiny tribe, the Tasaday, among the last remaining Stone Age people, in the remote Philippines jungle. Lindbergh admired the Tasaday for their ability to exist within nature, but was perplexed by their lack of curiosity over the wider world. He fretted over disturbing their primeval idyll, but ruefully conceded that the Tasaday's time was fast expiring in the age of global travel and communication he had helped advance.

Lindbergh died of cancer on August 25th, 1974, after refusing life support. As a holder of the Congressional Medal of Honor, he was entitled to interrment at Arlington National Cemetery in Washington, DC, but chose to be buried in a traditional Hawaiian tomb near his winter home on Maul. Questions about his support for Nazi Germany and public opposition to America's entry to the Second World War continue to darken his reputation even today, while public recognition for his environmental work faded, in part due to his own reluctance to court publicity for it.

At the height of his adulation, many Americans extolled Lindbergh's courage and conviction as the pioneer spirit manifest in the age of air travel. Lindbergh was one of a long line of archetypal American cultural figures, laconic, lonesome and marching to the measure of their own stride. He reflected upon many of the central issues of his age, and his resolute refusal to apologize for mistaken political views from the 1930s and 1940s, a product of the stubbornness that characterized him, was balanced against the actions he took in the 1960s and 1970s. Always in the vanguard, the exponent of technology had become its tireless opponent. An intensely private person, Lindbergh made few efforts to work with the news media to shape his image and agenda and treated reporters with antagonism. As a result, the press came to view him with suspicion. Eventually, he was largely ignored in the media, leaving unsung his accomplishments on behalf of environmentalism and relegating his energetic final years to obscurity.

Further Reading

A. Scott Berg, *Lindbergh* (Putnam's, 1998); Charles A. Lindbergh, *We* (Putnam's, 1927); Charles A. Lindbergh, *Autobiography of Values* (Harcourt Brace Jovanovich, 1978); Joyce Milton, *Loss of Eden: A Biography of Charles and Anne Morrow Lindbergh* (HarperCollins, 1993).

GLEN JEANSONNE is professor of American history at the University of Wisconsin-Milwaukee and the author of *Messiah of the Masses: Huey P. Long and the Great Depression* (Talman, 1995). **DAVID LUHRSSEN** is arts editor of the *Shepherd Express*, Milwaukee's weekly newspaper.

From *History Today*, January 2008, pp. 55–59. Copyright © 2008 by History Today, Ltd. Reprinted by permission.

Evolution on Trial

Eighty years after a Dayton, Tennessee, jury found John Scopes guilty of teaching evolution, the citizens of "Monkeytown" still say Darwin's for the birds.

STEVE KEMPER

In the summer of 1925, when William Jennings Bryan and Clarence Darrow clashed over the teaching of evolution in Dayton, Tennessee, the Scopes trial was depicted in newspapers across the country as a titanic struggle. Bryan, a three-time presidential candidate and the silver-tongued champion of creationism, described the clash of views as "a duel to the death." Darrow, the deceptively folksy lawyer who defended labor unions and fought racial injustice, warned that nothing less than civilization itself was on trial. The site of their showdown was so obscure the *St. Louis Post-Dispatch* had to inquire, "Why Dayton, of all places?"

It's still a good question. Influenced in no small part by the popular play and movie *Inherit the Wind,* most people think Dayton ended up in the spotlight because a 24-year-old science teacher named John Scopes was hauled into court there by Bible-thumping fanatics for telling his high-school students that humans and primates shared a common ancestry. In fact, the trial took place in Dayton because of a stunt. Tennessee had recently passed a law that made teaching evolution illegal. After the American Civil Liberties Union (ACLU) announced it would defend anyone who challenged the statute, it occurred to several Dayton businessmen that finding a volunteer to take up the offer might be a good way to put their moribund little town on the map.

One morning in early May, the enterprising boosters interrupted a tennis game Scopes was playing behind the high school and invited him to join them at Robinson's Drug Store on Main Street. After treating him to a soft drink at the soda fountain, they asked the young teacher if he had ever use the state's standard biology textbook, which contained a section on evolution. Scopes said yes. The men then told him what they were up to and wanted to know if he was willing to be arrested for teaching evolution. Although Scopes, a recent graduate of the University of Kentucky, certainly believed Darwin's theory, it's unclear whether he ever actually taught it in his classroom. Nevertheless, he amiably agreed to go along with the scheme and then returned to the tennis court. Neither he nor his fellow conspirators had any idea, of course, what an uproar their gambit would create, let alone how badly it would backfire, or with what long-lasting repercussions.

Today, 80 years later, the Scopes trial is still reverberating in the nation's consciousness. After President Bush was reelected last fall, commentators invoked it to help explain the cultural divide between blue and red, urban and exurban, secular and religious, scientific and evangelical. Many pointed to the seemingly decisive boost given to Bush by those who voted for him because of their conviction that he stood for moral values. Historian Garry Wills called the vote "Bryan's revenge for the Scopes trial." Implicit in more than a few election postmortems was the notion that Bryan's creationists had somehow contrived to come back from the dead. In truth, they have been here all along, living in places like Dayton.

A century or so ago, Dayton was a prosperous farming and mining center with 2,000 people and a blast furnace. After the furnace closed in 1913, the community fell on hard times and since then has undergone many changes. The population is currently 6,180 and counting. The big employer these days is a La-Z-Boy plant; up-to-date emporiums like Blockbuster and Wal-Mart have arrived on the scene, and the long-dormant downtown area, dominated by the old courthouse square, shows signs of revitalization. But one thing about Dayton has not changed and probably never will: its bedrock fundamentalism. Even now, it's hard to find a teacher who goes along with Darwin. "We all basically believe in the God of creation," says the head of the high-school science department.

Many residents, however, do wince at the ridicule that comes with Dayton's place in history. H. L. Mencken, who coined the term "Bible Belt," covered the Scopes trial along with 200 other newspapermen. He called the locals "primates," not to mention yaps, yokels, morons and anthropoids. The mockery lingers still. "If something bad happens here to people from Memphis or Chattanooga," says lifelong resident Bobbie McKenzie, "they'll say, 'It's just a monkey-town anyway.' They associate Dayton with ignorance." Then she brightens up a bit. "Well, for us it's a blissful state. I'm so glad I was born here and raised my kids here."

Bobbie is sitting with her husband, James "Jimmy" McKenzie, Rhea County's family-court judge, in his office at the three-story brick courthouse where, right upstairs, his grandfather Ben, and uncle, Gordon, helped prosecute Scopes. "It gave Dayton a black eye," Judge McKenzie acknowledges, referring to the trial. But in spite of all the hoopla and history associated with it, he notes wryly, "the case didn't solve anything."

Bryan and the creationists claimed victory because the jury in Dayton upheld the state's ban against teaching evolution and, by implication, the right of parents to control what their children learned. Darrow and the evolutionists, on the other hand, believed that in exposing the ignorance behind creationism they had stymied its threat to academic freedom. Time has proved both sides wrong. "As a result of the Scopes trial, evolution largely disappeared in public school science classrooms," says historian Edward J. Larson, a professor at the University of Georgia and author of *Summer for the Gods,* a Pulitzer Prize-winning account of the trial and its aftermath. Larson acknowledges that there is "more mandated teaching of evolution now than ever before." But that doesn't translate into actual teaching. According to a recent report in the *New York Times,* many teachers simply ignore evolution or play it down to duck controversy.

The level of support among Americans for creationism—and for what is now called "intelligent design"—remains high. "Polls say it's stayed pretty stationary over time," says Larson. "About half answer with a creationist viewpoint." These true believers are continuing to press for curricular changes in schools across the country. As in the Scopes case, the new creationists tend to focus on textbooks. They've persuaded Alabama to place evolution disclaimers on its biology texts. Kansas removed evolution from its science standards in 1999; it was subsequently reinstated. Early last year, Georgia purged the word "evolution" from a proposed biology curriculum because, explained the state's superintendent of schools, Kathy Cox, it causes "a lot of negative reaction" by bringing up "that monkeys-to-man sort of thing." The resulting furor forced Cox to back down. Since 2002, however, schools in Georgia's Cobb County have been putting stickers in its biology textbooks stating that "evolution is a theory, not a fact." The ACLU, riding to the defense of evolution once again, sued to have the stickers removed, and in January a judge agreed. The school board is appealing the ruling.

"If something happens here to people from Memphis or Chattanooga," says a resident, they'll say, "it's just a monkeytown anyway."

With help from their main think tank, the Discovery Institute in Seattle, advocates of intelligent design have also tried to persuade school boards to add "alternative theories" and criticisms of evolution to their science curricula. Three years ago, Ohio required its biology teachers to "critically analyze" evolution. Last year, a Wisconsin school board followed suit, and a school board in Pennsylvania voted to mandate the teaching of intelligent design. "These local revolts are started by people who are upset by what they consider to be the dogmatism of Darwin," says Phillip E. Johnson, an emeritus professor at the University of California at Berkeley's school of law.

An adviser to the Discovery Institute, Johnson ignited the intelligent-design movement with his influential 1991 book, *Darwin on Trial.* He's published a number of anti-evolution books and has been instrumental in reframing creationism as a "fairness" issue—as in, it's only fair to listen to both sides of an argument. "The Darwinists insist that only fully naturalistic explanations can be considered, regardless of the evidence," he says. "I would describe this as a faith in naturalism as a philosophy, rather than in science as an investigative process that considers all possibilities toward which the evidence may point."

"The idea that evolution is shaky or just a theory—this is absolutely amazing to scientists," says Eugenie C. Scott, executive director of the National Center for Science Education in Oakland, California. Scott has made a career out of playing Clarence Darrow to Johnson's William Jennings Bryan. She spearheads the defense of basic science education, including evolution, and has won many public service awards from scientific organizations. "On the street, a theory is just an opinion, but in science, a theory is an explanation," she says. "The theory of gravity is not an opinion or an observation, it explains why things fall. Creationists point to scientific arguments about how evolution takes place and the mechanisms of it, and then say evolution is controversial, so 'teach the controversy,' as if scientists are arguing about whether evolution is true. And that's just plain bad education."

In the aftermath of the November election, Scott anticipates many more challenges to the teaching of evolution. Religious conservatives "feel empowered now," she says. "For another four years, federal district court judges will be appointed, and conceivably one or more Supreme Court judges. Basically, it's court decisions that have kept creationism out of the classroom. But the law evolves too, and we can't stay confident the courts will continue to interpret the First Amendment as courts have in the past."

At Dayton's Rhea County High School, students do learn that species can change over time, a process modern creationists call "micro-evolution." Joe Wilkey, a genial bear of a man who heads the science department, can't think of anyone on his staff of nine teachers who believes in "macro-evolution"—the evolutionary origins of all life—and no one teaches it. If a student asks why a textbook states that dinosaurs lived 65 million years ago when his parents and his minister have told him that God created the world 6,000 years ago, Wilkey answers that people disagree about the earth's origins, and that some scientists trace the fossil record to the biblical flood. He doesn't teach creationism; it's not part of the state curriculum. "But I do not believe it would hurt a thing to teach intelligent design."

Darrow and others would go to my grandfather's office at the end of the day and tell war stories. My daddy said it was a show.

The Scopes trial ran for eight days in the middle of a July heat wave. Dayton worked hard to get ready for it. The big courtroom got a new coat of paint and was outfitted with 500 additional seats and a platform for a newsreel camera. New microphones installed in the courtroom were connected to speakers out on the lawn, so the expected overflow crowds could follow the proceedings, and a Chicago radio station arranged to use those same microphones to broadcast the trial live. Western Union strung wire for 22 telegraph operators to transmit breaking news to newspapers and radio stations across the country. To meet increased demand, the Southern Railway expanded its passenger service to Dayton.

Although folks in town couldn't abide the notion of monkeys as kinfolk, they had no reservations about exploiting them for fun and profit. While vendors sold popcorn, ice cream and cold drinks, hucksters hawked monkey souvenirs, including a coin minted by the Progressive Dayton Club that featured a monkey wearing a boater. A circus sent a gorilla in a freight car and charged a dime to see it. At his drugstore, Frank Robinson entertained customers with a besuited chimp that sipped "simian soda" and played a toy piano. Other stores advertised their wares with monkey displays, and the constable decorated his motorcycle with a "Monkeyville Police" sign. Meanwhile, Mencken observed, the courthouse lawn was "peppered" with evangelists, "and their yells and bawlings fill the air with orthodoxy."

More than 3,000 visitors showed up for the trial and the monkeyshines, and they all needed a place to eat and sleep. Some Daytonians rented their houses and left town. Many others let out rooms or sold home-cooked meals. Ann Gabbert Bates, druggist Robinson's 61-year-old granddaughter, remembers her mother telling how her own mother fed lots of journalists, "except Mr. Mencken. He wasn't welcome."

The visiting members of the press did not ingratiate themselves with their hosts. When an elderly woman asked one of the two reporters staying with her why he wrote that people in Dayton said "hain't" and "sech" and wore ragged clothes, he told her his paper wanted him to add "color." The other reporter never even bothered going to the courthouse because, he said, "I know what my paper wants me to write."

Longtime resident Richard Cornelius, a retired English professor, used to get his hair cut at Wilkey's Barbershop, where older habitués still laughed about a trick that was cooked up there for the newspapermen. After George Rappleyea, one of the chief drugstore plotters, sauntered in one day and began praising evolution, his partner, Thurlow Reed, yelled, "You can't call my ancestors monkeys!" and pretended to attack him. The Northern reporters ate it up because it matched their preconceptions about volatile Southerners. When another Dayton jokester shot off his pistol in front of the barbershop one day, he generated still more colorful copy—and more local glee at the reporters' expense.

Eloise Reed, an elegant 92-year-old widow whose attractive home sits a few blocks from the courthouse, was 12 that summer. Her brother Crawford had been playing tennis with John Scopes when the schoolteacher was summoned to the drugstore. After Scopes returned to the tennis court, he told Crawford about the scheme, which the youngster relayed to the family that night at supper. "We laughed," Reed recalls. "It didn't seem like any big deal." But then Bryan announced he was coming, followed by Darrow, and the excitement started to build.

When Bryan gave a sermon against evolution at the Southern Methodist church one Sunday, Eloise Reed was sitting near the front. Later, she shook his hand. She saw him and Darrow many times. Bryan was taller, she says. "And he stood tall. Darrow draped a little." Darrow was indeed stooped, and he wore baggy clothes and colorful wide suspenders. In contrast to Bryan's orotund grandiloquence, Darrow's speaking style was conversational, down-home and cuttingly quick. Working pro bono for the ACLU, he led a team of big-city lawyers. Tom Stewart, the astute district attorney, directed the prosecution with help from, among others, Bryan, his son, William Jr., old Ben McKenzie and his son Gordon. Judge John Raulston, a conservative lay Methodist minister, presided. All but one of the jurors belonged to local evangelical churches. On the trial's opening day, Judge Raulston read aloud the first chapter of Genesis.

Bryan, 65, and Darrow, 68, shook hands like boxers before the bell. They had once been political allies, back in the days when Bryan, who served as Woodrow Wilson's secretary of state, was known as "the Great Commoner," a passionate advocate of corporate reform, female suffrage and a progressive income tax. Teddy Roosevelt, no admirer, called him "a professional yodeler, a human trombone." Bryan left politics to become a crusader against Darwinism, which he blamed for atheism and a host of social and corporate ills. By the time of the trial, Darrow, a fierce rationalist, had long since concluded that Bryan was hazardous to the country's intellectual health. He intended to demolish him. "Nothing will satisfy us but broad victory, a knockout which will . . . prove that America is founded on liberty and not on narrow, mean, intolerable and brainless prejudice of soulless religio-maniacs," Darrow said.

Darrow's strategy was aimed less at exonerating Scopes than in discrediting the anti-evolution law. He assembled a distinguished group of scientists and religious leaders to testify that there was no conflict between evolution and belief in God; that many devout people also believed in evolution, and that the state should not allow a particular religious viewpoint to dictate or censor public-school curricula. His opening speech lasted two hours and awed even the opposition. Ben McKenzie told Darrow it was "the greatest speech that I have ever heard on any subject in my life."

Though McKenzie wryly referred to all of the Northern attorneys as "foreigners," he and Darrow struck up a lasting friendship. Ben's grandson, Jimmy, recently came across the family copy of Darrow's 1932 autobiography, inscribed: "To my esteemed and valued friend . . . with the kindest remembrances." A black-and-white photograph in Jimmy's office at the Dayton courthouse shows Ben with his arm around Darrow. It was no secret both men liked to drink, Jimmy says. "Darrow and others would go to my grandfather's office at the end of the day and tell war stories. My daddy said it was a show."

Since the town was dry, the booze consumed during those raucous get-togethers had to be bootlegged. Mary Welch, a 72-year-old widow, heard all about that from her father-in-law,

Luther Welch. He was a road commissioner and a good Christian, she says, but he didn't mind having a drink once in a while. At the time of the trial, he was a teenager, she recalls, and "he would go to Chattanooga in an old farm truck to get liquor for the lawyers on both sides."

Prosecutor Tom Stewart didn't want Darrow's shrewd eloquence and all-star experts to derail the trial. As it wore on, he constantly reminded Judge Raulston the case wasn't about creationism or academic freedom but solely about whether Scopes had broken the law. After Raulston agreed to prevent Darrow's experts from testifying before the jury, Mencken and many of the other reporters decided that was it for Scopes, so they left town and missed out on the biggest fireworks of all.

On the seventh day, the trial was moved from the stifling courtroom to a platform beneath the big oak trees on the lawn. There, after challenging Bryan to take the stand, Darrow asked him a series of questions designed to show that belief in the literal truth of the Bible was preposterous in light of current knowledge, and also that the Bible was subject to interpretation. Did Joshua really make the sun stand still? If so, did Bryan think the sun revolved around the earth? Did Jonah really live inside a whale for three days?

In the 1960 film version of *Inherit the Wind,* the Bryan-based character (played by Fredric March) melts down on the stand—becomes pathetic and incoherent. Actually, Bryan acquitted himself quite well, answering Darrow (Spencer Tracy in the movie) with wit and clever evasion. But eventually he did reveal that he knew little or nothing about fossils, geology, ancient civilizations or world religions. Such things did not interest him, he explained, because the Bible sufficed: "I have all the information I want to live by and to die by."

When Tom Stewart realized Bryan was not helping himself or the prosecution's case, he asked Judge Raulston, "What is the purpose of this examination?"

"The purpose," answered Bryan, "is to cast ridicule on everybody who believes in the Bible."

"We have the purpose," retorted Darrow, "of preventing bigots and ignoramuses from controlling the education of the United States."

The next day, Raulston expunged Bryan's testimony as immaterial to the case. Darrow responded by asking the court to instruct the jury to go ahead and find Scopes guilty so he could proceed with an appeal. The jury returned its unanimous verdict nine minutes later.

Scopes never spent time in jail, but the judge did fine him $100. Darrow's appeal lost (although Scopes' conviction was eventually reversed on a technicality), and Tennessee's anti-evolution law stayed in force until 1967. The Dayton school board asked Scopes to stay on, and he also had offers from Hollywood and vaudeville, but instead he accepted a scholarship to study geology at the University of Chicago. He worked as a geologist in South America and later for an oil and gas company in Texas and Louisiana. He married, had two boys, John Jr. and William, and stayed out of the spotlight.

In 1960, Scopes returned to Dayton for the world première of *Inherit the Wind* at a local drive-in (the town's only movie theater was too small), and in 1967 he published a memoir, *Center of*

the Storm. He died three years later at 70. Son John Jr., 72, spent his entire career in the insurance business and now lives on Long Island. Son Bill, semi-retired at 69, also worked mainly in the insurance field. Speaking by phone from his home in Guntersville, Alabama, recently, he said: "If anybody ever got to Heaven, it was Dad. He was just a real nice person—easygoing, modest, well liked, tolerant." John senior did not talk about the trial when the boys were growing up, Bill says, and he never discussed evolution.

The Scopes case was one of Darrow's last major trials. He visited Dayton with his family a few years later to be feted by the business club of Dayton, which gave him a dinner at the Aqua Hotel. When Darrow noticed a new church across from the hotel, he quipped, "Well, I didn't do so much good here after all." He died of heart disease at age 80 in 1938.

Bryan died of apoplexy five days after the trial ended while taking a nap in a bedroom of the house on S. Market Street in Dayton where he had been staying. (The house burned down in the late 1920s and has long since been replaced by another.) Some wondered whether the trial had broken his spirit and contributed to his death, but in fact Bryan felt vindicated and energized, and was enthusiastically planning another lecture tour.

In 1930, funded by donations from creationists throughout the country, William Jennings Bryan Memorial University opened in Dayton to carry on his work. Now known as Bryan College, the 110-acre campus consists of a dozen or so brick buildings scattered across a hill overlooking the town. Last year, the undergraduate enrollment was 600. According to the college's catalog, the curriculum is "based upon unequivocal acceptance of the inerrancy and authority of the Scriptures."

Kurt Wise teaches science at Bryan. His credentials are impressive—an undergraduate degree in geology from the University of Chicago and a PhD from Harvard, where he studied with the late Stephen J. Gould, the eminent paleontologist and anti-creationist. Wise believes that God created the world and everything in it 6,000 years ago.

On this July day, he is leading a group on a field trip through Grassy Cove Saltpeter Cave. Wearing headlights, the students crawl through muddy tunnels, run their hands over rough limestone columns and peer at fossil shells embedded in rock. Wise tells his students that water may have carved this extensive cave in a matter of hours about 4,000 years ago, a few centuries after Noah's Flood. He thinks the same phenomenon sculpted the Grand Canyon, though that, he says, took about three weeks.

This "catastrophic" explanation radically compresses geologic history to make it fit a literal interpretation of the Bible. For instance, Wise puts the Cambrian rock layers, usually dated from 540 million to 505 million years ago, at 2500 B.C. He tells students that geological events don't require long timelines—limestone can be simulated in a lab in two days, wood will petrify rapidly under certain conditions. Basically, what Wise and other "young earth" creationists are attempting to do is empirically explain the world in light of Genesis. "God's truth should be used to interpret—to properly interpret—all the data of the universe," Wise writes in his 2002 book, *Faith, Form, and Time.* "All the stars of the universe, all the rocks of the earth, all the organisms on its surface must be reinterpreted, as well as all the world's literature, philosophies, and religions. They can and should be reinterpreted from a Christian perspective so all these things can be taken captive under the mind of Christ."

What do most other paleontologists and geologists think of this? "Absolute bunk!" says Wise with a laugh. Does he believe evolution is flawed in and of itself, or flawed because it contradicts Genesis? His answer could have come straight from the college's namesake himself: "Scripture trumps interpretations of physical data."

Though the Scopes trial made Dayton a laughingstock in some quarters, it also made it a tourist destination. A steady stream of people visits the old courthouse these days and a few stop at the plaque where Robinson's Drug Store used to stand. Every July, Dayton puts on a three-day Scopes Festival, a modest affair that faintly echoes the original event—a few musicians on the courthouse lawn; a few vendors selling food, crafts and monkey souvenirs. In the main event put on daily, local actors restage the trial in the courtroom, speaking dialogue culled from the transcript by the wife of a Dayton minister. This time around, Bryan fares much better.

H. L. Mencken said he expected "a squalid southern village," but found instead "a country town full of charm and even beauty."

Richard Cornelius, 70, helped start the festival as a sort of damage-control project. He attended Bryan College and has lived in Dayton since 1961, when he joined the faculty, and over the years he has interviewed eyewitnesses and written articles "to show that perhaps we don't need to be quite so embarrassed."

Actually, not all of the publicity Dayton received at the time of the trial or since has been embarrassing. Mencken said he expected "a squalid Southern village," but instead found "a country town full of charm and even beauty," where the "Evolutionists and the Anti-Evolutionists seem to be on the best of terms." The next day he reported that "there is an almost complete absence, in these pious hills, of the ordinary and familiar malignancy of Christian men. . . . There is absolutely no bitterness on tap. But neither," he added, "is there any doubt."

That description still applies. Dayton has more than 30 churches; Rhea Country, with 28,400 people, has more than 140. The semiweekly *Herald-News* runs a biblical quote on every front page, the Dayton Coffee Shop sells religious CDs near the Jesus posters, and evangelical preachers compete with each other on the radio day and night. Even so, many Daytonians cringe anytime the extremists among them reinforce old stereotypes, as happened last year when the county commissioners voted not only to oppose gay marriage, but to recommend that the state prosecute homosexuals for crimes against nature. Sure enough, most outside news stories mentioned the monkey trial, implying that history was repeating itself.

Mary Brooks says she is "a pretty strong Christian person," but she doesn't like "the way people get lumped into backwoods ignorant stereotypes. I know there's some of that here, but it's not the majority." As one of Dayton's new boosters, Brooks focuses on economic rather than religious revival. Seven years ago, she bought the empty hardware store near the courthouse and turned it into an upscale shop that sells antiques and home accessories, with a coffee bar on one side. The store did well enough that Brooks bought six more run-down buildings. One became a deli, another houses her daughter's bakery. Brooks' example has inspired other merchants to open their own specialty gift stores. "It's a work in progress," she says of the budding revival, "but I do think we're on our way. The other morning we must have had 40 kids in here from Bryan College getting cappuccinos and espressos."

After Scopes returned to the tennis court, he told about the scheme. "We laughed," Reed recalls. "It didn't seem like any big deal."

Those old soda fountain plotters would be every bit as proud of Dayton's progress as Bill Hollin, 68, who was the town's director of development and tourism until he retired last year. "Rhea County is going to change," he predicts. But Hollin knows as well as anyone that still more change in his fundamentalist neck of the woods will require some earnest soul-searching. Hollin is convinced, for example, that Dayton, which remains almost as dry as it was in John Scopes' time, needs "some medium-to-better" restaurants, like Applebee's or O'Charlies. "But it's hard to bring them in, because they can't make it without a bar," he acknowledges. Two years ago a neighboring town approved liquor-by-the-drink. "And now they've got all those major restaurants!" says Hollin, sounding envious. "Not that I can recommend liquor-by-the-drink," he quickly adds. "I'm a deacon."

STEVE KEMPER's book about the *Segway, Code Name Ginger,* has been reissued as a paperback entitled *Reinventing the Wheel.*

Remember the Roaring '20s?

If the crisis is beginning to sound familiar, maybe it rhymes.

ROBERT S. MCELVAINE

"History doesn't repeat itself, but it rhymes." Mark Twain was supposed to have said that, but even if he didn't, there's no denying we're seeing proof of the adage in today's financial crisis.

Consider this statement: "The extraordinary rate of default on residential mortgages forced banks and life insurance companies to 'practically stop making mortgage loans. . . .'" Sounds like 2008, doesn't it? It is in fact a comment from Ben S. Bernanke, current chairman of the Federal Reserve board. But when he wrote those words in 1983, he was talking about the Great Depression.

We've been hearing a lot of comparisons to the Great Depression lately, because today's crisis rhymes with that one to an extraordinary degree. At the most basic level, the cause of the current crisis is simple: Economists, business leaders and policymakers have all been ignoring the lessons learned from that early 20th-century calamity.

I've written extensively about the Great Depression, and in my view, the collapse of the "un-real" estate market of recent years was as predictable as the collapse of the Great Bull Market of the late 1920s. Even though some politicians insist otherwise, the fundamentals of our economy have not been strong, just as they weren't in 1929. And the principal reason is that, just as they were in the period leading up to the Great Depression, economic fundamentalists have been in charge.

It's one of the fascinating coincidences of history that Adam Smith's "The Wealth of Nations" was published in 1776, the year of the United States's birth. America then was seen as an unspoiled paradise, a "New Eden" where humans could return to what they imagined was a "state of nature." There was talk of an "American Adam" who roamed freely in this land where the "natural economy" of the free market that Smith postulated could operate, well, freely.

Almost from the start, many Americans have operated on the assumption that this American Adam's surname was Smith, and have taken the market as their economic god. The great irony, though, is that a new type of economy was being born in Great Britain at the same time. And industrialism would remove men and women from a state of nature more completely than ever before.

By the 1920s, the industrial economy was mass-producing at a rapid rate, which meant that its survival required the rise of mass consumption. Trying to play by the rules of Adam Smith's pin factory at a time when Henry Ford's massive River Rouge complex was closer to the true nature of the economy was a prescription for disaster. Such huge economic actors don't behave according to the "natural" laws of the simple economy of Smith's day; under modern circumstances, a more visible hand is needed to guide the market onto a course that benefits all. Yet both economists and political leaders of the time maintained their faith in market-god fundamentalism.

The task facing business in the 1920s was replacing the work ethic with a consumption ethic. If the American people were to be made into insatiable consumers, traditional values would have to be undermined and reversed. The means of accomplishing this? Advertising. The Mad Men of the '20s made over the traditional wisdom of "Waste not, want not" into the essential message of the consumption economy: "Waste and want." Bruce Barton of Barton, Durstine & Osborn, for instance, famously portrayed Jesus as the ultimate advertiser and businessman in his 1925 bestseller, "The Man Nobody Knows."

But wanting isn't enough. If the masses are going to be able to buy what they've been persuaded to want, they have to receive a sufficient share of total income to do so. Yet the opposite happened in the '20s. President Calvin Coolidge and his Treasury secretary, Andrew Mellon, drastically reduced taxes on the highest incomes. Meanwhile, anti-union policies produced less income for worker-consumers. The share of total national income going to the very richest grew enormously, peaking in 1928, just months before the economy began to contract in the summer of 1929. The top 10 percent of American earners then were getting 46 percent of total income.

Providing large tax cuts for the richest was precisely the wrong policy. To stimulate consumption, taxes should have been cut at lower income levels. Cutting taxes on higher incomes stimulated speculation instead. Sound familiar?

"Don't kill the goose that lays the golden eggs" is one of the favorite sayings (and warnings) of champions of high profits, low taxes on the rich, concentrating wealth and income at the top, and the rest of trickle-down economics. But when profits become too high and taxes on the very rich too low, the geese get obese, eventually stop laying eggs and develop coronary problems.

What the economy needed was an effective weight-loss program for the monetarily corpulent and a program to help underweight consumers put on a few pounds (i.e., dollars). Yet those who argued for such an approach, such as progressive Republican Sen. George Norris of Nebraska, were ridiculed by the followers of the god of the unfettered market.

Instead, 1920s financiers gave consumers an injection of the economic steroid known as credit. And the economy temporarily became extremely robust. Sales of automobiles, radios and other new products to people who couldn't actually afford them soared. The ratio of private credit to GDP nearly doubled between 1913 and 1929. During the '20s, short-term personal loans from personal finance companies ballooned by more than 1,200 percent.

But a steroid-induced burst of great strength is always likely to be followed by impotence. Sooner or later the limits of consumer credit are reached—consumers find themselves with more debt than they can repay, sales decline and banks, left holding bad loans, begin to fail.

"Sooner or later" arrived in October 1929, as it did again in September 2008.

Today isn't an exact replay of the 1920s, but it's a pretty good rhyme. Over the last three decades, top-end tax rates have been slashed; unions' power has become diluted; top corporate pay has skyrocketed; the minimum wage has been allowed to fall in real terms and the average wage has flatlined. And the credit bubble on which the economy has been riding in recent years is vastly larger than the one in which Americans danced the Charleston and drank bathtub gin 80 years ago.

After a long period of less income inequality from the 1940s through the 1970s, inequality began to increase again in the 1980s and has continued to rise almost continually ever since. By 2005, income concentration slightly exceeded the levels of just before the Great Depression: The richest 1 percent of Americans were receiving nearly 22 percent of the nation's income, and the top 10 percent took in more than 48 percent.

Yet there are some significant differences between the 1920s and today. Some make our current situation more dangerous. These include today's huge federal budget deficits (compared with the more or less balanced budgets of the late 1920s) and the war in Iraq, which has undermined confidence in the administration and, along with other policies and the flood of federal red ink, makes a stimulus through a massive deficit difficult, if not impossible. There's also the trade imbalance: In the 15 years preceding the 1929 collapse, U.S. exports exceeded imports by $25 billion. Now the trade imbalance is decidedly in the other direction.

On the other hand, we learned a good deal from what happened in the Great Depression, so the consequences of a major collapse may be less severe. We came to understand that we live in an economy far removed from a state of nature and that the market can't be allowed to rule over us without any restraints. And although they've been weakened in recent years, we have in place many regulations and countercyclical programs from the New Deal, including unemployment insurance and Social Security.

Here's the main lesson the Great Depression taught us: Capitalism is the best economic system just as democracy is the best political system, but both contain inherent dangers that require checks and balances to ensure that they work properly. One of the most prominent dangers of capitalism is that income will become too concentrated at the top, undermining the functioning of a consumer-based economy. The fruits of this lesson were put into effect during the New Deal through higher taxes on the rich, support for unions to help working people get a larger share of the national income, social programs to aid the poor, and such regulatory agencies as the Securities and Exchange Commission. A system of regulated capitalism was in place and worked very well from World War II to 1980.

Then economic fundamentalism staged a revival—and once again got us into a mess. The only thing that can begin to get us out of it is replacing it with the sort of reasonable, balanced policies that produced a long period of widespread prosperity through the middle of the 20th century.

Bottom line: The fundamentalists of the economy are wrong.

ROBERT S. MCELVAINE, a professor of history at Millsaps College, is the author of "The Great Depression" and, most recently, "Grand Theft Jesus: The Highjacking of Religion in America."

From *The Washington Post National Weekly Edition*, October 6–12, 2008, p. 27. Copyright © 2008 by Robert S. McElvaine. Reprinted by permission of the author.

UNIT 4

From the Great Depression to World War II

Unit Selections

Key Points to Consider

- Describe the personality and character of Franklin D. Roosevelt. What made him such an effective president? Why was his first fireside chat so important?

- Discuss the "repatriation" of people of Mexican ancestry during the Great Depression?. What justifications were used for these blatant violations of human rights and what methods were employed?

- What is a "sit-down" strike? How effective were sit-down strikes both in the short and long run? What other means of bettering their pay and working conditions did laboring people have at the time?

- Discuss the difficulties women had in being recognized as capable fliers who deserved being treated just as servicemen were. Why were they treated so badly?

- Why was General Dwight Eisenhower's decision to go ahead with the invasion of Europe on June 6, 1944 so important? Why did he simply not wait until the weather got better a few days or weeks later?

Student Website

www.mhhe.com/cls

Internet References

Works Progress Administration/Folklore Project
    www.lcweb2.loc.gov/ammem/wpaintro/wpalife.html
Hiroshima Archive
    www.lclark.edu/~history/HIROSHIMA/
The Enola Gay
    www.theenolagay.com/index.html

After a brief postwar depression, the economy took off during the 1920s. Sales of relatively new products such as automobiles, radios, and telephones mushroomed. Farmers, who sold their goods on a fluctuating market, tended not to fare as well as others but even many of them were purchasing the sundry goods pouring off assembly lines. Successive Republican administrations understandably took credit for this prosperity—attributing it to their wise economic and financial policies. They proclaimed the 1920s as a "New Era." When people ran out of things to buy and still had money left over they dabbled in the stock market in ever-increasing numbers. As stock prices rose dramatically, a kind of speculative mania developed in the latter half of the decade. In the past, most people had bought stocks as long-term investments. That is, they wanted to receive income from the dividends reliable companies would pay over the years. Speculators had no interest in the long run; they bought stocks on the assumption that they would make money when they were sold on the market in a matter of months or even weeks. Rumors abounded, some of them true, about individuals who had earned fortunes "playing" the market.

By the end of the 1920s, stock market prices had soared to unprecedented heights. So long as people were confident that they would continue to rise, they did. There were a few people warning that stocks were overpriced, but they were denounced as doomsayers. Besides, had not the highly regarded President Herbert Hoover predicted that "we are on the verge of a wave of never ending prosperity"? No one can say why this confidence began to falter when it did and not months earlier or later, but on October 24, 1929 the market crashed. "Black Thursday" set off an avalanche of selling as holders dumped their shares at whatever price they could get, thereby driving prices even lower. Some large banks tried to shore up confidence by having representatives appear at the stock exchange where they ostentatiously made large purchase orders. Despite such efforts, prices continued to tumble in the months following.

President Herbert Hoover tried to restore confidence by assuring the public that what had happened was merely a glitch, a necessary readjustment of a market that had gotten out of hand. The economy of America was sound, he claimed, and there was no reason business should not go on as usual. His reassurances met with increasing disbelief as time went on. Businessmen as well as stockholders were worried about the future. In order to protect themselves they laid off workers, cut back on inventory, and put off previous plans to expand or to introduce new products. But their actions, however much sense they made for an individual company, had the collective result of making the situation worse.

Hoover endorsed more federal programs than had any of his predecessors to combat the Depression, but they failed to stop the downward slide. Just as people tend to credit an incumbent when times are good, they also blame him when things go sour. He became the most widely detested man in America: trousers with patches on them were scoffingly referred to as "Hoover" pants and in every city the collection of shacks and shanties in which homeless people lived were called "Hoovervilles." In the presidential election of 1932, Hoover lost by a landside to

Democrat candidate Franklin D. Roosevelt. Although Roosevelt had compiled an impressive record as governor of New York state, his greatest asset in the election was that he was not Hoover.

Roosevelt assumed the presidency without any grand design for ending the Depression. Unlike Hoover, however, he was willing to act boldly and on a large scale. His "first 100 days" in office resulted in passage of an unprecedented number of measures designed to promote recovery and to restore confidence. "15 Minutes that Saved America" discusses the first of what became known as Roosevelt's "Fireside Chats." FDR's reassuring manner and his ability to persuade people that he cared about them, the author argues, went a long way towards restoring confidence. "Lessons from the Great Crash" provides an overall assessment of the New Deal. If Roosevelt did not "save" capitalism, it concludes, "he at least steered it through its greatest crisis" by providing a package of reforms that got the economy moving again.

Unfortunately, FDR's "New Deal" mitigated the effects of the Depression but did not end it. Several articles discuss aspects of the 1930s. "When America Sent Her Own Packing" tells how the Depression fueled an anti-immigration frenzy that resulted in up to 1 million people of Mexican descent being driven across the border. "Labor Strikes Back" discusses "sit-down" strikes such as the one launched by the United Mine Workers against General Motors in 1936.

Massive purchases from abroad and the American preparedness program stimulated the economy as no New Deal legislation had been able to do. Unlike Woodrow Wilson, Roosevelt made no effort to remain neutral when conflict engulfed Europe and Asia. He believed the United States ought to cooperate with other nations to stop aggression, but had to contend with a Congress and public that was deeply influenced by those who thought the United States should remain aloof. After war broke out, Roosevelt took decidedly un-neutral steps when he transferred 50 overage destroyers to Great Britain and later pushed through Congress a "Lend Lease" program providing aid for those nations fighting the Axis Powers. Alarmed at Japan's attempt to conquer China, Roosevelt tried to use economic pressure to get Japan to back off. His efforts only stiffened the will of Japanese hardliners who planned and carried out the raid on Pearl Harbor on December 7, 1941. An aroused Congress almost unanimously approved the declaration of war Roosevelt requested.

Pearl Harbor and Germany's declaration of war against the United States a few days later united Americans in their determination to win the war. For the next six months, the Japanese ran rampant as they inflicted a string of defeats against British and American forces in the Pacific. The British suffered a humiliating setback at Singapore, and though American forces fought with greater determination in the Philippines they too had to surrender. The tide of Japanese expansion was halted during the summer of 1942 by the naval battles at the Coral Sea and at Midway. The United States launched its first offensive operations on Guadalcanal in the Solomon Islands. Though much bitter fighting remained, American military and industrial might rendered Japan's ultimate defeat inevitable.

Roosevelt and his military advisers agreed at the beginning of the war that the European theater should receive top priority. Offensive operations against the Germans and Italians began when U.S. forces invaded North Africa in November 1942, and Sicily and Italy during the next year. Still, the main effort against Germany was put off until June 6, 1944, when Allied forces invaded the French beaches at Normandy. "Ike at D-Day" tells of the agonizing decision Eisenhower made to "go" despite the possibility that bad weather might ruin the entire operation.

After tough going against determined German opposition, the invaders broke out across France and began approaching the German border. Hitler launched the last great German offensive in December. In what became known to Americans as "The Battle of the Bulge," the Germans initially made rapid advances but finally were stopped and then pushed back. After more months of fighting, with Germany caught between the western Allies and Soviet armies advancing from the east, Adolf Hitler committed suicide and Germany finally surrendered on May 8, 1945.

Meanwhile, American forces in the Pacific were steadily advancing toward the Japanese homeland. Capture of the Mariana Islands enabled the United States to mount massive air attacks against Japanese cities, and naval actions progressively strangled their war machine. Some historians have argued that President Harry S Truman could have attained a Japanese surrender by the summer of 1945 if only he had assured them that they could retain their sacred emperor. That is incorrect. The Japanese will to resist still ran strong, as the bloody battles of Iwo Jima and Okinawa during the first half of 1945 had shown. Indeed, Japanese generals claimed that they welcomed an invasion of the home islands, where they would inflict such staggering casualties that the United States would settle for a negotiated peace instead of unconditional surrender. The use of atomic bombs against Hiroshima and Nagasaki in August 1945 obviated the need for an invasion as the Japanese surrendered shortly thereafter.

Much has been written about the contributions of women to the war effort. They served in the armed forces as WACS, WAVES, and SPARS, and worked long hours in factories and on farms. "Flight of the Wasp" tells the lesser known story of the Women Airforce Service Pilots, who flew cargo, ferried planes, and towed aerial targets for male pilots. Despite its exemplary record, the organization was disbanded in 1944 and its members were not even officially recognized as veterans until the 1970s.

15 Minutes that Saved America

How FDR charmed the nation, rescued the banks and preserved capitalism.

H. W. BRANDS

Cold weather still gripped most of the country on Sunday, March 12, 1933, as President Franklin Delano Roosevelt prepared to speak to the American people from the White House. The radio networks of the National Broadcasting Company and Columbia Broadcasting System had agreed to suspend regular programming at 10 p.m. Eastern time, and millions of Americans huddled around their radios in kitchens, parlors and living rooms. Forced by hard times to skimp on home heating fuel, they bundled in blankets and overcoats on this late winter night waiting, with everyone else, to hear the president.

Moments before air time, the reading copy of Roosevelt's prepared remarks—triple-spaced and typed by assistant Grace Tully with a special blue ribbon—disappeared. Staff members flew about trying to find it, but Roosevelt calmly retrieved one of the smudged, single-spaced mimeographed copies that had been prepared for the press, and read from that.

Roosevelt spoke quietly, even soothingly. There was no levity in his words, but neither was there obvious gravity.

"I want to talk for a few minutes with the people of the United States about banking," he began. Listeners recognized the voice, but it sounded different tonight. Roosevelt's tenor typically rose when he projected to large crowds; now it retained its conversational tone. He spoke quietly, even soothingly, like a favorite uncle telling a bedtime story. There was no levity in his words or his inflection, but neither was there obvious gravity. A traveler from a distant country, unfamiliar with the crisis facing America, would never have guessed how much hung on Roosevelt's every word as he delivered his first fireside chat to the nation just eight days after his inauguration.

Echoes of the crisis Roosevelt inherited when he took office 75 years ago can be heard today in news reports of home foreclosures and tottering financial institutions. But what resonates more deeply across the decades is an abiding faith in the long-term resilience of the American economy—a faith that Roosevelt helped foster during a brief radio address delivered amid a run on banks that raised troubling questions about credit, the value of the dollar and the future of capitalism. The story of how Roosevelt stopped a nationwide panic and restored Americans' confidence in the banking system is a case study in presidential theatrics and the remarkable power of moral suasion when exercised by a visionary leader.

Presidents had been speaking to the American people since the birth of the republic. The inaugural addresses of every president from George Washington to Warren Harding had been pitched at the entire nation, although they were heard only by those in attendance at the inaugural ceremonies. Presidents' annual messages to Congress functioned similarly: delivered to a discrete audience but intended for Americans at large. Yet during the century between Thomas Jefferson and William Howard Taft, the annual messages had been delivered to the Senate and House in writing and were read to the legislators by clerks. Woodrow Wilson revived the practice of delivering the annual message orally, but even then the American people had to wait to read the speech in their local papers. The president's words were history before they reached their ultimate audience.

The rise of radio created new possibilities for connecting with the people. Calvin Coolidge gave his inaugural address on the radio to a patchwork of stations connected by telephone lines. Yet Coolidge was dubbed Silent Cal for a reason, and neither he nor his successor, Herbert Hoover, seriously explored radio's technological potential.

Nor did they explore radio's psychological potential. Radio continued a shift in the political center of gravity in Washington that had been underway for decades. During the 18th and 19th centuries, the great communicators in American politics had been members of Congress. Listeners swooned at the soaring phrases of Henry Clay, Daniel Webster and John Calhoun, not at the pedestrian utterances of Martin Van Buren, Millard Fillmore and Ulysses Grant. Abraham Lincoln's rare gems—his Gettysburg address, his second inaugural—were the exceptions that proved the rule of executive forgettability in American public speaking.

Things changed under Theodore Roosevelt. The master of the "bully pulpit" understood the moral and emotional power of the presidency, and his speeches sounded like sermons as he lashed the "criminal rich" and "malefactors of great wealth" for conspiring against the public. Wilson sermonized, too, although mostly about foreign affairs. Wilson summoned Americans to war in 1917 in order to make the world "safe for democracy," and he offered his Fourteen Points as a guide to a better future for humanity.

Franklin Roosevelt studied his predecessors closely. During visits to the White House during the presidency of Theodore Roosevelt, his fifth cousin and his uncle by marriage, Franklin mentally tried the residence on for size. FDR patterned his political career on TR's, starting with a stint in the New York legislature, followed by service with the Navy Department and then the governorship of New York. The navy posting afforded Roosevelt a good opportunity to observe the inner workings of the Wilson administration. For 7 ½ years, as assistant navy secretary, he noted Wilson's successes and failures, and he paid particular attention as Wilson toured the country to enlist popular support for the Treaty of Versailles and the League of Nations. Everywhere Wilson went, he stirred audiences with his vision of American leadership in the world. He might well have forced a skeptical Senate to accept the treaty and the League, but a stroke felled him and his magnificent voice went silent.

Roosevelt was still reflecting on Wilson and the power of presidential words when his own turn came. Not since Lincoln had a president assumed office under such disheartening circumstances. The stock market crash of 1929 had presaged the implosion of the American economy. Industrial production had fallen by half; industrial construction by nine-tenths. The steel industry, long a mainstay of America's might, was staggering along at barely 10 percent of capacity. Unemployment topped 12 million, and even this figure understated the problem, for it ignored those too discouraged to continue seeking work. Commodity prices had collapsed, forcing farmers to struggle ever harder to make ends meet, until the prices fell so far that the farmers couldn't afford to harvest their wheat and corn, and let it rot in the fields.

Hundreds of thousands of families lost their homes; as many as 2 million men, women and children wandered the highways of America seeking shelter. Homeless communities, called Hoovervilles in derision of the Republican president, sprang up in cities all across the country. The shantytowns at first hid under bridges and in gulches but eventually spilled into plain sight. Manhattan's homeless claimed the shore of the Hudson River from 72nd Street to 110th.

Hunger stalked the land, visibly afflicting the crowded shantytowns, invisibly sapping the strength of sufferers on isolated farms and in end-of-the-road hamlets. Some of the starving were reduced to an animal existence; they fought over scraps behind restaurants and in garbage dumps. "We have been eating wild greens," an out-of-work Kentucky coal miner reported unemotionally. "Such weeds as cows eat."

"You could smell the depression in the air," one survivor remembered, before switching metaphors: "It was like a raw wind; the very houses we lived in seemed to be shrinking, hopeless of real comfort." A journalist in Washington remarked at the time: "I come home from the hill every night filled with gloom. I see on the streets filthy, ragged, desperate-looking men, such as I have never seen before."

In the month before Roosevelt's inauguration on March 4, 1933, the crisis centered on the nation's financial sector. The stock market crash had punished many banks, as borrowers defaulted on loans they had used to underwrite speculation, and as speculating banks suffered from their own bad investments. Weak banks dragged stronger ones down when panicked depositors demanded their money, which the banks, having loaned it out, couldn't deliver. Five thousand banks had folded by the time Roosevelt took office, and perhaps 10 million Americans had lost their savings.

In several states the entire banking industry ground to a halt as governors suspended bank operations. The governor of Louisiana locked the bank doors in his state in early February; the governors of Michigan, Maryland, Indiana, Arkansas and Ohio did likewise during the next two weeks. Roosevelt reached Washington 48 hours ahead of his inauguration and took the presidential suite at the Mayflower Hotel; the walls there were festooned with slips of paper detailing the unfolding debacle: "Boise, Idaho: Acting Governor Hill today declared a fifteen-day bank holiday. . . . Salem, Oregon: Governor Meier declared a three-day bank holiday. . . . Carson City, Nevada: A four-day legal holiday. . . . Austin, Texas. . . . Salt Lake City, Utah. . . . Phoenix, Arizona. . . ."

The dollar losses were staggering. The Federal Reserve reported an outflow of more than $700 million in seven days ahead of the inauguration as surviving banks scrambled frantically to meet their depositors' demands. The bleeding escalated to $500 million in the final two days before the inauguration.

Gold grew more precious than ever and scarcer. An all-time record of $116 million of gold was withdrawn from the Fed banks in a single day, as foreign account holders lost faith in the dollar and insisted on the yellow metal. Domestic holders of dollars began to get nervous. They fingered their Federal Reserve notes and wondered whether and how the government would honor the promise engraved on each: "Redeemable In Gold On Demand At The United States Treasury, Or In Gold Or Lawful Money At Any Federal Reserve Bank."

Roosevelt presented a curious mix of reassurance and challenge to the nation in his inaugural address. "The only thing we have to fear is fear itself," he said. Yet he proceeded to catalog some dauntingly real reasons for fear. "The means of exchange are frozen. . . . The withered leaves of industrial enterprise lie on every side. . . . Farmers find no markets for their produce. . . . The savings of many years in thousands of families are gone." Roosevelt likened the nation's dire economic predicament to a war and promised bold action. Americans must operate in unison, he said, "as a trained and loyal army."

Roosevelt then promptly moved to stanch the hemorrhage of gold from the banks by doing what the governors had done but on a broader scale. Inauguration Day was Saturday; on Sunday all the banks were closed. At

1 o'clock on Monday morning, March 6, he issued a decree declaring a national bank holiday. During the suspension, all normal banking operations would be barred. No bank was allowed to "pay out, export, earmark, or permit the withdrawal or transfer in any manner or by any device whatsoever, of any gold or silver coin or bullion or currency."

The move took the country's breath away. Without consulting Congress or, apparently, the Constitution, the president had declared economic martial law. Deposits were frozen; customers of the country's 18,000 banks were prevented from even trying to get their money out. The embargo on gold effectively took the United States off the gold standard, at least for the duration of the bank holiday.

Roosevelt cited an obscure law most people thought had lapsed—the 1917 Trading With the Enemy Act (which gave the president the wartime power to prohibit hoarding gold)—as justification for his diktat. Opinions differed sharply on whether the law was still in force, let alone whether it supported a peace-time stroke of the magnitude Roosevelt had just delivered.

Yet so desperate was the country for decisive action that almost no one in political or business circles seriously challenged the president. Even the *Wall Street Journal* approved. "A common adversity has much subdued the recalcitrance of groups bent upon self-interest," the de facto mouthpiece of the financial sector observed. "All of us the country over are now ready to make sacrifices to a common necessity and to accept realities as we would not have done three months ago."

The bank holiday bought Roosevelt time but only a little. He immediately set his advisers to writing a remedy to the financial panic. William Woodin, the Treasury secretary, led the effort. "We're on the bottom now," Woodin told reporters in a rare break between drafting sessions. This was supposed to be reassuring. "We are not going any lower," he said.

Woodin and the others—including governors of the Federal Reserve, chairmen of private banks, members of key congressional committees, and academic and professional economists—worked until 2 o'clock each morning at the White House. They went home for a few hours' sleep before returning for more of the same. The pressure was tremendous. "We're snowed under, we're snowed under," Francis Await, the comptroller of the currency, muttered. But Woodin kept them on track. "Not once did his grey toupee slip askew in the excitement," a reporter remarked.

Roosevelt wanted to have a bill by Thursday morning, March 9. He had summoned an emergency session of Congress, and he wished to present the lawmakers with a finished product as they gathered that noon. But the myriad intricacies of the money question defied such rapid solution, and when the session convened, the administration's measure was still at the printer's shop. Congress went ahead nonetheless and, employing a folded newspaper as a proxy for the actual bill, approved it on the president's recommendation and that of those lawmakers who had seen a draft of the legislation. The measure stamped retroactive approval on the bank closure and the gold embargo, and it authorized the president to reopen the banks when he deemed appropriate and to reorganize the national banking system to protect strong banks from the weak.

Roosevelt signed the bill that Thursday evening and shortly announced a timetable for reopening the banks. The 12 Federal Reserve banks would open on Monday, March 13, along with the other banks in those 12 cities. Banks in most other cities would open on Tuesday. Banks in small towns and villages would open on Wednesday.

There was less to the bank law than met the eye. Roosevelt had needed to stem the panic, and closing the banks did so. The bank law made the process look legal and planned. But the question on which everything hung—the condition of American finance, the direction of the economy, even the fate of America's distinctive mix of capitalism and democracy—was whether confidence could be restored by the time the banks reopened. If it was restored, the rescue operation would succeed. Prosperity might remain some distance off, but the country could begin moving in that direction.

If confidence was not restored, all the effort would have been wasted. Pessimists noted that democracy was failing in other countries that couldn't solve their economic problems. Germany had installed Adolf Hitler as chancellor a month before Roosevelt was inaugurated. A week before the American inauguration, Nazi agents burned the Reichstag and blamed the German Communists. Hours before Roosevelt closed the American banks, German elections returned a parliamentary majority for Hitler's coalition. Hitler demanded, and quickly received, dictatorial powers from the intimidated legislature.

Roosevelt's foremost objective as he began his first fireside chat on March 12 was to sound a note of calm. Millions had tuned in to his inaugural address, just a week before, but that speech had been delivered to a live audience in Washington, D.C., with the radio listeners merely eavesdropping. Now the radio listeners were the president's sole audience, aside from the few family members and administration officials sitting with him in the Oval Office, as he offered a matter-of-fact explanation of what had precipitated the banking crisis. "Because of undermined confidence on the part of the public, there was a general rush by a large portion of our population to turn bank deposits into currency or gold—a rush so great that the soundest banks could not get enough currency to meet the demand," he said. "The reason for this was that on the spur of the moment it was, of course, impossible to sell perfectly sound assets of a bank and convert them into cash except at panic prices far below their real value."

To remedy the situation, Roosevelt said, he and Congress had taken two important steps. First, he had declared the bank holiday, to give bankers, depositors and everyone else a chance to catch their breath. Second, Congress had approved the bank bill, confirming his authority over the banking system and allowing him to reopen the banks in an orderly fashion.

Roosevelt explained the timetable for the reopenings, and he asked for special patience on the part of depositors. "There is

We have provided the machinery to restore our financial system; it is up to you to support it and make it work.

an element in the readjustment of our, financial system more important than currency, more important than gold, and that is the confidence of the people," he said. "Confidence and courage are the essentials of success in carrying out our plan. You people must have faith; you must not be stampeded by rumors or guesses. Let us unite in banishing fear. We have provided the machinery to restore our financial system; it is up to you to support and make it work. It is your problem no less than it is mine. Together we cannot fail."

Whether it was his tone of voice, his choice of words, the nature of the medium or a sudden desire on the part of Americans to please their new president, Roosevelt's 15-minute talk evoked a stunningly positive response. Thousands of telegrams poured into the White House overnight. "Created feeling of confidence in me and my family," one said. Another asserted: "Going direct to the people with the facts has inspired every confidence in the reopening of the banks." A third called the talk "a masterpiece in the circumstances and worthy of the historical precedent it established."

Editors and pundits fell over themselves in praise of Roosevelt's performance. *The New York Times* sensed a sudden change in the popular mood: "His simple and lucid explanation of the true function of a commercial bank; his account of what had happened, why it had happened, and the steps taken to correct the mischief were admirably fitted to cause the hysteria which had raged for several weeks before the banks were closed to abate if not entirely to subside."

Will Rogers labeled the speech a "home run" and considered it a model of straightforward eloquence. "Some people spend a lifetime juggling with words, with not an idea in a carload," the popular cowboy humorist observed. "Our President took such a dry subject as banking (and when I say 'dry' I mean dry, for if it had been liquid he wouldn't have had to speak on it at all). Well, he made everybody understand it, even the bankers." Sen. James Lewis marveled at the powerful emotional impact of the president's remarks. "I have never seen within my political life

such a real transformation in sentiment from discouragement to encouragement, from despair to complete hope and to immediate new trust and new hope," the Illinois Democrat declared.

Roosevelt was pleased at the praise but cared more for the financial effect of his message. The evidence from this direction was irrefutable. As the banks reopened, the negative currency flows of the previous weeks were reversed: Depositors stopped withdrawing funds and started returning the money they had pulled out. Bank balances began growing again, engendering additional confidence and further deposits. By the time the last banks opened, the crisis had passed.

The expeditious rescue of the banks didn't end the pressure on the larger economy. The grim statistics on national income, production and employment remained as dismal as ever. Central questions about the value of the dollar, the future of gold, the security of deposits and the structure of the industrial system were still to be answered.

But the emergency of the moment had been surmounted by Roosevelt's brilliant act of political theater. Raymond Moley, one of Roosevelt's advisers, later remarked that "capitalism was saved in eight days." He could have been more specific. The essence of the crisis was distilled into the quarter-hour of Roosevelt's fireside chat. Had the president failed to win the confidence of America that Sunday evening, the bank runs would have resumed and the downward spiral would have continued. But he didn't fail, and the banks, and capitalism, were saved.

In the bargain, Roosevelt fashioned a new link between presidents and the American people. *The New York Times,* in the same editorial in which it lauded the efficacy of Roosevelt's words, commented on the method of their delivery: "The President's use of the radio for this purpose is a fresh demonstration of the wonderful power of appeal to the people which science has placed in his hands. When millions of listeners can hear the President speak to them, as it were, directly in their own homes, we get a new meaning for the old phrase about a public man 'going to the country.'" Roosevelt went to the country without leaving the White House, and American politics would never be the same.

From *American History,* October 2008, pp. 36–41. Copyright © 2008 by Weider History Group. Reprinted by permission.

Lessons from the Great Crash

The New Deal turns 75 as the United States faces another credit crisis requiring government measures to restore confidence.

JAMES PIERESON

It was 75 years ago, on March 4, 1933, that Franklin Delano Roosevelt appeared on the steps of the Capitol to take the presidential oath, declaring in his inaugural address that "the only thing we have to fear is fear itself" and promising "direct, vigorous action" to confront the unprecedented economic crisis facing the nation.

Roosevelt's speech was short on specifics about his bold new measures, and he did not use the term "New Deal"—though he had used it extensively during his presidential campaign. But the "New Deal" soon became the catchall phrase for the philosophy and the legislative accomplishments by which his administration is known. Roosevelt's leadership during those difficult years turned him into the most popular figure of his era, an authentic hero in the eyes of liberals and Democrats—and for many Republicans, a sinister demagogue and a traitor to his class.

The passage of time has not settled the controversies that grew up around the New Deal. It is easy today to find enthusiasts who look back on it as the foundation of the American welfare state and critics who see it as an attack on American capitalism. There are leftwing historians who think Roosevelt should have gone much further in the direction of public ownership and welfare provision, and there are respected economists who say that the New Deal actually impeded recovery from the Depression. Ronald Reagan was accused of trying to roll back the New Deal, though this was manifestly untrue; if he tried to roll back anything, it was Lyndon Johnson's Great Society. Eminent liberals like Arthur Schlesinger Jr. and John Kenneth Galbraith claimed that the Depression discredited free market capitalism. They must have thought that history was playing a cruel joke when Reagan led a revival of market doctrines during the 1980s.

There is little political support today for rolling back any of the New Deal programs that continue to operate. (President Bush got nowhere with his modest proposal to introduce private savings accounts into Social Security.) But the New Deal remains an ideological touchstone in any debate about the appropriate role for government in our economy.

Roosevelt sounded an urgent populist theme in his inaugural address, placing the blame for the Depression squarely on the shoulders of bankers and industrial leaders who had put profit above the public interest. "The money changers have fled from their high seats in the temple of our civilization," he said. "We may now restore that temple to ancient truths. The measure of restoration lies in the extent to which we may apply social values more noble than mere monetary profit." Somewhat more ominously, he suggested that if the nation's inherited constitutional arrangements should prove inadequate to the task, he was prepared to call for a "temporary departure from that normal balance of public procedure." Roosevelt would pound on these two themes—hostility to big business and a readiness to break with tradition—throughout the 1930s.

The fact that Roosevelt's rhetoric was warmly received is a measure of the desperation felt by many Americans at the time. The dimensions of the catastrophe were overwhelming by any known measure. Following the stock market crash of 1929, real economic output in the United States declined by 30 percent and unemployment rose from 4 percent to 25. Stocks fell from a high of 381 in September of 1929 to 42 in mid-1932, turning Wall Street into a virtual ghost town and wiping out investors large and small. The dollar value of U.S. exports fell by two-thirds between 1929 and 1933. Nearly half of the banks in the United States had either failed or merged with other banks by the time Roosevelt came to office in 1933. In the process, millions lost everything. Worse, they saw little hope of getting it back.

> **After the stock market crash of 1929, economic output in the United States declined by 30 percent, while unemployment rose from 4 percent to 25 percent. Stocks fell from a high of 381 in September of 1929 to 42 in mid-1932. Millions lost everything they had. Worse still, they saw little hope of getting it back.**

The Depression was viewed in many circles as a sign of the impending doom of the capitalist order. Few were confident that the economy could be revived on the basis of the old principles. Intellectuals began to choose sides between socialist and fascist solutions to the crisis. Socialist parties received more than a million votes in the 1932 presidential election. Once in office, Roosevelt was attacked from both ends of the spectrum by extremists like Huey Long and Father Coughlin demanding measures to "share the wealth." Fascist and Communist parties advanced abroad in the wake of the worldwide economic collapse. Hitler came to power in Germany only five weeks before Roosevelt's inauguration.

Viewed in this context, Roosevelt's New Deal measures do not appear quite so radical. He would eventually say in response to critics that it had been his own actions "which saved the system of private profit and free enterprise after it had been dragged to the brink of ruin." He had a point. Among the industrial nations of the time, the United States was one of the few that did not eventually take the socialist path. From the distance of seven decades, it seems fair to suggest that the New Deal did far more to modernize and stabilize American capitalism than it did to undermine it.

Roosevelt's first term is conventionally divided into two periods: the so-called First New Deal, which was largely enacted in 1933 during Roosevelt's first hundred days in office, and the Second New Deal of 1935, in which Roosevelt pushed into territory that went well beyond the immediate economic crisis of the time.

The First New Deal was made up of measures designed to stabilize the banking system, to restore agricultural production, and to provide relief to the destitute. Few of them were radical in nature, and there was no clear ideological pattern.

> **The First New Deal consisted primarily of measures to stabilize the banking system, to restore agricultural production, and to provide jobs and relief to the destitute. Few of these measures could be called radical in nature, with one exception being Roosevelt's National Industrial Recovery Act, later ruled unconstitutional.**

Reversing the cascade of bank failures was an especially high priority for the New Deal, and in the process Roosevelt modernized the American banking system. He took the United States off the gold standard (one of the last nations to do so), provided for a system of deposit insurance, regulated the public sale of securities by requiring the registration of stocks and the disclosure to markets of pertinent information, and created a wall of separation between commercial and investment banking—the latter arising from the conviction that many bank failures had been caused by inappropriate speculation in stocks.

Most of these reforms, though crafted to deal with the immediate crisis, remain with us today. Deposit insurance, securities regulation, and the federal regulation of banks remain pillars of the modern system of credit and capital. The abandonment of the gold standard, while criticized by bankers at the time as an attack on sound money, is generally viewed as a necessary step to reverse the credit contraction. Central bankers, when faced with speculative attacks on their currencies, generally responded by raising interest rates and tightening credit in order to preserve exchange values in relation to gold—moves which only worsened the Depression. (The Glass-Steagall Act, which separated commercial from investment banking, was repealed in 1999.)

The New Deal is closely associated among critics with large-scale public employment programs and with heavy-handed regulatory initiatives that sought to create a centrally managed economy. What is important to note is that none of these highly controversial programs survived Roosevelt's terms in office, and they cannot be regarded as parts of the New Deal legacy.

Two major public employment programs, the Civilian Conservation Corps (CCC)—the model for Lyndon Johnson's poverty program—and the Public Works Administration (PWA), were erected during Roosevelt's first hundred days. The CCC created more than 1,000 work camps to provide jobs for the young in various conservation efforts (reforestation, flood control, and management of public parks). The PWA put unemployed adults to work building roads, dams, and public buildings. These programs were augmented in 1935 by the Works Progress Administration, which also employed several million workers in the late 1930s. Yet all of these programs were out of business by 1943, when mobilization for the war made them unnecessary.

One clear exception to the pattern of legislation under the First New Deal was the National Industrial Recovery Act (NIRA), which created a regulatory body (the National Recovery Administration) with broad powers to regulate wages, prices, and competitive practices. The act originated in the belief that the Depression had been caused by price cutting and unfair competitive practices in major industries (yes, competitive price cutting was thought to be unfair). NIRA reflected the corporatist outlook of Roosevelt advisers like Rexford Tugwell who believed that some form of economic planning was needed to prevent another collapse. The planners had their way as they hammered out complex wage and price codes in consultation with major manufacturers and labor unions. Yet the system rapidly proved to be too complex to be workable. NIRA is an obvious source of the New Deal's reputation for ham-fisted regulation. It was also short-lived; in 1935 the Supreme Court struck it down, by unanimous decision, as an unconstitutional delegation of power from Congress to the executive branch.

The Second New Deal took shape in 1935 following the 1934 midterm elections in which the Democrats added to their majorities in the House and Senate. The election was a mandate, Roosevelt said, and proved "that we are on the right track." The Second New Deal added two pillars to the nation's political economy: the Social Security Act, which established old-age insurance, unemployment insurance, and welfare benefits for widows and orphans, and the Wagner Act, which provided federal mechanisms for organizing unions and for collective bargaining in private industry. Over the long term, these proved to be the most politically potent of the New Deal measures.

Little needs to be said about the popularity of Social Security and the difficult challenges faced even today by reformers who would adjust the system. The Wagner Act greatly facilitated the formation of unions in major industries in the late 1930s much to the consternation of big business. Union membership expanded in the United States, from around one million in 1935 to nearly 10 million in 1940 and continuing upwards through the 1960s—a period during which industrial unions were key elements of the Democratic political coalition.

With these measures, Roosevelt laid the basis for the New Deal's long-running political appeal and influence. They established a precedent for building political majorities through federal programs and employment. Here, then, was a legacy of the New Deal that, in retrospect, was far more influential than its various regulatory measures.

The legislative breakthroughs of 1935 marked the high point of the New Deal. Roosevelt, in keeping with his political practice, saw the landslide election of 1936 as a mandate to make another bold step, this time in taking on the Supreme Court which had declared unconstitutional his farm program and NIRA and seemed on the verge of striking down both the Wagner and the Social Security Acts. Roosevelt's proposal to expand the Court to give him as many as six new appointments drew immediate opposition from members of Congress and the public, who appeared ready to draw the line on the New Deal when it came to fundamental alterations of the Constitution. The court-packing plan was a fiasco for Roosevelt and effectively marked the end of the creative period of the New Deal.

Fortunately for Roosevelt, Justice Owen Roberts switched his vote in key decisions in 1937, turning a 5-4 majority against the New Deal into a similar majority in support. An early sign of this shift was the Court's decision in April 1937 to uphold the constitutionality of the Wagner Act. When conservative justice Willis Van Devanter retired at the end of the 1937 term, FDR was given the appointment he needed to place his own stamp on the Court.

Though critics and supporters alike have said that the New Deal laid the foundations for the American welfare state, it is more accurate to say that it set up a social insurance state. The enduring pillars of the New Deal—old-age insurance, deposit insurance, unemployment insurance—were not redistributionist measures but insurance provisions compatible with traditional notions of individual responsibility. Even the welfare provisions of the Social Security Act were drawn up to aid only widows and orphans. The New Dealers were borrowing from the various insurance provisions that were enacted in Germany in the 1880s under Bismarck who saw in them a means to outmaneuver the socialists who were calling for more extreme measures on behalf of workers. In the battle within the New Deal—between the collectivists and planners on the one hand and the advocates for traditional ideals of individual responsibility—the individualists clearly had their way on the most important questions.

Rather than laying the foundations for a welfare state, it is more accurate to say that the New Deal set up a social insurance state. The enduring pillars of the New Deal–old-age insurance, deposit insurance, unemployment insurance–were not redistributionist measures but insurance provisions compatible with traditional notions of individual responsibility.

Despite their best efforts, however, the New Dealers were unable to pull the economy out of depression. While it began to grow again after 1933 and the unemployment rate fell to 14 percent by 1937, a recession that year provoked Roosevelt and fellow New Dealers into ever more extreme attacks on the business community. Roosevelt denounced the rich for bringing about the recession through a "capital strike"—precisely the kind of nonsense that would later give the New Deal a bad name among business leaders. Many economists argue that New Deal policies, to the extent that they promoted unionization and imposed new taxes on business, created an environment that discouraged business investment and thus impeded full recovery from the Depression.

The New Deal was based on a couple of propositions about the Depression that appear in retrospect to have been highly questionable. The first was that the Depression was a crisis of overproduction

that led to falling prices and unemployment, a proposition that was the basis for the industrial codes of the NIRA and of the New Deal's agricultural programs, which sought to limit farm production even as people around the country were in need of food. The second proposition was that the crisis had been caused by the malfeasance of bankers and stock manipulators in tandem with the monopoly power exercised by industrialists, a conviction which encouraged much of the anti-business rhetoric of the New Deal. This latter proposition was incorporated into the official histories of the period written by luminaries like Schlesinger *(The Crisis of the Old Order)* and Galbraith *(The Great Crash)*. When these two propositions were joined, they suggested that the old order of individualism and competition was discredited and should be replaced by a system of managed capitalism. Though this was not the actual agenda of the New Deal as it developed, it was thought by some to be the logical next step beyond it.

The Great Depression was actually caused by the restrictive interest-rate policies followed by the Federal Reserve Board in 1928 and 1929. Milton Friedman and Anna Schwartz pioneered this interpretation in their *Monetary History of the United States* (1963). The economic crisis, which they termed "the great contraction," was triggered when the Federal Reserve Board began to tighten interest rates in 1928 to discourage speculation in stocks and then continued a tight money policy even after the stock market collapsed and banks began to fail. Things were exacerbated by the failure of the monetary authorities to step in with infusions of capital to rescue failing banks and by political decisions like the Smoot-Hawley tariff bill which shut down trade and led to more restrictive credit policies around the world. The New Deal attacks on big business were nothing more than so much flailing in the wind.

This interpretation of the Depression is held by no less a figure than Ben Bernanke, the current chairman of the Federal Reserve Board and a careful student of the crisis. At a testimonial occasion to mark Milton Friedman's 90th birthday, Bernanke went so far as to say to the economist: "Regarding the Great Depression, you were right. We [the Federal Reserve Board] did it. We're very sorry. But thanks to you, we won't do it again."

In the end, the constitutional system that Roosevelt sought to alter imposed its limits on the New Deal, casting aside its more extreme measures while digesting its more constructive elements. By the time Republicans returned to power in the 1950s, New Deal programs were no longer seen as radical or even controversial. If Roosevelt did not "save" capitalism, he at least steered it through its greatest crisis by engineering a package of moderate and constructive reforms that, for the most part, met the test of time. For this reason alone, he richly earned the admiration of Americans at the time and a place in the pantheon of America's great presidents.

JAMES PIERESON, a senior fellow at the Manhattan Institute, is the author of *Camelot and the Cultural Revolution: How the Assassination of John F. Kennedy Shattered American Liberalism* (Encounter Books).

When America Sent Her Own Packing

**Fueled by the Great Depression, an anti-immigrant frenzy
engulfed hundreds of thousands of legal American citizens
in a drive to 'repatriate' Mexicans to their homeland.**

STEVE BOISSON

A 9-year-old girl stood in the darkness of a railroad station, surrounded by tearful travelers who had gathered up their meager belongings, awaiting the train that would take her from her native home to a place she had never been. The bewildered child couldn't know she was a character in the recurring drama of America's love-hate relationship with peoples from foreign lands who, whether fleeing hardship or oppression or simply drawn to the promise of opportunity and prosperity, desperately strive to be Americans. As yet another act in the long saga of American immigration unfolds today, some U.S. citizens can recall when, during a time of anti-immigrant frenzy fueled by economic crisis and racism, they found themselves being swept out of the country of their birth.

Emilia Castañeda will never forget that 1935 morning. Along with her father and brother, she was leaving her native Los Angeles. Staying, she was warned by some adults at the station, meant she would become a ward of the state. "I had never been to Mexico," Castañeda said some six decades later. "We left with just one trunk full of belongings. No furniture. A few metal cooking utensils. A small ceramic pitcher, because it reminded me of my mother . . . and very little clothing. We took blankets, only the very essentials."

As momentous as that morning seemed to the 9-year-old Castañeda, such departures were part of a routine and roundly accepted movement to send Mexicans and Mexican-Americans back to their ancestral home. Los Angeles County-sponsored repatriation trains had been leaving the station bound for Mexico since 1931, when, in the wake of the Wall Street crash of 1929 and the economic collapse and dislocation that followed, welfare cases skyrocketed. The county Board of Supervisors, other county and municipal agencies and the Chamber of Commerce proclaimed repatriation of Mexicans as a humane and utilitarian solution to the area's growing joblessness and dwindling resources. Even the Mexican consul stationed in Los Angeles praised the effort, at least at the outset, thanking the welfare department for its work "among my countrymen, in helping them return to Mexico." The Mexican government, still warmed by the rhetoric of the 1910 revolution, was touting

the development of agricultural colonies and irrigation projects that would provide work for the displaced compatriots from the north.

By 1935, however, it was hard to detect much benevolence driving the government-sponsored train rides to Mexico. For young Castañeda's father, Mexico was the last resort, a final defeat after 20 years of legal residence in America. His work as a union bricklayer had enabled him to buy a house, but—like millions of other Americans—his house and job were lost to the Depression. His wife, who had worked as a maid, contracted tuberculosis in 1933 and died the following year. "My father told us that he was returning to Mexico because he couldn't find work in Los Angeles," Castañeda said. "He wasn't going to abandon us. We were going with him. When L.A. County arranged for our trip to Mexico, he and other Mexicans had no choice but to go."

Francisco Balderrama and Raymond Rodríguez, the authors of *Decade of Betrayal,* the first expansive study of Mexican repatriation with perspectives from both sides of the border, claim that 1 million people of Mexican descent were driven from the United States during the 1930s due to raids, scare tactics, deportation, repatriation and public pressure. Of that conservative estimate, approximately 60 percent of those leaving were legal American citizens. Mexicans comprised nearly half of all those deported during the decade, although they made up less than 1 percent of the country's population. "Americans, reeling from the economic disorientation of the depression, sought a convenient scapegoat," Balderrama and Rodríguez wrote. "They found it in the Mexican community."

D uring the early years of the 20th century, the U.S. Immigration Service paid scant attention to Mexican nationals crossing the border. The disfavored groups among border watchers at the time were the Chinese, who had been explicitly barred by the Chinese Exclusion Act of 1882, criminals, lunatics, prostitutes, paupers and those suffering from loathsome and contagious diseases. In actuality, the Mexican immigrant was often a pauper, but he was not, in the law's language, "likely to become a public charge." Cheap Mexican labor was in great demand by a host of America's burgeoning industries. The railroads, mining companies and agribusinesses sent agents to greet immigrants at the border, where they extolled the rewards of their respective enterprises. Border officials felt no duty to impede the labor flow into the Southwest.

The Mexican population in the United States escalated during the years following 1910. By 1914, according to author Matt S. Meier, the chaos and bloodshed of the Mexican revolution had driven as many as 100,000 Mexican nationals into the United States, and they would continue to cross the border in large numbers legally and illegally. Immigration laws were tightened in 1917, but their enforcement at the border remained lax. While laws enacted in 1921 and 1924 imposed quotas on immigrants from Europe and other parts of the Eastern Hemisphere, quotas were not applied to Mexico or other Western nations. This disparity found its detractors, particularly East Texas Congressman John C. Box, who was a vocal proponent of curtailing the influx from the south.

Though none of Box's proposals became law, his efforts drew favorable coverage in the *Saturday Evening Post* and other journals that editorialized against the "Mexicanization" of the United States. When a Midwestern beet grower who hired Mexican immigrants appeared at a House Immigration Committee hearing, Box suggested that the man's ideal farm workers were "a class of people who have not the ability to rise, who have not the initiative, who are children, who do not want to own land, who can be directed by men in the upper stratum of society. That is what you want, is it?"

"I believe that is about it," replied the grower.

Those who exploited cheap Mexican labor, argued Box and his adherents, betrayed American workers and imperiled American cities with invading hordes of mixed-blood foreigners. Those who railed against quotas should visit the barrios in Los Angeles, wrote Kenneth L. Roberts in the *Saturday Evening Post,* "and see endless streets crowded with the shacks of illiterate, diseased, pauperized Mexicans, taking no interest whatever in the community, living constantly on the ragged edge of starvation, bringing countless numbers of American citizens into the world with the reckless prodigality of rabbits."

U pon taking office in 1929, President Herbert Hoover had to face the raging debate. He resisted imposing the quotas demanded by Box and others, as Hoover probably feared they would rankle the Mexican government and thus threaten American business interests there. Instead, Hoover, hoping to appease the restrictionists, chose the less-permanent option of virtually eliminating visas for Mexican laborers and by bolstering the Immigration Service, which had grown from a minor government operation to a force that included a border patrol of nearly 800 officers.

After the Depression set in, the removal of foreigners who were taking jobs and services away from cash-strapped, struggling Americans seemed to be a salient solution, perhaps the only tangible recourse to the desperation that had swept the country. Under the direction of William N. Doak, Hoover's newly appointed secretary of labor, immigration officers dredged the country for illegal aliens. They raided union halls, dances, social clubs and other ethnic enclaves where people without papers might be found. Their tactics favored intimidation over legal procedure. Suspects were routinely arrested without warrants. Many were denied counsel, and their deportation "hearings" were often conducted in the confines of a city or county jail. Frightened and ignorant of their rights, many suspects volunteered to leave rather than suffer through deportation.

While Mexicans were not the only target in the drive against illegal aliens, they were often the most visible. This was certainly true in Los Angeles, which, at that time had some 175,000 inhabitants of Mexican descent, second only to Mexico City. In early 1931, Los Angeles newspapers reported on an impending anti-alien sweep led by a ranking immigration officer from Washington, D.C. Walter Carr, the federal Los Angeles district director of immigration, assured the press that no single ethnic group was under siege, but raids in the Mexican communities of El Monte, Pacoima and San Fernando belied that official line. The final show of force occurred with a raid on La Placita, a downtown Los Angeles park that was popular with Mexicans and Mexican-Americans. On February 26, an afternoon idyll on Olivera Street was shattered by an invasion of immigration agents and local police. Agents searched every person on the scene for proof of legal residence. Though hundreds were hauled off for questioning, few were ultimately detained. The message was in the bluster, not the busts.

As recounted in *Decade of Betrayal,* Labor Secretary Doak's efforts proved to be highly successful: Deportees outnumbered those who entered the United States during the first nine months of 1931. There were, however, some detractors. A subcommittee formed by the Los Angeles Bar Association found that Carr's tactics, such as inhibiting a suspect's access to counsel, fell outside the law. Cart dismissed these charges as nothing more than sour grapes over a lost client base and justified the deprivation of counsel on the grounds that lawyers merely sold false hopes in exchange for cash squeezed from needy immigrants.

Immigration officers raided union halls, dances, social clubs and other ethnic enclaves where people without papers might be found.

Investigations into the alleged abuses began on a national level, as well, by the National Commission on Law Observance and Enforcement, which was appointed by President Hoover in 1929. Named for its chairman, former U.S. Attorney General George W. Wickersham, the Wickersham Commission had made front-page news with its investigations into the rackets of Al Capone and others. Like the L.A. Bar Association, the commission also found the methods employed by Doak's underlings to be unconstitutional. Regardless of the legality or illegality of the practices, one thing was clear: Mexican immigrants were departing in great numbers. According to a report by Cart, by May 1931, "There have been approximately forty thousand aliens who left this district during the last eighteen months of which probably twenty percent [were] deportable." Even those who were here legally, he allowed, had been driven out by fear.

A child in 1932, Rubén Jiménez remembers, 'We were not a burden to the U.S. government or anybody.'

In retrospect, other options were available. The Registry Act of 1929, for example, ensured permanent residency status—a version of amnesty—to those who had been in the United States continuously since 1921 and had been "honest, law-abiding aliens." While this surely would have applied to many Mexicans, the act's provisions were utilized mostly by European or Canadian immigrants. In many cases, institutionalized hostility prevailed over legal rights. Anti-Mexican sentiments convinced the father of author Raymond Rodríguez to return to Mexico. His mother met with a local priest, who assured her that, as a mother of five American children and a legal resident, she could not be forced to leave. "So he left and we stayed," says Rodríguez, who never saw his father again.

Instead of driving Mexican aliens underground—as was often the result of raids and other scare tactics—it became apparent to anti-immigrant proponents that it was more expedient simply to assist them out of the country. "Repatriation" became a locally administered alternative to deportation, which was a federal process beyond the purview of the county and municipal officials. "Repatriation is supposed to be voluntary," says Francisco Balderrama, *Decade's* co-author. "That's kind of a whitewash word, a kind of covering up of the whole thing."

Some 350 people departed on the first county-sponsored repatriation train to leave Los Angeles in March 1931. The next month, a second train left with nearly three times as many people, of which roughly one-third paid for their own passage. The repatriates were led to believe that they could return at a later date, observed George F. Clements, manager of agriculture of the Los Angeles Chamber of Commerce. In a memo to the chamber's general manager, Arthur G. Arnoll, Clements, who wanted to keep the cheap labor, wrote, "I think this is a grave mistake because it is not the truth." Clements went on to state that American-born children leaving without documentation were "American citizens without very much hope of ever coming back into the United States."

Los Angeles later developed a highly efficient repatriation program under the direction of Rex Thomson, an engineer who had impressed members of the Board of Supervisors with his nuts-and-bolts know-how while advising them on the construction of the Los Angeles General Hospital. After the county welfare caseload nearly doubled from 25,913 cases during

1929–30 to 42,124 cases in 1930–31, the board asked the pragmatic Thomson to serve as assistant superintendent of charities. "It was one of the highest paying public jobs in California," Thomson recalled during an interview nearly 40 years later. Having lost a bundle in failed local banks, he continued, "I was interested in a job."

Thomson proved to be a tough administrator who excised bureaucratic fat and made welfare money work for the county. Men dug channels in the Los Angeles River in exchange for room and board. He put the unemployed to work on several local projects: building walls along Elysian Park, grading the grounds around the California State Building. When Thomson visited Congress in Washington, D.C., to seek funding for his public works program, he challenged the feds to "send out people to see if we aren't worthy of this federal help." By the end of the week, he later reported: "I'll be darned if they didn't agree. The government got the idea, and started this Works Progress [Administration], but they didn't always impose the discipline that was necessary."

Along with putting the unemployed to work on government-sponsored projects, repatriation would become another of Thomson's social remedies that would merit emulation. Thomson would later describe his program: "We had thousands of Mexican nationals who were out of work. I went to Mexico City and I told them that we would like to ship these people back—not to the border but to where they came from or where the Mexicans would send them if we agreed it was a proper place. We could ship them back by train and feed them well and decently, for $74 a family. So I employed social workers who were Americans of Mexican descent but fluent in the language, or Mexican nationals, and they would go out and—I want to emphasize—offer repatriation to these people."

A child in 1932, Rubén Jiménez remembers one such social worker, a Mr. Hispana, who convinced Jiménez's father to exchange his two houses in East Los Angeles for 21 acres in Mexicali. "We were not a burden to the U.S. government or anybody," says Jiménez, whose father worked for the gas company and collected rental income on his property. Still, Hispana convinced the man that it was best for him to turn over his bungalow and frame house and depart with his family to Mexico, where their 21 acres awaited them. "We camped under a tree until Dad built a shack out of bamboo," Jiménez recalls. Since there was no electricity available, his parents traded their washing machine and other appliances for chickens, mules, pigs and other necessities for their new life.

In the clutches of the Depression's hard times, families sold their homes at low prices. In some cases, the county placed liens on abandoned property. "While there is no direct authority for selling the effects and applying their proceeds," a county attorney informed Thomson, "we fail to see how the county can be damaged by so doing."

"They are going to a land where the unemployed take all-day siestas in the warm sun," wrote the Los Angeles *Evening Express* in August 1931, which described children "following their parents to a new land of promise, where they may play in green fields without watching out for automobiles." The reality proved to be far less idyllic. Emilia Castañeda first glimpsed

Mexican poverty in the tattered shoes on the old train porter who carried her father's trunk. "He was wearing huaraches," she recalled. "Huaraches are sandals worn by poor people. They are made out of old tires and scraps." Along with her father and brother, Castañeda moved to her aunt's place in the state of Durango, where nine relatives were already sharing the one-room domicile. "There was no room for us," she said. "If it rained we couldn't go indoors." She quickly learned that running water and electricity were luxuries left back in Los Angeles. She took baths in a galvanized tub and fetched water from wells. The toilet was a hole in the backyard. "We were living with people who didn't want us there," Castañeda said. "We were imposing on them out of necessity." They left after her father found work. In time her brother would be working also and, to her great dismay, shuffling around in huaraches.

Contrary to what was being propagated, Mexicans in Los Angeles did not impose a disproportionate strain on welfare services during the Depression. This is according to *Decade* and Abraham Hoffman, whose dissertation and subsequent book, *Unwanted Mexican Americans in the Great Depression,* examined repatriation from a Los Angeles perspective. Based on the county's own figures, Mexicans comprised an average of only 10 percent of those on relief. Nonetheless, repatriation was promoted and widely viewed as an effective means of diminishing welfare rolls, and Mexico's proclaimed plans for agricultural expansion conveniently complemented the movement. Indeed, Thomson traveled extensively throughout Mexico to survey proposed work sites and hold negotiations at various levels of the Mexican government, including the ministry of foreign affairs and the presidency. Some Mexican officials were so eager to get Thomson's repatriates, he later recalled, he was personally offered a bounty of land for each. "One time I was met by the governor of Quintaneroo. He offered me 17 and a half hectares (44 acres) for every repatriated individual I sent there to cut sisal and I said 'Absolutely no.' " Thomson claimed repatriates were in high demand across the border. "They brought across skills and industrial discipline," he said. "At that time, if you could repair a Model T Ford, that was quite an art."

Thomson's program—and its seemingly fantastic results—attracted the attention of state and local leaders from around the country, and his practice of engaging the Mexican government was copied as well. In the fall of 1932, Ignacio Batiza, the Mexican consul in Detroit, urged his compatriots to return home and "accept this opportunity which is offered them." While Batiza may have believed his country's promises of cooperation, others did not. A pamphlet circulated by a group called the International Labor Defense warned that thousands of workers choosing to return to Mexico would die of hunger. This was the end of 1932, and the feasibility of Mexico's grand plans was not yet widely challenged.

With a population of less than 15 million in the early years of the Depression, Mexico needed more workers to attain its goal of land transformation. Even as the Depression took hold, the Mexican government proceeded with its agricultural development plans, which would include repatriated nationals—especially those with farming skills. During that time, "They are proclaiming workers' rights," Balderrama explained. "If they're not accepting of the repatriates, that calls into question what they're all about." In the end, however, the government's post-revolutionary zeal eclipsed a hard reckoning of the facts. The returning mass of impoverished pilgrims from the United States would strain an already fragile economy. Officially, at least, the government welcomed the compatriots from the north, underscoring its proclamation of Mexicanism and support for workers rights.

Mexico struggled to cope with the deluge of new arrivals. Hungry and sick travelers crowded into border towns such as Ciudad Juárez and Nogales, where paltry food and medical supplies ensured a daily death count. There are many accounts of border towns crowded with people, as the train connections were not well organized. One repatriado reported: "Many that come here don't have any place to go. They don't have any idea of where they are going or what they'll do. Some families just stayed down at the railway station."

Forced relocation 'prevented me from completing my education and advancing for better employment.'

In an attempt to manage the crisis, Mexican governmental agencies joined several private organizations to create the National Repatriation Committee in 1933. The first colonization project undertaken by this august assembly was Pinotepa Nacional, located in a fertile tropical area of southern Mexico. Modern farming equipment and mules, along with food and other provisions, were made available to the farmers, who were to earn their equity through produce. And while the crops grew quickly, this highly touted proletarian collective proved to be a disastrous failure beset with complaints about mistreatment and meager food rations. The project's final undoing came from disease, as the land was rife with poisonous insects. Sixty people died within 20 days, according to a settler who had left after one month, taking his three small sons with him. "Some have families and can't leave very well," he told one researcher. "But my boys and I could. We walked to Oaxaca. It took us eight days."

Though the government welcomed repatriates, the general citizenry often did not. "Most of us here in Mexico do not look on these repatriates very favorably," remarked one Mexico City landlady. "They abandoned the country during the revolution, and after getting expelled from the north, they expected their old compatriots . . . to greet them with celebrations of fireworks and brass bands." Castañeda remembers children taunting her as a "repatriada." "The word was very offensive to me," she recalled. "It was an insult, as is calling someone a gringo or a wetback." As one Mexican ranch worker asked a repatriate in Torreón in the northeastern state of Coahuila: "What you doing here for? To eat the little bread we have?"

As news about the harsh conditions in Mexico traveled north, it became more difficult to convince people to leave the United States. President Franklin D. Roosevelt's New Deal provided work for some Mexicans, such as veterans of the U.S. military, and welfare was allotted to those who were barred from the work projects. But, back in Los Angeles, Thomson remained resolute in his efforts to repatriate Mexicans, eventually turning his attention to nursing homes and asylums in his desire to purge what he considered welfare leeches. In some cases, the bedridden were sent out on the back of a truck.

Many American children of repatriates never lost their desire for a true repatriation of their own. Emilia Castañeda, who had relocated 17 times while living in Mexico, decided to return to Los Angeles as her 18th birthday approached, some nine years after that dark morning in 1935. Her godmother in Boyle Heights forwarded Castañeda's birth certificate, along with money for the train ride. Ironically, this American citizen was again subjected to humiliation. At the border crossing, immigration officials asked to see her tourist card. "I had to pay for a tourist card because, according to them, I was a tourist. Can you imagine? Me, a tourist, for nine years." It was 1944, and the train was crowded with soldiers. "I sat on my suitcase in the aisle. The seats were reserved for servicemen, but some were kind and they offered me their seats. I spoke very little English by then. Here was this American girl coming back to the United States."

Castañeda relearned English in the same school she had attended as a child. As she would later admit, her forced relocation "prevented me from completing my education and advancing for better employment." Rubén Jiménez had attended school in Mexico, walking 12 miles a day to a one-room structure where six grades shared one teacher. When he returned to the States, the transition back into Los Angeles schools was difficult. A high school sophomore at age 17, Jiménez dropped out and joined the Army, serving as a radar operator during World War II. After several years, he completed college and eventually retired as a parole investigator.

While many American citizens who were caught up in the repatriation movement returned and struggled to readjust to their native country, thousands who had left without documentation had no legitimate proof of citizenship and were denied reentry. "We talked to one lady, part of her family came back, and part of it, unable to prove their residency, settled along the border so they could get together sometimes," recalls Rodríguez. "But the whole family was not able to make it back. And that was not an unusual circumstance."

In 1972 Hoffman noted that the history of Mexicans in the United States was largely ignored. "A case in point is that of the repatriation phenomenon," he said. "When I started working on it as a dissertation there was really nothing. Historians had neglected it as a topic, as they did essentially everything that today we call ethnic studies. I was interested in the topic because I was born in East L.A., and although I am not a Mexican American, I did have some concerns about what had been going on in an area where I had grown up."

Repatriates often tried to forget the experience, and they did not speak about it to their children. Many saw themselves as victims of local vendettas rather than scapegoats of a national campaign. "They really didn't understand the broad aspects," says Rodríguez. "They thought it was an individual experience. It wasn't something pleasant. It wasn't something they could be proud of."

The silence, however, did not dissuade a new generation from seeking answers. "I knew that my father had spent his childhood in Mexico, despite the fact that he was born in Detroit, and I always had questions about it," says Elena Herrada, a union official and activist in Detroit. While at Wayne State University in the '70s, Herrada and other students began collecting oral histories from elders in the community, a practice she continues today. "All we wanted to do was get the story told in our own families, and in our own communities, so that we would have a better understanding of why we don't vote, why we don't answer the census, why we don't protest in the face of extreme injustice. It just explains so many things for us."

In the summer of 2003, the subject of Mexican repatriation went beyond the confines of family and academic circles and returned to the scrutiny of government. A hearing was held in Sacramento, Calif., presided over by state Senator Joe Dunne, who had been inspired by *Decade of Betrayal*. The book's authors spoke at the session, and Rodríguez's voice faltered as he recalled his own father's flight to Mexico in 1936. Other scholars spoke, as did local politicians and two repatriates. A class action lawsuit on behalf of those who had been unfairly expelled from California was filed in July, with Castañeda as the lead plaintiff. The suit was eventually withdrawn, as two consecutive governors vetoed bills that would have funded research and expanded statutory limitations.

For a time, however, the civil action and the forgotten history behind it were national news. This, in a way, was the beginning of a more lasting restitution: an acknowledgment of the past. "My idea is for it to be in the history books," says Emilia Castañeda, "for children to learn what happened to American citizens."

Labor Strikes Back

What was good for General Motors wasn't always good for GM workers. Sit-down strikes at the company's Michigan plants sparked a wave of similar actions in workplaces across the country.

ROBERT SHOGAN

'Sitting-down has replaced baseball as a national pastime.'

The Detroit News, 1937

It was the height of the Saturday shopping rush in the big F.W. Woolworth's five-and-ten-cent store in the heart of downtown Detroit. Customers thronged the aisles surveying the vast array of hair combs and knitting needles, lampshades and face creams, nearly everything on sale for only a nickel or a dime. The clerks stood by their counters as usual. All seemed normal. But this was February 27, 1937, more than seven years deep into the Great Depression, and what had once passed for normal had long since vanished from the American workplace. Suddenly, the bargain-hunting shoppers were startled by the screech of a whistle blown by a union organizer. The 150 women clerks knew just what to do. All of them, the lunch counter brigade in their white short-sleeved uniforms, and the others in their long, fitted skirts and knitted tops, stepped back from their counters and folded their arms, halting work in unison. "The jangle of cash registers stopped," reported the *Detroit News,* "and bewildered customers found themselves holding out nickels and dimes in vain."

The intrepid Woolworth clerks held their ground day and night for an entire week, taking command of the store. Confounded, the company rewarded the strikers with a 20 percent raise and gave their union a say in hiring.

The locally organized work stoppage in Woolworth's was only one of many examples of the potency of a novel weapon—the sit-down strike—that thousands of workers were taking up and using against their bosses across the land. The strikers demanded and frequently won higher wages, shorter working hours and, most commonly, recognition for their unions. Sparked by the signal triumph of the upstart United Auto Workers' (UAW) sit-down strike against General Motors in December 1936, "sit-downers" were causing Americans to take organized labor more seriously than ever before.

Entrenched corporate interests, the indifference of lawmakers and the outright opposition of the courts had combined to beat back the organizing campaigns of labor unions for years. The Great Depression and the launching of President Franklin Roosevelt's New Deal offered unions hope for contending against big business on a more level playing field. But Roosevelt's key legislative act in support of labor, a federal guarantee of collective bargaining, was torpedoed by the U.S. Supreme Court along with the rest of the National Recovery Administration (NRA), the centerpiece of FDR's reform program. The high court held that the NRA represented an unconstitutional grant of power over the economy to the executive branch of government. Meanwhile, the nation's great corporations continued to use every weapon at their disposal to throttle and disrupt the union movement.

Workers were growing desperate. And nowhere was despair deeper than in the auto industry, particularly at General Motors, then the nation's largest corporation. The pressure of the assembly line had always been a point of contention for autoworkers. But it became even harder to bear when GM stepped up the tempo to take advantage of the boost in the economy achieved by the early New Deal programs. Workers complained about what they considered the assembly line's unbearable pace, which some claimed made them ill or so dizzy that when they left the plant, they could not remember where they had parked their cars.

Well aware that such conditions made its factories a breeding ground for labor unions, GM did all it could to crush any such movement before it could start. Since the beginning of 1934, the automaker had spent about $1 million for private detectives to spy on union activities. A Senate committee, probing interference with union organizing efforts, called GM's espionage operation "a monument to the most colossal super-system of spies yet devised in any American corporation."

Spurred by unrest among the rank and file, UAW leaders on December 16, 1936, sought a meeting with General Motors to discuss working conditions. The company declined to meet with the union. Frustrated and angry, the workers were attracted to the sit-down idea, with its guerrilla war motif. A song composed by a UAW leader caught the mood of the workers:

When they tie the can to a union man, Sit down! Sit down!

When they give him the sack they'll take him back, Sit down! Sit down!

When the speed up comes, just twiddle your thumbs, Sit down! Sit down!

When the boss won't talk don't take a walk, Sit down! Sit down!

As auto industry national union strategists, led by the head of the Committee of Industrial Organizations (CIO), United Mine Workers president John L. Lewis, were still mulling over when to call a strike, the rank-and-file workers and their local leaders took the decision into their own hands. The catalyst was GM's plan for relocating the dies—the cutting tools used to shape the bodies of Chevrolets and Oldsmobiles—from the Fisher Body plant No. 1 in Flint, Mich., to other plants that were relatively free from UAW penetration.

O n the night of December 30, 1936, the local UAW leaders sounded the alarm to their assembled workers at a hastily called lunch break meeting by alerting them to GM's plans for transferring the dies. The response was unanimous and swift. "Them's our jobs!" one worker cried out about the crucial equipment. "Shut her down, shut the goddamn plant down!" another worker shouted. Others took up the call and began sitting down at their machinery, just as the starting whistle was set to blow. Within an hour the production line had shut down. "She's ours!" one striker yelled. For good measure, sit-downers also seized control of the much smaller Fisher Body plant No. 2 nearby.

Sit-downs were by no means a brand-new tactic. As early as 1906, General Electric workers sat down at a Schenectady, N.Y., factory, and European workers staged various forms of sit-ins after World War I. But it was during the hard times and frustration of the Depression years that sit-downs caught on and mushroomed as never before.

As the Flint strike soon proved, the sit-down strategy offered great advantages to labor. It made it possible for a relatively small number of workers to completely shut down a huge factory. No more than 1,000 took over Fisher No. 1, and fewer than half that number controlled the smaller No. 2 plant. But their presence, standing guard at the machinery, was enough to keep management from using strikebreakers to reopen plants. While companies could get a court injunction against strikers, enforcing the order would mean driving the sit-downers out of the plant they controlled, a move that was hard to do without the violence and bloodshed that politicians wanted to avoid.

Grasping the sit-down's potential, Lewis and the CIO plunged into the fray, hoping to get a foothold in mass production industries such as autos, which had resisted the efforts of the craft-based American Federation of Labor. A hulking figure of a man, with a personality to match, Lewis saw the unplanned sit-down

of the Flint UAW as a golden opportunity. On New Year's Eve 1936, barely 24 hours after the Flint sit-downs started, Lewis went on the radio to bolster the strikers' cause and to demand the help of President Roosevelt, to whose reelection the CIO had been a major contributor.

For GM the stakes were just as high as they were for Lewis, the CIO and the New Deal. The automaker could not ignore the fact that the strike was metastasizing across its vast empire.

In the week following the seizure of the Flint plants, UAW sit-downs and walkouts had closed the other GM plants throughout the Midwest. But none of those were as menacing to the company's profit margin as the sit-down at the Flint Fisher Body plants, the biggest producers of bodies and parts for all of GM.

Sit-downs made it possible for a small number of workers to completely shut down a huge factory.

On January 11, 1937, the 12th day of the strike, GM staged an assault on Fisher No. 2, the more lightly held of the two UAW bastions. A platoon of company guards rushed a group of workers handing food in through the main gate of the plant, overpowering them and slamming the gate shut. At the same time, with the outdoor temperature at just 16 degrees above zero, GM turned off the heat in the plant.

Union headquarters was alerted, and hundreds of workers rushed to the scene, reinforcing the union picket line outside the plant. To bolster the outnumbered company guards, Flint police soon arrived, brandishing revolvers and tear gas guns, laying siege to the plant. But the strikers inside dragged fire hoses to the windows and drenched the "bulls," as they called the company agents and police, while bombarding them with tools and hardware, including two-pound car door hinges. To make matters worse for the police, strong winds blew the tear gas they had fired at the strikers back into their faces, forcing them to call off their attack.

Their victory in the "Battle of the Running Bulls," as the union forces dubbed the confrontation, energized the strikers and buttressed their support among autoworkers in Flint and elsewhere. Just as important, the fracas at Fisher No. 2 brought Michigan's newly elected pro-labor Governor Frank Murphy into the picture. His interest carried with it the promise of an even more important development—the potential for increasing involvement on the part of President Roosevelt, Murphy's political patron as well as the beneficiary of union leader Lewis' largesse during his 1936 reelection campaign.

Murphy mobilized the National Guard and vowed to preserve order. But he also made clear that he did not intend to use the Guard to evict the strikers, but only to quell violence that the local police could not control.

For their part, the strikers organized themselves into committees to deal with food, sanitation and health, safety and entertainment. Every worker had a specific duty for six hours a day, which he performed in two three-hour shifts. Every night at 8, the strikers' six-piece band—three guitars, a violin, a mouth organ and a squeezebox—broadcast over a loudspeaker for the strikers and the women and children outside. Spirituals and country tunes made up most of their repertoire, but they always closed with "Solidarity Forever," the anthem of the labor movement, sung to the tune of "The Battle Hymn of the Republic," taking heart from its rousing chorus: "Solidarity forever, for the union makes us strong."

The sit-downers themselves were all men, but women played a major role in the effort. Wives came to the plant windows to distribute food, which went immediately into the general commissary, and clean laundry. Women were not allowed to enter, but children were passed through the windows for brief visits with their fathers.

The tenacity of the strikers and their families made it possible, within a month after the Battle of the Running Bulls, for the UAW to celebrate an even more significant victory. Facing an imminent collapse of its production schedule for the entire year, GM, prodded by Roosevelt and bulldozed by Lewis, came to an agreement with the UAW that paved the way for the long-term, quasi-partnership role the union would ultimately play in the auto industry.

The UAW's triumph inspired an epidemic of sit-down strikes the likes of which neither the United States, nor any other country, had ever seen. Shipyards and textile mills, college campuses and even coffin factories all were hit in one town or another. The number of sit-downs, which had nearly doubled from 25 in January 1937 to 47 in February, made a quantum leap in March to 170. This figure was more than three times the total for 1936, and represented strikes involving nearly 170,000 workers. In Detroit, the center of the storm, "sitting-down has replaced baseball as a national pastime," the *Detroit News* reported, "and sitter-downers clutter the landscape in every direction."

Sit-downs were by no means confined to the workplace. At penitentiaries in Pennsylvania and Illinois, inmates sat down to get better treatment—but failed. In Zanesville, Ohio, housewives occupied the office of the director of public services, protesting against a dusty neighborhood street.

The spree had its lighter side. In the town of Neponset, Ill., schoolchildren sat down in the local drugstore demanding free candy—until a generous resident resolved their grievance with a $5 check to the storeowner. A divorced woman sat down in her ex-husband's apartment demanding that he pay the back alimony he owed her. And in New York's Madison Square Garden, the New York Rovers amateur hockey team kept 15,000 fans waiting for half an hour while they sat down in their dressing room because they had been denied the free tickets promised them.

But most strikes were in deadly earnest, sometimes accompanied by violence. In the Fansteel Metallurgical Corp. plant south of Waukegan, Ill., a two-hour battle raged with more than 100 sit-downers beating back a like number of police and deputy sheriffs who tried to drive them out of their plant. The police and deputies then besieged the plant, sent for reinforcements and a

few days later launched another attack. This time they forced the strikers to evacuate.

Nevertheless, the pace of sit-downs continued to quicken. On one single day, March 8, 1937, 300 members of the United Electrical Workers sat down at the Emerson Electric plant in St. Louis, while in Springfield, Ohio, 300 workers at the Springfield Metallic Casket Company stopped production, and in Pittsburgh 200 workers at the American Trouser Company refused to work. The union demanded a return to the 1929 wage scale of $16 a week for a 40-hour week and intended to organize all 700 pants makers in the city.

Later in the same week, 215 strikers sat down at four stores of the H.L. Green department store chain in New York City. They presented the company with a 22-point program calling for union recognition, a 40-hour workweek and a minimum weekly wage of $20. While negotiations went forward, the union's food distribution system provided workers at the largest of the stores in Manhattan with 85 pounds of veal, which they cheerfully made into goulash. At night a nearby Greek restaurant sent in dinner.

But the major battleground continued to be the starting point for the year's imbroglios—Michigan and the auto industry. This time the principal target of the United Auto Workers was Chrysler, then the second largest of the auto companies. The struggle between the union and Chrysler soon reached the bitter intensity of the previous battle with GM.

The UAW's victory over GM had led to concrete gains—pay raises, the rehiring of fired workers, the retiming of jobs to eliminate the speed-up—all of which helped fuel the UAW drive against Chrysler. The leaders of the Chrysler strike had sent observers to Flint and learned from the sit-down there. But so had Chrysler. When 6,000 strikers took over eight Chrysler plants in the Detroit area, the company lost no time in getting an injunction, giving the workers two days to evacuate.

The UAW's friend, Michigan Governor Murphy, was on the spot. While vowing to support the law, he was reluctant to bring force to bear against the strikers, and with good reason. Neither police nor sheriff's deputies were up to the job, and to call on the National Guard would result in a bloody battle.

So the sit-downs continued, appearing to some to threaten chaos, not only in Detroit but also in other major cities. On March 16, 1937, the same day the Chrysler strikers defied the courts and challenged their governor, taxicab drivers battled strikebreakers and police in the heart of Chicago's Loop as thousands watched from office windows. A mounted policeman who rode into the mob was pulled from his horse and beaten; nearby another officer chased away strikers by leveling a shotgun at them. The strikers stopped cabs driven by scab drivers, threw passengers into the street and in one case set a cab on fire.

In New York City, perhaps inspired by their peers' success with their strike in Detroit, Woolworth clerks caught the sit-down fever. At a downtown Manhattan store of the five-and-ten-cent chain, union supporters clambered up onto a second-story ledge above the store entrance, opened windows and threw food, blankets and other provisions to the strikers inside, while private police tried in vain to stop them. The sit-downers sent a cablegram rebuking the Woolworth heiress Barbara Hutton Mdivani

Haugwitz-Reventlow, whose extravagant lifestyle had become an embarrassment to the company's executives. "Babs," as the tabloids called her, had just recently bought $2 million worth of jewelry, two Rolls Royces, a 157-foot yacht and a mansion in London. The strikers condemned her profligacy in the face of the Depression-driven hunger and poverty that prevailed in New York and elsewhere in the country.

In Clifton, N.J., 150 employees of the Pacific Slipper Company sat down to demand higher wages and, among other things, cleaner toilets. The company appealed to the state's governor, Republican Harold Hoffman, who had previously likened sit-down strikers to "gangsters" and vowed to crush any such outbreaks in his state with force. But Hoffman, like Democrat Murphy, was not eager to back up his words with actions. Dealing with sit-down strikes, he declared, was a matter best left to the courts.

But in the U.S. Senate, some decided that the time for dithering had passed. On March 17, 1937, with Chrysler under siege and smaller companies beset everywhere by sit-down strikes, one of the Senate's aging lions, California Republican Hiram Johnson, called the outbreak of sit-downs "the most ominous thing in our national economic life today." If public officials permit the strikes to go on, he declared, "then the warning signals are out, and down that road lays dictatorship." Democrat James Hamilton Lewis of Illinois picked up on that theme, warning, "In every hour such as this there awaits another Hitler and there lurks in the shadows another Mussolini."

Other voices joined the chorus in the chamber until Arkansas' venerable Joseph Robinson, the Democratic majority leader of the Senate, unable to find any other way to silence the critics of the sit-down, adjourned the Senate. But adjournment came too late to erase the impact of the anti-sit-down oratory. The next day's front page of *The New York Times* carried, along with more news of the continued Chrysler strike in Detroit and other sit-downs, a streaming headline that declared "SIT-INS HOTLY DENOUNCED IN SENATE," with even more alarming subheads: "CHAOS IS FORESEEN" and "FASCISM HELD POSSIBLE."

Labor's friends in the Senate tried to counterattack by blaming the U.S. Supreme Court. The high court's conservative majority had bedeviled Roosevelt, leading him to shock the nation with his controversial "court-packing" scheme. This would have allowed FDR to blunt the anti–New Deal thrust of the court by appointing six more justices, one for each of the present justices over age 70. Noting that the court had so far failed to rule on the constitutionality of the Wagner Act, which had been passed to reestablish the protections for union organizing that had been voided earlier by the Supreme Court, Democratic Senator Sherman Minton of Indiana quipped, "Apparently there is a sit-down strike over there."

But such lame sarcasm was drowned out by the crash of events. In Detroit on March 19, city police broke up sit-down strikes in seven downtown shoe stores, smashing the glass doors to gain entrance when the strikers refused to leave. And as the Chrysler strike dragged on, sit-downers warned that if an attempt were made to evict them, they would meet force with force. Roosevelt privately fretted to his confidant, Interior Secretary

Harold Ickes, that the political storm stirred by the sit-down strikes might add to the difficulties facing his already beleaguered plan to overhaul the Supreme Court. He had more reason for anxiety on March 26, when a group of New England civic and business leaders, headed by Harvard University's president emeritus, A. Lawrence Lowell, wired Vice President John Nance Garner demanding an end to what newspaper headlines were now calling the "sit-down revolt." If such defiance of established authority and property rights continued, the distinguished group warned, "then freedom and liberty are at an end, government becomes a mockery, superseded by anarchy, mob rule and ruthless dictatorship."

In Garner, who promised he would present the statement to the Senate at its next session, the Lowell group could not have found a more enthusiastic messenger. Though typically he did not speak out publicly on issues, he made no secret of his views within the administration's inner councils. The sit-down strikes, he told Roosevelt's erstwhile campaign manager, Jim Farley, were "mass lawlessness" and "intolerable" and would lead to "great difficulty if not destruction." Garner was so frustrated about Roosevelt's failure to lambaste the sit-down strikers, as Garner thought he should, that he let his feelings erupt during a Cabinet meeting. The vice president stood behind Labor Secretary Frances Perkins and berated her for being insufficiently rigorous in opposing such outbreaks, causing the nation's first woman Cabinet secretary to weep.

Meanwhile, Lewis and other union leaders were not deaf to the outcry against the sit-downs. Fearful his political allies might desert him, Lewis went along with a compromise offered by Governor Murphy that ultimately led to a union agreement with Chrysler similar to the UAW's landmark deal with General Motors.

In mid-April 1937, the Supreme Court at last handed down its ruling on the Wagner Act, upholding the rights the new law granted to union organizing efforts. The decision was a stunning reversal of the court's previous labor decisions. Writing in his diary, Roosevelt's Attorney General Homer Cummings called the ruling "amazing," and court watchers speculated that the justices, already under pressure from Roosevelt's court-packing scheme, had decided to do what they could to ease the labor turmoil roiling the nation.

By the fall of 1937, 70 percent of Americans disapproved of sit-downs.

That same April, sit-down strikes began to decline for the first time that year. With the backing of the Wagner Act, workers were now finding the drastic action of the sit-down less necessary, and at the same time much riskier because of increased public resentment. Public opinion pollster George Gallup found that by the fall of 1937 about 70 percent of Americans disapproved of sit-downs, a negative view that colored overall public attitudes toward labor unions in general. By December, the sit-downs declined from their all-time high to a mere four, involving only a handful of workers.

In 1939 the Supreme Court put an end to the tactic by finding it illegal. Ruling on a case stemming from the 1937 sit-down at the Fansteel metallurgical factory in Illinois, the court ruled that although the company had violated provisions of the Wagner Act in dealing with its employees, the sit-down staged by its workers was "a high handed proceeding without shadow of a legal right."

But for labor, it was a great ride while it lasted. In a few stormy months in 1937, the sit-down strikers wrote a new chapter in the annals of American labor. They helped John L. Lewis fulfill his vision of industrial unionism, gaining the opportunity for unions to participate in decision-making within the American economy for decades to come. Just as important, they emboldened individual workers in their struggle for a living wage, the right to organize and a voice in working conditions.

The passion that infused the sit-down strikers faded over the years as the gains they helped to achieve came to be taken for granted by workers. Today some critics blame those gains for contributing to the decline and threatened financial ruin of the great auto giants of the past—GM, Ford and Chrysler. But, as organized labor once again faces stiff challenges from a combination of forces and foes, including a more competitive global economy, others feel that it is time for the union movement to recall the faith expressed in the opening verse of Ralph Chaplin's theme song for the sit-down strikers, "Solidarity Forever":

> When the union's inspiration through the workers blood shall run,
> There can be no power greater anywhere beneath the sun.
> Yet what force on earth is weaker than the feeble strength of one,
> But the union makes us strong.

This article is adapted from **ROBERT SHOGAN**'s new book, *Backlash: The Killing of the New Deal,* published by Ivan R. Dee.

Flight of the Wasp

The Women Airforce Service Pilots seemed strange and exotic to World War II America. In fact, not even the military could quite figure out what to do with them.

VICTORIA POPE

Curiosity, patriotism, and even a hint of scandal lured the residents of Sweetwater, Texas, to the outskirts of town one April morning in 1943. The townspeople made a day of it, setting out picnic lunches near the military training base at Avenger Field and searching the sky for incoming aircraft. "Cars lined old Highway 80 for two miles in each direction from the Main Gate," recalled 17-year-old Hershel Whittington.

The first sightings came in mid-afternoon, and then dozens of planes, open cockpit and single propeller, began passing over the rolling plains of tumbleweed and cactus beyond town on the way to the base. "Here comes one," someone shouted. "And here's another!"

The planes belonged to members of the Women Airforce Service Pilots (WASP), a band of roughly 1,000 women flyers that served as a homefront Army auxiliary during World War II. But their program might have come too soon for an Army establishment—and a country—that was still wary about women in the military. From the moment of its creation to its abrupt end two years later, the WASP program met with skepticism despite a stellar record of ferrying B-17s, B-29s, B-26s, and other airplanes. One Pentagon official described the program as "an experiment" to test women's abilities to withstand duress and handle the physical demands of the military.

Some WASP pilots started flying hard-to-handle B-26s and B-29s.

The curious residents of Sweetwater may have had more in common with their high-profile visitors than either group realized. America's entry into war had brought sweeping cultural changes: women took on roles vacated by the men joining the military, leaving their kitchens to work on assembly lines and factory floors. Sweetwater experienced an influx of wartime newcomers, including the high-spirited women pilots, while the women found themselves pushing against the boundaries of society's frontiers.

The newly arrived trainees, outfitted in ill-fitting khaki jumpsuits they called zoot suits, seemed unusual indeed to the people of Sweetwater. "They were aloof, self-contained, self-assured, and self sufficient; at least so it seemed to me then," remembered Helen Kelly, a young girl when the WASP flyers came to town. She watched them in the women's dressing room at the town pool, where "they stripped and walked around naked, unashamed. We had never seen anyone do that. Every Sweetwater female changed in and out of her bathing suit barricaded behind the firmly locked door of a dressing booth." Even their speech seemed different. "They used words we didn't," Kelly recalled; "some long and fancy words, some short and pungent words. They even cursed openly, something which no proper lady in Sweetwater would do."

Blue Bonnet Hotel's Charles Roberson recalled how they poured in on the weekends to have their shoes shined. Most customers would give a small tip, or perhaps nothing at all; these women arrived with pocketfuls of change. Digging into their pant pockets—they did not carry handbags—they paid him with whatever they pulled out, often a fistful of coins. He remembers looking forward to their weekend visits, not for their extravagance of spending but for the extravagance of their spirit.

That kind of spirit was something they shared with Jacqueline Cochran, the program's guiding light, and a household name in her own right. An accomplished racing pilot, she had earned a victory in 1938's cross-country Bendix flying competition. A striking blonde, Cochran also ran her own cosmetics firm and created such popular products as Wonda-matic mascara. Born Bessie Lee Pittman in the Florida Panhandle, she had escaped poverty by moving to New York City, changing her name, and working in a Fifth Avenue hair salon. Through her well-heeled clients she met and later married Floyd Odlum, a man of great wealth and quiet influence. Odlum bought Cochran her first plane and encouraged her aspirations as a flyer and businesswoman.

Cochran wrote to First Lady Eleanor Roosevelt in 1939 about an idea she had for a corps of women Army reserve pilots. "Should there be a call to arms it is not my thought that women pilots will go and engage in combat, for I'm sure they won't," she wrote. "But every trained male pilot will be needed in active service. The 'lady birds' could do all sorts of helpful back of the lines work. Every woman pilot who can step into the cockpit of an ambulance plane or courier plane or a commercial or transport plane can release a male pilot for more important duty."

Using women pilots, the Pentagon said, was "utterly unfeasible."

The U.S. War Department had already broached the idea of using women pilots as early as 1930. The Pentagon's reply: "utterly unfeasible." Women, as a memo explained, were "too high strung for wartime flying." In 1936 a member of the 99s, a prominent women's aviation organization, suggested women should join the military as pilots, but was promptly rebuffed. In the summer of 1941, Cochran, armed with a letter that the First Lady had helped her extract from President Franklin Roosevelt, made the rounds of the Pentagon. Henry "Hap" Arnold, the commanding general of the U.S. Army Air Forces, turned down her plan, stating that the Army had an adequate number of pilots. He also questioned whether Cochran could assemble enough qualified fliers. And, he asked, what about finding proper facilities for training women? "The use of women pilots presents a difficult situation as to the housing and messing of personnel at Air Corps Stations," he wrote to her.

But with the number of male pilots dwindling further every month, Arnold reversed his position. At roughly the same time, the head of the Army Air Transport Command, Col. William H. Turner, approved the plan of an accomplished flyer, Nancy Harkness Love, to assemble a group of highly experienced women pilots to ferry planes. Cochran, in contrast, sought full military training for her women pilots. She began recruiting women who could compare favorably with the average cadet both in intellect and, as she put it, "coordination." For consideration, applicants could be no shorter than 5 feet 2½ inches tall, no younger than 18 and a half years, and must have flown no fewer than 200 hours. Cochran looked for "clean-cut, stable appearing girls." Conservative in many respects, Cochran wedded her views on female abilities with the conventional views of the period. "A woman, to accomplish all she can, must present herself at an absolute peak of attractiveness, just as she must keep herself in good health and her brain growing and alert," she told *Ladies Home Journal* in 1941. "Her beauty is not a frivolous irrelevancy but a touchstone to a full life." She looked askance at black WASP candidates—there was at least one—because, she argued, they would attract far too much prejudice for them to succeed.

Even in the chaotic atmosphere of wartime America, the recruitment process struck prospective WASP candidates as surprisingly informal. Cochran threw cocktail parties and receptions, sometimes making verbal offers after only short conversations. "How many of you would be willing to fly for your country?" she asked a gathering of women in Washington, D.C. A month after that meeting, Jane Straughan was startled to receive a wire that instructed her to report immediately for duty. While more than qualified, she had not even filled out an application form.

Determined applicants found ways around the physical requirements. At 98 pounds, Caro Bayley was simply too small, but she pinned her father's fishing weights under her clothes to add weight. Her examiner passed her. Called "Little Gear" by her classmates, Bayley had trouble reaching the pedals but nonetheless became

one of the best acrobatic pilots in the program with the aid of a small stack of pillows. Some challenged the height requirement by hanging upside down by their heels to stretch themselves out, while others simply begged the examiners to pass them anyway.

The program got under way slowly at Howard Hughes Field in Houston in November of 1942. It was a haphazard start. The 319th Army Air Force Women's Flying Training Detachment (WFTD) lacked classrooms, a cafeteria, and even the military planes to train in, instead relying on ordinary civilian carriers painted olive drab. To eat or use the restrooms, the trainees had to walk to the Houston Municipal Airport a half mile away. Without set uniforms, they dressed in whatever they wanted—cowboy boots, loafers, and saddle shoes. One pilot, Marion Florsheim, wore bedroom slippers with pompoms. The only WFTD-issued item was a hairnet required for flying, because the Washington brass worried that long hair would hinder flight training.

In April the training operation shifted to Avenger Field. By then Sweetwater's residents weren't the only ones who found the fliers unusual. Many of the women pilots themselves felt transformed, noting in diaries and letters that their friends and family might not recognize them because they had grown so rough-and-tumble. Living together in barracks and following a rigorous regimen—beginning with reveille at 6 A.M., followed by Morse code, Link (flight simulation) training, and flight training—did not allow time for primping. Gallows humor became a coping mechanism as well as a form of bonding between the pilots, who sometimes had to withstand slights from bullying instructors. Winifred Wood described how her class grew more confident of its military bearing but felt deflated after performing as the honor guard for visiting generals Barton K. Yount and Barney Giles. After the inspection, Giles had turned to his wife and said, "Aren't they cute!"

The oddity of women in the military made good copy for the American press. In late April 1943 the *Houston Post* ran an Associated Press report on the WASP's move to Sweetwater, dubbing them the "Lipstick Squadron." Reporter Hugh Williamson described the pilots as "sun-bronzed, trim as the streamlined planes," but also quoted Cochran as saying that the program was hard work with little glamour. Field supervisor Maj. L. E. McConnell told Williamson that "gentler treatment" was the only change required for the instruction of women students. As for fighting in actual combat, McConnell said they could learn gunnery and "take their place in the front if called upon to do it." Cochran shared her worries with Williamson that combat would harden and brutalize the women, who still needed to be wives and mothers after the war. Nonetheless, if events called for it, women could fly combat missions. "When aroused, women make the nastiest fighters," she said.

The WASP pilots that graduated from Avenger fanned out to air bases throughout the United States, where they flew cargo, transported new airplanes from factories, and assumed other aviation roles. One elite group, formed from Cochran's best flyers, received an assignment to tow aerial targets at Camp Davis in South Carolina. Cochran hoped the assignment would serve as a stepping stone to bigger responsibilities, perhaps even overseas. "[Cochran] told us the wonderful news that 25 of us were to be used as an experiment and trained on bigger equipment to see just what women can do," WASP Dora Jean Dougherty wrote in her diary. "Will fly almost everything including B-26s and sounds wonderful. She couldn't tell us everything. . . . None of us could sleep for [we] were too excited."

But at Camp Davis, it almost seemed as though the WASP themselves were the targets. The commanding officer of the 3rd Tow Target Squadron, Lovick Stephenson, made it clear that he did not support women in the military. Male pilots already assigned to tow-target duty felt threatened by the new arrivals. Some enlisted men even requested transfers. Although correspondence plainly stated that the 25 women "would be given every opportunity to demonstrate their ability to replace a proportion of, or all, men tow target pilots," Stephenson instead gave them busy work—administrative paperwork or tracking flights in light planes such as the L-5 Stinson liaison planes and Cubs. It was a big comedown.

In time, the women would fly the big planes they came to fly and win the respect they deserved, but ill will was palpable, as one story in *Flying Magazine* made clear. "Isabel Fenton of West Springfield, Mass. was flying a Vega Ventura about 6,000 feet over the dunes off Camp Davis the other day, hauling an airplane target for a battery to shoot at. In 20 rounds the 90's got the target and the target fell blazing into the sea. There were cries of Ah and Oh and Good Shooting from the gallery of press and radio representatives and officers. But as the Ventura wiggled its wings and swung off for its base, a grizzled colonel mumbled into his moustache, 'Hell, they missed the girl.' "

Cochran did not let the summer's challenges slow her down. She offered the WASP another groundbreaking assignment—a chance to fly the B-26 Marauder "Widowmaker," a twin-engine bomber so named for its proclivity for crashing during takeoff. Soon afterward they began flying the country's newest, biggest bomber—the B-29 Superfortress, another plane with a reputation for being hard to handle. Cochran told General Arnold that her pilots had shown that the concerns about those planes were overstated. "The obvious conclusion was that if a woman could do it so could a man," Cochran said, with understated irony.

But things were changing for the WASP and for the world at large. By 1944 the war had turned in the Allies' favor. New, long-range fighters could now destroy German Luftwaffe planes on the ground, making the skies even safer for the Allies. The United States required fewer combat pilots in the European theater, so the Army Air Force began shutting down both its War Training Service and its civilian flight training program. The civilian pilots reacted by charging women pilots with stealing their jobs. Columnist Drew Pearson launched a virulent campaign against the WASP program, writing that "Jackie's glamour girls" were benefiting from "a racket." Sen. Harry Truman, the head of a committee investigating war waste, asserted that the cost of training a WASP flyer was a hefty $22,000. It was a wildly inflated figure; a truer estimate for both female and male cadets was $12,000.

In February 1944 Rep. John Costello of California submitted a bill to confer Army Air Force commissions on all on-duty women pilots. It failed a House vote on June 19, with 188 voting against, 169 for, and 73 abstaining. It marked the beginning of the end for the WASP. Congress did approve the necessary appropriation for another year, but Cochran decided to close down the program because full military status—which had been given to the Women's Army Corps (WAC) and other branches of the military—was not forthcoming.

At Avenger Field, the final WASP class learned that its training would be abbreviated. Trainee Peggy Daiger was dispirited by the resulting collapse of general field operations. "Those employed at Avenger Field were draft exempt; they hurried away in droves to find other draft-exempt jobs before the December deadline." The changes became evident immediately. "Maintenance was sloppy; instructors became harried; food declined to the almost inedible. I remember one chill day's evening chow that consisted solely of warmed-over boiled potatoes, gummy macaroni, and milk that had been kept next to something less tasty in the refrigerator. One graduate WASP, on the field for only a day's business, carefully loaded her tray with this mess and then slammed the whole thing against the wall. We applauded mentally but nobody smiled."

More than 100 pilots stationed at bases across the country returned for the final graduation on December 4, 1944, a powerful sign of support for a class of graduates with no base assignments awaiting them, who would receive wings they could not wear in military flight. Cochran predicted that the women would return to more conventional paths: "Their careers will be marriage." And overnight, with the abrupt end of the WASP, that assessment seemed accurate.

At the official ceremony, Cochran stuck to a colorless script, thanking the generals and expressing pride in the program's accomplishments. But then Arnold gave the WASP a meaningful sendoff, saying, "Frankly I didn't know in 1941 whether a slip of a young girl could fly the controls of a B-17 in the heavy weather they would naturally encounter in operational flying." The unusually expansive general concluded, "Well, now in 1944, more than two years since the WASP first started flying with the Air Forces we can come to only one conclusion: It is on the record that women can fly as well as men."

In 1976, the Air Force announced that it would accept women cadets.

Arnold's summation was soon forgotten. The WASP pilots themselves were in a sense responsible, soft pedaling their experience and declining to speak about it when husbands and brothers recalled their supposedly more important wartime experiences. But the women kept in touch, and they eventually launched a campaign for full military recognition. In 1976 the U.S. Air Force announced that it would begin accepting women cadets into their corps, a decision hastened by the end of the draft. Once again women had been invited into the military to counterbalance a shortage of men—but as the WASP alumnae knew, despite media reports, this would not mark the first time women had flown for the U.S. military. Motivated by the new developments, they began a campaign to receive the military status that they had been denied 30 years earlier. Congress finally passed such a bill in 1977 that President Jimmy Carter signed into law. But the law did not make many of the military benefits retroactive. Two years later the secretary of the Air Force announced a further step toward recognition. The members of the WASP program—the women who had served in a service that wasn't ready to accept them—were now considered to be veterans.

Ike at D-Day

The rain he worried about. The Camel cigarettes he chain-smoked. The letters he wrote in case of failure. Gen. Dwight Eisenhower's defining moment comes to life in an excerpt from Michael Korda's best-selling new biography.

MICHAEL KORDA

All over England the vast task of loading the invasion fleet was going on. Rural roads were lined with ammunition dumps, and huge numbers of vehicles, from heavy tanks to jeeps, motorcycles and bicycles, were being assembled—for the invasion was like an intricate jigsaw puzzle: everything had to be packed and loaded so that it all would come off in the right order on the beaches. Tanks had to be laboriously backed into the LSTs, or landing-ship tanks, so they could come down the ramp onto the beach with their heavier frontal armor facing the enemy and their guns ready to fire; ammunition and medical supplies had to be placed so they would arrive on the beach at the same time as the first troops; hundreds of thousands of two-way radios had to have their frequencies set so they could communicate with each other. The tasks were endless.

Nothing, it seemed, had been left to chance. The only thing over which the supreme commander, Gen. Dwight D. Eisenhower, had no control—was the weather.

All the same, late on the evening of June 5, when the great fleet bearing almost 170,000 men was already at sea, and the paratroopers were already on their way through the dark night sky to their drop zones in Normandy, and the midget submarines were rising to the surface to mark the boundaries of the invasion beaches, Winston Churchill, getting ready to go to bed with tears running down his cheeks, said to his wife, Clementine, "Do you realize that by the time you wake up in the morning, 20,000 men may have been killed?"

On no pair of shoulders did these concerns rest more heavily than those of the supreme commander himself. Eisenhower commanded some 3 million men—nearly 1.7 million of them American; 1 million British and Canadian; the rest Free French, Polish, Norwegian, Czech, Belgian and Dutch. This was the largest international alliance ever assembled.

Only two things could stop the invasion. The first was the possibility that the Germans had discovered where and when the landings would take place, but from intercepted German radio traffic and clandestine broadcasts from French resistance groups, there appeared no evidence of this. The enormous fleet put to sea without any sign that the Germans had even noticed it—another consequence of the Allies' control of the air, and another example of the failure of Hermann Göring's *Luftwaffe*. Had some of the new German jet fighters been modified as high-altitude, high-speed photoreconnaissance aircraft like the Royal Air Force's PR Mosquitoes and Spitfires, the fate of the invasion might have been very different; but on Hitler's orders the jet fighters were being converted into light bombers.

The weather, and particularly the tides, were Eisenhower's greater concern. The invasion could take place only when the tides were at their lowest ebb, in order to expose the mined obstacles that Field Marshal Erwin Rommel had placed in the water in such staggering quantities, even though the price for this was to increase the distance the troops would have to cross over open beaches in the face of enemy machine-gun fire once they were onshore. Also, there had to be sufficient moonlight the night before the invasion to enable the transport and glider pilots to find drop zones for the paratroopers and for the paratroopers and glider pilots to see where they were landing.

Low visibility might be an advantage for troops landing on the beaches, but it would hamper airmen flying the bombers and fighter bombers, and perhaps make parachute drops impossible. High winds would raise surf on the beaches and again might make it necessary to cancel the parachute drops; but a totally windless morning would shroud the beaches in smoke and make it difficult for warships to reach enemy targets accurately with their big guns. In short, to succeed, the invasion required a remarkably complex combination of factors, and these would be available only on certain days of each month. June offered only three possible dates: June 5, 6 and 7.

At first, the onslaught had been fixed for dawn on June 5. As the ships were loaded and the troops moved south, Eisenhower himself moved from his headquarters outside London closer to the invasion fleet at Southwick, outside Portsmouth, where Gen. Bernard Montgomery, commander of ground forces, and Adm. Bertram Ramsay, the naval commander in chief, had their headquarters. By June 1, the intricate operation was in motion: the great battleships were at sea, the men were on the move, the vehicles were loaded and the systematic bombing of key points of the French railroad system was already in progress. The only difficulty was the weather: low clouds, high winds, intermittent heavy rain and rough seas, with more of the same forecast for the foreseeable future.

Late on June 3, Eisenhower reluctantly made the decision to postpone the invasion by 24 hours, from June 5 to June 6, even though much of the invasion force was already at sea, and the troops were packed in the ships like sardines, adding seasickness to their woes. Eisenhower was aware of their misery, and he was even more conscious that every hour the fleet was at sea increased the chance that it might be discovered by a German E-boat or submarine.

The morning of June 4 offered no visible improvement. Rain poured down; wind rattled the windowpanes of the headquarters at Southwick; low clouds scudded past, driven by high winds. The sea was a dark gunmetal gray, with heavy surf breaking on the beaches and a heavy swell farther out, where the ships of the invasion fleet rolled and pitched. Uncomfortable at the best of times, the troopships were now a nightmare, with toilets backed up; men vomiting anyplace they could; and the sour odor of dense cigarette smoke, vomit and unwashed bodies permeating the low, crowded, dimly lit compartments in which the troops, their bulky equipment and weapons were densely packed. Many of the men actually looked forward to the moment when they could clamber down rope nets into the Higgins boats below and head for shore. They were wrong, however—as they would shortly discover. Being packed into a tiny, open Higgins boat in a rough sea, with waves breaking over the sides, was no picnic; nor was moving down the ramp onto the beach while carrying almost 100 pounds of gear and ammunition straight into steady, well-aimed German machine-gun fire—if you were lucky enough to make it to the beach, that is, rather than being dumped into water above your head by a coxswain too eager to get his boat away to wait until it touched ground, or being blown into the sea when the boat touched a mine or was hit by German artillery fire.

All these things were on Eisenhower's mind on the morning of June 4. Although Southwick House, the Operations Center at naval headquarters, had been until recently a luxurious mansion, the supreme commander had elected to set up his battle headquarters—consisting of his own trailer, a cluster of tents for conferences, and trailers for his personal staff—in a park a few miles away. The comparative solitude gave Eisenhower a chance to take long walks and think. But he was by no means isolated. The white-and-gold walls of Southwick House were now covered with big maps, on which Wrens (members of the Women's Royal Navy Service) plotted the position of each unit of the invasion fleet to the sound of ringing telephones and clattering teletypes. A red telephone in the spare, cramped bedroom of his trailer linked Eisenhower to a secure, scrambled line to Washington; a green telephone to 10 Downing Street; a black one to his chief of staff, Maj. Gen. W. Bedell Smith.

Despite all this, Eisenhower was under no obligation to consult with anyone. His orders read simply, "You will enter the continent of Europe and, in conjunction with the other United Nations, undertake operations aimed at the heart of Germany and the destruction of her armed forces." The decision to invade, to postpone, even to call off the invasion if need be, was his and his alone.

Perhaps the only sign of Ike's nervous tension was the increasingly rapid rate of his chain-smoking. Every ashtray in the trailer was full to overflowing with smoldering ashes, one of his staff noticed, as the general restlessly lit one Camel cigarette from another without stubbing out the first, pausing only to take another gulp of black coffee. From time to time, he stood up, put his hands on his hips and stared out the window of the trailer at the rain, or stood at the door of the trailer and looked up at the sky.

He knew that by the end of the day he would have to make the decision about whether to go on June 6. Through most of the day, Eisenhower stayed in his trailer, occasionally leaving to take a walk, waiting restlessly for the weather to change. It was still windy and pouring rain that evening when he left for Southwick House.

Waiting for him in the library were his senior commanders and their chiefs of staff—12 uniformed men in all, though Montgomery wore his trademark baggy corduroy trousers and roll-neck pullover. The big library had once been an elegant room, but the bookshelves were empty now, and most of the furniture had been removed. A large table covered with green baize cloth was placed in the center of the room. Heavy blackout curtains covered the windows but did little to keep out the noise of wind and rain.

Promptly at 9:30 Eisenhower entered the room and asked the others to sit down. There was no small talk. They all knew why they were there and shared the same concerns. There was a haze of tobacco smoke in the room—it was an age when almost everybody smoked, except Montgomery, who rarely allowed anybody to smoke in his presence except King George VI, Churchill and Eisenhower. The door opened and the three senior meteorologists came in, led by their chief, RAF Group Capt. J. M. Stagg.

Stagg began on a note of cautious optimism: weather aircraft far out over the Atlantic had detected a high-pressure front moving rapidly east. Tomorrow, June 5, would see periods of gradual clearing over southern England and the invasion beaches, with dropping winds. These conditions would improve through the night of June 5, enabling bombers to operate and airborne operations to take place, and would continue through the morning of June 6; but later in the day, conditions would begin to deteriorate. In short, there would be a window of 24 hours or less.

Once Stagg and his staff had been dismissed, Eisenhower asked his commanders to give him their opinions. Predictably, the air commander, Trafford Leigh-Mallory, was pessimistic about the airborne operations, having already expressed his fear that they would result in a disastrous blood bath. Leigh-Mallory had been a pessimist about the airborne operations from the start, even if weather conditions were perfect—to the great annoyance of the British and American airborne commanders, who were impatient for an opportunity to demonstrate that large-scale parachute and glider operations were feasible at night. Failure to play a major—and successful—role in the coming invasion would very likely lead to the airborne units' being broken up to provide replacements for regular infantry units, so not just honor but survival was at stake.

Montgomery was succinct as usual. "I would say go," he said simply.

A. W. Tedder, Eisenhower's deputy, for once agreed with his fellow air marshal Leigh-Mallory. This must have dismayed Eisenhower, who placed a good deal of confidence in Tedder's judgment. Leigh-Mallory's opinion would not have surprised him—indeed, Eisenhower had already had a long and painful conversation with Leigh-Mallory, during which he had warned him that while he was entitled to his opinion, he must not let it affect the troops' morale—but Tedder's doubts were something Eisenhower would have to take more seriously.

It was left to Admiral Ramsay to give the group the naval facts of life. If the invasion was postponed again, he pointed out, it would be necessary to bring many ships back to refuel. A naval operation of that size, spread across ports all over southern England, might easily be picked up by the Germans. In any case, it would take far more than 24 hours to refuel the ships and get them back in place again. If the invasion did not go forward on June 6, he saw no practical likelihood that it could do so on June 7—it would have to be postponed until late in June or sometime in July.

Postponing the invasion by another 24 hours was bad enough, but postponing it until the end of June or the first week of July would be catastrophic. Politically, it would reawaken Joseph Stalin's not altogether dormant suspicion that the invasion would never take place; both President Franklin Roosevelt and Churchill were anxious to avoid such a reaction. Militarily, the risks were worse. Could 170,000 men be brought back to England without being noticed by a German spy or without starting rumors? And what would be the effect on morale? Most of the men had already been briefed about the invasion beaches, which meant they would have to be held virtually incommunicado on their airfields, in their barracks or on their ships. Postponement until July, Ike thought, was simply "too bitter to contemplate" and probably impossible.

There was a long silence, broken only by the spatter of rain against the windows, the noise of the wind and the ticking of a clock. Eisenhower sat at the baize-covered table, his hands clasped in front of him, while the others waited for him to speak. It was Eisenhower's decision now, and even Montgomery, usually keen to press his own case, sat silently, looking at him.

Nearly five minutes passed, and then Eisenhower said in a low voice, "I am quite positive we must give the order. . . . I don't like it, but there it is. . . . I don't see how we can do anything else."

Then he stood up and walked to the door. The order had been given.

The invasion would take place on the sixth of June.

When asked what kind of generals he liked, Napoleon is said to have replied, "Lucky ones." Nobody in the room could have known it, but luck was about to strike Eisenhower.

Across the English Channel, the Germans were suffering, once again, from the difficulties of the Luftwaffe. Unlike the British and the Americans, the Germans had no aircraft that could safely patrol the Atlantic beyond Iceland to report on the weather. As a result, the high-pressure front that Stagg had reported to Eisenhower was unknown to them. Their meteorological forecast was for the bad weather to continue uninterrupted through June 6 and beyond—poor visibility, low cloud cover, rain, high winds, a heavy swell at sea, and strong surf on the French beaches.

Field Marshal Gerd von Rundstedt concluded that nobody in his right mind would order an invasion as long as the weather remained bad. That being the case, he set off with his immediate staff for a four-day inspection tour, and allowed Field Marshal Rommel to take a few days of leave. Rommel wished to spend his wife's birthday, June 6, with her in Germany, and he left early in the morning of June 4 in his Horch touring car, sitting in front, with his chauffeur, Daniel, at the wheel and two of his staff officers seated behind him. His birthday present for his beloved Lucie was beside him on the seat: a pair of elegant suede shoes he had bought in Paris—for even in the fourth year of the German occupation, Paris remained the center of haute couture, the place where everybody who could afford to do so still came to buy shoes, gloves, perfume, hats and lingerie. Even the commander of the 21st Panzer Division, Gen. Edgar Feuchtinger, a fanatic Nazi and a particular favorite of Adolf Hitler's, decided that it would be safe to spend the nights of June 5 and 6 in Paris with his mistress.

As for the Führer, he too was taking a vacation, at his home in Berchtesgaden, high above the Obersalzburg, accompanied by his staff and his mistress, Eva Braun.

Eisenhower's tiny trailer bedroom was littered with ashtrays and paperback westerns—virtually his only form of relaxation. Having made his decision, he left his commanders at Southwick House to get on with implementing it and went back to the trailer for a few hours of sleep. He was not the kind of man to waste time second-guessing himself once a decision was made.

All over Britain, the decision that Eisenhower had made at 9:45 had triggered a frenzy of activity RAF bombers were revving up their engines to strike vital targets in France, while all across southern England, thousands of transport aircraft had to be given last-minute checks, as well as the gliders aligned in long rows, just so, with their long towlines arranged in a zigzag pattern in front of them; everywhere ground crews worked through the night, loading bombs, rockets and long belts of ammunition into combat aircraft—the belts of .50-caliber ammunition for the heavy machine guns of the American bombers were 27 feet long (whence the expression "the whole nine yards"). Troops moved south by rail and truck toward the embarkation ports, following a complicated schedule that would take them and their equipment in phases to the beaches once these had been secured on D-Day. The British midget submarines that had been in place off the beaches, resting on the sea bottom since June 4—their crews now suffering from cramps, exhaustion and lack of air inside the tiny, crowded hulls—were given, at last, the order to surface before dawn on June 6 and raise a telescopic mast with a signal light, to mark the boundaries of the five invasion beaches for 7,000 ships in five separate fleets.

Eisenhower woke early in the morning of June 5 to the familiar sound of rain and wind. He had slept soundly, but apparently the thought that the invasion might fail was on his mind, for the moment he was dressed, he sat down at his little desk in the trailer and wrote out a kind of brief aide-mémoire of what he would tell the news correspondents if it did. This is one of the most extraordinary documents of the war, dignified, modest and truthful. Eisenhower takes on himself full responsibility for the failure:

> *Our landings in the Cherbourg-Havre area have failed to gain a satisfactory foothold and I have withdrawn the troops. My decision to attack at this time and place was based upon the best information available. The troops, the air, and the Navy did all that bravery and devotion to duty could do. If any blame or fault attaches to the attempt it is mine alone.*

He folded the piece of paper carefully, put it in one of the breast pockets of his short uniform jacket (already known as an Eisenhower jacket) and buttoned the flap. It was there if needed—he would not be at a loss for what to say if the worst happened. Then he went off to a final, last-minute briefing, at which Stagg gave yet another cautiously optimistic weather forecast.

Eisenhower spent most of the day in his trailer, receiving a steady stream of what were beginning to be called VIP visitors—among them Churchill and Gen. Charles De Gaulle. The rain slowly diminished, the cloud cover began to lighten and the wind dropped.

In late afternoon, Eisenhower decided to visit the airborne troops, who would soon be loading up. It was about them that Eisenhower had the sharpest concern. Nobody had ever attempted a night drop on this scale before, and Leigh-Mallory had predicted that casualties might be as high as 80 percent. From the beginning, Eisenhower had insisted on the airborne drops, despite the possibility of catastrophic losses, since these drops were the only way to secure both flanks of the invasion during the first few crucial hours, when the troops on the beach would be at their most vulnerable, trying to fight their way through the German defenses inland. Eisenhower had faced the problem squarely: if the three airborne divisions—one British, two American—had to be sacrificed to make the invasion possible, so be it. He hated the idea; he hoped that Leigh-Mallory was wrong; but the airborne drops were indispensable to success. On the other hand, he felt the need to go and see the men whose lives he might be sacrificing and look them in the eyes; and he felt, too, perhaps, that the sight of him would reassure them.

Shortly before 6, he stepped into his olive-drab Packard, with Kay Summersby, who by now had become his driver, hostess, social secretary and confidante, at the wheel. He told her not to fly the flag from the hood of the car and to cover up the plates bearing his four stars—he wanted no pomp or ceremony. As they set off, the weather began to clear, the sky turning a

glorious red as the sun set. "Red sky at night, sailor's delight," Summersby recited to herself as she watched it and felt a stirring of optimism.

It was nearly 50 miles from Portsmouth to Newbury, where the U.S. 101st Airborne was spread out at several airfields, some of the men getting ready to board waiting C-47S, others to board the gliders that would be towed by the transport aircraft. Greenham Common was the first airfield Eisenhower visited, and 31 years later, Summersby would remember the troops cheering, whistling and shouting, "Good old Ike!" as the supreme commander appeared.

Ike just started walking among the men. when they realized who it was, everyone went crazy. The roar was unbelievable.

"Ike," she remembered, "got out and just started walking among the men. When they realized who it was, the word went from group to group like the wind blowing across a meadow, and then everyone went crazy—the roar was unbelievable. . . . There they were, these young paratroopers in their bulky combat kits with their faces blackened so that they would be invisible in the dark of the French midnight. Anything that could not be carried in their pockets was strapped on their backs or to their arms and legs. Many of them had packages of cigarettes strapped to their thighs. They looked so young and brave. I stood by the car and watched as the General walked among them. . . . He went from group to group and shook hands with as many men as he could. He spoke a few words to every man as he shook his hand, and he looked the man in the eye as he wished him success. 'It's very hard really to look a soldier in the eye,' he told me later, 'when you fear that you are sending him to his death.'"

Summersby drove Eisenhower to two more of the 101st Airborne's airfields, but then there was no time left to continue, so she drove him back to Greenham Common to watch the aircraft there take off. It was dark now, but an American correspondent saw tears running down Eisenhower's cheeks as he watched, one after another, the C-47s roll down the runway and vanish into the night.

On the way back to Southwick in the car, he said to Summersby, "I hope to God I know what I'm doing."

At 6:30 in the morning, underwater demolition engineers ("frogmen") began to demolish the mined obstacles that protected the beaches, and the first "swimming tanks" were already going onshore to support the infantry. By 7, the assault troops in the first wave were beginning to wade through waist-high water onto the beaches, while overhead a fearsome naval bombardment—the heaviest in history—began to pound German defenses from Cabourg on the left to Quinéville on the right. A German officer reported back to his headquarters that he was looking at "ten thousand ships," and was warned not to exaggerate; but gradually, as the full extent of what was happening made its way up the German communications system, doubt was extinguished except at the very top.

Field Marshal von Rundstedt, breakfasting at his headquarters outside Paris, still thought that the landings were a diversion, and that the real invasion would take place in the Pas de Calais, though he took the precaution of alerting two of four Panzer divisions. Hitler was asleep in Berchtesgaden; his naval aide decided not to wake him until more information was available. Field Marshal Rommel was home in Herrlingen, and in the confusion nobody thought to call him until 10:15. He alone understood at once that this was not a diversion, but the real thing—the invasion he had been preparing for. "How stupid of me," he repeated as his aide gave him the details over the phone. By 1 in the afternoon, he was in his car on the way back to France, urging his driver on—*Tempo! Tempo! Tempo!* (Faster! Faster! Faster!) he called out, as the big Horch sped down the road.

Cautiously, the most Ike would say was that the landings were going "fairly well"; but at 9:33 in the morning he at last ordered his press aide, Col. Ernest Dupuy, to announce: "Under the command of General Eisenhower, Allied naval forces, supported by strong air forces, began landing Allied armies this morning on the northern coast of France."

Characteristically, Ike did not make the announcement himself, but this made no difference—around the world people stopped what they were doing to listen to the radio. In Britain work ceased and men and women stood and sang "God Save the King" spontaneously. In Philadelphia the Liberty Bell was rung, and church bells rang out in jubilation all across the United States, the United Kingdom and Canada. In America so many people called friends and families to tell them the news that telephone switchboards were jammed across the nation. In the House of Commons, Churchill, artfully keeping the members in suspense as he told them of the liberation of Rome, said, at last, "I have also to announce to the House that during the night and the early hours of this morning the first of the series of landings in force upon the European continent has taken place—in this case the liberating assault fell upon the coast of France." He went on to say "There is a brotherhood in arms between us and our friends of the United States. . . . There is complete confidence in the Supreme Commander, General Eisenhower." From all over the world—except, as Churchill would say "in the abodes of the wicked"—congratulations poured in. Even Stalin cabled, "It brings joy to us all." The normally staid *London Times* commented, "At last the tension has broken."

> *Eisenhower was vindicated in his belief that an airborne operation was critical to the success of D-Day. Some 18,000 paratroopers were dropped overnight behind German lines to secure the flanks, enabling the invasion to go forward. Although the nearly 80 percent casualty predictions did not materialize, some 3,700 of the 23,000 airborne troops sent into combat on the night of June 5 and on D-Day itself were killed, wounded or missing.*

As for the men who made the initial assault on the beaches of Normandy: total Allied losses that day have never been totally confirmed, but appear to have been more than 10,000, with American losses, including the paratroopers, totaling 6,577.

MICHAEL KORDA's previous books include the biography *Ulysses S. Grant* and a memoir, *Charmed Lives*.

As seen in *Smithsonian*, December 2007, pp. 50–56, 58. From *Ike: An American Hero* by Michael Korda (HarperCollins, 2007). © 2007 by Success Research Corporation. Published by permission of HarperCollins Publishers.

UNIT 5

From the Cold War to 2010

Unit Selections

Key Points to Consider

- What was the Marshall Plan and why did U.S. policymakers believe it was necessary? How effective was it in trying to restore European nations to prosperity?

- Why did the launching of a Soviet space satellite in 1957 seem so important to Americans at the time? Discuss both the scientific and military aspects.

- Why did some of Martin Luther King, Jr.'s supporters become alarmed by his views on social and economic issues and the Vietnam War?

- What did Bill Clinton accomplish during his presidency? Which of his objectives eluded him? How did his personal failings destroy his presidency?

- Discuss the President Bush/Karl Rove strategy to achieve a permanent Republican majority? Why did it fail?

- Most other advanced nations have had public health insurance programs for a long while. What is there about American institutions that make it so difficult to enact controversial reforms?

Student Website

www.mhhe.com/cls

Internet References

Coldwar
www.cnn.com/SPECIALS/cold.war
The American Experience: Vietnam Online
www.pbs.org/wgbh/amex/vietnam/
The Gallup Organization
www.gallup.com/
STAT-USA
www.stat-usa.gov/stat-usa.html
U.S. Department of State
www.state.gov/

President Franklin D. Roosevelt sought to build a working relationship with Soviet leader Josef Stalin throughout World War II. Roosevelt believed that the wartime collaboration had to continue if a lasting peace were to be achieved. At the Yalta Conference of February 1945, a series of agreements were made that FDR hoped would provide the basis for continued cooperation. Subsequent disputes over interpretation of these agreements, particularly with regard to Poland, raised doubts in Roosevelt's mind that Stalin was acting in good faith. Roosevelt died on April 12, 1945, and there is no doubt that he was moving toward a "tougher" position during the last weeks of his life. Harry S Truman assumed the presidency with little knowledge of Roosevelt's thinking. Truman had not been part of the administration's inner circle and had to rely on discussions with the advisers he inherited and his own reading of messages passed between FDR and the Soviets. Aside from an ugly encounter with Soviet Foreign Minister V. M. Molotov at the White House only eleven days after Roosevelt's death, Truman attempted to carry out what he believed were Roosevelt's intentions: be firm with the Soviets, but continue to seek accommodation. He came to believe that Foreign Minister V. M. Molotov was trying to sabotage U.S.-Soviet relations and that the best way to reach agreements was to negotiate directly with Stalin. This he did at the Potsdam Conference during the summer of 1945, and left the talks believing that Stalin was a hard bargainer but one who could be trusted.

Events during the late summer and early autumn eroded Truman's hopes that the Soviets genuinely wanted to get along. Disputes over Poland and other Eastern European countries, the treatment of postwar Germany, and a host of other issues finally persuaded Truman that it was time to stop "babying" the Soviets. A militant public speech by Stalin, which one American referred to as the "declaration of World War III," appeared to confirm this view. Increasingly hostile relations led to what became known as the "Cold War," during which each side increasingly came to regard the other as an enemy rather than merely an adversary. Meanwhile the United States had to cope with the problems of conversion to a peacetime economy. Demobilization of the armed forces proved especially vexing as the public clamored to have service men and women, stationed virtually all over the world, brought home and discharged as quickly as possible. When the administration seemed to be moving too slowly, the threat "no boats, no votes" became popular. Race riots, labor strife, and inflation also marred the postwar period.

Relations with the Soviets continued to deteriorate. Perceived Soviet threats against Greece and Turkey led to promulgation of the "Truman Doctrine" in 1947, which placed the United States on the side of those nations threatened with overt aggression or internal subversion. That same year Secretary of State George C. Marshall sketched the outlines of what would become known as the "Marshall Plan," an even more ambitious effort to prevent economic chaos in Europe. "Dollar Diplomacy" evaluates this program that has been described as "among the most noble experiences in human affairs."

How had things gotten to such a sorry state only a few years after the dragons of fascism and Japanese militarism had been slain? Some people began alleging that, as dangerous as the

Library of Congress/Historicus, Inc.

Soviet Union was, internal subversion was an even greater problem. Opponents of Roosevelt's "New Deal" and Truman's "Fair Deal" cited various allegations of spying on the part of former government officials to bolster their claims that Democrat administrations had been shot-through with subversion. Liberals cried frame up. Some of these allegations have been shown to be true, but what became known as "McCarthysim" (after a Wisconsin senator who was a prominent "Commie hunter") cast a pall of suspicion over the society.

In 1950, a scant five years after the end of World War II, the United States found itself at war again. The North Korean invasion of the South in June of that year appeared to American leaders as a Soviet-inspired probe to test Western resolve. Failure to halt aggression there, many believed, would embolden the Soviets to strike elsewhere just as Hitler had done in the 1930s. President Truman's decision to send American troops to Korea was almost universally applauded at first, but discontent arose as the war dragged on. Americans were not used to fighting "no win" wars. David Halberstam's "Command Performance" tells how General Matthew B. Ridgway reorganized dispirited American troops after China entered the war.

Domestically, the 1950s offered a mixed bag. Social critics denounced the conformity of those who plodded up the corporate ladder, purchased tract homes that all looked alike, or who had no greater ambition than to sit in front of their television sets every night. Beneath the veneer of tranquility, however, there were stirrings over civil rights and liberties that would erupt into prominence during the 1960s. "Crisis at Central High" analyzes the attempt to integrate schools in Little Rock, Arkansas, in 1957. That same year Americans were shocked when the Soviet Union announced that it had launched the first space satellite in history. "Launch of a New World" discusses how *Sputnik* shattered assumptions about American technological superiority and had grave military implications as well.

The election of John F. Kennedy to the presidency in 1960 appeared to many as a turning point in American history. His charm and good looks, as well as his liberal agenda, provided a marked contrast to the Eisenhower era. Kennedy did sponsor some significant legislation and moved hesitantly on civil rights, but his assassination in 1963 leaves us only to speculate on what he might have accomplished had he served his full term and perhaps a second. Recent historians have given mixed grades to his presidency. They point to the Bay of Pigs fiasco and to the fact that he was the one to first send combat troops to Vietnam.

There was a great deal of social unrest during the latter part of the 1960s. In addition to protests against the war, racism, and social inequities, there were virtual revolutions with regard to sex, music, and to the use of drugs. "Will the Left Ever Learn to Communicate Across Generations?" recounts the struggle among generations of radicals to determine the direction and leadership of protest movements. "King's Complex Legacy" shows how this civil rights leader became even more controversial when he embraced what some deemed extreme social and economic goals, and began opposing the Vietnam War.

Social ferment began to subside during the latter part of the 1970s, causing some observers to regard these years as dull and relatively uneventful. Not so, Kenneth S. Baer argues in "The Spirit of '78, Stayin' Alive." He claims that one must look at 1978 to "see the beginnings of the world we live in today."

Three articles deal with presidential conduct in more recent decades. "Soft Power: Reagan the Dove" argues that in spite of his militant rhetoric against the Soviets, Ronald Reagan played a key role in ending the Cold War because of his commitment to peace. "The Tragedy of Bill Clinton" discusses this extremely talented but flawed president. Author Gary Wills believes it would have been better for him and for his programs had he resigned from office. "The Rove Presidency" contends that President George W. Bush's key adviser, Karl Rove, had "the plan, the power, and the historic chance to remake American politics." This seemed especially true after 9/11. The vision of creating a permanent Republican majority dissipated through a series of blunders. "Bush will leave behind a legacy long on ambition," the author writes, "and short on positive results."

Public health insurance has been one of the most controversial issues of President Obama's administration. "Good Health for America?" provides a history of earlier attempts to enact this reform and tells why they failed. American institutions, the author claims, make it extremely difficult to achieve "deep and contentious reforms."

Dollar Diplomacy

How much did the Marshall Plan really matter?

NIALL FERGUSON

It was "the most generous act of any people, anytime, anywhere, to another people," its chief administrator declared. It was "among the most noble experiences in human affairs," its representative in Europe said. It was "the most staggering and portentous experiment in the entire history of our foreign policy," the young Arthur Schlesinger, Jr., who served on its staff, wrote. Foreigners concurred. It was "like a lifeline to sinking men," according to the British Foreign Secretary Ernest Bevin. It "saved us from catastrophe," a manager at Europe's largest tire factory declared. Sixty years after Secretary of State George C. Marshall outlined the need for economic aid to stimulate European recovery, in a speech at Harvard University's commencement on June 5, 1947, the plan named after him continues to be fondly remembered in donor and recipient countries alike. In our own time, liberal internationalists have periodically called for new Marshall Plans. After the collapse of Communism, some economists maintained that the former Soviet Union was in need of one. More recently, there has been desultory talk of Marshall Plans for Afghanistan, Iraq, and even the West Bank and Gaza. When critics lament the allegedly modest sums currently spent by the American government on foreign aid, they often draw an unfavorable contrast with the late nineteen-forties. Yet some people, at the time of its inception and since, have questioned both the Marshall Plan's motivation and its efficacy. Was it really so altruistic? And did it really avert a calamity?

More popular history is written about war than about peace, and very little concerns itself with economics. Greg Behrman's "The Most Noble Adventure: The Marshall Plan and the Time When America Helped Save Europe" (Free Press; $27) is admirable for bringing to the potentially arid story of America's biggest aid program all the literary verve and drama one associates with the best military and diplomatic history. Behrman's approach recalls that of Margaret MacMillan in her recent book "Paris 1919," about the Paris Peace Conference after the First World War. Like "Paris 1919," "The Most Noble Adventure" is an account in which individual actors predominate over economic calculations. But, whereas MacMillan's book had few, if any, unalloyed heroes, Behrman's has a surfeit. I counted five.

There is Marshall himself, truly a titan among public servants. As Chief of Staff of the U.S. Army during the war, he had been, in Churchill's phrase, the "organizer of victory," and, as Secretary of State, he approached Europe's postwar reconstruction with the same sangfroid and self-discipline. There is William Clayton, the Under-Secretary of State for Economic Affairs, a Southerner who had made his fortune in cotton and his political reputation in wartime procurement. Clayton was another formidable workhorse, whose only weakness was his demanding wife, Sue, who hated his absence on government business and vetoed a succession of more senior appointments he was offered. (To crown it all, she divorced him a year after he retired, only to remarry the hapless fellow two months later.) A third hero is Arthur H. Vandenberg, a leading Republican in the Senate, who had been converted from isolationism to internationalism by the experience of war. Without him, Behrman suggests, the Marshall Plan might have been stymied by Republican opposition. The fourth member of Behrman's quintet is W. Averell Harriman, the imperious tycoon who, as Commerce Secretary, headed the President's Committee on Foreign Aid and then became the European Recovery Program's Special Representative in Europe. His contribution was to broker the diplomatic deals within Europe, whereby aid was subtly tied to other American objectives. Finally, there is Paul Hoffman, the indefatigable automobile salesman and president of Studebaker, whom Truman press-ganged into the job of Marshall Plan administrator. It was Hoffman, more than anyone else, who sold the Plan to Americans. (Richard Bissell, whom Hoffman summoned from M.I.T. to act as his chief economist, comes close to being a sixth hero—something of a rehabilitation for a figure now mostly recalled as one of the C.I.A. men behind the Bay of Pigs invasion.)

Flitting across this crowded stage are some better-known figures: Harry Truman, who declined to call the program the "Truman Plan" not out of modesty but for fear of riling Republican opponents; Josef Stalin, whose aggressive action toward Czechoslovakia greatly helped Vandenberg to overcome congressional resistance; Ernest Bevin, the overweight, ebullient, and ineffably proletarian British Foreign Secretary, who was the Plan's biggest fan; and the diarist and wit Harold Nicolson, whose condescending characterization of the United States ("a giant with the limbs of an undergraduate, the emotions of a spinster, and the brain of a pea-hen") now reads like postimperial sour grapes. The United States in 1945 was a giant, all right, but with the wealth of a Harriman, the altruism of a Marshall, and the sheer dedication of men like Clayton, Vandenberg, Hoffman, and Bissell, it was surely a benign colossus.

What, exactly, was Marshall's plan? To answer that question, as Behrman's diligent research shows, we need to go back to the speech at Harvard. More than two years after the end of the Second World War in Europe, Marshall bluntly informed his audience that "the rehabilitation of the economic structure of Europe" would "require a much longer time and greater effort than had been foreseen." The division of labor between town and country was "threatened with breakdown" in Europe because "town and city industries are not producing adequate goods to exchange with the food-producing farmer." Consequently, European governments were obliged to import essentials from the United States, using precious hard-currency reserves that would be better spent on capital goods for reconstruction. Marshall declared:

> The truth of the matter is that Europe's requirements for the next three or four years of foreign food and other essential products—principally from America—are so much greater than her present ability to pay that she must have substantial additional help or face economic, social, and political deterioration of a very grave character.

The alternative to intervention was "hunger, poverty, desperation, and chaos." The aim of the United States, then, should be to restore "the confidence of the European people in the economic future of their own countries and of Europe as a whole." But it was left up to the Europeans to decide whether or not to accept the offer of American aid and for what purposes they would like it to be used. "The initiative must come from Europe," Marshall stated. This new policy (Marshall himself did not use the word "plan") was "directed not against any country or doctrine." However, "any government which maneuvers to block the recovery of other countries" would be denied American assistance. And any political parties or groups that sought to "perpetuate human misery" for their own nefarious political purposes would "encounter the opposition of the United States."

Four things are especially striking about Marshall's speech, which he read (Behrman tells us) in a barely audible monotone from a seven-page typescript. The first is its economic premise: Europe urgently needed American aid so that urban consumers could be fed without exhausting hard-currency reserves, but the longer-term objective should be to restore European confidence, productivity, and self-sufficiency. The second is its disavowal of unilateralism: this was an invitation to Europeans to specify the help they needed. The third is the European scope of the speech: victors and vanquished were henceforth to be regarded as an integral unit. The fourth is Marshall's thinly veiled allusion to the Soviet Union and to Communism: anyone who opposed this new policy would get short shrift.

Even at the time, not everyone in the United States was convinced. "We are through being 'Uncle Sap,'" Senator Alexander Wiley, of Wisconsin, declared. To Senator Homer Capehart, of Indiana, the Marshall Plan was "state socialism." To Congressman Frederick Smith, of Ohio, it was "outright communism." Not to be outdone, Senator Joseph McCarthy, of Wisconsin, later called it a "massive and unrewarding boondoggle" that had turned the United States into "the patsy of the modern world." The very fact of McCarthy's denunciation could be taken as a powerful argument in the Plan's favor, and it is tempting, at this distance, to see such critics as blinkered isolationists, partisan hacks, or incurable xenophobes. But a significant number of eminent economic historians—notably, the British scholar Alan Milward—have questioned just how vital Marshall Aid really was for Europe's postwar recovery. According to Milward, recovery was under way well before the advent of the Marshall Plan, and reconstruction of damaged infrastructure was far advanced before the funds reached Europe. The program was also too small to have a significant effect on Europe's capital stock. The total aid package was equivalent to less than three per cent of the recipient countries' combined national income, and it represented less than a fifth of their gross investment.

To gauge the true importance of the Marshall Plan, it is crucial to get a sense of the amounts involved. Behrman writes, "From June 1947 to its termination at the end of 1951, the Marshall Plan provided approximately $13 billion to finance the recovery . . . of Western Europe." This was less than half the Europeans' initial request and four billion dollars less than President Truman's initial proposal to Congress, but it was still serious money. Behrman computes that, in today's dollars, "that sum equals roughly $100 billion, and as a comparable share of U.S. Gross National Product it would be in excess of $500 billion." That's actually an understatement. In fact, the total amount disbursed under the Marshall Plan was equivalent to roughly 5.4 per cent of U.S. gross national product in the year of Marshall's speech, or 1.1 per cent spread over the whole period of the program, which, technically, dated from April, 1948, when the Foreign Assistance Act was passed, to June, 1952, when the last payment was made. A Marshall Plan announced today would therefore be worth closer to seven hundred and forty billion dollars. If there had been a Marshall Plan between 2003 and 2007, it would have cost five hundred and fifty billion. By comparison, actual foreign economic aid under the Bush Administration between 2001 and 2006 totalled less than one hundred and fifty billion, an average of less than 0.2 per cent of G.D.P.

Yet even these calculations understate the magnitude of the Marshall Plan. There had been American economic assistance to Europe before, through the United Nations Relief and Rehabilitation Administration, which spent about $2.5 billion, and ad-hoc measures like the loan of $3.75 billion to Britain that was negotiated in 1946. But none of these expedients addressed the fundamental problem of the "dollar gap"—the fact that an exhausted Europe could not earn the foreign exchange it needed to pay for indispensable U.S. imports. As Behrman demonstrates, Marshall Aid solved this problem. A French farmer who needed an American-manufactured tractor would buy it with French francs. The Economic Cooperation Administration (the Plan's executive arm) would then vet the transaction in consultation with the French government. If it was approved, the U.S. tractor manufacturer would be paid out of Marshall Plan funds. The French farmer's francs, meanwhile, would go to the French central bank, enabling the French government to spend the money on reconstruction. Marshall Aid thus did "double duty," relieving the pressure on the French balance of payments while at the same time channelling money into the French government's own recovery plan. It thereby had a "multiplier effect," a term borrowed from John Maynard Keynes. According to one contemporary, each dollar of Marshall cash stimulated four to six dollars' worth of additional European production.

This positive reassessment echoes the argument advanced in the early nineties by Brad DeLong and Barry Eichengreen (in an article that is absent from Behrman's bibliography). Marshall Aid was indeed vital, but more in terms of political economy than macroeconomics. It helped get the European economies through a balance-of-payments crisis, to be sure. More important, though, it helped European governments balance budgets and reduce inflation. It forced them to shift from wartime controls to free-market mechanisms. And it played an important part in moving Europe from a dysfunctional system of labor relations based on strike action and class conflict to one based on wage restraint and productivity growth. In all of this, the Marshall Plan resembled the "structural adjustment programs" the International Monetary Fund imposed on borrowers in the developing world during the nineties, but on a larger scale and with much better public relations. As Marshall had foreseen, tackling the food bottleneck was beneficial both materially and psychologically. One Dutch baker displayed a sign that read, "More than half of your daily bread is baked with Marshall wheat." Wherever the red-white-and-blue Marshall shield could be seen, its motto resonated: "For European Recovery: Supplied by the United States of America." The most important strings attached to such supplies were the ones tying Europe to the new American model of managerial capitalism.

Behrman goes still further, however. He also sees the Marshall Plan as having been instrumental to the process of European economic integration, presaging today's European Union in the Organization for European Economic Cooperation. And he accepts the claim that the Marshall Plan defused potentially revolutionary situations in Western Europe and helped prevent a Communist tide from engulfing West Berlin, Italy, and perhaps even France. He has no interest in the once fashionable arguments of Cold War revisionists that the Plan was—in the memorable phrase of Stalin's economic adviser Yevgeny Varga— "a dagger pointed at Moscow." If the Soviets chose to decline Marshall Aid for themselves and their clients, more fools they. The notion that Marshall and his colleagues aimed at "economic and political subjugation of European countries to American capital," to quote another Soviet source, is presented as unworthy of serious consideration.

This is a timely book, reminding us of the good things that the United States has achieved within living memory. Not for nothing do economists call aid payments "unrequited transfers." It is also useful to recall just how poisonously partisan Washington was after 1947, as Joseph McCarthy's witch hunt gathered momentum. This was no golden age of cross-party consensus.

Yet there is a need for caution. Historians have a duty to immerse themselves in contemporary testimony, as Behrman has clearly done. But they must also beware of uncritically accepting contemporary judgments.

One way of avoiding this is to pose counterfactual questions. "What would it cost not to aid Europe?" one congressman asked. That remains the key question. If there had been no Marshall Plan, would Western Europe's economies have failed to recover from the postwar crisis? It would seem not (though there would probably have been more currency volatility and more labor unrest). Under the Marshall Plan, grants and loans were received by sixteen different countries. Britain received more than twice the amount given to West Germany. Yet no European economy performed more dismally in the postwar period than Britain's. A crucial difference between the two was the success of the German currency reform of 1948, which saw the birth of the enormously successful Deutsche Mark, compared with the ephemeral stimulus of the British devaluation of 1949, the first of several vain attempts to revive the U.K. economy by cheapening exports.

If there had been no Marshall Plan, would Western Europe have remained economically fragmented? No, because the Europeans did not need America to come up with their own plan for a six-nation Coal and Steel Community, the decisive first step toward economic integration. By comparison, the American-sponsored O.E.E.C. was a cul-de-sac. Notice, too, that among the recipients of Marshall Aid were a number of countries that even today remain outside the European Union: Iceland, Norway, and Turkey. And no amount of American pressure could persuade the British to participate in the first wave of European integration. As one British official complained, "We are being asked to join the Germans, who started two world wars, the French, who had in 1940 collapsed in the face of German aggression, the Italians, who changed sides, and the Low Countries, of whom not much was known but who seemed to have put up little resistance to Germany."

If there had been no Marshall Plan, would American industry have enjoyed less access to European markets? Again, no: European recovery did not especially benefit American manufacturers, for whom domestic markets were vastly more important. In 1953, Britain still accounted for only 5.2 per cent of U.S. exports and Germany for just 2.3 per cent. As a whole, exports represented a modest share of U.S. G.D.P.—about three per cent even at the end of the nineteen-fifties, compared with roughly seven per cent today. Similarly, the French Communist paper *L'Humanité* exaggerated the threat of "Coca-colonization" of Europe by American capital. In fact, the volume of U.S. direct investment in Europe was relatively modest in the years following 1947.

Finally, if there had been no Marshall Plan, would Stalin have brought some or all of Western Europe into the Soviet imperium? Again, no; the principal deterrent to Stalin was not American dollars but American firepower. By the time the Plan had run its course, soft power was increasingly yielding to hard power in the struggle between the superpowers, particularly after the Soviet-sponsored North Korean invasion of South Korea. True, some Marshall Plan funds were channelled into the C.I.A.'s Office of Policy Coordination (a euphemism for covert operations). But these amounts were trivial compared with the sums being spent on more overt methods of containment. Ultimately, the North Atlantic Treaty mattered more than the Marshall Plan in checking the Soviet advance.

In all likelihood, then, Western Europe could have pulled through without the Marshall Plan. But it certainly could not have pulled through without the United States. At the time that Marshall made his speech in Harvard Yard, no one could be sure that all would turn out for the best in postwar Western Europe. No one could even be sure that the United States would deliver on Marshall's pledge. All people could remember was the sad sequence of events that had followed the previous World War, when Western Europe was swept by general strikes and galloping inflation, while the United States Senate reneged on Woodrow Wilson's "plan" for a new order based on collective security. The Marshall Plan was not the only difference between the two postwar eras, but, to West Europeans struggling to make ends meet, it was the most visible manifestation of American good will—and a mirror image of the Soviet policy of mulcting Eastern Europe. This, more than its macroeconomic impact, explains its endurance in the popular imagination. At a time when, according to the Pew Research Center, only thirty-nine per cent of Frenchmen and thirty per cent of Germans have a positive view of the United States, that is something worth remembering, and pondering.

Command Performance

With U.S. forces in Korea beleaguered and demoralized in 1950, American prestige and the future of South Korea hung in the balance. Then Gen. Matthew B. Ridgway took charge.

In August 1945, at the end of World War II, Russia and the United States divided the Korean peninsula at the 38th parallel into communist north and western-aligned south, setting the stage for one of the first great conflicts of the Cold War. After North Korea invaded the south on June 25, 1950, U.N. forces, led by the United States, entered the war on South Korea's behalf General Douglas MacArthur's daring landing at Inchon on September 15, 1950, pushed the North Koreans almost to the Yalu River on the Chinese border. MacArthur, however, had made a disastrous miscalculation—that the Chinese would not enter the war. In November 1950, 300,000 Chinese routed U.N. troops, forcing a retreat. It was at this dark hour, following the death of Lt. Gen. Walton Walker in a jeep accident, that Lt. Gen. Matthew B. Ridgway was ordered to Korea.

DAVID HALBERSTAM

I f ever an American officer was perfectly suited for a particular moment in American military history, it was Matthew Bunker Ridgway when he was summoned to take over the shambles of a dysfunctional Eighth Army. He was the flintiest of men, rather humorless, fiercely aggressive, as unsparing of himself as he was of others. The G.I.'s admired him, even if they did not love him. They knew that he did not play games, that he had a genuine feel for them and their hardships, and that he would be on their side if they had legitimate grievances.

One could not think of him except as a soldier—and not a peacetime soldier either. Though he had none of the grandiosity of MacArthur, he had his own mystique and his own very personal sense of his role in history. He believed that he and the men he commanded were the direct descendants of those who had gone before them, dating back to Valley Forge. It was as if George Washington and the men who fought with him were always looking over his shoulder. Ridgway sometimes talked in an almost mystical way of those who had fought in the Revolution or the Civil War, and of the need for his men to be worthy of the hardships they had suffered.

Though he was fiercely anti-Communist, he was not, like MacArthur, on an ideological crusade. The enemy was the enemy, to be analyzed on the basis of actual strengths and weaknesses. If ideology made the Chinese or North Koreans better, more committed soldiers, then attention should be paid to that fact.

Ridgway was in his own way a very serious hawk, but unlike MacArthur, he accepted that this was a limited war, that the civilians running it had pressures on them that officers in the field might not grasp and that the main battlefield might end up thousands of miles from Korea, most likely in Central Europe where the Soviets had placed so many armored divisions.

He was an imposing man, forceful and trim, 5-foot-10 but thanks to the sheer force of his personality, seemingly much bigger. He was a Spartan. He worried that America was in decline because of the country's ever greater materialism; he warned that it was becoming a place where people never walked anymore and that the nation's men were becoming softer every year. His views, ironically, were not all that different from those of the Chinese commanders who had launched their successful assault on American troops. He believed a loss of fiber had contributed to the disappointing early performance of our young men in Korea. They had become too dependent on their machines and their technology. The first thing he intended to do when he took over was get them out of the warmth of their jeeps and trucks and make them patrol exactly as their predecessors had done, climbing the hills on foot. If they shared nothing else with their enemy, they would share the cold.

Ridgway bristled with personal purpose: he had an innate sense of how to lead, of what motivated fighting men—and what did not. There were at least three moments in his career when his country had reason to think of him as someone who, by dint of intelligence and character, set himself apart from his peers. The first was when he led the airborne assault on France on D-Day in June 1944. The second was in 1954, after elite French forces had been trapped by the Vietminh at Dien Bien

Phu and pressures grew on the Americans to come to their aid. At that time, as Army chief of staff, he wrote a memo so forceful in assessing the extremely high cost of an American entry into the war in French Indochina (and the potential lack of popularity of such a war) that President Dwight Eisenhower put aside any idea of intervention. And the third was when he took over the shattered Eighth Army, in late December 1950, and in two short months reinvigorated it, thereby blunting a Chinese offensive that threatened to drive U.N. forces into the sea or push the Americans into using atomic weapons.

There was a constancy to his code of honor. He had been assigned to command the Eighteenth Airborne Corps in the final battle for Japan, but then the war had ended quickly. MacArthur had invited him to attend the surrender on the battleship *Missouri,* a great honor, but he declined—only the men who fought in the Pacific, he believed, should attend. Still, there was no false modesty to him—he knew he was good and that was not by happenstance. Bill Sebald, the American ambassador to Japan, wrote a draft speech that Ridgway was to give on his arrival in Tokyo at the moment in 1951 when he finally replaced MacArthur as the commander of all American forces in the Far East and de facto governor-general of Japan. In it, Sebald had him saying "with due humility" Ridgway edited the phrase out. "Bill, I'm humble only before my own God, not before the Japanese people or anyone else."

He was not caught up in the vainglory of war. He never tried to sugarcoat what war was about. When he nicknamed his first major Korean offensive Operation Killer, he received a note from Army chief of staff Joe Collins, suggesting that such a name might be difficult for the Army's public relations people to deal with. Ridgway was not moved by the objections of PR people on this or any other issue. The name, he had been told, was too bloodthirsty and lacked sex appeal. Later he wrote, "I did not understand why it was objectionable to acknowledge that war was concerned with killing the enemy. . . . I am by nature opposed to any effort to 'sell' war to people as an only mildly unpleasant business that requires very little in the way of blood."

"All lives on a battlefield are equal," Ridgway once said, "and a dead rifleman is as great a loss in the eyes of God as a dead General."

He was aware that he was in charge of the most precious kind of national resource—the lives of young men who were dear to their parents. "All lives on a battlefield are equal," he once said, "and a dead rifleman is as great a loss in the eyes of God as a dead General. The dignity which attaches to the individual is the basis of Western Civilization, and this fact should be remembered by every Commander." That did not mean he did not fight the enemy with full ferocity or take a certain pleasure from a battlefield littered with their dead, for he knew the alternative, a battlefield littered with American dead. After

the Battle of Chipyongni in February 1951, when the Chinese finally broke and the Americans killed thousands with air and artillery strikes, one company commander had spoken of the battlefield as covered with "fricasseed Chinese." Ridgway liked that phrase.

There was a vast unacknowledged difference in his and MacArthur's concepts of leadership, produced not merely by greatly different temperaments, but by different visions of leadership in very different eras. So much of MacArthur's own energy went into building the commander up as a great man—as if, for the men in the ranks, fighting under so great a general would in itself make them great as well. Ridgway's concept of leadership was better suited for a more egalitarian era. He intended to impose his will on his men, but to allow the men under him to find something within themselves that would make them more confident, more purposeful fighting men. It was, then, their confidence in themselves that would make them fight well, he believed, not so much their belief in him. His job was to teach them to find that quality in themselves. Like MacArthur, however, he knew the importance of myth and was skilled at creating his own. "Old Iron Tits" was his nickname, based on the belief that it was two grenades he had pinned to the harness on his chest—one was a grenade, the other a medical kit. But the message was clear—Matt Ridgway was always ready to fight.

Ridgway arrived in Korea on December 26, 1950. The first thing he remembered was the cold—"It stuck to the bone," he noted. He had already flown to Tokyo and met with MacArthur, who told him, "The Eighth Army is yours, Matt. Do what you think best." That statement of itself signaled the end of one phase of the Korean War—in the past, everything had been run out of Tokyo. Now the command was his. The question was: Could he keep his troops from being driven off the peninsula? Because Korea was such a grinding war, with such an unsatisfactory outcome, not many military men emerged from it as heroes. Grim wars that end in stalemates may produce men who are heroes to other soldiers, but not to the public at large. Thus Ridgway was revered in years to come not so much by ordinary Americans, who had largely turned away from the war, but by the men who fought there and knew what he had done. In Korea he was the soldier's soldier. Gen. Omar Bradley, a plain-spoken Midwesterner not readily given to superlatives, wrote years later of Ridgway's performance in Korea, "It is not often in wartime that a single battlefield commander can make a decisive difference. But in Korea, Ridgway would prove to be the exception. His brilliant, driving, uncompromising leadership would turn the battle like no other general's in our military history."

On arrival Ridgway almost immediately started to tour forward positions. He was appalled by what he found: defeatist attitudes on the part of his commanders, low morale and almost no military intelligence of any significance. He visited one corps commander who did not even know the name of a nearby river. "My God almighty!" he said later of that particular piece of ignorance. How could there be decent intelligence when all the American units had broken off contact with the enemy and were fleeing south? "What I told the field commanders in essence," he later wrote, "was that their infantry ancestors would roll over in their graves could they see how road-bound this army was, how often it forgot to seize the high ground along its route, how it failed to seek and maintain contact in its front, how little it knew of the terrain, and how [it] seldom took advantage of it." He was sickened by finding an army broken in spirit, "not in retreat, but in flight," as Lt. Col. Harold Johnson, who had been at Unsan, said. Ridgway thought the corps commanders shockingly weak, the division and regimental commanders too old and more often than not out of touch as well as ill-prepared for this war. Nothing enraged him more than the maps at the various headquarters he visited. Each American unit, it seemed, was surrounded by little red flags, each flag indicating a Chinese division. But many of his units simply had no idea how many Chinese were near them because they were not sending out patrols. Not to know the location and strength of the enemy was in his eyes as great a sin as a commander could commit. He changed that quickly. He was everywhere in those days. He visited each headquarters, not just division and regimental, but sometimes battalion and company, arriving in his little plane flown by pilot Mike Lynch, landing where he had no business showing up and often where no airstrip existed. What he wanted was for the most forward units to go out and find the enemy. They were to patrol, patrol, patrol: "Nothing but your love of comfort binds you to the roads," he kept repeating. "Find the enemy and fix him in position. Find them! Fix them! Fight them! Finish them!"

"Nothing but your love of comfort binds you to the roads," he kept repeating. "Find the enemy. . . . Find them! Fix them! Fight them! Finish them!"

Very quickly he promulgated a new Ridgway rule of mapping. He would look at the local map with a red flag or two on it and ask when the last time was that the unit had had contact with the Chinese. At first the usual answer was four or five days—for most American units were in fact staying as far away from the Chinese as possible. With a gesture of complete contempt, he would then reach out and take the flags off the map. The new rule was that a red flag could stay on a map only if the unit had made contact in the previous 48 hours. The unstated corollary of this rule was equally simple: if the commander of the Eighth Army, a known and feared hard-ass, returned and found the situation unchanged, it would quite likely not just be the little red flag that would disappear but the unit commander as well.

With Ridgway's arrival, MacArthur, his forces defeated by the Chinese along the Chongchon and Yalu rivers, had not only lost his great gamble but in effect his command as well. The two men spent an hour and a half together in Tokyo on December 26, 1950, much of the time taken up by a monologue delivered by MacArthur. It was quickly clear what the commander in the Far East wanted.

"There isn't any question that MacArthur wanted to go to war," Ridgway would say later, "full war with Communist China. And he could not be convinced by all the contrary arguments. . . . He reluctantly acted in accordance with the policy, but he never did accept it."

Ridgway knew the limits of the hand he had been dealt. Washington wanted to bring the Chinese to the negotiating table without investing significantly more resources in Korea. That, Ridgway knew, would be his job, and it would be a bloody one—to make the Chinese pay so high a price that victory would seem as out of reach to them as it already seemed to Washington.

If there was going to be an unspoken limit on the number of divisions allotted him, then he would compensate with far greater firepower, especially more artillery—which was why he so quickly pressed for more artillery units. He was shocked—given the enormous potential advantage that artillery offered and the limits that the Chinese and North Korean styles of warfare placed on them—that the Americans had not emphasized their advantage in big guns earlier. Now he asked for ten more National Guard and Reserve artillery battalions. The use of artillery as a key factor in the kind of grinding war he was already envisioning was obvious. After all, the United States was rich with weaponry and ammunition but wanted to conserve its manpower; and the Chinese were desperately limited in their ability to bring heavy guns, which, in any case, would be vulnerable to U.S. air power, to the battlefield. Ridgway intended to even out the demographics in the crudest, crudest way possible—with long-range guns. The new artillery units were ordered in country as quickly as possible.

From the start Ridgway believed the war could be fought as what he called a meat grinder. On January 11, just two weeks after he had arrived in country, he had written his friend Ham Haislip, the Army's vice chief of staff, "the power is here. The strength and the means we have—short perhaps of Soviet military intervention. My one overriding problem, dominating all others, is to achieve the spiritual awakening of the latent capabilities of this command. If God permits me to do that, we shall achieve more, far more than our people think possible—and perhaps inflict a bloody defeat on the Chinese which even China will long remember, wanton as she is with the sacrifice of lives."

His confidence was contagious—and those who did not share it would soon find themselves at other jobs. He was changing the Eighth Army as quickly as he could into an effective fighting force. He understood something that few others realized at the time: the physical damage to the Eighth Army was less than everyone imagined; the real damage had been psychological or emotional. Some divisions had lost a great deal of equipment yes, but that could be replaced. The surprise that had resulted from stumbling into a giant Chinese trap at the Chongchon and Yalu rivers and fighting a brand-new enemy in such poorly chosen terrain had magnified the sense of damage and the resulting defeat had crushed his army's morale. That was what had to be rebuilt—the spiritual or psychological side of his force.

Ridgway was unintimidated by those early Chinese victories and the awesome size of the Chinese force; he seemed to have his finger on the strength and weakness of every unit and was full of confidence about what his forces could do. That was the way he had commanded in World War II. He was, his talented World War II deputy Jim Gavin once said, always drawn to the cutting edge of battle. "He was right up there every minute. Hard as flint and full of intensity, almost grinding his teeth with intensity; so much so that I thought that man's going to have a heart attack before it's over. Sometimes it seemed as though it was a personal thing: Ridgway versus the Wehrmacht. He'd stand in the middle of the road and urinate. I'd say: 'Matt, get the hell out of there. You'll get shot.' No! He was defiant. Even with his penis he was defiant."

In contrast to MacArthur, who never spent a night in Korea and who saw the war primarily in theoretical terms, Ridgway was there all the time. He wanted the fighting men in the field to know that he shared their knowledge and their hardships, and he wanted field commanders to know that he could not be fooled. His presence put everyone to a constant test of excellence. The Corps chief of staff later said of that period, "Oh God! He came to *every* briefing *every* morning. . . . He'd go out all day with the troops, then when he came back at night, I'd have to brief him again—on *everything,* even minor things like which way the water drained in our sector." Soon three division commanders were on their way home. They would be praised for what they had done, given medals and honorable new jobs, but the Eighth Army was not going to retreat any more.

The other thing they were going to do was know their enemy—one more sign that the days of grandiose contempt for an Asian enemy, so racist in origins, were over. More than most senior American commanders of his era, Matt Ridgway had a passion for intelligence. The American Army had always taken its intelligence functions somewhat casually; the men assigned to intelligence duty tended to have been passed over in their careers, not quite good enough for the prized command positions. Perhaps it was the nature of the modern American Army—it had so much force and materiel that when it finally joined battle, intelligence tended to be treated as secondary, on the assumption that any enemy could simply be out-muscled and ground down.

There were a number of reasons for Ridgway's obsession with intelligence. Some of it was his own superior intellectual abilities; he was simply smarter than most great commanders. Some of it was his innate conservatism, his belief that the better your intelligence, the fewer of your own men's lives you were likely to sacrifice. A great deal of it was his training in the airborne, where you made dangerous drops behind enemy lines with limited firepower and were almost always outnumbered and vulnerable to larger enemy forces.

The CIA, blocked from the Korean theater by MacArthur and Brig. Gen. Charles Willoughby, was soon welcomed back; there was going to be a healthy new respect for the enemy. The Chinese had identifiable characteristics on the battlefield. They also had good, tough soldiers. Some units were clearly better than others, some division commanders better than others and it was vital to know which these were and where they were. Now he intended to study them. There would be no more windy talk about the Oriental mind. The questions would be: How many

miles could they move on a given night? How fixed are their orders once a battle begins? How much ammo and food do they carry into each battle—that is, how long can they sustain a given battle? The essential question was: How *exactly* can we tilt the battlefield to our advantage?

Ridgway now intended to play at least as big a role in the selection of the battlefield as his Chinese opposites. For a time, he started his day by getting in a small plane and, with Lynch at the controls, flying as low as they could, looking for the enemy. With that many Chinese coming at his army, there had to be signs of them, evidence that they existed, but he saw almost nothing. That he found nothing did not create a lack of respect for them—rather it brought greater respect for the way they could move around, seemingly invisible. Gradually he began to put together a portrait of who they were and how they fought— and so, how he intended to fight them. The Chinese were good, no doubt about that. But they were not supermen, just ordinary human beings from a very poor country with limited resources. Not only did the Chinese operate from a large technological disadvantage, they had significant logistical and communications weaknesses. The bugles and flutes announcing their attacks could be terrifying in the middle of the night, but the truth was that they could not react quickly to sudden changes on the battle field. Certain logistical limitations were built into any attack they made—the ammunition and food they could carry was finite. The American Army could re-supply in a way inconceivable to the Chinese and so could sustain a given battle far longer.

Ridgway spent his first few weeks in country pressing everyone for information about the Chinese fighting machine. By the middle of January, he felt he knew what he needed to know. This war, he decided, was no longer going to be primarily about gaining terrain as an end in itself, but about selecting the most advantageous positions, making a stand and bleeding enemy forces, inflicting maximum casualties on them. At a certain point, even a country with a demographic pool like China's had to feel the pain from the loss of good troops. He wanted to speed up that moment.

The first thing he realized was that it was a disaster to retreat once the Chinese hit. The key to their offensive philosophy was to stab at a unit, create panic, and then, from advantageous positions already set up in its rear, maul it when it retreated. All armies are vulnerable in retreat, but an American unit, because of all its hardware, condemned to the narrow bending Korean roads, was exceptionally so. Ridgway's long training as an airborne man was critical to the strategy he sought now. He meant to create strong islands of his own, sustain unit integrity with great fields of fire and then let the enemy attack.

What Ridgway wanted to do was start the Eighth Army moving north again—for reasons of morale as much as anything. In mid-January, he began the process, sending Col. Mike Michaelis' 27th Regiment Wolfhounds toward Suwon. He named this first offensive action Operation Wolfhound in their honor. Michaelis had known Ridgway before Korea, but not well. Still, he had been struck by Ridgway's fierce beetle-eyed glare—that was how he would later describe it—that went right through you. Ridgway had been in Korea only a few days when he called Michaelis in.

"Michaelis, what are tanks for?" he asked.

"To kill, sir."

"Take your tanks to Suwon," Ridgway said.

"Fine sir," Michaelis answered. "It's easy to get them there. Getting them back is going to be more difficult because they [the Chinese] always cut the road behind you."

"Who said anything about coming back?" Ridgway answered. "If you can stay up there 24 hours, I'll send the division up. If the division can stay up there 24 hours, I'll send the corps up." That, thought Michaelis, was the start of a brand-new phase of the war, the beginning of the turnaround. Without the Chinese leadership realizing it, a very different American and U.N. Army were coming together in Korea.

By March 1951, Ridgway's leadership and tactical brilliance had turned near-certain defeat of U.N. forces into stalemate.

On April 11, 1951, President Truman removed MacArthur from command; Ridgway succeeded him as Allied Commander of the Far East. A cease-fire was declared on July 27, 1953. The peninsula remained divided at the 38th parallel.

U.S. casualties numbered 33,000 dead and 105,000 wounded. The South Koreans suffered 415,000 killed and 429,000 wounded. The Chinese and North Koreans maintained secrecy about their casualties: estimates are 1.5 million dead. A state of tension endures between the two Koreas, poised on either side of a 2.5-mile wide demilitarized zone. The United States maintains a force of some 28,000, including soldiers and marines, in South Korea.

DAVID HALBERSTAM died in an automobile accident on his way to interview former quarterback Y. A. Tittle last April.

As seen in *Smithsonian,* November 2007, pp. 56, 58–59, 61, 64, 67. Excerpt from *The Coldest Winter* by David Halberstam (The Amateurs Ltd., 2007).

Crisis at Central High

John A. Kirk recalls the dramatic events at Little Rock, Arkansas, fifty years ago this month, when a stand-off over the granting of black students acess to integrated education brought the civil rights agenda to international attention.

JOHN A. KIRK

On the morning of Wednesday, September 4th, 1957, fifteen-year-old Elizabeth Ann Eckford prepared for her first day of classes at Central High School in Little Rock, Arkansas. Leaving anxious parents behind, she caught the bus and alighted just a short distance from the school. About 400 people were gathered at the main entrance. Trying to avoid the crowd, Elizabeth attempted to enter by a side entrance. She was stopped by armed National Guard troops who had formed a cordon around the school. They directed Elizabeth to the main entrance. She made her way through the crowd, but found her path to entry blocked again. Elizabeth suddenly realized that she was at the mercy of a mob. 'Lynch her! Lynch her!' someone shouted. 'No nigger bitch is going to get in our school. Get out of here!' another screamed. Elizabeth made for the nearest bus stop, pursued by the mob. A bus soon arrived and sped her away from the scene before she could be harmed.

Fifty years ago this month, Elizabeth Eckford's first day of classes marked the beginning of what would become known as the Little Rock crisis. For almost a month, Elizabeth and eight other students who endeavored to attend Central High— Minnijean Brown, Ernest Green, Thelma Mothershed, Melba Pattillo, Gloria Ray, Terrance Roberts, Jefferson Thomas and Carlotta Walls—found themselves in the middle of a tug-of-war between federal and state power. The students, who would go down in history as the 'Little Rock Nine', placed their lives on the line at a pivotal moment in the unfolding struggle for black freedom and equality.

The crisis arose as a result of the US Supreme Court's 1954 *Brown v Board of Education* ruling that outlawed segregation in schools. The case was decided on a class action comprising five suits brought by lawyers of the leading civil rights organization of the time, the National Association for the Advancement of Colored People (NAACP). *Brown* overturned the legal doctrine of 'separate but equal' established in the 1896 *Plessy v Ferguson* case. This doctrine stated that 'separate' facilities provided for blacks and whites were legally acceptable provided that they were of an 'equal' standard. Using evidence from the newly developing field of psychology, the Court found that segregation affected the 'hearts and minds' of black students 'in a way ever unlikely to be undone'. Therefore, the Court concluded, 'in the field of public education the doctrine of "separate but equal" has no place.' Although the ruling pertained only to schools, the questioning of 'separate but equal' threatened the whole edifice of segregation in the southern states.

The ruling gave rise to virulent opposition in states of the lower South with large black populations. Many whites vowed a campaign of 'massive resistance' to school desegregation. In the face of this opposition, the position of the Supreme Court was further weakened by the responses of other branches of federal government. President Dwight D. Eisenhower refused to back the Court decision strongly in public. In private, he confided that his recent appointment of Supreme Court Chief Justice Earl Warren, who had handed down the *Brown* decision, was the 'biggest damn fool mistake' he had ever made. Many in Congress, particularly powerful southern politicians, refused to back the decision. In March 1956, 101 southern Congressmen signed the 'Southern Manifesto' condemning *Brown* as a 'clear abuse of judicial power'.

Not everyone opposed *Brown*. Alabama governor James 'Big Jim' Folsom declared that 'when the Supreme Court speaks, that's the law'. Even Mississippi governor James P. Coleman appealed for 'cool thinking' on the matter. Many white southern newspaper editors echoed these more moderate sentiments.

The key battlegrounds were upper South states where there were fewer blacks. A number of school districts in these states immediately moved to desegregate, not least because of the financial burden imposed by running a separate school system for what could often be just a handful of black students.

Three such districts—Bentonville, Charleston and Fayetteville—were in Arkansas. As one observer from the NAACP put it, the state appeared to be, the 'brightest prospect among the southern states for integration'. In 1948, the University of Arkansas had been the first southern university to admit a black student voluntarily. In the state capital of Little Rock, tentative progress had been made in a number of areas. Limited desegregation had taken place at the city library and the city zoo. Some downtown stores had removed 'white' and 'colored' signs from their drinking fountains. In 1956, as blacks in Montgomery, Alabama, boycotted for thirteen months to end segregation on city buses amid white violence, public transportation in Little Rock desegregated without incident.

The initial signs were that school desegregation would proceed in a similar manner. Arkansas Governor Francis Cherry told reporters the state would 'obey the law'. The Little Rock school board was one of the first in the nation to draw up integration plans. These plans involved building two new schools, Horace Mann High in the predominantly black eastern part of the city, and Hall High in the affluent white suburbs of the west. Superintendent of schools, Virgil T. Blossom, stressed that the two new schools, in black and white residential areas respectively, would not have a set racial designation. He assured local blacks that the school board planned to desegregate all three of the city's high schools, Horace Mann, Hall High and Central High, along colour-blind attendance zones in 1957.

The Supreme Court's implementation order for *Brown,* handed down on May 31st, 1955, and known as *Brown II,* was a blow for advocates of desegregation. In 1954, the Court purposefully left to one side the question of implementing its decision. A year later, amid growing opposition, it appeared to back down. *Brown II* gave neither definite deadlines for when desegregation should begin nor firm guidelines for how it should be carried out. It devolved these responsibilities to local school boards and state judges, many of whom were at best lukewarm about desegregation. The Court ambiguously instructed them to make a 'prompt and reasonable start' to end segregation 'with all deliberate speed'.

Just before the Court handed down its implementation order, the Little Rock school board changed its desegregation plans. It introduced a transfer system to allow white students to opt out of attendance at Horace Mann High without giving black students the chance to transfer to the white Hall High. Moreover, it allocated an all-black teaching staff to Horace Mann and opened it as a segregated black school in February 1956, a year before it was due to desegregate. The Little Rock branch of the NAACP assisted thirty-three black students with applications for admission to white schools in the district. Their applications were turned down. On February 8th, 1956, local NAACP attorney Wiley Branton filed suit against the school board for desegregation under the title of *Aaron v. Cooper.*

When the NAACP sent its southwest regional attorney Ulysses Simpson Tare to assist Branton, Tare undermined the case of the local NAACP. Local blacks wanted the courts to uphold the school board's original desegregation plans. At the trial in August 1956, Tate ignored this and argued for the immediate and complete integration of all schools. The District Court backed the school board's modified school desegregation plan. In March 1957, the Appeals Court reaffirmed that decision, stating that the school board's proposals operated within a timetable that was reasonable under the guidelines of *Brown II.* However, it also ruled that the school board was now obliged to carry out its modified plan beginning in September 1957.

After further efforts to discourage black applications to white schools, Virgil Blossom managed to get the total number of applicants down to just seventeen. He decreed that they would be allowed only in to one school, downtown Central High, with 2,000 white students. After eight more students dropped out, only nine remained. The head of the state NAACP, journalist Daisy Bates, took on the job of counselling the nine students through their ordeal.

On the night of September 2nd, 1957, the day before Central High was due to desegregate, Governor Orval Faubus called out the National Guard to surround the school. Faubus had not up to now made his position on school desegregation clear. The son of a socialist, Faubus came from northwest Arkansas, an area with a relatively small black population. He had a track record as a liberal-leaning politician. Winning election for the first time in 1954, he had played down the school desegregation issue. But when his failure to take a strong stand for segregation became a political liability, Faubus slowly adopted segregationist rhetoric. This process accelerated when he was challenged for the governorship in 1956 by head of the Arkansas White Citizens' Council, James D. Johnson.

After winning re-election, however, Faubus dropped the facade. His actions in September 1957 were a calculated bid for political power when he finally decided that there were more votes in opposing desegregation than in supporting it. He was right: it won him an unprecedented six consecutive terms in office.

Elizabeth Eckford's lonely attempt to enroll at Central High on the morning of September 4th, was because of a lapse in communications with Daisy Bates. Bates had called the eight other students the night before to arrange a rendezvous with two white and two black church ministers who would act as their chaperones the following morning. Elizabeth's family did not have a telephone and therefore did not get the message. As Daisy and her husband, L.C. Bates, were driving to meet with the other eight students, they heard a radio report about Elizabeth's mobbing. Mortified, L.C. Bates leapt out of the car to go and find her. Daisy Bates went on to the prearranged meeting point. When they arrived at Central High, the students and the ministers, jostled and shoved by the mob, were refused entry by National Guardsmen.

Faubus's actions placed him in open defiance of the courts. A terse exchange of telegrams between President Eisenhower and the governor followed over the next few days. A face-to-face meeting between the two men at the President's Newport, Rhode Island, retreat on September 14th produced little consensus. Although Eisenhower verbally rebuked Faubus for his actions, he still refused to intervene.

A legal resolution of the matter appeared to be the most likely outcome. On the day of Elizabeth's mobbing, the Little Rock school board asked the District Court to suspend its integration order because of the violence and disorder that had occurred. On September 6th, attorney Wiley Branton demanded that desegregation proceed as planned. The next day, the court turned down the school board's request for a delay. On Monday morning, September 9th, a temporary replacement to the court bench from North Dakota, Judge Ronald Davies, received a full report on the situation in Little Rock from the office of US Attorney General Herbert Brownell. Davies indicated that the federal government should file a petition against Governor Faubus and National Guard commanders to prevent them from interfering with the court order.

Faubus absented himself from the trial on September 20th. In an extraordinary move, Faubus's attorneys declared that the governor did not recognize the District Court's authority. After the hearing, Davies granted an injunction prohibiting Faubus or anyone under his orders from interfering with school desegregation. Three hours later, Faubus conceded defeat and removed the National Guard. Refusing to accept any responsibility for the dire situation that his actions had created, Faubus removed himself from events by flying off to attend the Southern Governors' Conference at Sea Island, Georgia.

In the Eye of the Storm

Dale Hanks, a National Guardsman in Little Rock in 1957, Describes His Recollection of the Events at Central High

After a mob of a thousand outraged segregationists gathered at Little Rock Central High on September 23rd, 1957, and the police slipped the Nine in through a side entrance, a volcano of hate erupted in the rabble. By noon, the Little Rock police chief had quit. The President ordered the military into action, and by the end of the following day, 1,100 men from the 101st Airborne Division had arrived. These federal troops deployed around the school to enforce orders for integration of the school.

At the same time, President Eisenhower removed the Arkansas National Guard from Governor Faubus's control. The 101st Airborne troops were meant to be a temporary measure until National Guard units could be assembled to replace them. Eisenhower wanted these units to come from outside Little Rock to avoid cases of 'brother against brother'—and that is how my soldiers and I came to be at Central High.

Most of our troops lived either in Walnut Ridge, or Hoxie, 130 miles from Little Rock. Practically all of our soldiers were born and raised in northeast Arkansas as were their parents and grandparents. Our roster included rice and cattle farmers, laborers, truck drivers, mechanics, construction workers, gas station attendants, and other such jobs. All were male and white. Proud to wear their National Guard uniforms, they were committed to serving their state and country. They grimaced at the thought of 'federal interference' with their public schools.

As we made our way to Little Rock, it seemed that our troops' animosity was directed not so much at the blacks seeking school desegregation, but toward the federal government's efforts at 'race mixing.' In light of Governor Faubus's recent actions toward federal authority, it was not implausible that he intended to use the National Guard forcefully to remove the US Army troops from Central High. Such a move would have been catastrophic, but there was no doubt in my mind at the time that our National Guard soldiers would do their duty.

But, sadly for some, the match-up was not to be. We had been federalized and were now part of the US Army, no longer under the control of the Governor. I was relieved, but it was a pity for the radical element that itched for a fight with the Feds.

Our simple mission was easier said than done: 'To enforce the orders of the Federal Courts with respect to the attendance of the public schools in Little Rock of all those who are properly enrolled, and to maintain law and order while doing so.'

It was clear that the US Army's commander of the Arkansas Military District did not trust us and had conveyed his distrust to the regular army soldiers. I sensed a considerable amount of tension between us and the 101st troops as we met in a change of command ceremony.

As long as the National Guard kept the Nine out of Central High School, we were heroes to those opposed to desegregation. However, the day we arrived in Little Rock to be used as an instrument of school integration, we became traitors and turncoats. We were prepared for our military mission, but not for the abuse that was soon heaped upon us. Die-hard segregationists across the state grew to hate us with a passion.

Our new status was made public on a beautiful Thursday morning, October 3rd. As a young First Lieutenant, I waited to move out with a detachment of twenty Guardsmen, sons of the South who had grown up in a culture where racial segregation was socially respectable. Our soldiers, like most white Arkansans, agreed that if God had intended the races to be mixed, he would not have made people different colours.

As the nine students got out of the station wagon, our troops formed a V-shaped configuration like a wedge. This riot formation allowed the students to walk double file inside the V and to be protected from all sides. I was confident that my men had the physical capabilities to manage a mob, but I couldn't shake my concern about their mental readiness to take those nine black kids into the school.

These young Guardsmen were now closer to a black person than they had ever been. And they were about to commit the most appalling act of aiding and abetting racial integration while the whole world watched. After a lifetime in a deep-rooted segregationist culture, this was a bitter pill to swallow. Despite whatever misgivings my troops may have harboured, when I gave the command to move out, the sudden, determined look in their eyes told me that I had worried unnecessarily. They were ready.

Our adversaries, a pack of angry, white male students sporting fashionable duck-tail haircuts, saddle oxfords, white socks, and trademark jeans were digging in on the front steps of the school. They were ready to defend it head on. Like us, they had put their big guys up front. The large doors at the main entrance had become an important symbol of resistance. The previous two mornings they had successfully blocked the black students' access through the main entrance. The Nine finally gained entrance through a side door.

But this day, it would be different. As we set out on our course across the campus, I took my place behind the students inside the formation to cover their backs. Most of these National Guard kids were not much older than the black kids they were protecting, and close to the age of the white students they would soon confront. I was in my twenties, but feeling like an old man.

The hecklers grew quiet in disbelief that fellow Arkies would use brute force to take black folks into a white school. Not a sound could be heard but our marching feet.

With rifles at port arms and sheathed bayonets attached, we moved up the steep, wide steps and came face to face with the junior mob. If the hatred in their eyes could have killed, we would all have been instant casualties. We continued on through the fifty to sixty sullen students. One by one, they grudgingly gave way.

When we reached the front entrance at the top of the steps, the 101st troops inside the building opened the doors

(continued)

and assumed charge of security for the black students as they moved about the school during the day. An hour later a group of white students walked out of the building and set fire to an effigy of a black person on Park Street in front of the school.

The reaction to these events was violent: I was pursued on my way to a football game by four or five tough guys in a beat-up green Pontiac, and the next day a grim-faced guy in a big black Buick slammed into my rear and took several other runs at me. But the animosity toward us was age and gender-free. A few days later, I took twenty soldiers to a barber shop for haircuts. We were approached by two little old ladies who proceeded to rebuke us every step of the way for two whole blocks.

Their language was rich and full-bodied, 'You no-count sonsabitches'; 'You dirty, rotten, lowdown, goddam, traitors;' 'You turncoat bastards'. In the midst of this chaos, my guys kept their wits about them, and remained true to their mission. They never quit.

It was not until February 23rd, 2007, that the Little Rock School District was released from federal court supervision of its desegregation efforts—almost fifty years after my young men and I escorted the Little Rock Nine into Central High School.

I moved to Virginia. I have been to Little Rock since, and likely will go there another time. But I can tell you this: next time I visit and talk to the folks there, I still will not divulge this small claim to fame.

The following Monday morning, September 23rd, all nine black students were with Daisy Bates at her home waiting for news about what would happen next. The Little Rock police department, which in the absence of Faubus and the National Guard was charged with upholding law and order in the city, telephoned with a warning that a mob of over 1,000 whites was gathered at Central High. The police agreed to meet Bates and the nine students near the school to provide an escort into a side entrance.

Bates told black reporters based at her home to go on ahead to Central High. When they arrived, the mob mistook them for the student entourage. 'Here they come!' shouted one. 'Get the niggers! Get 'em.' At the precise moment that the mob descended upon the black reporters and started to beat them, the nine students arrived and were swiftly taken into the school through the side entrance. Realizing what had happened, a mob member shouted 'They're in! The niggers are in!'

Throughout the morning a white female student supplied a series of false reports to media correspondents about the mobbing of black students inside the school. The reports were broadcast unchecked and unsubstantiated. This was terrifying for the parents of the nine, who had been told to stay away from the school. Indeed, not all of them knew about their offspring's plans to attend Central. Gloria Ray's father, Harvey, had been kept in the dark by his daughter and her mother, since they feared what it would do to the sixty-eight-year-old who had a heart condition. He first learned his daughter was one of the nine while watching his television set at home. Easing tensions a little, white attorney Edwin Dunaway, a friend of both Daisy Bates and the assistant chief of police, acted as an intermediary to provide regular reassurance that the students were unharmed. Yet as the morning wore on, the mob refused to disperse and began to overpower the police. Eventually the students were removed for their own safety.

The scenes of lawlessness brought an angry response from President Eisenhower. He issued a statement condemning the behaviour of the mob as 'disgraceful' and sent out a proclamation commanding 'all persons engaged in such obstruction of justice to cease and desist'. The next day, a defiant mob again assembled outside Central High. Eisenhower had little choice but to act. He issued Executive Order 10730, bringing the Arkansas National Guard under his command and sending in an additional thousand soldiers of the 101st 'Screaming Eagles' Airborne Division of the US Army.

On September 25th, federal troops arrived at Daisy Bates' home to take the nine black students to Central High. The Bates and the parents of the nine waved them off, proud at the courage of the young students in refusing to be intimidated by the mob. At the school, a mob again gathered waiting for the students to arrive. When a federal officer asked them to disperse, they refused. Federal troops then moved them on at bayonet-point. A host of international, national and local media representatives watched the nine students enter Central High flanked by twenty-two armed federal troops. After school, federal troops took the students back home again. The escort would become part of the students' daily routine.

Entry into Central High was, the nine students soon discovered, not an end to their troubles. Over the ensuing weeks, the students were subject to 'threatening notes, verbal insults and threats, crowding, bumping and jostling in the halls'. Having lost the battle to keep the black students out of the school, segregationists turned their attention, and tried to encourage white students to do the same, to making life for the nine so unbearable inside the school that they would withdraw voluntarily. They failed. One student, Minnijean Brown, was expelled for retaliating to her tormentors in February 1958, although no white students were ever expelled for their actions. The rest of the nine survived the school year. In May 1958, Ernest Green became the first black student to graduate from Central High. Civil rights leader Martin Luther King, Jr. attended the graduation ceremony in support.

Outside school, the adults in the black community were also subject to white hostility. A number of parents of the nine were dismissed from their jobs. The Bates' home was regularly attacked. State agents of the Internal Revenue Service began to take a special interest in their finances. Arkansas Attorney General Bruce Bennett applied pressure to try to get Daisy Bates to identify NAACP members, which she resisted on the basis that they would be targeted for 'reprisals, recriminations and unwarranted hardship'. The hardest blow segregationists struck was in encouraging white advertisers to boycott the newspaper co-owned by the Bates, the *Arkansas State Press,* which led to the paper's eventual collapse in October 1959.

In early 1958, attention switched back to the courts. The school board appealed to the District Court for a two-and-half-year delay of their desegregation plan, by which time they erroneously believed Faubus would be out of office. On June 21st, the court upheld the request. On August 18th, the Appeals Court overruled that decision. School board attorneys then indicated that they would take their case to the US Supreme Court. On August 28th, the Court met in a special session to hear the case. On September 12th, in the landmark ruling of *Cooper v. Aaron,* the Court said that violence and disruption were not justifiable reasons for delaying school desegregation.

Governor Faubus again intervened. He called a special session of the Arkansas General Assembly and rushed through a battery of pro-segregation legislation. One bill allowed Faubus to close any school forced to integrate by federal order. With the school closed, voters in the local district would then participate in a referendum to decide if the school should reopen on an integrated basis. On the day that the Court ordered integration to proceed, Faubus closed all of the city's schools. In the referendum held on September 27th, the governor handily stacked the cards in his favour by providing a stark choice between keeping the schools closed or accepting 'complete and total integration'. By a margin of 19,470 to 7,561 votes, the electorate decided to keep the schools closed.

The disarray finally prompted Little Rock's white elite to mobilize to rescue the schools from the segregationists. At the referendum election, a group of influential white women had organized the Women's Emergency Committee to Open our Schools (WEC). Though unsuccessful, they continued to pressure white businessmen and professionals to act, not least on the grounds of the negative financial impact events were having on the city. Prior to September 1957, Little Rock's economy had been booming. Since then, outside investment had dried up altogether. The WEC successfully lobbied for a slate of business-backed candidates to stand against segregationist candidates at the school board elections in December 1958. The results produced a divided board of three segregationists and three business-backed candidates. In May 1959, segregationist school board members proposed not to renew the contracts of forty-four school district employees perceived as unsympathetic to their cause. This precipitated a recall election at which business candidates finally wrested control out of the segregationist's hands. The new board then drew up plans to integrate schools on a token basis in August 1959. When August arrived, five black students peacefully integrated two city schools.

The re-opening of schools was a victory, but not an end to the struggle over school desegregation in Little Rock or elsewhere. Numerous plans for achieving meaningful desegregation were debated nationally through the 1960s. The next major milestones were two US Supreme Court rulings in 1968 and 1971 which introduced much more stringent measures for school desegregation. The 1968 *Green v. New Kent County* decision said that school boards had a duty to end segregation 'root and branch' by achieving 'unitary status'—that is, by eliminating racial discrimination altogether. The 1971 *Swann v. Charlotte-Mecklenburg Board of Education* decision permitted the 'busing' of black and white students city-wide to achieve this.

Such measures only fuelled 'white flight' out of city school districts and into suburban private schools. This coincided with longer-term urban renewal projects drawn up by city planners, which had been underway since the late 1940s, to create more geographical segregation, by manipulating construction plans and the housing market. In Little Rock, during the 1960s and 1970s, 41,000 whites moved from east to west of the city, while 17,000 blacks moved—or were moved—in the opposite direction. This figure represented about a third of the city's total population. In 2003, the *Arkansas Democrat-Gazette* reported a tipping point had been reached and Little Rock had become 'a city of mostly black public schools and mostly white private schools'.

In February 2007, the courts finally declared the Little Rock school district 'unitary', bringing to an end five decades of litigation. From being a 25 per cent black minority school district in 1957, it has become a 25 per cent white minority school district in 2007. In effect, the courts ruled on the basis that there were no white students left to integrate. Recent rulings of a much more conservative US Supreme Court have curtailed the means by which integration can lawfully be achieved. There are those who claim the spirit of *Brown* has now been undermined altogether. On the fiftieth anniversary of the Little Rock crisis, national and local remembrance of events will focus on the overcoming of racial hatred and the successful integration of Central High School. The Little Rock Nine, presented with Congressional Gold Medals in 1999 by an Arkansas President, Bill Clinton, are quite rightly feted as heroes. But there is another side to the story. As events since 1957 illustrate, Little Rock remains part of an ongoing struggle to deliver justice and equality for all America's schoolchildren. Whether that will ever be achieved remains to be seen.

Reference

Daisy Bates, *The Long Shadow of Little Rock: A Memoir* (David McKay Company, Inc., 1962, repr. University of Arkansas Press); Melba Pattillo Beals, *Warriors Don't Cry: A Searing Memoir of the Battle to Integrate Little Rock's Central High* (Pocket Books, 1994); Tony A. Freyer, *Little Rock on Trial: Cooper v Aaron and School Desegregation* (University Press of Kansas, 2007); Elizabeth Jacoway, *Turn Away Thy Son: Little Rock, the Crisis that Shocked a Nation* (Free Press, 2007); John A. Kirk, *Beyond Little Rock: The Origins and Legacies of the Central High Crisis* (University of Arkansas Press, 2007); John A. Kirk, *Redefining the Color Line: Black Activism in Little Rock Arkansas, 1940–70* (University Press of Florida, 2002); Roy Reed, *Faubus: The Life and Times of an American Prodigal* (University of Arkansas Press, 1997).

JOHN A. KIRK is a Professor of US History at Royal Holloway, University of London.

Launch of a New World

Fifty years ago, Sputnik transformed the way Americans viewed our planet.

Joel Achenbach

News flash, Oct. 4, 1957: The Russians have launched a tiny moon. It is an artificial satellite, 184 pounds, a pumpkin-size sphere polished to a shine. The Russians call it Sputnik. As it passes over the United States it transmits a signal—surely the most ominous beep-beep-beep that any American has ever heard.

"The communists were going to rule," recalled Homer Hickam, who was 14 when he saw Sputnik in the sky above his home town of Coalwood, W.Va., and who would go on to become a spacecraft designer. "And the proof of this was this shiny little bauble that flew around the world every 90 minutes."

Rocket engineer Julian Davidson, dismayed at being beaten into space, remembers a radio commercial that night—an ad for a new Gillette razor. "The Russians just launched a satellite," he says, "and I'm listening to an ad for a great technology the Americans had for making razor blades."

Sputnik and its aftermath are a familiar tale at this point—the story of a fat and happy superpower suddenly finding itself in a full-blown existential crisis but shaking free of its torpor, revamping science and math education, and winning the race to the moon.

Fifty years later, however, the standard narrative of disaster, recovery and triumph is being overhauled by historians. They're more likely to speak of Sputnik's impact as a shock to the system that incited political maneuverings and media misinformation. Much that seemed certain in October 1957 turned out to be misunderstood or purely illusory.

Humans have not set up space colonies or left boot prints on Mars, as widely predicted, but we have launched a stunning number of new Sputniks—thousands of satellites for communications, navigation and surveillance that have changed everything from how we fight wars to how our rental cars guide us to our hotels.

One result of Sputnik had nothing to do with space. It was the creation of the Pentagon's Defense Advanced Research Projects Agency, a technology think tank that went on to develop a computer network called Arpanet. Arpanet evolved into the Internet.

"The great irony is that what we actually saw in space, what we actually accomplished in space, was strikingly different but ultimately more significant than what was anticipated," says Roger Launius, senior curator at the National Air and Space Museum.

More broadly, the Space Age, so famously inaugurated by Sputnik, has taken on new shadings in recent years. The "conquest of space" has never played out according to script: Sputnik signaled the moment when humankind escaped the gravity well of the planet, but rather than propelling us to the stars, space technology keeps turning back toward terrestrial needs and desires.

"Is spaceflight about leaving this planet," asks Launius, "or is spaceflight about making this planet more humane and a better place for humans to reside?"

In 1957 anyone who read popular culture knew of the coming age of space travel. Space buffs had devoured a series of articles in *Collier's* magazine written by Wernher von Braun, the former Nazi scientist who had been invited to come to the United States to work on rockets. Von Braun envisioned space colonies, moon missions and astronauts on Mars.

Americans presumed that the space era would begin with the launch of Vanguard, a small U.S. satellite, as part of a global scientific program called the International Geophysical Year. The Soviets announced their own intentions to put up a satellite, but few people gave the claim any credence.

The big event scheduled in the United States for Friday night, Oct. 4, was the premiere of a CBS television series, "Leave It to Beaver."

Nikita Khrushchev, the Soviet leader, had taken his son Sergei, then a 22-year-old engineering student, to a meeting of Ukrainian officials in Kiev. It was nearing midnight, Sergei Khrushchev recalled, when an aide summoned his father to the phone. He soon returned, smiling broadly, and announced the launch of Sputnik.

Not everyone was surprised that Sputnik Night. Ernst Stuhlinger, a rocket scientist, now 93, had followed von Braun to the United States along with 116 other German scientists. On Sept. 27, 1957, Stuhlinger warned Army Gen. John Medaris, head of the Army Ballistic Missile Agency in Huntsville, Ala., that the Soviets were on the verge of launching a satellite. Medaris told him the Soviets weren't yet capable.

Stuhlinger, now 93, remembers being in a taxi in Barcelona when the Sputnik bulletin came over the radio. "I told you so," he said to himself.

Sputnik made the popular President Dwight D. Eisenhower suddenly appear out of touch, almost semi-retired. Paul Dickson's "Sputnik: The Shock of the Century" reports that Eisenhower played golf five times during the week of Sputnik's launch.

But Eisenhower had his own geopolitical calculations that the public knew nothing about. He wanted to avoid the militarization of space and insisted that the first American satellite would use a nonmilitary rocket. He knew that the United States would soon have spy satellites for observing the Soviets.

What he didn't anticipate was the public relations disaster that the "Red moon" would become for him. Even the Soviets underplayed the achievement initially. Their 15-paragraph announcement was matter-of-fact, except for the concluding sentence:

"Artificial earth satellites will pave the way for space travel and it seems that the present generation will witness how the freed and conscious labor of the people of the new socialist society turns even the most daring of man's dreams into reality."

Sputnik's polished aluminum exterior made it visible from the ground after dusk and before dawn as the satellite reflected the sun's rays. Many Americans lacked any understanding of the Newtonian mechanics of orbiting objects. They wondered why Sputnik didn't fall to the ground.

The political and media riot lasted for months. People suspected that Sputnik was spying on the United States. Was the beep-beep-beep a secret code? Pundits decried the softness of an American society that cared more about the size of automobile tail fins than the long struggle against the communists. Democrats in Congress saw political opportunity, and aerospace corporations envisioned new profits. Lyndon B. Johnson, the Senate majority leader, warned that the Soviets would soon build space platforms and drop bombs on America "like kids dropping rocks onto cars from freeway overpasses." Sen. Mike Mansfield declared, "What is at stake is nothing less than our survival."

A month after Sputnik I came Sputnik II, with a massive payload of more than 1,000 pounds and containing an ill-fated dog named Laika. "Soviets Orbit Second Artificial Moon; Communist Dog in Space," read one headline. A *Life* magazine column ran under the banner "Arguing the Case for Being Panicky."

The United States tried to launch its own satellite, Vanguard, but as the nation watched on live television, the rocket rose just four feet and exploded. Johnson called it "one of the best publicized—and most humiliating—failures in our history."

Many Americans literally went to ground, building bomb shelters. "The public relations impact of Sputnik in October of '57 never faded away until the election of 1960," says William Ewald, who was one of Eisenhower's speechwriters. "Everyone's speeches—'The Russians are coming, they're 10 feet tall,

they're 12 feet tall, they're ahead of us in outer space.' People were talking about the missile gap, which did not exist."

Today we know that the United States wasn't behind the Soviet Union technologically. One reason the Soviet Union had bigger rockets was that, unlike the United States, it didn't have the technology to miniaturize the nuclear weapons that intercontinental missiles would deliver.

A new book on Sputnik, "Red Moon Rising" by Matthew Brzezinski, reports that the Soviets were desperately afraid that the United States would launch a preemptive nuclear attack. The satellite Sputnik was never as important as the R-7 rocket that delivered it—and that served notice that the Soviets potentially could strike America with intercontinental missiles.

"Sputnik was never about space or the satellite. It was always about the missile, the rocket it rode on," Brzezinski said in an interview.

In 1957, many basic features of space were unknown. No one knew if Venus or Mars or any other planets in the solar system were habitable. Textbooks still taught that the shifting surface characteristics of Mars, observed through telescopes, might be the seasonal fluctuations of vegetation. Robotic probes eventually showed that they are caused by dust storms.

Half a century ago, no one could have predicted the boom-and-bust nature of human spaceflight. But now the Apollo triumph looks in retrospect like a heroic Cold War stunt. "Beating the Russians was everything. Going into space was almost secondary," says Hickam, author of the book "Rocket Boys," which was adapted for the movie "October Sky."

No human beings have gone beyond low Earth orbit since 1972. The international space station, a version of which was envisioned as long ago as the early 1950s, has yet to be completed.

There are bold plans at NASA for a return to the moon near the end of the next decade, about the time of the 50th anniversary of Apollo 11. But the space agency will have to achieve this feat on a tight budget, using spacecraft architecture that resembles that of Apollo. Much of the glory of post-Apollo spaceflight has belonged to unmanned probes and orbiting telescopes.

Perhaps satellites have been the real story of spaceflight all along.

"I thought eventually we'd have a few satellites in orbit, but not hundreds," says Konrad Dannenberg, 95, another of the German scientists on the von Braun team.

About 6,600 satellites of one kind or another have been launched since Sputnik, according to Jonathan McDowell, an astronomer at the Harvard-Smithsonian Center for Astrophysics. He says 850 to 920 are in active operation, and of those, 568 are for communications.

Sergei Khrushchev, now a senior fellow at Brown University, cites the proliferation of satellites when he speaks of the historical significance of Sputnik Night:

"It is the beginning," he says, "of the new world."

On the 50th anniversary of the Space Age, few people use the term "Space Age" anymore. It's the Information Age now, and the era of globalization. Space technology has played a key role in the creation of a highly networked, accelerated, communications-saturated civilization.

People who have grown up in the age of satellites may find them no more remarkable than streetlights or storm sewers. They're infrastructure.

Sputnik plus the Internet equals Google Maps. Click on "Satellite," zoom in, and you can see your house from space.

From *The Washington Post National Weekly Edition,* October 8–14, 2007, p. 13. Copyright © 2007 by Washington Post Writers Group. Reprinted by permission via PARS International Corp.

Will the Left Ever Learn to Communicate across Generations?

Maurice Isserman

When 32-year-old Michael Harrington, a veteran socialist activist, first met 20-year-old Tom Hayden at a student conference on civil rights in Ann Arbor, Mich., in the spring of 1960, he found him "unprepossessing, a nondescript youth of no great presence," yet burning with "an intense leftist commitment." Harrington tried without success to recruit Hayden, a University of Michigan undergraduate, into the Young People's Socialist League, the youth affiliate of the Socialist Party that was Harrington's political home at the time. Hayden declined. "Socialism" seemed a needlessly esoteric word to the younger man, Harrington recalled: "He wanted to speak American."

Hayden would go on two years later to do just that by writing the Port Huron Statement, the founding document of Students for a Democratic Society. Harrington had mixed feelings about that document, approving of its moral passion for change, its support of civil rights, and its call for the creation of a "participatory democracy" in the United States, but disapproving of Hayden's apparent lack of anti-Soviet zeal. At the conference that adopted the manifesto, Harrington wound up alienating SDS leaders by attacking them in a famously intemperate political diatribe.

When 28-year-old Tom Hayden, by then a veteran New Left activist, first met 20-year-old Mark Rudd in the midst of the Columbia University student strike in the spring of 1968, he found him "a new type of campus leader," who could be "disarmingly personal, a young boy," but at the same time possessed by "an embryo of fanaticism." Rudd, leader of the so-called "action faction" of Columbia's SDS chapter, "considered SDS intellectuals impediments to action," according to Hayden. Hayden felt "slightly irrelevant in his presence."

I wish Harrington and Hayden had found a better way to sort out their differences at Port Huron in 1962. I also wish Rudd had been less impatient with his SDS elders in 1968. When Rudd first arrived at Columbia three years earlier, he had read the Port Huron Statement admiringly, but at the time of the Columbia strike he had abandoned the belief expressed in the statement, and central to the early SDS's political vision, that the American New Left "must be, in large measure, a left with real intellectual skills, committed to deliberativeness, honesty, reflection as working tools."

> **Some of the history of the 1960s might have worked out differently if the politics of the American left had been less marked by striking generational discontinuities.**

Some of the history of the 1960s might have worked out differently, and for the better, if the politics of the American left had been less marked by such striking generational discontinuities. As another SDS leader, Todd Gitlin, would write in his look back at the decade, *The Sixties: Years of Hope, Days of Rage* (1987), in the early years of the decade Harrington was key to the future of the New Left "because he was the one person who might have mediated across the generational divide." At a moment when a new generation of young radicals is gathering strength on some college campuses—sometimes grouped under the banner of a revived SDS—there may be value in reviewing this cautionary tale of miscommunication.

Harrington, who died in 1989 at the age of 61, is best remembered as author of *The Other America: Poverty in the United States* (1962), the book credited with sparking Lyndon Johnson's War on Poverty. But he also left another important legacy: the scores of disciples he inspired to take on the steady work of democratic radicalism. Harrington thought a great deal about the challenges of passing on his political insight and experience to younger generations. He had a real gift as a political talent spotter, and numerous "Harringtonites" (a term never used in his lifetime, but descriptive nonetheless) can be spotted in the labor movement, in elected office, and in progressive organizations and publications, as well as among the ranks of what critics have called "tenured radicals."

A number of the latter, myself included, gathered at a symposium late last year at New York University's Tamiment Library & Robert F. Wagner Labor Archives to mark the opening of Harrington's papers, the latest addition to its collection on radical history. In my comments on Harrington's political career and legacy, I focused on his arrival in New York in 1949, at 21, and the steps that led him steadily leftward over the next several years. Harrington's letters from that period, part of the

Tamiment holdings, offer a case study in youthful enthusiasm, indecision, identity crisis, and the beginnings of a lifelong commitment to the cause of social justice.

In those early letters, the young author reveals himself as very much a work in progress, still signing off with his childhood nickname "Ned." Shortly after Christmas 1949, he wrote his conservative Roman Catholic parents back home in St. Louis from his apartment in Greenwich Village. Edward and Catherine Harrington disapproved of their son's New York venture, as they had when he had, in rapid succession, dropped out of Yale Law School and the graduate program in English at the University of Chicago. Harrington's reason for moving to New York—in the great tradition of young men and women of literary inclination and Midwest origins—was to become a writer. But in his letter, he confessed to having made a terrible mistake. The only thing Greenwich Village offered, he now understood, was a setting designed to ruin artists. "It no longer means artistic freedom, it now means sexual freedom," he said. "In this short time, I have grown afraid of these people who sit around in bars and talk literature all the time, talk of creating all the time, and never get to anything more than sitting around in bars."

Contrite, Harrington promised to re-enroll in the English department at Chicago for the spring semester. But in the weeks that followed, he would change his mind yet again; he was to remain a New Yorker and a Villager (the latter at least in spirit) for the rest of his life.

Before another year had passed, Harrington had acquired his first girlfriend in New York (there would be quite a few successors)—a young woman who fortunately held on to many of his love letters, which finally made their way to the Tamiment. He had been on a "Dostoevsky kick," he wrote her in 1950. In another letter to her that year, he revealed that he was considering leaving the Catholic Church: "I need God as I need food and sleep, but tracing his face with my fingers seems a long way off—a terribly long way."

There's no reason to doubt Harrington's spiritual anguish, for after years of Jesuit education, in high school and at Holy Cross University, he took such concerns seriously. But God and Dostoevsky were not the only things on his mind; his friends from the era remember a bright, funny, irrepressible young man, obviously intended to accomplish great things when he finally found himself.

Consider, finally, this letter in the Tamiment archives, written in January 1952 to a former classmate from the University of Chicago. A year earlier, Harrington had decided to return to the church, and what's more, to join the Catholic Worker movement, a spiritual and political group led by the redoubtably saintlike Dorothy Day. In March 1951, he moved to St. Joseph's House of Hospitality, the Catholic Worker headquarters, soup kitchen, and residence on the Lower East Side. Catholic Workers were committed to a life of rigorous religious devotion and voluntary poverty. Harrington embraced the ascetic ideals and lifestyle with the zeal of a new convert and quickly became a favorite of Day's: Within weeks of arriving at St. Joseph's, he became one of the editors of the monthly *Catholic Worker* newspaper. But as he approached the first anniversary of his arrival, he was drawn to explore some heretical notions.

At "the heart of Christianity," Harrington wrote his friend, "is an uncomfortable, radical proposition—do good and avoid evil. This proposition does not make any reference to pragmatism." That was the standard and, indeed, essential Catholic Worker viewpoint. To compromise the movement's commitment to its deeply spiritual, anarchist, and pacifist principles in a bid for political gain, allies, or respectability was seen as the first step down the slippery slope to a worldly and morally dubious opportunism. "However, in general, morality is usually pragmatic," Harrington wrote. "Therefore, a social phenomenon is evil, i.e., should be absolutely shunned, when the means are such that they clearly and inevitably lead to an evil end. Thus war. However, the state, the union, etc., though containing evil elements, are not inevitably tending toward evil." He added, "In this situation it is possible to cooperate with the means in the hope of forming them toward the good."

Though Harrington's point was a little obscure, he was "howevering" himself right out of the Catholic Workers, coming to the conclusion that the quest for individual spiritual perfection had cut the group off from the possibility of influencing the institutional mechanisms by means of which social justice on a mass scale had been achieved historically.

Later that spring, Harrington signed on to the Young People's Socialist League. And before the year was over, without many qualms and with little of the drama of his earlier decisions, he left St. Joseph's, the Catholic Worker movement, and the church. Democratic socialism became the defining allegiance of the remainder of his life.

Skipping ahead 10 years to 1962, Harrington's hopes for the emergence of a New Left in America (a term he had been using since 1958) were being realized. SDS had taken form in the past two years as a vital new campus organization, largely inspired by the rise of the Southern civil-rights movement. Hayden, the SDS president, had described Harrington in a 1961 article for *Mademoiselle* as one of three radicals over the age of 30 who had "won [the] respect" of New Leftists (the other two were Norman Thomas and C. Wright Mills). And when Hayden sat down in the spring of 1962 with an early draft of what would become the Port Huron Statement, he had Harrington's example much in mind, writing to fellow SDSers: "A moral aspiration for social equality, unaccompanied by a political and economic view of society, is at best wistful (I think I mimic Harrington) and, at worst, politically irresponsible. But an economic and political analysis, without an active, open moral pulse, dwindles to uninspired and uninspiring myopia."

The dilemma that Hayden wrestled with in 1962—striking the proper balance between principle and expedience, vision and pragmatism—was basically the same Harrington had confronted in 1952. Harrington, leaning toward the pragmatic, had concluded that it was "possible to cooperate with the means" of established institutions like the unions and the federal government, "in the hope of forming them toward the good." Hayden, leaning toward the visionary, wanted to wed "economic and political analysis" with "an active, open moral pulse." Their emphases may have differed, but the two were clearly in dialogue.

That is, until they met at Port Huron later that spring, and Harrington blew up. The details have been chronicled many times since, perhaps most definitively in James Miller's *Democracy Is in the Streets: From Port Huron to the Siege of Chicago* (1987). Basically, Harrington misread Hayden's attempt to offer an evenhanded analysis of cold-war tensions as a neo-Stalinist apology for the Soviet Union. In doing so, he violated his own rules for effective cross-generational communication. Writing in the democratic-socialist journal *Dissent* a few months before, Harrington had cautioned "veterans of the radical movement" not to overreact when young radicals displayed naïve attitudes on topics like Fidel Castro's revolution in Cuba. Although mistaken attitudes had to be confronted by democratic leftists, he argued, that "cannot be done from a lecture platform, from a distance. Rather the persuasion must come from someone who is actually involved in changing the status quo." At Port Huron, as Harrington later wrote, he "treated fledgling radicals trying out their own ideas for the first time as if they were hardened faction fighters."

Hayden, in his *Reunion: A Memoir* (1988), accurately described Harrington's Port Huron outburst as a disaster for all concerned. SDS members "learned a distrust and hostility to the very people we were closest to historically, the representatives of the liberal and labor organizations who had once been young radicals themselves," he said. "In retrospect, I regret that the extreme overreaction to SDS by its elders left me numb to potentially valuable lessons of their experience."

Skip ahead another half-dozen years to 1968 and the Columbia strike. Thanks to the Vietnam War, SDS was a much larger and angrier group than it had been in 1962; the few hundred members of the Port Huron era had grown to tens of thousands. At the chapter level in 1968, rank-and-file members represented a remarkable diversity of radical viewpoints, including a left-leaning liberalism, a counterculturally flavored anarchism, and 57 varieties of Marxism. But at the national level, SDS leaders showed an increasing preference for commanding small vanguard parties of revolutionaries rather than presiding over a large, ideologically sloppy, ill-disciplined, and multi-tendency student movement. That was the very outcome that Harrington had feared at Port Huron.

SDS leaders showed a preference for commanding small vanguard parties of revolutionaries rather than presiding over a large, ideologically sloppy, ill-disciplined student movement.

Hayden was in New York when Columbia students took over a number of buildings on the campus to protest the university's plans to build a gym in a Harlem park, and to demand an end to war-related research on the campus. He rode the subway up to Columbia to see what was going on and wound up leading

one of the building occupations for the next five days. Although "leading" is perhaps not the right term. "After all," he would write in *Reunion*, "the slogan I believed in was 'Let the people decide.' I was not [at Columbia] to lecture anyone on the Port Huron Statement." On April 23, 1968, he was arrested along with more than 700 other strikers.

Afterward, Hayden wrote an article titled "Two, Three, Many Columbias" for *Ramparts,* the title echoing the call by the recently martyred Che Guevara for the world's revolutionary left to create "Two, Three, Many Vietnams" to defeat U.S. imperialism. If Hayden had any residual concerns about the "embryo of fanaticism" he would later claim to have detected in the student leader Rudd, they did not appear in the article. In fact, Hayden had no criticisms at all of what happened at Columbia. The stance he adopted, at least rhetorically, was that of a loyal and deferential supporter of whatever young people on campuses decided they needed to do to challenge war and racism. It seemed to him, he wrote self-deprecatingly, that "issues being considered by 17-year-old freshmen at Columbia University would not have been within the imagination of most 'veteran' student activists five years ago."

I remember that article well. I read it during the summer of 1968, as I prepared to go off to Reed College in the fall to become one of those 17-year-old freshmen whose political acuity Hayden flattered. I signed up for SDS as soon as I got to the campus, prepared to re-enact the Columbia strike as soon as the proper issue presented itself (to my disappointment, it never quite did, although it was a stormy year at Reed). I also read the Port Huron Statement that year, mostly because I was interested in the early history of the New Left. It didn't seem nearly as relevant or enthralling as "Two, Three, Many Columbias." It was only in later years that I came to appreciate the earlier document's virtues, particularly its vision of the university as a "potential base and agency in a movement of social change," a movement in which "action" would "be informed by reason." By 1968, in contrast, student radicals at Columbia and elsewhere tended to dismiss the university as simply part of the war machine. And, as Hayden said at the conclusion of his *Ramparts* article, it was time to "bring the war home," a rhetoric and strategy that placed disruption and confrontation over appeals to reason.

"Two, Three, Many Columbias" was a primer for a politics that valued the gut instinct of young radicals over experience, continuity, and historical perspective and, sadly, proved to be one of the most influential pieces Hayden would write in the 1960s. He may have intended to "bring the war home" in a purely symbolic fashion, but the phrase took on a darker meaning: In March 1970, Ted Gold, a veteran of the Columbia strike, would be among a small group of the Weathermen of SDS building a nail-studded dynamite bomb in the basement of a Greenwich Village townhouse when it inadvertently went off, killing him and two others. In his 1988 memoir, Hayden sought to own up to a measure of responsibility for encouraging the turn toward fanaticism in SDS that he later deplored. It is interesting in that regard that he did not include "Two, Three, Many Columbias" in a recently released anthology, *Writings for a Democratic Society: The Tom Hayden Reader* (City Lights, 2008).

When young people turn to radical doctrines and movements, whether in 1952, 1962, 1968, or 2008, they are apt to bring with them a mixed collection of motives and impulses: simultaneously craving autonomy and validation, guidance and self-definition. For their radicalism to be anything more than a youthful fling, they need to find within it both a meaningful sense of personal identity and a sustainable vision of how to bring about social change. They can learn from their elders, but they also need to bring a critical scrutiny to bear on received wisdom.

When young people turn to radical doctrines and movements, whether in 1952, 1962, 1968, or 2008, they are apt to bring with them a mixed collection of motives and impulses.

The 1960s offer mostly cautionary examples of what to avoid when one generation on the left tries to influence the next. In the early 1960s, Michael Harrington, violating his own precepts on listening for the good emotions behind bad theories, squandered his opportunity to contribute to the future development of SDS and instead indulged in a blustering, condescending, and all-out political assault on the young radicals gathered at Port Huron. In the late 1960s, Tom Hayden offered young campus revolutionaries flattery and deference, refrained from saying anything that would sound like a lecture, and wound up at best "irrelevant," and at worst contributing to the emergence of the Weathermen.

Is there a happy middle ground for radical elders to take with their juniors, located somewhere between unproductive confrontation and unprincipled capitulation? As a guiding principle, one could do worse than bear in mind the young Harrington's "uncomfortable radical proposition" of 1952: "Do good and avoid evil."

MAURICE ISSERMAN is a professor of American history at Hamilton College. Among his books are *The Other American: The Life of Michael Harrington* (PublicAffairs, 2000), and *America Divided: The Civil War of the 1960s* (3rd, rev. ed., Oxford University Press, 2007), with Michael Kazin.

King's Complex Legacy

Scholars assess the nation's progress toward his social and economic goals.

KEVIN MERIDA

Near the end of his life, the Rev. Martin Luther King Jr. felt cornered and under siege. His opposition to the Vietnam War was widely criticized, even by friends. He was being pressured both to repudiate the black power movement and to embrace it. Some of his lieutenants were urging him to jettison his urgent new campaign to uplift the poor, believing that King had taken on too much and was compromising support for the civil rights struggle.

Today students learn of his powerful "dream" that children be judged not "by the color of their skin but by the content of their character." Politicians and private citizens of all ideologies summon King's soaring oratory as the inspiration that challenged the nation to better itself. But this beleaguered young man—he was only 39 when he died—was not just the icon celebrated at Martin Luther King Day programs and taught in U.S. schools.

His life, like those of other historical figures—Abraham Lincoln, Franklin D. Roosevelt—has been simplified, scholars say, his anger blurred, his militancy rarely discussed, his disappointments and harsh critiques of government's failures glossed over.

Forty years after King was gunned down by an assassin in Memphis, it is this sharper-edged figure who has come into focus again. To mark today's anniversary, several scholarly reports have been released charting the nation's uneven social and economic progress during the past 40 years. Some scholars and former King associates are using the occasion to zero in on the two issues—war and poverty—that were consuming him at the time of his death.

Both have particular resonance now: The United States is engaged in a war in Iraq that has grown increasingly unpopular, and the poor—despite the concerns highlighted by Hurricane Katrina and the subprime mortgage crisis—are as voiceless as they were in King's day, advocates contend.

"His challenge was much bigger than being nice," says Taylor Branch, author of a three-volume history, "America in the King Years." "It was even bigger than race. It was whether we take our national purpose seriously, which is the full promise of equal citizenship."

King's legacy, Branch says, should have been to give the nation confidence that it can address big problems such as the crumbling economy, the endangered environment and ending the war. "Instead, our sense of what we can do has kind of atrophied," he says. "We're still imprisoned by the myths of the 1960s"—that it was a period when the country went off the rails and government overreached.

If King could look across the landscape today, he would see a mixture of progress and regression on the issues he cared about: The overall poverty rate hasn't changed much since 1968, though there has been a big drop among the elderly. Wider income disparities exist between the richest and poorest Americans, but opportunities for educational advancement have broadened and workplaces have become more diverse.

The number of African Americans in prison or local jails, currently more than 900,000, is nearly six times the number incarcerated in 1970. But the growth in the number of black elected officials is even greater, from 1,469 in 1970 to an estimated 10,000 now. One of them, Democratic Sen. Barack Obama of Illinois, is given a serious chance of becoming the next president.

King was not a fan of fawning testimonies to his greatness, but in the years since his death about 770 streets and 125 schools have been named after him, according to research by Derek H. Alderman, an East Carolina University geographer. The street-namings are fitting tributes to King's legacy, Alderman says, because so much of the civil rights movement unfurled in the streets. Roads link our homes to our schools to our jobs, "the three areas where we struggle the most to negotiate our differences," Alderman says.

But there is an uneasy irony to these tributes: Most of the King avenues run through black communities, often in low-income neighborhoods. In some cities, attempts to rename major thoroughfares—streets that cross racial and economic boundaries—after King were met with political resistance.

"Here was this man whose life was committed to bridging races," Alderman says, "and in death his commemoration is largely segregated."

King was the son, grandson and great-grandson of preachers, and he grew up studying and practicing what messages might work best on people. In 1958, Branch says, he traveled 250,000 miles delivering sermons and speeches. As Branch put it, King thought he could preach America out of segregation.

Lawrence E. Carter, dean of the Martin Luther King Jr. International Chapel at Morehouse College, King's alma mater, says that he "recognized the humanity even in people who oppressed him," adding: "He saw in them something that could be redeemed."

But King was not meek, nor were his words always soothing. He called for boycotting discriminatory businesses, sometimes demanding that they advertise in black newspapers and deposit some of their money in black savings and loan associations. He spoke of "cultural homicide" committed against blacks, how their worth and achievements were diminished in schools while white superiority was promoted. In one speech, he even noted that there were 60 "offensive" synonyms for blackness in Roget's Thesaurus, and 134 "favorable" synonyms for whiteness.

But King reserved some of his toughest assessments for the U.S. government, which he called "the greatest purveyor of violence" in the world.

"His admonishments to us of how we ought to live seem to be reflected in his social consciousness, and that is rooted in his understanding of Jesus and the social gospels," says Carter, who met King on four occasions. "When he chastised us for being the greatest perpetrator of violence in the history of the world, think about Jeremiah Wright"—Obama's former long-time Chicago pastor, who came under fire recently for controversial statements in his sermons.

In a 1967 speech at Riverside Church in New York, exactly one year before his death, King explained his opposition to the Vietnam War and tied it to his advocacy on behalf of the poor. The war buildup had "continued to draw men and skills and money like some demonic, destructive suction tube," King said. "So I was increasingly compelled to see the war as an enemy of the poor and to attack it as such."

"Perhaps a more tragic recognition of reality took place when it became clear to me that the war was doing far more than devastating the hopes of the poor at home. It was sending their sons and their brothers and their husbands to fight and to die in extraordinarily high proportions relative to the rest of the population. We were taking the black young men who had been crippled by our society and sending them 8,000 miles away to guarantee liberties in Southeast Asia which they had not found in southwest Georgia and East Harlem. So we have been repeatedly faced with the cruel irony of watching Negro and white boys on TV screens as they kill and die together for a nation that has been unable to seat them together in the same schools."

Clayborne Carson, a King historian at Stanford University, says he was "politically isolated" in the final years of his life.

"The white liberals had kind of abandoned him because of his Vietnam speech and his decision to take on the war on poverty," says Carson, who was selected by the late Coretta Scott King to edit her husband's papers. "They were attacking him. [President Lyndon B.] Johnson thought he had gone off the deep end. And most black people in the civil rights movement thought he had gone off the deep end. I think it took a toll on him."

"The white liberals had kind of abandoned him because of his Vietnam speech and his decision to take on the war on poverty," says Clayborne Carson, a King historian at Stanford University.

Not many Americans, Carson noted, seem aware of the tremendous pressures King faced on so many fronts.

"King sometimes gets suspended in time at the March on Washington in '63," Carson added. "It's kind of a way of Americans patting themselves on their backs."

But Carson sees in King a real paradox. "He was very discouraged. On the other hand, I think he was exhilarated. He was finally doing what he felt he was on this Earth to do—preach the social gospel, help the poor."

Some of King's aides didn't share his enthusiasm for a planned Poor People's Campaign for jobs and income in Washington in April 1968. King envisioned leading a "multiracial army of the poor" to demonstrate and camp out in tents around the city. But first, there would be an unscheduled detour through Memphis.

Taylor Rogers, now 82, remembers what it was like to haul garbage in Memphis in 1968: "You could work a 40-hour week and be eligible for welfare." Rogers had eight children and no benefits. "We had nothing, just work." And the work, done for $1.80 an hour, was messy and degrading.

"You would go back in people's back yards, put the garbage in tubs and bring the tubs back out to the truck," he recalled. "The tubs had holes in them, and garbage would leak all over you. Sometime you had to take your clothes off to keep them maggots off."

On Feb. 1, 1968, during a heavy rain, two black sanitation workers were crushed when their garbage truck's compressing mechanism was triggered. Less than two weeks later, 1,100 of Memphis's 1,300 sanitation and sewer workers walked off the job in what would become a 65-day strike for increased wages and better working conditions.

"We just couldn't take no more," says Rogers, who started as a sanitation worker in 1958 and continued for 34 years. "We decided we were going to stand up and be men."

The workers staged regular nonviolent marches, led by the Rev. James Lawson and local ministers. King made his first appearance in support of the sanitation workers on March 18. He returned 10 days later to lead a march, which turned into chaos when militant youths smashed storefront windows and started looting, and police responded with force. The violence left at least one dead, 62 injured and 218 arrested, according to local news reports.

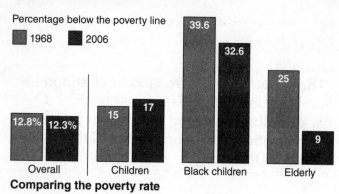

Percentage below the poverty line
■ 1968 ■ 2006

Overall	Children	Black children	Elderly
12.8% / 12.3%	15 / 17	39.6 / 32.6	25 / 9

Comparing the poverty rate

Source: Eisenhower Foundation and "Beyond the Mountaintop: King's Prescription for Poverty," by William E. Spriggs of Howard University and Steven C. Pitts of the University of California at Berkeley.

King was despondent after the day's events, which increased pressure on him from close aides and Memphis officials to leave the strike alone.

But King was determined to return to lead another, better-planned nonviolent march—what was billed as a "dress rehearsal" for his anti-poverty drive in Washington.

Back in Memphis on April 3, the night before he was killed, King decided to skip a rally at Bishop Charles Mason Temple. The weather was stormy, there were early reports of a thin crowd, and King was not in the best of moods. He sent a close friend and adviser, the Rev. Ralph Abernathy, to speak for him.

But when Abernathy and other King aides arrived, and felt the energy in Mason Temple and the mounting anticipation by sanitation workers of a King speech, Abernathy phoned King and told him to get over to the rally quickly.

It was there that King gave his final speech, "I've Been to the Mountaintop," which many have described as prescient. He mentioned the threats against his life, the talk about "what would happen to me from some of our sick white brothers." But he went on to say: "It really doesn't matter with me now, because I've been to the mountaintop. . . . And I've looked over, and I've seen the Promised Land. I may not get there with you. But I want you to know tonight, that we as a people, will get to the Promised Land."

The Rev. Samuel "Billy" Kyles, a local minister and King friend who was there that night, believes King was forecasting his own death. "I am so certain he knew he would not get there," Kyles says. "He didn't want to say it to us, so he softened it—that he *may not* get there." Later, Kyles would tell people that King "had preached himself through the fear of death."

What is often unremarked upon about that speech, however, is how resolute King was in his prescriptions for fighting the injustices suffered by the poor. He urged those at the meeting to tell their neighbors: Don't buy Coca-Cola, Sealtest milk and Wonder Bread. Up to now, only the garbage workers had been feeling pain, King noted. "Now we must kind of redistribute the pain."

The next day, King was in a good mood, almost giddy, Kyles remembered. Kyles was hosting a dinner for King at his home that evening. "I told him it was at 5 because he was never in a hurry."

But when Kyles knocked on King's door, at Room 306 of the Lorraine Motel, to hurry him along, King let him know he had uncovered the little ruse: He had found out the dinner was actually at 6. So they had some time, and King invited Kyles to sit down. Abernathy was there, too. King liked to eat and was anticipating a lavish soul-food feast, so he couldn't resist razzing Kyles. "I bet your wife can't cook," King told his friend. "She's too pretty."

Just to tease a little more, King asked Kyles: Didn't you just buy a new house? He then told the story of an Atlanta preacher who had purchased a big, fancy home and had King and Coretta over for dinner. "The Kool-Aid was hot, the ham was cold, the biscuits were hard," Kyles recalled King jiving. "If I go to your house and you don't have a decent dinner, I'm going to tell the networks that the Rev. Billy Kyles had a new house but couldn't afford to have a decent dinner."

It was about 5:45 when King and Kyles left the room and stepped onto the second-floor balcony. Abernathy stayed put. King leaned over the rail to gaze at a busy scene in the parking lot eight feet below, exchanging words with his young aide Jesse Jackson, among others. Kyles was just about to descend the steps, with King behind him, when he heard the shot. "And when I looked around, he had been knocked from the railing of the balcony back to the door," Kyles recalled. "I saw a gaping hole on the right side of his face."

Kyles ran back into the room and tried to call for an ambulance, but no one at the motel switchboard answered. He took a bedspread and draped it over King's body.

King was pronounced dead at 7 P.M. at St. Joseph's Hospital.

"Forty years ago, I had no words to express my feelings; I had stepped away from myself," recalled Kyles, now 73, the pastor at Monumental Baptist Church in Memphis. "Forty years later, I still have no words to describe my feelings."

For years, Kyles struggled with an internal question: "Why was I there?" And at some point, he can't remember when, "God revealed to me, I was there to be a witness. Crucifixions have to have a witness."

As for Rogers, one of the sanitation workers King fought for, he retired in 1992 after serving 20 years as the local union president. Forty years after the strike, wages and conditions have improved for Memphis sanitation employees—crew chiefs and truck drivers can make upwards of $37,000; workers have uniforms, showers and no more leaking tubs to carry. Residents must roll their garbage carts to the curb for pickup.

"The sanitation workers, their jobs are much better," Rogers says. "They can almost wear a suit to work."

Not that some struggles don't continue.

"There are a lot of things we have to work on," Rogers says. "Race relations, for one. Like I say, there is always room for improvement. But Dr. King really didn't die in vain."

Washington Post staff researchers Meg Smith and Bob Lyford contributed to this report.

The Spirit of '78, Stayin' Alive

Kenneth S. Baer

Everyone seems to be telling us that if you want to understand 2008, you have to look back 40 years to 1968. "It's the year that changed everything," wrote *Newsweek* last November. Seen through tie-dye-tinted glasses, Iraq is the new Vietnam, Barack Obama is the new Bobby Kennedy, and bloggers are the new student activists.

But are we commemorating the right year? If we really want a time that defined the way we live now, we should look back not to the romance and trauma of the '60s but to the gloriously tacky '70s, to the year that made modern America—1978. Look beyond the year's bad disco and worse clothes; if you peer deeply into the polyester soul of 1978, you can see the beginnings of the world we live in today.

Start with politics. Two weeks into that year, on Jan. 13, former vice president Hubert H. Humphrey died, but it took six more months before the big-government liberalism that he embodied was buried. In June, California voters backed Proposition 13, which slashed property taxes and capped tax increases, thereby marking the start of conservatism's rebirth—and the beginning of the long end of New Deal liberalism.

People had good reason to be irked at Washington, too. Voters were fed up with rising tax rates (heavily fueled by inflation) and an inefficient government that was seen as wasting their dollars. The Yankelovich poll found that 78 percent of Americans agreed with the statement, "Government wastes a lot of money we pay in taxes," an 18-point jump from 1968.

This anti-government sentiment propelled successful efforts to limit taxing and spending in 13 states and prompted 23 state legislatures to call for a constitutional convention to consider a balanced-budget amendment to the Constitution. The sour public mood, especially after the passage of Prop 13, triggered a stampede of elected officials to the right, and those who didn't dart quickly enough were run over—such as Massachusetts Gov. Michael S. Dukakis, who lost his party's gubernatorial primary.

In fact, it was in November 1978 that the modern Republican Party—which had been on the verge of extinction after Watergate—was born. In the midterm elections, the GOP gained three Senate seats, 12 House seats and six governorships. The anti-tax, small-government worldview of its right wing was suddenly ascendant—and has dominated American politics until the present day. (Note that, even with President Bush and his party on the ropes, neither Barack Obama nor

Hillary Rodham Clinton was willing to back the sort of nationalized health care that every other industrialized democracy enjoys or mention raising taxes to get rid of the massive deficit that Bush is leaving behind.)

Our year also set the contours of today's civil rights battles. In *Regents of the University of California v. Bakke,* the Supreme Court ruled that rigid race quotas for university admissions were unconstitutional but that affirmative action policies designed to ensure a diverse student body were not. Americans have battled over the implications of this decision ever since, but we have come to accept diversity as a virtue in universities, corporations and throughout American life. That began with Bakke in 1978.

Of course, today's most contentious civil rights battles aren't over race but over sexual orientation. Here, too, 1978 was pivotal. As the year began, a handful of communities had ordinances on the books banning discrimination against gays in employment and housing. But as these measures passed, opposition mobilized, often led by the singer Anita Bryant. In 1978, the citizens of Eugene, Ore.; St. Paul, Minn.; and Wichita, Kan., voted overwhelmingly to repeal these gay-friendly laws. Even in liberal New York, Mayor Ed Koch's effort to expand a ban on discrimination on the basis of sexual orientation for municipal hiring never got out of the relevant city council committee.

But the most bizarre and important incident happened, perhaps unsurprisingly, in San Francisco. The city had passed its own anti-discrimination law in March. On Nov. 27, Daniel White, the lone city supervisor to oppose the ordinance, walked into Mayor George Moscone's office and shot him dead, then proceeded to the office of Supervisor Harvey Milk—the country's first openly gay official of any consequence—and killed him, too.

More than 30,000 San Franciscans took to the streets to mourn Milk and Moscone, blaming their deaths on the anti-gay backlash. One person held a sign stating: "Are you happy, Anita?" If this didn't galvanize the gay community, the light sentence that White received did. That year, the gay community's first Washington lobbyist was hired, and its long struggle for equality was underway.

Politics wasn't the only thing that began to change in 1978. Are you reading this article on your BlackBerry? That's only possible because, in 1978, Illinois Bell rolled out the first cellular phone system—a radical new technology that promised to break the 10-year waiting list for mobile phones. That same year, the first computer bulletin-board system was created, and the first piece of e-mail spam was sent over the ARPANET, the forerunner to today's Internet, inviting users to a computer company's product demonstration. (No word on whether it promised to enhance the attendees' virility.)

Computers were quickly becoming more pervasive, too. VisiCalc, an early spreadsheet program, was introduced in 1978 and quickly became the first commercially successful piece of software, giving personal computers mass rather than just geek appeal. "Eventually, the household computer will be as much a part of the home as the kitchen sink," *Time* magazine boldly predicted in February 1978.

E-mail spam went largely unnoticed at the time, but the year's advances in biotechnology certainly did not. Late on the evening of July 25, in the small city of Oldham in northwest England, the first "test-tube baby" was born. Louise Brown's arrival after in vitro fertilization touched off a worldwide ethical debate about whether and how we should be fooling with Mother Nature. Thirty years later, IVF is commonplace, and genetic science has leapt astonishingly forward, but the scope of the debates—now focused on stem cells and cloning—remains the same.

Other eerily familiar issues from today's headlines first appeared three decades ago. Wiretapping and national security? The Foreign Intelligence Surveillance Act—whose overhaul triggered a contentious debate last week on Capitol Hill—was signed into law by President Jimmy Carter in October 1978. Skyrocketing gas prices and national reliance on foreign oil? The country's first comprehensive national energy program was signed into law at the end of 1978—but only after 18 months of contentious logrolling in Congress.

You can find the roots of some of today's biggest foreign policy challenges in 1978, too. A Middle East roiled by Islamist extremism? Nineteen seventy-eight marked the beginning of the end for the shah of Iran, soon to be swept aside by the Shiite radicals led by Ayatollah Ruhollah Khomeini—a man whose example would help pave the way for a new generation of Sunni fanatics also angry about the U.S. role in the Middle East. But while 1978 was a rotten year for U.S. efforts to prop up the shah, it was a far better one for Arab-Israeli peacemaking. Not only did the otherwise hapless Carter help broker the watershed Israeli-Egyptian peace treaty at Camp David, the summit also produced "A Framework for Peace in the Middle East," a much more ambitious document explaining how Israelis, Palestinians and Jordanians would work out their own conflicts over the next five years. That time horizon proved a little ambitious, but a precedent had been set: Since 1978, Arabs and Israelis have expected the U.S. president to be personally and deeply involved in any painful deal-making.

Then as now, the Middle East got the most headlines, but it was what was happening in the Far East that would most radically shape the world. After years of near-total isolation, China decided to join the rest of the world, setting out on what its rulers called a "New Long March" to become a world power by the end of the century. Under the leadership of Deng Xiaoping, Mao's heir, China ratified a peace and friendship treaty with Japan and reached out to its traditionally wary Asian neighbors. At home, it took momentous early steps toward capitalism by beginning to dismantle its agricultural communes, allowing peasants to sell their crops and pocket the profits.

The most dramatic sign of China's new openness was announced simultaneously in Beijing and Washington in December: The United States formally recognized China, broke its longstanding recognition of Taiwan and normalized relations with the communist titan. This momentous decision helped propel China into the modern world, turn it into a rival—if not an enemy—of the United States and intertwine the two countries' economies. Last year, U.S. trade with China was $386 billion, up from $1 billion in 1978. There is not a person reading this article who doesn't own a Chinese product.

The rise of China may not be as sexy as the student uprisings of 1968, and the passage of Prop 13 may not pack the same emotional punch as the tragic campaign of RFK. But from politics to technology, from civil rights to foreign policy, 1978 marked the start of the age we live in. Thank God, disco didn't survive.

KENNETH S. BAER, a former senior speechwriter for Vice President Al Gore, is co-editor of *Democracy: A Journal of Ideas.*

Soft Power
Reagan the Dove

VLADISLAV M. ZUBOK

D eath, not surprisingly, has secured Ronald Reagan's place in history. In recent days, policy veterans, journalists, and scholars have placed him among the top ranks of twentieth-century presidents. In a *New York Times* op-ed written shortly after Reagan's death, Mikhail Gorbachev, the former Soviet leader, acknowledged Reagan's role in bringing about the end of the cold war. Reagan's conservative admirers go even further. They proclaim him the architect of "victory" against the USSR, citing his support of the anti-communist mujahedin in Afghanistan, of the anti-Soviet Solidarity movement in Poland, and, above all, his Strategic Defense Initiative (SDI). Former White House Chief of Staff Donald Regan told CNN seven years ago that Gorbachev's failure to convince President Reagan to give up SDI at the Reykjavik summit in 1986 meant it was "all over for the Soviet Union." A memorial plaque in the court of the Ronald Reagan Presidential Library in Simi Valley, California, flatly states that Reagan's SDI brought down Soviet communism.

Newly released Soviet documents reveal that Reagan indeed played a role in ending the cold war. Yet, it was not so much because of SDI or the support of anti-Soviet forces around the world. Rather, it was the sudden emergence of another Reagan, a peacemaker and supporter of nuclear disarmament—whom conservatives opposed—that rapidly produced a new U.S.-Soviet détente. This détente facilitated Gorbachev's radical overhaul of Soviet domestic and foreign policy—changes that brought the USSR crashing down and that would have been impossible had Reagan remained the hawk conservatives now celebrate.

I n retrospect, it's hard to see SDI as anything but a bit player in the final act of the cold war. In 1983, the year Reagan announced the program to stop Soviet missiles in space (immediately dubbed "star wars"), the Soviet leadership convened a panel of prominent scientists to assess whether SDI posed a long-term security threat. The panel's report remains classified, but various leaks point to the main finding (one that mirrored the assessment of independent U.S. scientists): In the next decade or even beyond, SDI would not work. The rumor circulating in politburo circles was that "two containers of nails hurled into space" would be enough to confuse and overwhelm U.S. anti-missile defenses. In a compromise decision between Kremlin leaders and military commanders reached by 1985, a number of R&D labs received limited funds to look into possible countermeasures to SDI. The budget of the Soviet "anti-SDI" program, a fraction of the huge allocations to the Soviet military-industrial complex, remained at the same modest level through the rest of the '80s.

Gorbachev feared SDI less for the military threat it posed to the USSR than for the practical threat it posed to his political agenda. The young general secretary belonged to a generation shaped by the denunciations of Stalinist crimes, the cultural liberalization of the 1960s, and East-West détente; this generation wanted to reform the Soviet Union and end the confrontation with the United States. But the reformists remained a minority and operated in a milieu of anti-American paranoia. As a result, Gorbachev was frustrated by the Reagan administration's hawkish actions—such as increased military assistance to Afghanistan, provocative naval exercises near Soviet coasts, and the CIA's unrelenting "spy war" against the KGB.

The Soviets interpreted SDI as an outgrowth of this renewed American aggressiveness, which made it harder for Gorbachev to push his reforms. As Boris Ponomarev, a Communist apparatchik, grumbled in early 1986, "Let the Americans change their thinking instead. . . . Are you against military strength, which is the only language that imperialism understands?" Gorbachev admitted in his memoirs that he was initially too cautious to resist this pressure. At the politburo, he adopted hard-line language, describing the American president as a "troglodyte" in November 1985.

Still, the early interactions between Gorbachev and Reagan revealed that there might be enough common ground between the two leaders to allow Gorbachev to press ahead: As it happened, both men were closet nuclear abolitionists. For all his outward toughness, Reagan connected nuclear threats to the prophecy of Armageddon and, under the influence of his wife, Nancy, who saw ending the cold war as an opportunity to save the president's legacy from the taint of Iran-Contra, wanted to be remembered as a peacemaker. Gorbachev, likewise, saw eliminating the danger of nuclear confrontation between the superpowers as his top priority. When Gorbachev participated in a strategic game simulating the Soviet response to a nuclear attack shortly after coming to power, he allegedly refused to press the nuclear button "even for training purposes."

Though the continuing U.S.-Soviet confrontation obscured the common anti-nuclear agenda for much of the '80s, the shared goal surfaced suddenly in a dramatic exchange at the Reykjavik summit in October 1986. Gorbachev proposed eliminating all ballistic missiles. When Reagan demurred, Gorbachev raised the ante. Both leaders then began proposing that more and more categories of weapons be abolished until they had agreed upon total disarmament. But Gorbachev refused to cut anything if SDI remained, prompting the frustrated Reagan to interject: "What the hell use will anti-ballistic missiles or anything else be if we eliminate nuclear weapons?" The Soviet leader held firm, at which point the summit collapsed and Reagan returned home feeling angry and cheated.

Though conservatives lauded Reagan for courageously avoiding what they saw as a Soviet trap, administration insiders were furious at the president for even broaching the idea of a nuclear-free world. They were right to be concerned. By the end of 1987, Reagan had begun to distance himself from the extreme hawks who opposed any negotiations (the most prominent of them, Secretary of Defense Caspar Weinberger, left the administration in 1987) and was relying increasingly on the pragmatic advice of Secretary of State George Shultz. In December 1987, the president and Gorbachev met in Washington to sign a treaty eliminating intermediate-range missiles. And, by June 1988, Reagan was kissing Russian babies in Red Square and had nonchalantly dropped the "evil empire" label he had affixed to the Soviet Union in 1983.

For his part, Gorbachev used the increasingly warm encounters with Reagan as capital for domestic reforms. Soviet journalists, as well as the entire international media, covered the summits, transforming Gorbachev into a TV star. Back home, millions of Soviets felt proud of their leader for the first time in years. Reykjavik, in particular, increased Gorbachev's domestic standing; the Soviet audience appreciated his tough talk with Reagan, but not as much as his "struggle for peace." This enhanced stature allowed Gorbachev to make a series of crucial changes in the aftermath of various U.S.-Soviet summits: the release of the Nobel Laureate and political prisoner Andrei Sakharov in December 1986 and the introduction of glasnost came on the heels of Reykjavik; the withdrawal of troops from Afghanistan in January 1988 came just after the Washington summit the previous December; the liberalization of the communist political system began with the announcement of parliamentary elections during the summer of 1988, just after Reagan's visit to Moscow.

It was perhaps inevitable that some of Reagan's former advisers would begin to rewrite his legacy using their hardline script. Back in the '80s, however, this script produced nothing but new cold war crises, an accelerated arms race, and a huge budget deficit. With the notable exception of the support of Polish Solidarity, U.S. measures to "bleed" the Soviet Union only bred mutual fears of war. The most notorious symbol of U.S. "victory" in the cold war, SDI, still remains an unfulfilled promise 20 years later.

It is not clear how much vision regarding the end of Soviet communism Ronald Reagan had. What Reagan certainly had in abundance was luck and instinct. He was lucky that a new reformist leadership came to power in Moscow looking for a partner to end the cold war. He sensed a historic opportunity in his relationship with Gorbachev and finally seized on it. It was Reagan the peacemaker, not the cold warrior, who made the greatest contribution to history. One only wishes more Americans were aware of this paradox as they pay homage to their fortieth president.

VLADISLAV M. ZUBOK, a professor of history at Temple University, is the author of the forthcoming book *The Enemy That Went Home* (University of North Carolina Press).

The Tragedy of Bill Clinton

GARRY WILLS

So far, most readers of President Clinton's book seem to like the opening pages best, and no wonder. Scenes of childhood glow from many memoirs—by Jean-Jacques Rousseau, Henry Adams, John Ruskin, John Henry Newman, and others. It is hard to dislike people when they are still vulnerable, before they have put on the armor of whatever career or catastrophe lies before them as adults. In fact, Gilbert Chesterton advised those who would love their enemies to imagine them as children. The soundness of this tactic is proved by its reverse, when people become irate at attempts to imagine the childhood or the youth of Hitler—as in protests at the Menna Meyjez film *Max*. So it is hard, even for his foes, to find Clinton objectionable as a child. Yet the roots of the trouble he later had lie there, in the very appeal of his youth.

Another reason we respond to narratives of childhood is that first sensations are widely shared by everyone—the ways we became aware of the world around us, of family, of school, of early friends. One might expect Clinton's pineywood world to be remote from people who did not grow up in the South. But since he experienced neither grinding poverty nor notable privilege, there is an everyman quality to what he is writing about. His relatives were not blue-collar laborers but service providers—as nurse (mother and grandmother), heavy equipment salesman (father), car dealer (first stepfather), hairdresser (second stepfather), food broker (third stepfather). This was no Dogpatch, as one can tell from the number of Clinton's childhood friends who went on to distinguished careers. (The daughters of one of his ministers became, respectively, the president of Wellesley and the ombudsman of *The Washington Post*.)

Admittedly, Clinton's family was notably fissiparous, with a litter of half-relatives filling the landscape—but even that is familiar to us in this time of frequent divorce and divided custodies. It may seem out of the ordinary for Clinton's father to have been married four times by the age of twenty-six, his first stepfather to have been married three times (twice to Clinton's mother), his second stepfather to have been married twice (with twenty-nine months in jail for fraud bridging the two). His mother, because of the mortality rate of her husbands, was married five times (though two of the times were to the same man). Clinton, who has had the gift of empathy throughout his life, remained astonishingly close to all the smashed elements of this marital kaleidoscope—even to his stepfather, whose abuse of his mother Clinton had to stop with physical interventions and calls to the police. He took time from college to give his stepfather loving care at the end of his life. The most recurrent refrain in this book is "I liked him," and it began at home.

Clinton usually looked at the bright side. What the jumble of marriages gave him as a boy was just more relatives to charm and be cosseted by. Later the same people would be a political asset. The first time he ran for office, "I had relatives in five of the district's twenty-one counties." Later still, he could rely on "a big vote in south Arkansas, where I had lots of relatives." One might think he was already preparing for a political career when he got along so well with all his scattered families. But he was, even then, a natural charmer, with an immediate gratification in being liked, not looking (yet) for remoter returns from politics. Clinton won others' affection for a reason Aristotle famously gave—we enjoy doing things that we do well.[1]

Clinton claims that his sunny adaptability as a child was a front, that he lived a secret "parallel life" imposed on a "fat band boy" by his father's violence and alcoholism. He is preparing his explanation of the Monica Lewinsky affair as a product of this secret life. It is true that we all have a public self and several private ones. It is also true that childhood and adolescence prompt dark or lonely moments in most people. But the India-rubber-man resiliency of Clinton makes it hard to believe his explanation-excuse for later aberrations. "Slick Willie," the nickname he says he dislikes most, was always an unlikely brooder. The thing that would impress others about Clinton's later philandering, which long preceded the Monica stuff, was its lack of secrecy, its flamboyant risk-taking.

His attempt at a Dickensian shoe-black-factory childhood is therefore unconvincing. One of the afflictions he says he had to bear in silence was going to church in shoes his mother bought him; "pink and black Hush Puppies, and a matching pink suede belt." But since he shared his mother's idolatry of Elvis, his S-C (sartorially correct) attitude is probably retrospective. In fact, the "fat band boy" was very popular, with a wide circle of friends who stayed true to him (and he to them) ever after. His ability to enthrall others would become legendary, and one the pleasures of his book is watching him get around ob by force of personality and cleverness:

—As a Yale law student organizing New Haven
McGovern campaign, Clinton goes to the city's

Arthur Barbieri, who tells him he has the money and organization to crush the McGovern insurgency:

> I replied that I didn't have much money, but I did have eight hundred volunteers who would knock on the doors of every house in his stronghold, telling all the Italian mothers that Arthur Barbieri wanted to keep sending their sons to fight and die in Vietnam. "You don't need that grief," I said. "Why do you care who wins the nomination? Endorse McGovern. He was a war hero in World War II. He can make peace and you can keep control of New Haven."

Barbieri is struck by this law student—he and Matty Troy of New York are the only old-line bosses to endorse McGovern in the primary.

—Wanting to take Hillary Rodham to a special exhibit in the Yale art gallery for their first date, he finds the gallery locked, but talks his way in by telling the custodian that he will clean up the litter in the gallery courtyard if he lets them go through the exhibit.

—Fresh from law school, Clinton hears his application for a teaching job is turned down by the dean of the University of Arkansas Law School because he is too young and inexperienced, and he says those qualities are actually a recommendation:

> I'd be good for him, because I'd work hard and teach any courses he wanted. Besides, I wouldn't have tenure, so he could fire me at any time. He chuckled and invited me to Fayetteville for an interview.

He gets the job.

—After doing the whole Lamaze course to assist his wife when their first child is born; he learns that she must have a Caesarean section because the baby is "in breech." No one is allowed in the operating room during surgery. He pleads that Hillary has never been in a hospital before and she needs him. He is allowed to hold her hand during the delivery. Can no one say no to this man?

Persuasiveness on Clinton's scale can be a temptation. The ability to retrieve good will can make a person careless about taking vulnerable steps. Indeed, a certain type will fling himself over a cliff just to prove he can always catch a branch and crawl back up to the top. There is nothing, he begins to feel, for which he cannot win forgiveness. This kind of recklessness followed by self-retrieval is what led Clinton to think of himself as "the comeback kid" (the use of the word "kid" is probably more indicative than he intended). Famous charmers are fun to be around, but they are not people to depend on.

shington

der at his sniffiest declared that Clinton was a social
shington: "He came in here and he trashed the
not his place."[2] Clinton was simply "not one
Broder he had gone to school there. From
ington as a high school member of Boys
t Kennedy's hand, Clinton wanted to
lacement counselor, Edith Irons,

told me she urged him to apply to several colleges, not just one. But he filled out forms only for Georgetown—not because it was a Jesuit school, or a good school. Because it was in Washington. And so ingratiating was this Southern Baptist in a cosmopolitan Catholic school that he quickly became class president as a freshman and sophomore. He did not run for the office in his third year because by then he was an intern in Arkansas senator William Fulbright's office. He had to be given security clearance because he ran classified documents from place to place on Capitol Hill. Already he was a Washington insider.

Some of the freshest pages in the book register Clinton's impressions of the senators he observed. These were models against which he was measuring his future career, and the images were printed deep in him. He saw Carl Hayden of Arizona, whom a friend called "the only ninety-year-old man in the world who looks twice his age." The senior senator from his own state, John McClellan, had sorrows "drowned in enough whiskey to float the Capitol down the Potomac River." Clinton was especially interested in Senator Robert Kennedy, brother to his own fallen hero:

> He radiated raw energy. He's the only man I ever saw who could walk stoop-shouldered, with his head down, and still look like a coiled spring about to release into the air. He wasn't a great speaker by conventional standards, but he spoke with such intensity and passion it could be mesmerizing. And if he didn't get everyone's attention with his name, countenance, and speech, he had Brumus, a large, shaggy Newfoundland, the biggest dog I ever saw. Brumus often came to work with Senator Kennedy. When Bobby walked from his office in the New Senate Building to the Capitol to vote, Brumus would walk by his side, bounding up the Capitol steps to the revolving door on the rotunda level, then sitting patiently outside until his master returned for the walk back. Anyone who could command the respect of that dog had mine too.

One of Clinton's housemates at Georgetown worked in Robert Kennedy's office, and another was in Henry "Scoop" Jackson's office. A Georgetown girl he was dating hated Kennedy because she was working for his rival, Eugene McCarthy, whose lassitude Clinton compared unfavorably with Kennedy's energy. He especially admired his own boss, Senator Fulbright:

> I'll never forget one night in 1967 or '68. I was walking alone in Georgetown when I saw the Senator and Mrs. Fulbright leaving one of the fashionable homes after a dinner party. When they reached the street, apparently with no one around to see, he took her in his arms and danced a few steps. Standing in the shadows, I saw what a light she was in his life.

Oxford

Clinton not only worked for Fulbright in Washington but drove him around Arkansas. He sincerely admired his opposition to the Vietnam War—among other things it gave him an excuse for avoiding the war. The flap over Clinton's "draft dodging" looks quaint in retrospect. He first tried to do what George W. Bush did, join the National Guard, but he did not have the contacts to be accepted. The differences are that he, unlike Bush, did not support the war, and he is honest in saying that he was trying to avoid combat. He was in his first term as a Rhodes Scholar at Oxford, and a friend and housemate of his (Frank Aller) was defying the draft as a conscientious objector. Aller said Clinton should risk the draft in order to have a political career, though he could not do that himself.

A man much admired by his Oxford contemporaries but tortured by his scruples, Aller later committed suicide. Robert McNamara, who came to know of Aller's anguish, wrote Clinton when he was elected president:

> By their votes, the American people, at long last, recognized that the Allers and the Clintons, when they questioned the wisdom and morality of their government's decisions relating to Vietnam, were no less patriotic than those who served in uniform.

After Clinton failed to get into the National Guard, his uncle tried to get him into a navy program (which would involve less danger, and a delay in enlistment). Clinton's third try was as an ROTC law student at the University of Arkansas in Fayetteville, which would have given him three to four years' delay in actual service—but would have kept him from continuing at Oxford. Only when he drew a low number in the draft did he take his chances on staying in England rather than going to Fayetteville. The famous letter he wrote to explain why he was not going to show up for the ROTC spot was a typical act of ingratiation with the man who had admitted him into the program, Colonel Eugene Holmes. He said that he would "accept" the draft (he did not say he had been given a low number) only "to maintain my political viability within the [political] system." The ingratiation worked, at first. Colonel Holmes, when asked about Clinton's relations with ROTC, said for years that there was nothing abnormal about them. Only in the 1992 campaign did he write a letter denouncing Clinton as a draft dodger. Clinton suggests that Holmes may have had "help" with his memory from his daughter, a Republican activist in the Arkansas Bush campaign. Clinton's best biographer, David Maraniss, goes much further, and says that national officials of the Bush campaign "reviewed the letter before it was made public."[3]

C linton's time in Oxford led to many silly charges against him. He was said to have been a protester in Arkansas, at a time when he was in England—an accusation that came up in his campaigns for state office. Much was made of his confession that he tried marijuana but "did not inhale." *Could* not inhale would have been more truthful—his allergies had kept him from smoking any kind of cigarette, and the respected British journalist Martin Walker, who was with Clinton at the time, confirmed that he and others tried to teach Clinton to inhale, but he could not—he would end up "leaning his head out an open window gasping for fresh air." The problem with a reputation for being "slick" is that even the simple truth can look like a ploy.

Clinton's asthma and allergies stood in his way during his first political campaign, but charm overcame the problem when two local figures he wanted to campaign for him in Arkansas took him out from town in a truck, pulled out a pack of Red Man chewing tobacco, and said, "If you're man enough to chew this tobacco, we'll be for you. If not, we'll kick you out and let you walk back to town." Clinton hesitated a moment, then said: "Open the damn door." The two men laughed and became his campaigners for many years.

A more serious charge arising from his two years at Oxford came from his trip to Russia, which would later be called treasonous—a charge that the senior Bush's campaign tried to verify by breaking its own rules on passport and embassy reports. Clinton's interest in Russia came from the fact that his housemate and fellow Rhodes Scholar, Strobe Talbot, was already such an expert on the Russian language and history that he was translating the memoirs of Khrushchev, smuggled out to him by Jerry Schecter, the Moscow correspondent for *Time*. Clinton learned more about America than about either England or Russia during his time at Oxford, where his fellow Rhodes Scholars talked endlessly about their country and the war. Clinton gave up a third year and a degree in England to get back to the Yale Law School and antiwar activities, first in Joseph Duffey's failed Connecticut campaign for senator and then in McGovern's campaign for the presidency. In the latter cause, he had an ally in Hillary Rodham.

Yale

Clinton refers to various women he dated or traveled with in Europe, and he drops some indirect references to his reputation as a ladies' man—as inoculation, I suppose. He says he "had lived a far from perfect life," and carried "more baggage than an ocean liner." "The lies hurt, and the occasional truth hurt more." He even admits that when he proposed to Hillary, "nothing in my background indicated I knew what a stable marriage was all about." With women before Hillary, he was the one not seeking a commitment; but he pursued Hillary relentlessly. As law students, after they began living together, they traveled to Europe and the American West. He first proposed to her in England's Lake Country, but she said no. When she spent the summer of 1968 as an intern for a law firm in Oakland, California, he turned down an offer to organize the McGovern campaign in Miami and went with her to California for the whole summer. He was afraid he would lose her. What their marriage proves is that even a lecherous man can have the one great love affair of his life.

Lechery

In this book Clinton misleads not by equivocation but by omission. He gives a long account of his decision not to run for president in July of 1988—how he summoned friends with wide experience to Little Rock and weighed all the options. He admits that Gary Hart had withdrawn from the race two months earlier, and that "after the Hart affair, those of us who had not led perfect lives had no way of knowing what the press's standards of disclosure were." Clinton had to be paying close attention to the Hart campaign that year. He had worked closely with Hart on the McGovern team—in fact, Hart had rebuked him for paying too much attention to his "girl friend" (Hillary) during the campaign.[4] What Clinton leaves out of the account of his decision in 1988 is the brutal candor of the advice given him by his longtime aide, Betsey Wright. According to David Maraniss,

> Wright met with Clinton at her home on Hill Street. The time had come, she felt, for Clinton to get past what she considered his self-denial tendencies and face the issue squarely. For years, she told friends later, she had been covering up for him. She was convinced that some state troopers were soliciting women for him, and he for them, she said. Sometimes when Clinton was on the road, Wright would call his room in the middle of the night and no one would answer. She hated that part of him, but felt that the other sides of him overshadowed his personal weaknesses.
>
> . . . She started listing the names of women he had allegedly had affairs with and the places where they were said to have occurred. "Now," she concluded, "I want you to tell me the truth about every one." She went over the list twice with Clinton, according to her later account, the second time trying to determine whether any of the women might tell their stories to the press. At the end of the process, she suggested that he should not get into the race. He owed it to Hillary and Chelsea not to.[5]

No one who has seen Clinton with his daughter can doubt that he loves her deeply, and he does say that concern for her kept him out of the 1988 race, when she was eight years old. "Carl Wagner, who was also the father of an only daughter, told me I'd have to reconcile myself to being away from Chelsea for most of the next sixteen months." The same problem would arise, of course, four years later, when Chelsea would be twelve—yet he would run then. Wagner's advice is given a much different sense in his account to Maraniss. Wagner, who was a friend of Betsey Wright and had been given a job by her when he arrived in Little Rock, knew about her concerns, and shared them. After the conference with advisers, he stayed while the others left, to tell Clinton:

> When you reach the top of the steps, walk into your daughter's bedroom, look at her, and understand that if you do this, your relationship with her will never be the same. I'm not sure if it will be worse or better, but it will never be the same."[6]

Wagner was not worried about Clinton's absence from Chelsea, but about the presence of shadowy women in her young mind.

When Clinton ran in 1992, he admits that he anticipated trouble. A man in George H. W. Bush's White House, Roger Porter—with whom Clinton had worked on the President's "education initiative"—called him to say that "if I ran, they would have to destroy me personally."

> He went on to say the press were elitists who would believe any tales they were told about backwater Arkansas. "We'll spend whatever we have to spend to get whoever we have to get to say whatever they have to say to take you out. And we'll do it early."

Of course, this is Clinton's version of the phone call; it has the ring of a Lee Atwater campaign, although it can even be interpreted as kindly meant. Clinton was being forewarned that he could not expect to get a free pass on his background. Clinton presents his decision to run despite this warning as a brave refusal to be blackmailed: "Ever since I was a little boy I have hated to be threatened."

On Gennifer Flowers, Clinton did resort to equivocation. In the famous post–Super Bowl interview on *60 Minutes,* Steve Kroft asked about "what she calls a twelve-year affair with you." Clinton said, "That allegation is false" (referring to the twelve-year aspect). So, said Kroft, "you're categorically denying that you ever had an affair with Gennifer Flowers?" Clinton answered, "I've said that before, and so has she." Both answers were technically correct, though six years later he would admit that they were "misleading"—he did have an affair. Most people forget that Clinton's trouble with women taping their phone calls did not begin with Monica Lewinsky. In 1992 Flowers was taping him, at a time when she was publicly denying claims of their affair. When he called her after defeating Sheffield Nelson for governor, Clinton mocked Nelson for denying that he had charged Clinton with infidelity: "I knew he lied. I just wanted to make his asshole pucker. But I covered you," Clinton said on a tape that became public.[7]

The Lewinskiad

Clinton claims that he does not offer excuses for his past life in this book. But he now says that he lied because he was confused, fatigued, and angry at being surrounded by bloodhound prosecutors, a hostile Congress, and a barking press: "And if there had been no Kenneth Starr—if we had different kind of people, I would have just said, 'Here are the facts. I'm sorry. Deal with it however you please.'" Here all the contrived contrition is forgotten—it was Ken Starr who made him lie. But what was he lying about? For that he has another excuse, his "parallel life" in which he kept embarrassing things secret. Well, we all do that. But why did he do the reckless things with Lewinsky that he had to keep secret? With both Dan Rather and Charlie Rose he said: "I think I did something for the worst possible reason, just because I could. I think that's the most—just about the most morally indefensible reason that anybody could have for doing anything, when you do something just because you could." Here he is applying to himself what Newt Gingrich said to him when Clinton asked why the Republicans shut down the government in 1995. The answer: "Because we could." Later Clinton says the prosecutors hunted him "because they could."

As applied to him, the answer is nonsense. First of all, he *couldn't* do it, if that meant doing it with impunity—as he found out. Moreover, that is not the worst possible reason for doing anything. There are far worse reasons—hatred, revenge, religious fanaticism, sadism. He avoids saying that he did it because he wanted to, but that is the only honest answer. He did it from lechery. And the absurdity of it, the risk, just spiced the matter with danger. He was not withdrawing into a secret self but throwing himself outward in flamboyant bravado. Clinton, like his mother, is a gambler. He does not, as she did, play the ponies. He dares the lightning. He knew he had numerous hunters and trackers circling him about. He knew that he already had to cope with Gennifer Flowers, Paula Jones, and Kathleen Willey. The young woman he was adding to the list was not likely to be discreet—she boasted of earning her presidential kneepads, and wangled thirty-seven entrances to the White House, and snapped her thong, and preserved the candied semen. (DNA technology is still a comparatively young discipline, but it is not likely for some time to get a stranger exercise than testing the effluvia of presidential fellation.)

Flirting with ever greater peril, he repeatedly telephoned Lewinsky. He sent her presents (*Leaves of Grass* as Seducer's Assistant). He wore her present. He lied in risky forums. He put in jeopardy political efforts he cared about, as well as the respect and love of his wife and daughter. It was such a crazy thing to do that many of us could not, for a long time, believe he had done it. But Betsey Wright, from her long experience of the man, knew at once: "I was miserably furious with him, and completely unable to communicate with him from the time the Lewinsky stuff was unfolded on the national scene. This was a guy I had given thirteen years of my life to."[8]

Starr

Though Clinton's conduct was inexcusable, it does pale next to the deep and vast abuses of power that Kenneth Starr sponsored and protected. He is a deceptively sweet-looking fellow, a dimpled, flutily warbling Pillsbury Doughboy. But he lent himself to the schemes of people with an almost total disregard for the law. A man of honor would not have accepted his appointment by a right-wing judge to replace Robert Fiske, a Republican general counsel who was a distinguished prosecutor. Not only did Starr have no prosecutorial experience; he had already lent support to Paula Jones's suit against the President. He continued private practice for right-wing causes with right-wing funding. Five former presidents of the American Bar Association said that he had conflicts of interest for which he should recuse himself. At one point in his investigation, a *New York Times* editorial said he should resign. His own chosen ethics adviser, Sam Dash, left him in protest at his tactics. The American Civil Liberties Union had to bring an end to the "barbaric" conditions he imposed on the imprisoned Susan McDougal.[9]

Starr raised again the suspicion that Vince Foster was murdered, after his predecessor had disposed of that claim. This was a favorite cause of the man funding much of the right-wing pursuit of Clinton, Richard Mellon Scaife, who is a principal donor to Pepperdine College, where Starr now holds a chair. The list of Starr's offenses is long and dark. Congressman Barney Frank questioned him about the fact that he released his damning "sex report" on Clinton before the 1998 elections though he held findings that cleared Clinton of other charges—findings reached months earlier—until after the election. After Starr made several attempts at evading the question, Frank said, "In other words, you don't have anything to say [before an election] unless you have something bad to say."[10]

Starr prolonged his investigations as charge after charge was lengthily discredited, until the right-wing Rutherford Institute's lawyers, representing Paula Jones, could trap Clinton in a confession of his contacts with Monica Lewinsky, to which Starr then devoted his frenzied attention. The wonder is that Starr got away with all his offenses. For that he needed a complicit press, which disgraced itself in this period, gobbling up the illegal leaks that flowed from his office. The sniffy Washingtonians went so berserk over the fact that Clinton was Not One of Us that they bestowed on Starr an honorary Oneness with Usness. Sally Quinn wrote in *The Washington Post* that "Beltway Insiders" were humiliated by Clinton, and that "Starr is a Washington insider, too."[11]

Starr was one thing that made some people stay with Clinton, who says Starr's unfairness helped bring Hillary back to his side. Paul Begala admitted he was disgusted by what Clinton had done, but determined that he would not let Starr accomplish a "coup d'etat." That does not describe what a Starr success would have meant. Conviction on impeachment charges would not have brought in a Republican administration. Succession would have gone to Vice President Al Gore in Clinton's own administration. But Clinton agrees with Begala. He presents his fight with Starr as a defense of all the things the right wing disliked about him—his championship of blacks, and gays, and the poor. He works himself up to such a righteous pitch that he says his impeachment trial was a "badge of honor."

Honor

Actually, the honorable thing for Clinton would have been to resign. I argued for that in a *Time* magazine article as soon as he revealed that he had lied to the nation.[12] I knew, of course, that he wouldn't. He had thrown himself off the highest cliff ever, and he had to prove he could catch a last-minute branch and pull himself, improbably, back up. And damned if he didn't. He ended his time as president with high poll numbers and some new accomplishments, the greatest of the Kid's comebacks—so great that I have been asked if I still feel he should have resigned. Well, I do. Why? Partly because what Ross Perot said in 1996 was partly true—that Clinton would be "totally occupied for the next two years in staying out of jail." That meant he would probably go on lying. He tried for as long as possible to "mislead" the nation on Gennifer Flowers. He still claims that Paula Jones and Kathleen Willey made false charges. Perhaps they did, but he became unbelievable about personal behavior after lying about Flowers and Lewinsky. I at first disbelieved the story Paula Jones told because it seemed too bizarre; but the cigar-dildo described by Monica Lewinsky considerably extended the vistas of the bizarre.

Though Clinton accomplished things in his second term, he did so in a constant struggle to survive. Unlike the current president, his administration found in Sudan the presence of a weapon of mass destruction (the nerve gas precursor Empta) and bombed the place where it had existed—but many, including Senator Arlen Specter and the journalist Seymour Hersh, said that Clinton was just bombing another country to distract people from his scandal.[13] "That reaction," according to Richard Clarke, "made it more difficult to get approval for follow-up attacks on al Quaeda."[14] Even when Clinton was doing things, the appearance of his vulnerability made people doubt it. It was said in the Pentagon that he was afraid to seize terrorists because of his troubles; but Clarke rebuts those claims—he says that every proposal to seize a terrorist leader; whether it came from the CIA or the Pentagon, was approved by Clinton "during my tenure as CSG [Counterterrorism Security Group] chairman, from 1992 to 2001."

We shall never know what was not done, or not successfully done, because of Clinton's being politically crippled. He has been criticized for his insufficient response to the ethnic cleansing in Kosovo. Michael Walzer said of the bombing raids Clinton finally authorized that "our faith in airpower is . . . a kind of idolatry."[15] But Clinton was limited in what he could do by the fact that the House of Representatives passed a resolution exactly the opposite of the war authorization that would be given George W. Bush—it voted to deny the President the power to commit troops. Walzer says that Clinton should have prodded the UN to take action; but a Republican Congress was not going to follow a man it distrusted when he called on an institution it distrusted.

At the very end of Clinton's regime, did Arafat feel he was not strong enough in his own country to pressure him into the reasonable agreement Clinton had worked out and Ehud Barak had accepted? Clinton suggests as much when he says that Arafat called him a great man, and he had to reply: "I am not a great man. I am a failure, and you have made me one."

Clinton had a wise foreign policy. But in an Oval Office interview, shortly before he admitted lying to the nation, he admitted that he had not been able to make it clear to the American people. His vision had so little hold upon the public that Bush was able to discard it instantly when he came in. Clinton summed up the difference between his and Bush's approach for Charlie Rose by saying that the latter thinks we should "do what we want whenever we can, and then we cooperate when we have to," whereas his policy was that "we were cooperating whenever we could and we acted alone only when we had to." The Bush people are learning the difference between the two policies as their preemptive unilateralism fails.

Clinton claims that he was not hampered in his political activity by scandals. He even said, to Charlie Rose, that "I probably was more attentive to my work for several months just because I didn't want to tend to anything else." That is improbable a priori and it conflicts with what he told Dan Rather about the atmosphere caused by the scandal: "The moment was so crazy. It was a zoo. It was an unr—it was—it was like living in a madhouse."

Even if he were not distracted, the press and the nation were. His staff was demoralized. The Democrats on the Hill were defensive, doubtful, absorbed in either defending Clinton or deflecting criticism from themselves. His freedom to make policy was hobbled.

Clinton likes to talk now of his "legacy." That legacy should include partial responsibility for the disabling of the Democratic Party. There were things to be said against the Democratic Leadership Council (Mario Cuomo said them well) and the "triangulation" scheme of Dick Morris, by which Clinton would take positions to the right of most congressional Democrats and to the left of the Republican Party. But Clinton, as a Southerner, knew that the party had to expand its base back into sources of support eroded by the New Right. This was a defensible (in fact a shrewd) strategy as Clinton originally shaped it. He could have made it a tactical adjunct to important strategic goals. But after the scandals, all his maneuvering looked desperate—a swerving away from blows, a flurried scrambling to find solid footing. His very success made Democrats think their only path to success was to concede, cajole, and pander. Al Gore began his 2000 campaign unhappy about his association with Clinton but trying to outpander him when he opposed the return of the Cuban boy Elian Gonzalez to his father. There is a kind of rude justice to the fact that the election was stolen from Gore in the state where he truckled to the Cubans.

Clinton bequeathed to his party not a clear call to high goals but an omnidirectional proneness to pusillanimity and collapse. This was signaled at the very outset of the new presidency. The Democrats, still in control of the Senate, facing a president not even strong enough to win the popular vote, a man brought into office by linked chicaneries and chance (Kathleen Harris, Ralph Nader, Antonin Scalia), nonetheless helped to confirm John Ashcroft as attorney general. The senators knew Ashcroft well; they were surely not impressed by his acumen or wisdom.

A whole series of capitulations followed. While still holding a majority in the Senate, the Democrats did not use subpoenas and investigative powers to challenge Dick Cheney's secret drafting of energy policy with Enron and other companies. A portion of the Democrats would support the welfare-to-billionaires tax cut. They fairly stampeded to support the Patriot Act and the presidential war authorization—with John Kerry, John Edwards, and Hillary Clinton at the front of the pack. The party had become so neutered that Al From and others from the Democratic Leadership Council called Howard Dean an extremist for daring to say what everyone is now saying about the war with Iraq—that it was precipitate, overhyped, and underprepared, more likely to separate us from the friends needed to fight terrorists than to end terrorism.

What would have happened had Clinton resigned? Gore would have been given a "honeymoon" in which he could have played with a stronger hand all the initiatives Clinton had begun, unashamed of them and able to bring them fresh energy. That is what happened when Lyndon Johnson succeeded John Kennedy. Clinton himself may have reaped a redeeming admiration for what he had sacrificed to recover his honor. Before him would have lain all the opportunities he has now, and more. Hillary Clinton's support of him in this act of real contrition would have looked nobler. Clinton's followers were claiming that it was all and only about sex. Clinton could have said, "Since that is what it is about, I'll step aside so more important things can be addressed." All the other phony issues Starr had raised would have fallen of their own insubstantiality.

Of course, this is just one of many what-ifs about the Clinton presidency. By chance I saw a revival of Leonard Bernstein's musical *Wonderful Town,* just before getting my copy of the Clinton book. All through the 957 pages of it, a song from the show kept running through my head: "What a waste! What a waste!"

Notes

1. Aristotle, *Nichomachean Ethics,* 1097–1098.

2. Sally Quinn, "Not in Their Backyard: In Washington, That Let Down Feeling," *The Washington Post,* November 2, 1998.

3. David Maraniss, *First in His Class: A Biography of Bill Clinton* (Simon and Schuster, 1995), p. 205.

4. Garry Wills, "Lightning Rod," *The New York Review,* August 14, 2003.

5. Maraniss, *First in His Class,* pp. 440–441.

6. Maraniss, *First in His Class,* p. 441.

7. Maraniss, *First in His Class,* p. 457.

8. Interview in the Harry Thomason and Nicholas Perry film *The Hunting of the President* (Regent Entertainment, 2004).

9. The despicable treatment of Susan McDougal is movingly presented in *The Hunting of the President,* a film that has many trivializing touches (like intercut clips of old Hollywood melodramas). McDougal's story is backed up by a very impressive woman, Claudia Riley, the wife of Bob Riley, the former Arkansas governor and college president, who stayed with McDougal through her ordeal and describes the bullying tactics she witnessed.

10. Sidney Blumenthal, *The Clinton Wars* (Farrar, Straus and Giroux, 2003), p. 512.

11. Quinn, "Not in Their Backyard: In Washington, That Let Down Feeling."

12. Garry Wills, "Leading by Leaving," *Time,* August 31, 1998.

13. See the important work by two former National Security Council antiterrorist directors, Daniel Benjamin and Steven Simon, *The Age of Sacred Terror: Radical Islam's War Against America* (Random House, 2002), pp. 352–360. See also Richard Clarke, *Against All Enemies: Inside America's War on Terror* (Free Press, 2004), pp. 146–147.

14. Clarke, *Against All Enemies,* p. 189.

15. Michael Walzer, *Arguing About War* (Yale University Press, 2004), p. 99.

The Rove Presidency

Karl Rove had the plan, the power, and the historic chance to remake American politics. What went wrong?

JOSHUA GREEN

With more than a year left in the fading Bush presidency, Karl Rove's worst days in the White House may still lie ahead of him. I met Rove on one of his best days, a week after Bush's reelection. The occasion was a reporters' lunch hosted by *The Christian Science Monitor* at the St. Regis Hotel in Washington, a customary stop for the winning and losing campaign teams to offer battle assessments and answer questions.

Kerry's team had glumly passed through a few days earlier. Afterward his chief strategist, Bob Shrum, boarded a plane and left the country. Rove had endured a heart-stopping Election Day (early exit polls indicated a Kerry landslide) but had prevailed, and plainly wasn't hurrying off anywhere. "The Architect," as Bush had just dubbed him, had spent the week collecting praise and had now arrived—vindicated, secure of his place in history—to hold court before the political press corps.

When Rove entered the room, everyone stood up to congratulate him and shake his hand. Washington journalism has become a kind of Cult of the Consultant, so the energy in the room was a lot like it might have been if Mickey Mantle had come striding into the clubhouse after knocking in the game-winning run in the World Series. Rove was pumped.

Before taking questions, he removed a folded piece of paper from his pocket and rattled off a series of numbers that made clear how he wanted the election to be seen: not as a squeaker but a rout. "This was an extraordinary election," Rove said. "[Bush won] 59.7 million votes, and we still have about 250,000 ballots to count. Think about that—*nearly 60 million votes!* The previous largest number was Ronald Reagan in 1984, sweeping the country with 49 states. We won 81 percent of all the counties in America. We gained a percentage of the vote in 87 percent of the counties in America. In Florida, we received nearly a million votes more in this election than in the last one." Rove was officially there to talk about the campaign, but it was clear he had something much bigger in mind. So no one missed his point, he invoked Franklin Roosevelt's supremacy in the 1930s and suggested that something similar was at hand: "We've laid out an agenda, we've laid out a vision, and now people want to see results."

The Early Birds

At dawn they start again, the early birds, as if they'd left some bitter things unsaid the day before. The sharp notes rise in thirds. I wake up knowing that I'll soon be dead, and that's no worse than justice, as is just. The kindest words are almost never meant. Most fond endearments fill us with disgust. To lie is sometimes all too eloquent; but, as I stumble toward that unknown date, even the lies may be inadequate.

—William Logan

William Logan's most recent book of essays and reviews, *The Undiscovered Country*, received the 2005 National Book Critics Circle Award in Criticism. His most recent book of poetry is *The Whispering Gallery* (2005).

One of the goals of any ambitious president is to create a governing coalition just as Roosevelt did, one that long outlasts your presidency. It's the biggest thing you can aim for, and only a few presidents have achieved it. As the person with the long-term vision in the Bush administration, and with no lack of ambition either, Rove had thought long and hard about achieving this goal before ever arriving in the White House, and he has pursued it more aggressively than anyone else.

Rove has always cast himself not merely as a campaign manager but as someone with a mind for policy and for history's deeper currents—as someone, in other words, with the wherewithal not just to exploit the political landscape but to reshape it. At the *Christian Science Monitor* lunch, he appeared poised to do just that. It was already clear that Social Security privatization, a longtime Rove enthusiasm, was the first thing Bush would pursue in his second term. When things are going well for Rove, he adopts a towel-snapping jocularity. He looked supremely sure of his prospects for success.

But within a year the administration was crumbling. Social Security had gone nowhere. Hurricane Katrina, the worsening war in Iraq, and the disastrous nomination of Harriet Miers to the Supreme Court shattered the illusion of stern competence that had helped reelect Bush. What surprised everybody was how suddenly it happened; for a while, many devotees of the Cult of Rove seemed not to accept that it had. As recently as last fall, serious journalists were churning out soaring encomiums to Rove and his methods with titles like *One Party Country* and *The Way to Win*. In retrospect, everyone should have been focusing less on how those methods were used to win elections and more on why they couldn't deliver once the elections were over.

The story of why an ambitious Republican president working with a Republican Congress failed to achieve most of what he set out to do finds Rove at center stage. A big paradox of Bush's presidency is that Rove, who had maybe the best purely political mind in a generation and almost limitless opportunities to apply it from the very outset, managed to steer the administration toward disaster.

Years from now, when the major figures in the Bush administration publish their memoirs, historians may have a clearer idea of what went wrong than we do today. As an exercise in not waiting that long, I spent several months reading the early memoirs and talking to people inside and outside the administration (granting anonymity as necessary), in Congress, and in lobbying and political-consulting firms that dealt directly with Rove in the White House. (Rove declined requests for an interview.) The idea was to look at the Bush years and make a first pass at explaining the consequential figure in the vortex—to answer the question, How should history understand Karl Rove, and with him, this administration?

Fifty years ago, political scientists developed what is known as realignment theory—the idea that a handful of elections in the nation's history mattered more than the others because they created "sharp and durable" changes in the polity that lasted for decades. Roosevelt's election in 1932, which brought on the New Deal and three decades of Democratic dominance in Washington, is often held up as the classic example. Modern American historians generally see five elections as realigning: 1800, when Thomas Jefferson's victory all but finished off the Federalist Party and reoriented power from the North to the agrarian South; 1828, when Andrew Jackson's victory gave rise to the modern two-party system and two decades of Jacksonian influence; 1860, when Abraham Lincoln's election marked the ascendance of the Republican Party and of the secessionist impulse that led to the Civil War; 1896, when the effects of industrialization affirmed an increasingly urban political order that brought William McKinley to power; and Roosevelt's election in 1932, during the Great Depression.

Academics debate many aspects of this theory, such as whether realignment comes in regular cycles, and whether it is driven by voter intensity or disillusionment. But historians have shown that two major preconditions typically must be in place for realignment to occur. First, party loyalty must be sufficiently weak to allow for a major shift—the electorate, as the political scientist Paul Allen Beck has put it, must be "ripe for realignment." The other condition is that the nation must undergo some sort of triggering event, often what Beck calls a "societal trauma"—the ravaging depressions of the 1890s and 1930s, for instance, or the North-South conflict of the 1850s and '60s that ended in civil war. It's important to have both. Depressions and wars throughout American history have had no realigning consequence because the electorate wasn't primed for one, just as periods of electoral unrest have passed without a realignment for lack of a catalyzing event.

Before he ever came to the White House, Rove fervently believed that the country was on the verge of another great shift. His faith derived from his reading of the presidency of a man most historians regard as a mediocrity. Anyone on the campaign trail in 2000 probably heard him cite the pivotal importance of William McKinley's election in 1896. Rove thought there were important similarities.

"Everything you know about William McKinley and Mark Hanna"—McKinley's Rove—"is wrong," he told Nicholas Lemann of *The New Yorker* in early 2000. "The country was in a period of change. McKinley's the guy who figured it out. Politics were changing. The economy was changing. We're at the same point now: weak allegiances to parties, a rising new economy." Rove was suggesting that the electorate in 2000, as in 1896, was ripe for realignment, and implying, somewhat immodestly, that he was the guy who had figured it out. What was missing was an obvious trigger. With the economy soaring (the stock-market collapse in the spring of 2000 was still months away) and the nation at peace, there was no reason to expect that a realignment was about to happen.

Instead, Rove's idea was to use the levers of government to create an effect that ordinarily occurs only in the most tumultuous periods in American history. He believed he could force a realignment himself through a series of far-reaching policies. Rove's plan had five major components: establish education standards, pass a "faith-based initiative" directing government funds to religious organizations, partially privatize Social Security, offer private health-savings accounts as an alternative to Medicare, and reform immigration laws to appeal to the growing Hispanic population. Each of these, if enacted, would weaken the Democratic Party by drawing some of its core supporters into the Republican column. His plan would lead, he believed, to a period of Republican dominance like the one that followed McKinley's election.

Rove's vision had a certain abstract conceptual logic to it, much like the administration's plan to spread democracy by force in the Middle East. If you could invade and pacify Iraq and Afghanistan, the thinking went, democracy would spread across the region. Likewise, if you could recast major government programs to make them more susceptible to market forces, broader support for the Republican Party would ensue. But in both cases the visionaries ignored the enormous difficulty of carrying off such seismic changes.

The Middle East failure is all too well-known—the vaulting ambition coupled with the utter inability of top administration figures to bring about their grand idea. What is less appreciated is how Rove set out to do something every bit as audacious with domestic policy. Earlier political realignments resulted from historical accidents or anomalies, conditions that were recognized and exploited after the fact by talented politicians.

Nobody ever planned one. Rove didn't wait for history to happen to him—he tried to create it on his own. "It's hard to think of any analogue in American history," says David Mayhew, a Yale political scientist who has written a book on electoral realignments, "to what Karl Rove was trying to do."

Rove's style as a campaign consultant was to plot out well in advance of a race exactly what he would do and to stick with it no matter what. But he arrived in the White House carrying ambitions at striking variance with those of a president whose stated aims were modest and who had lost the popular vote. The prevailing view of Bush at the time seems impossibly remote today. But the notion that he wanted nothing more than "to do a few things, and do them well," as he claimed, seemed sensible enough. Nothing suggested that radical change was possible, much less likely, and the narrow margins in Congress meant that any controversial measure would require nearly flawless execution to prevail.

And yet at first it appeared that Bush might be capable of achieving big things. His first initiative, the No Child Left Behind Act, unfolded as a model of how to operate in a narrowly divided environment. Bush had made education a central theme of his campaign, an unlikely choice given that the issue strongly favors Democrats. Accountability standards had been one of his signature accomplishments as governor of Texas, and he made a persuasive pitch for them on the campaign trail. Rove likes to point out that people who named education as their top issue voted for the Democrat over the Republican 76–16 percent in the 1996 presidential election, but just 52–44 in 2000. His point is that Bush moved the electorate.

As the top political adviser in the White House, Rove orchestrated the rollout of Bush's legislative agenda. In December, even before the inauguration, he put together a conference in Austin that included key Democrats who went on to support the education bills that sailed through Congress and became the first piece of Rove's realignment. At the time, everybody assumed this was how Bush would operate—"as a uniter, not a divider," his method in Texas, where he left behind a permanent-seeming Republican majority.

In retrospect, everyone should have been focusing less on how Rove's methods were used to win elections and more on why they couldn't deliver once the elections were over.

It's not clear why Bush abandoned the moderate style that worked with No Child Left Behind. One of the big what-ifs of his presidency is how things might have turned out had he stuck with it (education remains the one element of Rove's realignment project that was successfully enacted). What did become clear is that Rove's tendency, like Bush's, is always to choose the most ambitious option in a list and then pursue

it by the most aggressive means possible—an approach that generally works better in campaigns than in governing. Instead of modest bipartisanship, the administration's preferred style of governing became something much closer to the way Rove runs campaigns: Steamroll the opposition whenever possible, and reach across the aisle only in the rare cases, like No Child Left Behind, when it is absolutely necessary. The large tax cut that Bush pursued and won on an almost party-line vote just afterward is a model of this confrontational style. Its limitations would become apparent.

By late summer of his first year, the early burst of achievement had slowed and Bush's approval ratings were beginning to sag. Ronald Brownstein of *The Los Angeles Times* dubbed him the "A4 president," unable even to make the front page of the newspaper. He did not seem the likely leader of a realignment.

That September 11 was both a turning point for the Bush administration and an event that would change the course of American history was immediately clear. It was also clear, if less widely appreciated, that the attacks were the type of event that can instantly set off a great shifting of the geological strata of American politics. In a coincidence of epic dimensions, 9/11 provided, just when Rove needed it, the historical lever missing until then. He had been presented with exactly the sort of "societal trauma" that makes realignment possible, and with it a fresh chance to pursue his goal. Bob Woodward's trilogy on the Bush White House makes clear how neoconservatives in the administration recognized that 9/11 gave them the opening they'd long desired to forcefully remake the Middle East. Rove recognized the same opening.

After 9/11, any pretense of shared sacrifice or of reaching across the aisle was abandoned. The administration could demand—and get—almost anything it wanted, easily flattening Democratic opposition, which it did with increasing frequency on issues like the PATRIOT Act and the right of Department of Homeland Security workers to unionize. The crisis atmosphere allowed the White House to ignore what normally would have been some of its most basic duties—working with Republicans in Congress (let alone Democrats) and laying the groundwork in Congress and with the American public for what it hoped to achieve. At the time, however, this didn't seem to matter.

Rove's systematic policy of sharply contrasting Republican and Democratic positions on national security was a brilliant campaign strategy and the critical mechanism of Republican victory in the 2002 midterms. But he could not foresee how this mode of operating would ultimately work at cross-purposes with his larger goal. "What Bush went out and did in 2002," a former administration official told me, "clearly at Karl's behest, with an eye toward the permanent Republican majority, was very aggressively attack those Democrats who voted with him and were for him. There's no question that the president helped pick up seats. But all of that goodwill was squandered."

From the outset, Rove's style of pursuing realignment—through division—was in stark contrast to the way it had happened the last time. In *Franklin D. Roosevelt and the New Deal*, the historian William E. Leuchtenburg notes that Roosevelt mentioned the Democratic Party by name only three times in his entire 1936 reelection campaign. Throughout his presidency, Roosevelt had large Democratic majorities in Congress but operated in a nonpartisan fashion, as though he didn't. Bush, with razor-thin majorities—and for a time, a divided Congress—operated as though his margins were insurmountable, and sowed interparty divisions as an electoral strategy.

Rove never graduated from college. He dropped out of the University of Utah and campaigned for the chairmanship of the College Republicans, a national student organization whose leaders often go on to important positions in the party. He won, placing himself on a fast track to a career in politics. But he was and remains an autodidact, and a large part of his self-image depends on showing that his command of history and politics is an order of magnitude greater than other people's. Rove has a need to outdo everybody else that seems to inform his sometimes contrarian views of history. It's not enough for him to have read everything; he needs to have read everything and arrived at insights that others missed.

This aspect of Rove was on fuller-than-usual display during a speech he gave at the University of Utah, titled "What Makes a Great President," just after the Republicans swept the 2002 elections. The incumbent presidential party typically loses seats in the off-year election, so winning was a big deal to Rove, who actively involved himself in many of the campaigns. Overcoming historical precedent seemed to feed his oracular sense of himself, and during his speech and the question-and-answer period that followed he revealed a lot about how he thinks and where he imagined his party was going.

In his speech, he described a visit to the White House by the revisionist historian Forrest McDonald, who spoke about presidential greatness. Rove expressed delight at discovering a fellow McKinley enthusiast, and said that McDonald had explained in his talk, "Nobody knows McKinley is great, because history demanded little of him. He modernized the presidency, he modernized the Treasury to deal with the modern economy, he changed dramatically the policies of his party by creating a durable governing coalition for 40 years"—this last part clearly excited Rove—"and he attempted deliberately to break with the Gilded Age politics. He was inclusive, and he was the first Republican candidate for president to be endorsed by a leader in the Catholic hierarchy. The Protestant Anglo-Saxon Republicans were scandalized by his 1896 campaign, in which he paraded Portuguese fishermen and Slovak coal miners and Serbian iron workers to Canton, Ohio, to meet him. He just absolutely scandalized the country."

In this way of telling it, McKinley alone understood what everybody else was missing: A political realignment was under way, and by harnessing it, though it might "scandalize" conventional thinking, McKinley would not only carry the presidency but also bring about an unprecedented period of dominance for his party. The subtext seemed to be that Rove, too, recognized something everybody else had missed—the chance for a Republican realignment—just as he recognized the overlooked genius of William McKinley. He joked to the audience, "This tripled the size of the McKinley caucus in Washington—it was Bob Novak, me, and now Forrest McDonald."

After the speech a member of the audience asked a question that took as its premise the notion that America was evenly divided between Republicans and Democrats. Rove insisted this was not the case, pouring forth a barrage of numbers from the recent midterm elections that seemed to lay waste to the notion. "Something is going on out there," Rove insisted. "Something else more fundamental . . . But we will only know it retrospectively. In two years or four years or six years, [we may] look back and say the dam began to break in 2002."

Like his hero McKinley, he alone was the true visionary. Everyone else looked at the political landscape and saw a nation at rough parity. Rove looked at the same thing and saw an emerging Republican majority.

From Rove's vantage point after the 2002 elections, everything seemed to be on track. He had a clear strategy for achieving realignment and the historical conditions necessary to enact it. His already considerable influence within the administration was growing with the Republican Party's rising fortunes, which were credited to his strategy of aggressive divisiveness on the issues of war and terrorism. But what Rove took to be the catalyst for realignment turned out to be the catalyst for his fall.

September 11 temporarily displaced much of what was going on in Washington at the time. The ease with which Republicans were able to operate in the aftermath of the attacks was misleading, and it imbued Rove, in particular, with false confidence that what he was doing would continue to work. In reality, it masked problems—bad relationships with Congress, a lack of support for Bush's broader agenda—that either went unseen or were consciously ignored. Hubris and a selective understanding of history led Rove into a series of errors and misjudgments that compounded to devastating effect.

He never appreciated that his success would ultimately depend on the sustained cooperation of congressional Republicans, and he developed a dysfunctional relationship with many of them. This wasn't clear at first. Several of the administration's early moves looked particularly shrewd, one of them being to place the White House congressional liaisons in the office suite of the majority whip, Tom DeLay of Texas. At the time, DeLay was officially third in the Republican House leadership hierarchy, but as everyone knew, he was the capo of House Republicans and the man to see if you wanted to get something done.

Things never clicked. Republicans on the Hill say that Rove and DeLay, both formidable men who had known each other in Texas, had a less-than-amiable relationship. When I asked DeLay about their history, he let out a malevolent chuckle and told me that his very first race had pitted him against one of Rove's candidates. "They were nasty to me," DeLay recalled. "I had some payroll tax liens against me, as most small businessmen do, and I was driving a red Eldorado at the time. The taxes were paid, but they were running radio ads saying I was a deadbeat who didn't pay my taxes." DeLay still remembered the ad: "He wants to drive his red Cadillac to Washington on the backs of the taxpayers."

XYZ

The cross the fork the zigzag—a few straight lines
For pain, quandary and evasion, the last of signs.
　　　　　　　　　　　　　　　　　　—Robert Pinsky

Robert Pinsky's new collection of poems, *Gulf Music*, will be published this fall. He served three terms as the United States poet laureate and currently teaches at Boston University.

DeLay made a point of saying he didn't hold a grudge. ("That wouldn't be Christian of me.") But he did allow that Rove had been extremely aggressive in trying to impose his ideas on Congress. "Karl and I are sort of the same personality," he explained, "so we end up screaming at each other. But in the end you walk out of the room with an agenda." DeLay insists he didn't mind Rove's screaming, but if that's true, he belongs to a truly Christian group.

Rove's behavior toward Congress stood out. "Every once in a while Rove would come to leadership meetings, and he definitely considered himself at least an equal with the leaders in the room," a Republican aide told me. "But you have to understand that Congress is a place where a certain decorum is expected. Even in private, staff is still staff. Rove would come and chime in as if he were equal to the speaker. Cheney sometimes came, too, and was far more deferential than Rove—and he was the vice president." Other aides say Rove was notorious for interrupting congressional leaders and calling them by their first name.

Dick Armey, the House Republican majority leader when Bush took office (and no more a shrinking violet than DeLay), told me a story that captures the exquisite pettiness of most members of Congress and the arrogance that made Bush and Rove so inept at handling them. "For all the years he was president," Armey told me, "Bill Clinton and I had a little thing we'd do where every time I went to the White House, I would take the little name tag they give you and pass it to the president, who, without saying a word, would sign and date it. Bill Clinton and I didn't like each other. He said I was his least-favorite member of Congress. But he knew that when I left his office, the first schoolkid I came across would be given that card, and some kid who had come to Washington with his mama would go home with the president's autograph. I think Clinton thought it was a nice thing to do for some kid, and he was happy to do it." Armey said that when he went to his first meeting in the White House with President Bush, he explained the tradition with Clinton and asked the president if he would care to continue it. "Bush refused to sign the card. Rove, who was sitting across the table, said, 'It would probably wind up on eBay," Armey continued. "Do I give a damn? No. But can you imagine refusing a simple request like that with an insult? It's stupid. From the point of view of your own self-interest, it's stupid. I was from Texas, and I was the majority leader. If my expectations of civility and collegiality were disappointed, what do you think it was like for the rest of the congressmen they dealt with? The Bush White House was tone-deaf to the normal courtesies of the office."

Winning the 2002 elections earned Rove further distinction as an electoral strategist. But it didn't change the basic dynamic between the White House and Congress, and Rove drew exactly the wrong lesson from the experience, bringing the steamroller approach from the campaign trail into his work in government. Emboldened by triumph, he grew more imperious, worsening his relations with the Hill. With both houses now in Republican hands, he pressed immigration reform and Social Security privatization. A congressional aide described a Republican leadership retreat after the midterms where Rove whipped out a chart and a sheaf of poll numbers and insisted to Republican leaders that they pursue a Social Security overhaul at once. Making wholesale changes to a beloved entitlement program in the run-up to a presidential election would have been a difficult sell under the best of circumstances. Lacking goodwill in Congress and having laid no groundwork for such an undertaking, Rove didn't get a serious hearing on the issue—or on immigration, either.

A revealing pattern of behavior emerged from my interviews. Rove plainly viewed his standing as equal to or exceeding that of the party's leaders in Congress and demanded what he deemed his due. Yet he was also apparently annoyed at what came with his White House eminence, complaining to colleagues when members of Congress called him to consult about routine matters he thought were beneath his standing—something that couldn't have endeared him to the legislature.

When Bush revived immigration reform this past spring and let it be known that Rove would not take part in the negotiations, the president seemed to have belatedly grasped a basic truth about congressional relations that Armey summed up for me like this: "You can't call her ugly all year and expect her to go to the prom with you."

Another important misjudgment by Bush, prodded by Rove, was giving Rove too much power within the administration. This was partly a function of Rove's desire to control policy as well as politics. His prize for winning the reelection campaign was a formal role and the title of deputy chief of staff for policy. But his power also grew because the senior policy staff in the White House was inept.

In an early scene in Ron Suskind's book *The Price of Loyalty*, Treasury Secretary Paul O'Neill, not yet alive to the futility of his endeavor, warns Dick Cheney that the White House policy process is so ineffectual that it is tantamount to "kids rolling around on the lawn." Had O'Neill lasted longer than he did (he resigned in 2002), he might have lowered his assessment. Before she left the White House in humiliation after conservatives blocked her nomination to the Supreme Court, White House Counsel Harriet Miers had also served as deputy chief of staff for policy. The president's Domestic Policy Council was run by Claude Allen, until he, too, resigned, after he was caught shoplifting at Target.

Rove was and remains an autodidact, and a large part of his self-image depends on showing that his command of history and politics is an order of magnitude greater than other people's.

The weakness of the White House policy staff demanded Rove's constant involvement. For all his shortcomings, he had clear ideas about where the administration should go, and the ability to maneuver. "Where the bureaucracy was failing and broken, Karl got stuff done," says a White House colleague. "Harriet was no more capable of producing policy out of the policy office she directed than you or I are capable of jumping off the roof of a building and flying to Minneapolis."

As a result, Rove not only ran the reelection campaign, he plotted much of Bush's second-term agenda, using the opportunity to push long-standing pet issues—health-savings accounts, Social Security privatization—that promised to weaken support for Democrats, by dismantling Medicare and Social Security. But this also meant committing the president to sweeping domestic changes that had no public favor and had not been a focus of the 2004 campaign, which had centered almost exclusively on the war.

Bush's reelection and Rove's assumption of a formal policy role had a bigger effect than most of Washington realized at the time. It is commonly assumed (as I assumed) that Rove exercised a major influence on White House policy before he had the title, all the time that he had it, and even after it was taken away from him in the staff shake-up last year that saw Josh Bolten succeed Andrew Card as chief of staff.

Insiders don't disagree, but say that Rove's becoming deputy chief of staff for policy was still an important development. For the purposes of comparison, a former Bush official cited the productiveness of the first two years of Bush's presidency, the period that generated not just No Child Left Behind but three tax cuts and the Medicare prescription-drug benefit. At the time, Bolten was deputy chief of staff for policy, and relations with Congress had not yet soured. "Josh was not an equal of Karl's with regard to access to the president or stature," says the official. "But he was a strong enough intellect and a strong enough presence that he was able to create a deliberative process that led to a better outcome." When Bolten left to run the Office of Management and Budget, in 2003, the balance shifted in Rove's favor, and then shifted further after the reelection. "Formalizing [Rove's policy role] was the final choke-off of any internal debate or deliberative process," says the official. "There was no offset to Karl."

Rove's greatest shortcoming was not in conceptualizing policies but in failing to understand the process of getting them implemented, a weakness he never seems to have recognized in himself. It's startling that someone who gave so much thought to redirecting the powers of government evinced so little interest in understanding how it operates. Perhaps because he had never worked in government—or maybe because his standing rested upon his relationship with a single superior—he was often ineffective at bringing into being anything that required more than a presidential signature.

As the September 11 mind-set began to lose its power over Washington, Rove still faced the task of getting the more difficult parts of his realignment schema through Congress. But his lack of fluency in the art of moving policy and his tendency to see the world through the divisive lens of a political campaign were great handicaps. There was an important difference between the administration's first-term achievements and the entitlement overhauls (Social Security and Medicare) and volatile cultural issues (immigration) that Rove wanted to push through next. Cutting taxes and furnishing new benefits may generate some controversy in Washington, but few lawmakers who support them face serious political risk. (Tax cuts get Republicans elected!) So it's possible, with will and numbers alone, to pass them with the barest of majorities. Rove's mistake was to believe that this would work with everything.

Entitlement reform is a different animal. More important than reaching a majority is offering political cover to those willing to accept the risk of tampering with cherished programs, and the way to do this is by enlisting the other side. So the fact that Republicans controlled the White House and both houses of Congress after 2002—to Rove, a clinching argument for confrontation—actually *lessened* the likelihood of entitlement reform. Congressional Republicans didn't support Rove's plan in 2003 to tackle Social Security or immigration reform because they didn't *want* to pass such things on a party-line vote. History suggested they'd pay a steep price at election time.

Rove's idea was to use the levers of government to create a realignment—to force an effect that ordinarily occurs only in the most tumultuous periods in American history.

To understand this, Rove need not have looked back any farther than the last Republican president who had attempted something on this order. Before he was president, Ronald Reagan talked about letting people opt out of the Social Security system, a precursor of the plan Rove favors. In 1981, in the full tide of victory, Reagan proposed large cuts—and the Republican Senate refused even to take them up. The mere fact that they had been put forward, however, was enough to imperil Republicans, who took significant losses in 1982.

The following year, Reagan tried again, this time cooperating with the Democratic speaker of the House, Tip O'Neill. He now understood that the only way to attain any serious change on such a sensitive issue was for both parties to hold hands and jump together. To afford each side deniability if things fell apart, the two leaders negotiated by proxy. O'Neill chose Robert Ball, a widely respected Social Security commissioner under three presidents, while Reagan picked Alan Greenspan, the future chairman of the Federal Reserve. Key senators in both parties were looped in.

As Ball and Greenspan made headway, it was really O'Neill and Reagan who were agreeing. To assure both sides political cover, the negotiations were an all-or-nothing process. The plan that was eventually settled on addressed the solvency problem by raising the retirement age (which pleased Republicans) and taxing Social Security benefits for the first time (which pleased Democrats). Unlike in 1981, Republicans in Congress weren't left exposed. Democrats couldn't attack them for raising the retirement age, because Tip O'Neill had signed on. Republicans couldn't complain about higher taxes, because Democrats had supported Ronald Reagan's plan.

At the *Christian Science Monitor* lunch just after the reelection, Rove, then at the apogee of his power, had no time for nostrums like bipartisanship or negotiation. Armed with his policy title and the aura of political genius, he pressed for the Social Security changes so far denied him. In many ways, this decision was the fulcrum of the Bush presidency. Had Bush decided not to pursue Social Security or had he somehow managed to pursue it in a way that included Democrats, his presidency might still have ended up in failure, because of Iraq. But the dramatic collapse of Rove's Social Security push foreclosed any other possibility. It left Bush all but dead in the water for what looks to be the remainder of his time in office.

Rove pursued his plan with characteristic intensity, running it out of the White House from the top down, like a political campaign, and seeking to enlist the network of grassroots activists that had carried the Bush-Cheney ticket to a second term. Bush gave Social Security prominence in his State of the Union address, then set out on a national road show to sell the idea. But after an election fought over the war, Social Security drew little interest, and in contrast to the effect Bush achieved on education in the 2000 campaign, public support didn't budge. (It actually worsened during his tour.)

Unlike Reagan, Bush did not produce a bill that could have served as a basis for negotiation—nor did he seriously consult any Democrats with whom he might have negotiated. Instead, Rove expected a bill to emerge from Congress. The strategy of a president's outlining broad principles of what he'd like in a bill and calling on Congress to draft it has worked many times in the past. But Rove had no allies in Congress, had built no support with the American public, and had chosen to undertake the most significant entitlement reform since Reagan by having Bush barnstorm the country speaking before handpicked Republican audiences with the same partisan fervor he'd brought to the presidential campaign trail—all of which must have scared the living daylights out of the very Republicans in Congress Rove foolishly counted upon to do his bidding. The problems buried for years under the war and then the presidential race came roaring back, and Bush got no meaningful support from the Hill. He was left with a flawed, unpopular concept whose motive—political gain—was all too apparent.

Within months it was clear that the Social Security offensive was in deep trouble and, worse, was dragging down Bush's popularity at a time when he needed all the support he could muster for Iraq. Every week, the political brain trust in the Bush White House gathers under Rove for what is known as the "Strategery Meeting" (an ironic nod to Bush's frequent malapropisms) to plot the course ahead. What transpires is usually a closely held secret. But two former Bush officials provided an account of one meeting in the late spring of 2005, in the middle of the Social Security push, that affords a remarkable glimpse of Rove's singularity of purpose.

He opened the meeting by acknowledging that the Social Security initiative was struggling and hurting the president's approval ratings, and then announced that, despite this, they would stay the course through the summer. He admitted that the numbers would probably continue to fall. But come September, the president would hit Democrats hard on the issue of national security and pull his numbers back up again. Winning on Social Security was so important to Rove that he was evidently willing to gamble the effectiveness of Bush's second term on what most people in the White House and Congress thought were very long odds to begin with. The gamble didn't pay off. Even before Hurricane Katrina hit New Orleans on the morning of August 29, what slim hope might have remained for Social Security was gone.

Hurricane Katrina clearly changed the public perception of Bush's presidency. Less examined is the role Rove played in the defining moment of the administration's response: when Air Force One flew over Louisiana and Bush gazed down from on high at the wreckage without ordering his plane down. Bush advisers Matthew Dowd and Dan Bartlett wanted the president on the ground immediately, one Bush official told me, but were overruled by Rove for reasons that are still unclear: "Karl did not want the plane to land in Louisiana." Rove's political acumen seemed to be deserting him altogether.

An important theme of future Bush administration memoirs will be the opportunity cost of leading off the second term with the misguided plan to overhaul Social Security. "The great cost of the Social Security misadventure was lost support for the war," says a former Bush official. "When you send troops to war, you have no higher responsibility as president than to keep the American people engaged and maintain popular support. But for months and months after it became obvious that Social Security was not going to happen, nobody—because of Karl's stature in the White House—could be intellectually honest in a meeting and say, 'This is not going to happen, and we need an exit strategy to get back onto winning ground.' It was a catastrophic mistake."

It strains belief to think that someone as highly attuned as Rove to all that goes on in politics could have missed the reason for Bush's reelection: He persuaded just enough people that he was the better man to manage the war. But it's also hard to fathom how the master strategist could leave his president and his party as vulnerable as they proved to be six months into the second term. The Republican pollster Tony Fabrizio says, "People who were concerned about the war, we lost. People who were concerned about the economy, we lost. People who were concerned about health care, we lost. It goes on and on. Any of those things would have helped refocus the debate or at least put something else out there besides the war. We came out of the election and what was our agenda for the next term? Social Security. There was nothing else that we were doing. We allowed ourselves as a party to be defined by—in effect, to live and die by—the war in Iraq."

That Rove ignored a political reality so clear to everyone else can be explained only by the immutable nature of his ambition: Social Security was vital for a realignment, however unlikely its success now appeared. At the peak of his influence, the only person who could have stopped him was the one person he answered to—but the president was just as fixated on his place in history as Rove was on his own.

Moments of precise reckoning in politics are rare outside of elections. Snapshot polls don't tell you much about whole epochs. Even voter identification can be a misleading indicator. In 1976, the post-Watergate Republican Party would have appeared to be in existential peril, when in fact it was on the verge of setting the agenda for a generation. So the question of where exactly things stand right now is more complicated than it might appear.

As he nears the end of his time in government, Rove has been campaigning for the notion that Bush has been more successful than he's being credited for. But the necessity of adopting history's longer perspective to make his argument says a great deal. Of the five policies in his realignment vision, Social Security and immigration failed outright; medical-savings accounts and the faith-based program wound up as small, face-saving initiatives after the original ambitions collapsed; and the lone success, No Child Left Behind, looks increasingly jeopardized as it comes up for renewal in Congress this year, a victim of Bush's unpopularity. Rove no longer talks about realignment—though the topic is now very popular with Democrats, who have a good shot at controlling both houses of Congress and the presidency after the next election. On the face of things, the Republican Party is in trouble. In a representative example, voters in a recent NBC-*Wall Street Journal* poll preferred that the next president be a Democrat by 52–31 percent, and delivered the most negative assessment of the Republican Party in the surveys two-decade history. In 2002, Americans were equally split along partisan lines. A recent Pew study shows that 50 percent of the public identifies as Democratic or leaning that way, while just 35 percent identifies with the GOP.

Rove is a great devotee of the historian Robert H. Wiebe, who also emphasizes the pivotal quality of the 1896 election. Wiebe thought industrialization had launched a great sorting-out process in the 1880s and '90s that reached a dramatic culmination in 1896. He argues in his book *The Search for Order, 1877–1920* that "a decade's accumulated bitterness ultimately flowed into a single national election."

It seems highly unlikely, though not impossible, that historians will one day view 2000 or 2004 as the kind of realigning election that Rove so badly wanted. Ken Mehlman, a protégé of Rove's and one of the sharper minds in the Republican Party, is adamant that the analysis that led Rove to believe realignment was at hand remains fundamentally correct. "If you look back over the last few decades, an era of politics has run its course," Mehlman told me. "Both parties achieved some of their highest goals. Democrats got civil rights, women's rights, the New Deal, and recognition of the need for a cleaner environment. Republicans got the defeat of the Soviet Union, less violent crime, lower tax rates, and welfare reform. The public agrees on this. So the issues now become: How do you deal with the terrorist threat? How do you deal with the retirement of the Baby Boomers? How do you deliver health care with people changing jobs? How do you make sure America retains its economic strength with the rise of China and India? How that plays out is something we don't know yet." As far as what's happened since 2000, Mehlman says, "the conditions remain where they were."

In this view, America is still in the period of great churn, and the 1896 election hasn't happened yet.

Rove has no antecedent in modern American politics, because no president before Bush thought it wise to give a political adviser so much influence.

Premised as it is on the notion that the past seven years have been a wash, Mehlman's analysis has a self-justifying tinge. At least for now, Republicans have measurably fallen behind where they were in 2000. It's hard to sift underlying political views from temporary rage against Bush, or to anticipate what effect his presidency will have on the Republican Party's fortunes once he's gone. But the effect does seem certain to be less pronounced—less disastrous—than it is now. Considered in that context, Mehlman's analysis rings true.

When I asked Mark Gersh, one of the Democrats' best electoral analysts, for his view of how the political landscape has shifted, he basically agreed with Mehlman, and offered his own perspective on Rove's vision of realignment. "September 11 is what made them, and Iraq is what undermined them, and the truth lies in between the two—and that is that both parties are at parity," Gersh told me. "There was never any indication that the Republicans were emerging as the majority party. What was happening was that partisanship was actually hardening. Fewer people in both parties were voting for candidates of the other party." Gersh added that he doesn't believe Democrats are the majority party, and he gives Republicans "at worst a 4-in-10 chance" of holding the presidency in 2008. Even if Rove didn't create a generational shift to the Republican Party, so far at least he does not appear to have ushered in a Democratic one, either.

Nonetheless, certain painful, striking parallels between the presidencies of George Bush and William McKinley can't have been lost on Rove, even if he would be the last to admit them. Both originally campaigned almost exclusively on domestic issues, only to have their presidencies dominated by foreign affairs. Neither distinguished himself. *Policy inertia* is the term the historian Richard L. McCormick uses to characterize McKinley's presidency. David Mayhew, the political scientist, writes in his skeptical study *Electoral Realignments,* "Policy innovations under McKinley during 1897–1901 [McKinley was assassinated in 1901] probably rank in the bottom quartile among all presidential terms in American history." Both sentiments could be applied to Bush.

Perhaps the strangest irony is the foreign adventure that consumed much of McKinley's presidency. Though he lacked Bush's storm-the-barricades temperament, McKinley launched the Spanish-American War partly at the urging of his future vice president, Teddy Roosevelt, and other hawks. As the historian Eric Rauch way has pointed out, after American forces defeated the Spanish navy in the Philippines, the U.S. occupation encountered a bloody postwar insurgency and allegations of torture committed by U.S. troops. Roosevelt, who succeeded

McKinley, was hampered by questions about improper force size and commitment of troops and eventually came to rue his plight. "While I have never varied in my feeling that we had to hold the Philippines," he wrote in 1901, "I have varied very much in my feelings whether we were to be considered fortunate or unfortunate in having to hold them."

To understand Rove's record, it's useful to think of the disaster as being divided into foreign and domestic components. Rove had little say in foreign policy. Dick Cheney understood from decades of government experience how to engineer a war he'd pressed for, and still the administration failed to reshape the Middle East. More than anyone outside the Oval Office, Rove was responsible for much of what went wrong on the domestic front—partly because he had never served in government, and he lacked Cheney's skill at manipulating it. Both men came in believing they had superior insights into history and theoretical underpinnings so strong that their ideas would prevail. But neither man understood how to see them through, and so both failed.

Rove has proved a better analyst of history than agent of historical change, showing far greater aptitude for envisioning sweeping change than for pulling it off. Cheney, through a combination of stealth and nuance, was responsible for steering the Bush administration's policy in many controversial areas: redirecting foreign policy, winning a series of tax cuts, weakening environmental regulations, asserting the primacy of the executive branch. But his interests seldom coincided with Rove's overarching goal of realignment. And Rove, forever in thrall to the mechanics of winning by dividing, consistently lacked the ability to transcend the campaign mind-set and see beyond the struggle nearest at hand. In a world made new by September 11, he put terrorism and war to work in an electoral rather than a historical context, and used them as wedge issues instead of as the unifying basis for the new political order he sought.

Why did so many people get Rove so wrong? One reason is that notwithstanding his pretensions to being a world-historic figure, Rove excelled at winning elections, which is, finally, how Washington keeps score. This leads to another reason: Journalists tend to admire tactics above all else. The books on Rove from last year dwell at length on his techniques and accept the premise of Republican dominance practically on tactical skill alone. A corollary to the Cult of the Consultant is the belief that winning an election—especially a tough one you weren't expected to win—is proof of the ability to govern. But the two are wholly distinct enterprises.

Rove's vindictiveness has also cowed his critics, at least for the time being. One reason his standing has not yet sunk as low as that of the rest of the Bush administration is his continuing ability to intimidate many of those in a position to criticize him. A Republican consultant who works downtown agreed to talk candidly for this article, but suggested that we have lunch across the river in Pentagon City, Virginia. He didn't want to be overheard. Working with Rove, he explained, was difficult enough already: "You're constantly confronting the big, booming voice of Oz."

In ways small and large, Rove has long betrayed his lack of understanding of Washington's institutional subtleties and the effective application of policy, even for the rawest political objectives. The classic example is Rove's persuading the president in 2002 to impose steep tariffs on foreign steel—a ploy he believed would win over union workers in Rust Belt swing states, ordinarily faithful Democrats, in the next presidential election. This was celebrated as a political masterstroke at the time. But within a year the tariffs were declared illegal by the World Trade Organization and nearly caused a trade war. The uproar precipitated their premature and embarrassing removal.

"It is a dangerous distraction to know as much about politics as Karl Rove knows," Bruce Reed, the domestic-policy chief in Bill Clinton's administration, told me. "If you know every single poll number on every single issue and every interest group's objection and every political factor, it can be paralyzing to try to make an honest policy decision. I think the larger, deeper problem was that they never fully appreciated that long-term success depended on making sure your policies worked."

Rove has no antecedent in modern American politics, because no president before Bush thought it wise to give a political adviser so much influence. Rove wouldn't be Rove, in other words, were Bush not Bush. That Vice President Cheney also hit a historic high-water mark for influence says a lot about how the actual president sees fit to govern. All rhetoric about "leadership" aside, Bush will be viewed as a weak executive who ceded far too much authority. Rove's failures are ultimately his.

Bush will leave behind a legacy long on ambition and short on positive results. History will draw many lessons from his presidency—about the danger of concentrating too much power in the hands of too few, about the risk of commingling politics and policy beyond a certain point, about the cost of constricting the channels of information to the Oval Office. More broadly, as the next group of presidential candidates and their gurus eases the current crew from the stage, Rove's example should serve as a caution to politicians and journalists.

The Bush administration made a virtual religion of the belief that if you act boldly, others will follow in your wake. That certainly proved to be the case with Karl Rove, for a time. But for all the fascination with what Rove was doing and thinking, little attention was given to whether or not it was working and why. This neglect encompasses many people, though one person with far greater consequences than all the others. In the end, the verdict on George W. Bush may be as simple as this: He never questioned the big, booming voice of Oz, so he never saw the little man behind the curtain.

JOSHUA GREEN is a senior editor of *The Atlantic*.

From *The Atlantic*, September 2007, pp. 52–72. Copyright © 2007 by Joshua Green. Reprinted by permission of the author.

Good Health for America?

America has struggled to reform public health care for over 100 years and now has a byzantine, costly system controlled by powerful, money-hungry interest groups. Martin Gorsky wonders whether President Obama can deliver reform.

MARTIN GORSKY

When Barack Obama swept to power in November 2008, he seemed to promise a new start for domestic politics in the United States. High on his agenda was reform of the health care system, widely considered to be expensive, underperforming and unfair. America was spending a huge proportion of its national wealth on medical care—15 per cent in 2005, compared with eight per cent in Britain and 11 per cent in France. Yet unlike European countries with universal coverage, around 46 million US citizens lacked any health insurance. With Obama's thumping majority and a tide of goodwill towards him, expectations of change were high.

Since then reform politics have been a rollercoaster ride. The president's proposals had three basic goals: regulation of the private insurance market, a 'public option' of a state-run health insurance scheme and more compulsion on employers and individuals to purchase coverage. However, the plan quickly generated huge controversy with opponents saying it was tantamount to Soviet-style Communism. For European observers, long accustomed to tax-funded national health services or state-mandated social insurance, this is rather baffling. Why should so many Americans believe universal health coverage poses a fundamental threat to their liberty and why has it been so hard for Obama to deliver his legislation?

History can help us understand the choices which led the US to such a different approach to that of Europe. A useful concept in thinking about this is 'path dependency', the idea that decisions taken early on can significantly constrain possibilities for change later in time. With this in mind, we can look at why national health insurance was rejected by Americans from the early 20th century onwards.

Statutory sickness insurance originated in Germany in 1883, devised by civil servant Theodor Lohmann and implemented by the 'Iron Chancellor' Otto von Bismarck. The principle was that health coverage became obligatory for particular groups of waged workers, financed by employer contributions and employee payroll deductions. Bismarck's goals in delivering welfare benefits were partly to enhance the efficiency with which 'human capital' was managed in an era of dynamic industrial expansion and partly to head off the appeal of socialism.

As the system proved broadly successful, other countries began to consider their own versions of it. In Britain it was adopted in 1911 as part of the Liberal welfare reforms, which also included unemployment insurance and old age pensions.

In America, proposals for blue-collar health insurance were made in the 1910s by the American Association for Labor Legislation (AALL), a group typifying the 'progressive' strand in US politics which held that social intervention was needed to ameliorate the damage inflicted by untrammelled capitalism. The market, they suggested, had failed to protect the health of the workforce and American industrial productivity was suffering. But their strategy of presenting a model insurance law for state governments was rejected. Organised labour withheld support for the proposals, arguing that it was nothing but a ploy to avoid paying fair wages. Recent scholarship has also shown that the AALL underestimated the extent to which private insurance schemes were already providing sick pay coverage in many industries. Moreover, American wages were high and many workers could pay their medical bills. However, this 'labour rejection' analysis ignores the fact that trade unions in Britain and Germany had also been unenthusiastic, yet their opposition did not stop determined governments imposing such welfare laws.

So why not in America? Opinion is divided. Marxist historians emphasise that ruling classes used welfare legislation to wean proletarian loyalties away from the lure of socialism, represented in Germany by the Social Democrats and in Britain by the Labour Party. In America, however, socialist politics never took hold so there was no imperative for governments to undercut the left by advancing welfare entitlements.

Perhaps a better explanation lies with political structures and the power of pressure groups to influence law-making. In the US, there were various interests which stood to lose from state intervention. Doctors feared the loss of their freedom to treat and charge patients as they saw fit and their trade body, the American Medical Association (AMA), provided powerful opposition. Employers worried that expenditure on health insurance premiums might undermine competitiveness, while private insurers and pharmaceutical manufacturers anticipated a loss of business. These groups argued that the introduction of statutory health insurance would lead to dependency and to what economists now call 'moral hazard': unwarranted claims and high absenteeism. Such criticisms reached a head after America's entry into the First World War, with health insurance depicted as an insidious German innovation fundamentally at odds with the American way.

After America's entry into the First World War, health insurance was depicted as an insidious German innovation at odds with the American way.

The failure of the AALL meant that between the wars most working Americans relied instead on private and voluntary approaches to their health care needs. Public hospitals and asylums remained for the very poor. This system was tested by the Depression of the 1930s, when the medical marketplace was hit hard. Hospital income was rescued by locally-based non-profit insurance schemes called Blue Cross, while the associated Blue Shield provided cover for medical care. Meanwhile, industry-based pre-payment plans became more established. In 1938 the industrialist Henry Kaiser established a fund to provide medical care for workers building the Grand Coulee Dam in Washington State, which led to the birth of Kaiser Permanente, the forerunner of the later Health Maintenance Organisations (HMOs).

However, no progress was made in implementing statutory insurance despite growing support in the New Deal era of the 1930s. This was when the Democratic Party established key elements of America's welfare state, put in place to tackle the distress that followed the Wall Street Crash of 1929. President Franklin Roosevelt briefly considered whether national health insurance should be an element of his 1935 Social Security Bill, which introduced pension provisions and unemployment insurance. However, fearing that it might imperil the bill, he decided against including it. Pro-reform senators brought forward unsuccessful bills in 1939, 1943 and finally 1945, when President Truman lent his support. These repeated congressional defeats meant that, like FDR before him, Truman retreated from the reform agenda. Once again, America put its faith in a private and voluntary sector route towards universal and comprehensive health care.

At this point, the 'path dependency' explanation comes into play. In western Europe politicians and people were already accustomed to compulsory health insurance. Moreover, the resistance of groups such as doctors had been partly overcome. It was therefore not such a big leap to legislate in the 1940s for a larger state role, whether through the tax-funded NHS devised by Britain's Aneurin Bevan, or through extending the reach of insurance, as under France's Sécurité Sociale, introduced by President de Gaulle. In the US, by contrast, there was no prior popular acceptance and the fears of opponents were undimmed. Nor, unlike in Europe, had the political left entirely embraced the goal of a bigger welfare state. Instead,

American trade unions had accommodated themselves to the market by demanding that employers provide health benefits within remuneration packages. Thus the favourable labour market conditions of wartime had seen a huge expansion of voluntary coverage, so that by 1945 there were 15.7 million people enrolled in Blue Cross schemes.

That said, path dependency does not really explain why popular, competent politicians failed to overcome the odds against them. Why, despite Democratic electoral successes and the trauma of depression and war, could Roosevelt and Truman not assert their wills? A fuller explanation demands the 'institutionalist' and 'pressure group' explanations.

The key point is that the political institutions of the US tend to impede deep and contentious reforms. Indeed, the separation of powers between the executive, Congress and the Supreme Court was designed to provide checks and balances on overmighty presidents. Nor can US presidents always count on the support of their own members in Congress. Meanwhile pressure groups wield considerable influence over decision-making, with contributions to campaign funds giving politicians an incentive to block reform. Contrast this with Britain where the 'first past the post' system frequently delivers governments with clear working majorities.

In the 1930s and 1940s congressional opposition to the US president came from conservative Southern Democrats, who were expressing the political wishes of a range of interest groups, notably those of the AMA. National health insurance, US doctors worried, would curtail their medical autonomy and reduce them to the status of salaried employees. They launched a series of propaganda drives, a favourite theme being that national health insurance was 'un-American', the contrast drawn first with German medicine under Nazism then, as the Cold War began, with Soviet Communism.

In the 1960s, however, the US state finally extended its role through the Medicare and Medicaid programmes. Once again the Democrats were in power and once again a president, Lyndon B. Johnson, backed the proposals. This time, though, various factors undermined the capacity of interest groups to block change. First, demographic and scientific factors combined to expose the limits of markets as providers of health care: the elderly population was booming and technological and pharmaceutical innovation both increased costs and raised expectations about what medicine could deliver. The problem of health cover had therefore returned to the political limelight. The intellectual mood had also changed in the era of Kennedy progressives: President Eisenhower's Great Society of the 1950s, founded on industrial prosperity and mass consumerism, had not, they argued, solved all America's social problems. This time the reformers adopted a more subtle strategy, pressing not for universalism, but rather for incremental changes that would be politically more palatable. The economic context was also favourable with America enjoying a golden age of growth before the burden of Vietnam and the oil crisis of the 1970s. Finally, doctors were won round because the organisation of Medicare seemed to promise a fillip for their incomes, since the state would reimburse them according to their 'customary' fees.

So with this benign combination of factors, America had arrived by the mid-1970s at a mixed economy of health care which apparently satisfied all citizens: the poor through Medicaid and public hospitals, the elderly through the respectable channel of Medicare, the working and middle classes through HMOs (developed under legislation passed by President Nixon) and workplace-related insurance and the wealthy through private insurance or direct payment. Unfortunately, the cracks in the system soon began to appear. Public expenditure shot up to meet Medicare payments as both hospitals and physicians increased their activities. Meanwhile the structure of the private health care industry changed, with small institutions superseded by large, profit-hungry corporations running hospital chains. This was the point at which US health spending began its relentless upwards course, rising from 5.6 per cent of GDP in 1966 to 8.1 per cent in 1976 and reaching 13.2 per cent in 1996. Medicaid, meanwhile, remained an incomplete solution as the right of states to determine eligibility could lead to the exclusion of groups such as two-parent families, childless couples and widows. President Reagan acted in 1983 to stem the Medicare/Medicaid budgets, introducing the 'Prospective Payment System', which pegged costs of reimbursement to doctors. But this was only a partial brake.

The next attempt at a solution was the Clinton Plan of 1993, with its 'third way' goal of 'managed competition'. A more tightly regulated private health insurance sector would remain dominant, supplemented by new state-level 'health purchasing alliances', while mandatory employer contributions would ensure universal coverage. Once again though, the absence of party unity undermined support in Congress with conservative Democrats too ready to concede to the interests of employers on whom they depended for funding. The labour movement, bruised by the president's embrace of free trade, was also unsupportive and other groups which stood to gain, such as senior citizens, hung back for fear that Medicare might be cut to pay for the reform. Without a pro-reform coalition to foster support at the grassroots, public sentiment was easily swayed by the opposition which, true to historical form, swiftly entered the political arena with well-funded campaigning. Four other factors were in play: first, the level of government debt meant this was not an economically propitious moment for anything which might raise public expenditure; second, the detail of the plan was complicated and the president was slow to start explaining it to the people; third, he delegated the framing of the plan to Hillary Clinton and an inner circle of advisers rather than to Congress and thereby failed to forge a broader consensus; and fourth, the Republican Party seized on the health issue as a platform for a personal attack on Clinton, charging him with secretive policy-making and with imposing 'big government' on Americans.

President Obama has learnt enough from history to dodge some of Clinton's errors on health reform.

Where does all this leave Obama's America? The path dependency analysis tells us why health care reform is such a challenge. At each fork in the road the private health insurance industry emerged stronger and now forms a huge opposition lobby. This means that pro-reform politicians now regard a European-style NHS or social insurance scheme as unfeasible. The institutional structure still means the president can't count on party unity, which encourages the hostile propaganda of interest groups and Republican adversaries. They, in time-honoured fashion, maintain that a state plan would be un-American. Meanwhile the government debt racked up from bailing out the banks makes this, once again, an inopportune economic moment to propose a 'public option'. However, Obama has learnt enough from history to dodge some of Clinton's errors. He has set broad policy goals and then left it to congressional committees to work out the detail while actively selling his plan to voters. Then, with astute political management, he has swayed enough Democratic opponents to make a modified health care bill in 2010 a real possibility. Will this be the year that America finally breaks with the trajectory of the 20th century?

MARTIN GORSKY is Senior Lecturer in the History of Public Health at the London School of Hygiene and Tropical Medicine. For more articles on this subject visit www.historytoday.com/medicine

UNIT 6

New Directions for American History

Unit Selections

Key Points to Consider

- The United States is the most powerful nation in the world, both economically and militarily. What does author Niall Ferguson see as the greatest threat to its continued wealth and prestige?

- Frequently throughout our history, many of those who consider themselves "Americans" (even though *their* ancestors were immigrants) have become worried over "foreigners" and their impact on society. Is the concern over Mexican immigration any different?

- Scholars used to talk about American "exceptionalism": the idea that our history and people are unique. Beginning in the 1960s, this notion came under increasing fire. Historian Simon Schama bucks this trend. In what respects does he believe Americans *are* unique?

- Is global warming a genuine threat, or merely a case of crying wolf? If it is a threat, which nations are more likely to be affected? What should we be doing about it?

- What are "Baby Boomers"? Discuss the conditions under which they came to maturity, and how this has affected their attitudes toward the future?

Student Website

www.mhhe.com/cls

Internet References

American Studies Web
  www.georgetown.edu/crossroads/asw/
National Center for Policy Analysis
  www.public-policy.org/web.public-policy.org/index.php
The National Network for Immigrant and Refugee Rights (NNIRR)
  www.nnirr.org/
STANDARDS: An International Journal of Multicultural Studies
  www.colorado.edu/journals/standards
Supreme Court/Legal Information Institute
  www.supct.law.cornell.edu/supct/index.html

The breakup of the Soviet Union and the end of the Cold War could only be welcomed by those who feared a great power confrontation might mean all-out nuclear conflict. One scholar proclaimed that the collapse of Communism as a viable way of organizing society (only a few small Communist states remain. and China is Communist in name only) in effect signaled "the end of history." By that he meant that liberal democracy has remained as the only political system with universal appeal. Not so, argued another scholar. He predicted that the "clash of cultures" would engender ongoing struggles in the post-Cold War era. At the time of this writing, the United States is at war in both Iran and Afghanistan. Niall Ferguson's "An Empire at Risk" argues that the huge deficits we are incurring from these wars and other costs may well amount to "the fatal arithmetic of imperial decline."

Three articles in this section deal with the treatment of minorities. "What Do We Owe the Indians?" describes the activities of a new generation of educated Indians who are using the courts to get redress from the hundreds of treaties that have been broken or ignored. "Becoming Us" tells how successive waves of immigration in our history have alarmed people who felt that the newcomers might somehow taint our culture. The recent controversy over Mexican immigration has been no exception. Finally, "Ending the Slavery Blame-Game" deals with the question of paying reparations to black people for their centuries under the yoke of slavery. Author Henry Louis Gates points out even if one accepts the idea of reparations, the question of who should be responsible for paying them is enormously complex. He emphasizes the culpability of many Africans for the slave trade.

Historians have long debated the question of American "exceptionalism." That is, has the American experience been such as to create a people who are unique in their habits and outlook? Or is this just a patriotic fallacy? In "The American Character" author Louis Masur explains how well known historian Simon Schama argues that indeed Americans are "exceptional" in many ways, and he identifies four topics that he says "will inform America's future because they

National Archives & Records Administration/Historicus, Inc.

have indelibly shaped its past: war, religion, immigration and abundance."

Despite controversy over some irregularities in reports on global warming, most scientists in the field believe it constitutes a very real threat. Gregg Easterbrook, in "Global Warming: Who Loses—and Who Wins?" argues that it could cause a broad-based disruption of the global economy unparalleled by any event since World War II. He says that in all likelihood global warming will do the most damage to those nations already mired in poverty and might actually benefit the more affluent ones.

The last essay in this volume, "Boomer Century," refers to that generation born between 1946 and 1964, a period when the national birthrate skyrocketed. Baby Boomers were raised in a period of unprecedented prosperity, but now have to cope with a situation of more limited resources and diminished American power. Boomers, author Joshua Zeitz points out, have "long been defined by a vain search for satisfaction."

An Empire at Risk

We won the cold war and weathered 9/11. But now economic weakness is endangering our global power.

Niall Ferguson

C all it the fractal geometry of fiscal crisis. If you fly across the Atlantic on a clear day, you can look down and see the same phenomenon but on four entirely different scales. At one extreme there is tiny Iceland. Then there is little Ireland, followed by medium-size Britain. They're all a good deal smaller than the mighty United States. But in each case the economic crisis has taken the same form: a massive banking crisis, followed by an equally massive fiscal crisis as the government stepped in to bail out the private financial system.

Size matters, of course. For the smaller countries, the financial losses arising from this crisis are a great deal larger in relation to their gross domestic product than they are for the United States. Yet the stakes are higher in the American case. In the great scheme of things—let's be frank—it does not matter much if Iceland teeters on the brink of fiscal collapse, or Ireland, for that matter. The locals suffer, but the world goes on much as usual.

But if the United States succumbs to a fiscal crisis, as an increasing number of economic experts fear it may, then the entire balance of global economic power could shift. Military experts talk as if the president's decision about whether to send an additional 40,000 troops to Afghanistan is a make-or-break moment. In reality, his indecision about the deficit could matter much more for the country's long-term national security. Call the United States what you like—superpower, hegemon, or empire—but its ability to manage its finances is closely tied to its ability to remain the predominant global military power. Here's why.

The disciples of John Maynard Keynes argue that increasing the federal debt by roughly a third was necessary to avoid Depression 2.0. Well, maybe, though some would say the benefits of fiscal stimulus have been oversold and that the magic multiplier (which is supposed to transform $1 of government spending into a lot more than $1 of aggregate demand) is trivially small.

Credit where it's due. The positive number for third-quarter growth in the United States would have been a lot lower without government spending. Between half and two thirds of the real increase in gross domestic product was attributable to government programs, especially the Cash for Clunkers scheme and the subsidy to first-time home buyers. But we are still a very long way from a self-sustaining recovery. The third-quarter growth number has just been revised downward from 3.5 percent to 2.8 percent. And that's not wholly surprising. Remember, what makes a stimulus actually work is the change in borrowing by the whole public sector. Since the federal government was already running deficits, and since the states are actually raising taxes and cutting spending, the actual size of the stimulus is closer to 4 percent of GDP spread over the years 2007 to 2010—a lot less than that headline 11.2 percent deficit.

Meanwhile, let's consider the cost of this muted stimulus. The deficit for the fiscal year 2009 came in at more than $1.4 trillion—about 11.2 percent of GDP, according to the Congressional Budget Office (CBO). That's a bigger deficit than any seen in the past 60 years—only slightly larger in relative terms than the deficit in 1942. We are, it seems, having the fiscal policy of a world war, without the war. Yes, I know, the United States is at war in Afghanistan and still has a significant contingent of troops in Iraq. But these are trivial conflicts compared with the world wars, and their contribution to the gathering fiscal storm has in fact been quite modest (little more than 1.8 percent of GDP, even if you accept the estimated cumulative cost of $3.2 trillion published by Columbia economist Joseph Stiglitz in February 2008).

And that $1.4 trillion is just for starters. According to the CBO's most recent projections, the federal deficit will decline from 11.2 percent of GDP this year to 9.6 percent in 2010, 6.1 percent in 2011, and 3.7 percent in 2012. After that it will stay above 3 percent for the foreseeable future. Meanwhile, in dollar terms, the total debt held by the public (excluding government agencies, but including foreigners) rises from $5.8 trillion in 2008 to $14.3 trillion in 2019—from 41 percent of GDP to 68 percent.

In other words, there is no end in sight to the borrowing binge. Unless entitlements are cut or taxes are raised, there will never be another balanced budget. Let's assume I live another 30 years and follow my grandfathers to the grave at about 75. By 2039, when I shuffle off this mortal coil, the federal debt held by the public will have reached 91 percent of GDP, according to the CBO's extended baseline projections. Nothing to worry about, retort-deficit-loving economists like Paul Krugman. In 1945, the figure was 113 percent.

Well, let's leave aside the likely huge differences between the United States in 1945 and in 2039. Consider the simple fact that under the CBO's alternative (i.e., more pessimistic) fiscal scenario, the debt could hit 215 percent by 2039. That's right: more than double the annual output of the entire U.S. economy.

Forecasting anything that far ahead is not about predicting the future. Everything hinges on the assumptions you make about demographics, Medicare costs, and a bunch of other variables. For example, the CBO assumes an average annual real GDP growth rate of 2.3 percent over the next 30 years. The point is to show the implications of the current chronic imbalance between federal spending and federal revenue. And the implication is clear. Under no plausible scenario does the debt burden decline. Under one of two plausible scenarios it explodes by a factor of nearly five in relation to economic output.

Another way of doing this kind of exercise is to calculate the net present value of the unfunded liabilities of the Social Security and Medicare systems. One recent estimate puts them at about $104 trillion, 10 times the stated federal debt.

No sweat, reply the Keynesians. We can easily finance $1 trillion a year of new government debt. Just look at the way Japan's households and financial institutions funded the explosion of Japanese public debt (up to 200 percent of GDP) during the two "lost decades" of near-zero growth that began in 1990.

Unfortunately for this argument, the evidence to support it is lacking. American households were, in fact, net sellers of Treasuries in the second quarter of 2009, and on a massive scale. Purchases by mutual funds were modest ($142 billion), while purchases by pension funds and insurance companies were trivial ($12 billion and $10 billion, respectively). The key, therefore, becomes the banks. Currently, according to the Bridgewater hedge fund, U.S. banks' asset allocation to government bonds is about 13 percent, which is relatively low by historical standards. If they raised that proportion back to where it was in the early 1990s, it's conceivable they could absorb "about $250 billion a year of government bond purchases." But that's a big "if." Data for October showed commercial banks selling Treasuries.

That just leaves two potential buyers: the Federal Reserve, which bought the bulk of Treasuries issued in the second quarter; and foreigners, who bought $380 billion. Morgan Stanley's analysts have crunched the numbers and concluded that, in the year ending June 2010, there could be a shortfall in demand on the order of $598 billion—about a third of projected new issuance.

Of course, our friends in Beijing could ride to the rescue by increasing their already vast holdings of U.S. government debt. For the past five years or so, they have been amassing dollar-denominated international reserves in a wholly unprecedented way, mainly as a result of their interventions to prevent the Chinese currency from appreciating against the dollar.

Right now, the People's Republic of China holds about 13 percent of U.S. government bonds and notes in public hands. At the peak of this process of reserve accumulation, back in 2007, it was absorbing as much as 75 percent of monthly Treasury issuance.

But there's no such thing as a free lunch in the realm of international finance. According to Fred Bergsten of the Peterson Institute for International Economics, if this trend were to continue, the U.S.-current-account deficit could rise to 15 percent of GDP by 2030, and its net debt to the rest of the world could hit 140 percent of GDP. In such a scenario, the U.S. would have to pay as much as 7 percent of GDP every year to foreigners to service its external borrowings.

Could that happen? I doubt it. For one thing, the Chinese keep grumbling that they have far too many Treasuries already. For another, a significant dollar depreciation seems more probable, since the United States is in the lucky position of being able to borrow in its own currency, which it reserves the right to print in any quantity the Federal Reserve chooses.

Now, who said the following? "My prediction is that politicians will eventually be tempted to resolve the [fiscal] crisis the way irresponsible governments usually do: by printing money, both to pay current bills and to inflate away debt. And as that temptation becomes obvious, interest rates will soar."

Seems pretty reasonable to me. The surprising thing is that this was none other than Paul Krugman, the high priest of Keynesianism, writing back in March 2003. A year and a half later he was comparing the U.S. deficit with Argentina's (at a time when it was 4.5 percent of GDP). Has the economic situation really changed so drastically that now the same Krugman believes it was "deficits that saved us," and wants to see an even larger deficit next year? Perhaps. But it might just be that the party in power has changed.

History strongly supports the proposition that major financial crises are followed by major fiscal crises. "On average," write Carmen Reinhart and Kenneth Rogoff in their new book, *This Time Is Different,* "government debt rises by 86 percent during the three years following a banking crisis." In the wake of these debt explosions, one of two things can happen: either a default, usually when the debt is in a foreign currency, or a bout of high inflation that catches the creditors out. The history of all the great European empires is replete with such episodes. Indeed, serial default and high inflation have tended to be the surest symptoms of imperial decline.

As the U.S. is unlikely to default on its debt, since it's all in dollars, the key question, therefore, is whether we are going to see the Fed "printing money"—buying newly minted Treasuries in exchange for even more newly minted greenbacks—followed by the familiar story of rising prices and declining real-debt burdens. It's a scenario many investors around the world fear. That is why they are selling dollars. That is why they are buying gold.

Yet from where I am sitting, inflation is a pretty remote prospect. With U.S. unemployment above 10 percent, labor unions relatively weak, and huge quantities of unused capacity in global manufacturing, there are none of the pressures that made for stagflation (low growth plus high prices) in the 1970s. Public expectations of inflation are also very stable, as far as can be judged from poll data and the difference between the yields on regular and inflation-protected bonds.

So here's another scenario—which in many ways is worse than the inflation scenario. What happens is that we get a rise in the real interest rate, which is the actual interest rate minus inflation. According to a substantial amount of empirical research by economists, including Peter Orszag (now at the Office of Management and Budget), significant increases in the debt-to-GDP ratio tend to increase the real interest rate. One recent study concluded that "a 20 percentage point increase in the U.S. government-debt-to-GDP ratio should lead to a 20–120 basis points [0.2–1.2 percent] increase in real interest rates." This can happen in one of three ways: the nominal interest rate rises and inflation stays the same; the nominal rate stays the same and inflation falls; or—the nightmare case—the nominal interest rate rises and inflation falls.

Today's Keynesians deny that this can happen. But the historical evidence is against them. There are a number of past cases (e.g., France in the 1930s) when nominal rates have risen even at a time of deflation. What's more, it seems to be happening in Japan right now. Just last week Hirohisa Fujii, Japan's new finance minister, admitted that he was "highly concerned" about the recent rise in Japanese government bond yields. In the very same week, the government admitted that Japan was back in deflation after three years of modest price increases.

It's not inconceivable that something similar could happen to the United States. Foreign investors might ask for a higher nominal return on U.S. Treasuries to compensate them for the weakening dollar. And inflation might continue to surprise us on the downside. After all, consumer price inflation is in negative territory right now.

Why should we fear rising real interest rates ahead of inflation? The answer is that for a heavily indebted government and an even more heavily indebted public, they mean an increasingly heavy debt-service burden. The relatively short duration (maturity) of most of these debts means that a large share has to be rolled over each year. That means any rise in rates would feed through the system scarily fast.

Already, the federal government's interest payments are forecast by the CBO to rise from 8 percent of revenues in 2009 to 17 percent by 2019, even if rates stay low and growth resumes. If rates rise even slightly and the economy flatlines, we'll get to 20 percent much sooner. And history suggests that once you are spending as much as a fifth of your revenues on debt service, you have a problem. It's all too easy to find yourself in a vicious circle of diminishing credibility. The investors don't believe you can afford your debts, so they charge higher interest, which makes your position even worse.

This matters more for a superpower than for a small Atlantic island for one very simple reason. As interest payments eat into the budget, something has to give—and that something is nearly always defense expenditure. According to the CBO, a significant decline in the relative share of national security in the federal budget is already baked into the cake. On the Pentagon's present plan, defense spending is set to fall from above 4 percent now to 3.2 percent of GDP in 2015 and to 2.6 percent of GDP by 2028.

Over the longer run, to my own estimated departure date of 2039, spending on health care rises from 16 percent to 33 percent of GDP (some of the money presumably is going to keep me from expiring even sooner). But spending on everything other than health, Social Security, and interest payments drops from 12 percent to 8.4 percent.

This is how empires decline. It begins with a debt explosion. It ends with an inexorable reduction in the Army, Navy, and Air Force.

This is how empires decline. It begins with a debt explosion. It ends with an inexorable reduction in the resources available for the Army, Navy, and Air Force. Which is why voters are right to worry about America's debt crisis. According to a recent Rasmussen report, 42 percent of Americans now say that cutting the deficit in half by the end of the president's first term should be the administration's most important task—significantly more than the 24 percent who see health-care reform as the No. 1 priority. But cutting the deficit in half is simply not enough. If the United States doesn't come up soon with a credible plan to restore the federal budget to balance over the next five to 10 years, the danger is very real that a debt crisis could lead to a major weakening of American power.

42% of Americans say cutting the deficit in half is the administration's most important task—compared with 24% for health-care reform.

If the United States doesn't come up with a credible plan to balance the budget, the danger is a major weakening of American power.

The precedents are certainly there. Habsburg Spain defaulted on all or part of its debt 14 times between 1557 and 1696 and also succumbed to inflation due to a surfeit of New World silver. Prerevolutionary France was spending 62 percent of royal revenue on debt service by 1788. The Ottoman Empire went the same way: interest payments and amortization rose from 15 percent of the budget in 1860 to 50 percent in 1875. And don't forget the last great English-speaking empire. By the interwar years, interest payments were consuming 44 percent of the British budget, making it intensely difficult to rearm in the face of a new German threat.

Call it the fatal arithmetic of imperial decline. Without radical fiscal reform, it could apply to America next.

NIALL FERGUSON is Laurence A. Tisch professor of history at Harvard and the author of *The Ascent of Money*.

What Do We Owe the Indians?

For starters, a new generation of courthouse-savvy warriors insists we honor the solemn promises made in 371 active treaties, some of which predate the Constitution.

PAUL VANDEVELDER

The Yellowtail ranch, tucked into a narrow valley of soft-rock geology that separates the Big Horn Mountains from the surrounding plains on the southern border of Montana, is not the easiest place to find. Hang a right at Wyola, population 100, the home of the "Mighty Few" as Wyolians are known to their fellow Crow Indians, and head straight for the mountains. This is the rolling rangeland where Montana got its famous moniker, Big Sky Country. Eventually a red sandstone road will take you to a small log cabin on Lodge Grass Creek, 26 miles from the nearest telephone.

The Crow Indian Nation once stretched for hundreds of miles across this high plains grassland without a single road, fencepost or strand of barbed wire to mar the view. Then, in 1887, the federal government cast aside its treaty obligations to the Crow and other tribes and opened up their homelands to white settlers. Cattle soon replaced buffalo, and a hundred years later, about the same time the economics of the cattle industry began circling the drain, geologists discovered that the Big Horn Mountains are floating on a huge lake of crude oil. It wasn't long before guys in blue suits and shiny black cars were cruising the back roads of Crow country and gobbling up land and mineral rights for pennies on the dollar. By hook and crook, the Yellowtails managed to keep their 7,000-acre chunk of that petrochemical dream puzzle. "We just barely hung on to this ranch in the '80s," says Bill Yellowtail, who, in addition to being a cattleman, has been a state legislator, a college professor, a fishing guide and a regional administrator for the Environmental Protection Agency. "It was dumb luck, I guess. And stubbornness."

At 6 feet 2 inches tall and 250 pounds, Yellowtail is a prepossessing figure, and no matter where his life mission takes him, his spirit will always inhabit this place. When his eyes take in the 360-degree view of soaring rock and jack-pine forest and endless blue sky, he sees a wintering valley of 10,000 bones that has been home to his clan for nearly a millennium. And because his inner senses were shaped by this land, by this scale of things, his vision of the future is a big picture. "The battle of the 21st century will be to save this planet," he says,

"and there's no doubt in my mind that the battle will be fought by native people. For us it is a spiritual duty," says Yellowtail, sweeping his hand across the thunderous silence of the surrounding plains from the top of a sandstone bluff, "and this is where we will meet."

What Yellowtail describes with the sweep of his hand is not so much a physical place as a metaphorical landscape where epic legal battles over the allocation and distribution of rapidly diminishing natural resources are destined to be fought. Tacitly, those looming battles echo a question that Americans have finessed, deflected or avoided answering ever since the colonial era: What do we owe the Indian? Long before the United States became an independent nation, European monarchs recognized the sovereignty of Indian nations. They made nation-to-nation treaties with many of the Eastern tribes, and our Founders, in turn, acknowledged the validity of these compacts in Article VI, Clause 2 of the U.S. Constitution, which describes treaties as "the supreme law of the land." Once the Constitution was ratified, the new republic joined a pre-existing community of sovereign nations that already existed within its borders. Today, the United States recognizes 562 sovereign Indian nations, and much of what we owe them is written in the fine print of 371 treaties.

Indian lands hold 65 percent of the nation's uranium, 20 percent of its fresh water, millions of barrels of oil and a treasure chest of copper and zinc.

In 2009, Indians comprise about 1 percent of the population, and irony of ironies, the outback real estate they were forced to accept as their new homelands in the 19th century holds 40 percent of the nation's coal reserves. And that's just for openers. At a time when the nation's industrial machinery and extractive industries are running out of critical mineral resources, Indian lands hold 65 percent of the nation's uranium, untold ounces of gold, silver, cadmium, platinum and manganese, and billions of board feet of virgin timber. In the ground beneath that timber are billions of cubic feet of natural gas, millions of barrels of oil and a treasure chest of copper and zinc. Perhaps even more critically, Indian lands contain 20 percent of the nation's fresh water.

Tribal councils are well aware of the treasures in the ground beneath their boots and are determined to protect them. Fifteen hundred miles southwest of Yellowtail Ranch, Fort Mojave tribe lawyers thwarted a government nuclear waste facility in Ward Valley, Calif. Eight hundred miles east of Ward Valley, Isleta Pueblo attorneys recently won a U.S. Supreme Court contest that forced the city of Albuquerque to spend $400 million to clean up the Rio Grande River. Northwest tribes won the right to half of the commercial salmon catch in their ancestral waterways, including the Columbia and Snake rivers. And, after a 20-year-long legal battle, the Potawatomi and Chippewa tribes of Wisconsin prevented the Exxon Corporation from opening a copper mine at Crandon Lake, a battle Indian lawyers won by enforcing Indian water rights and invoking provisions in the Environmental Protection Agency's Clean Air Act.

The Indian Wars of the 19th century were largely fought over land because the federal government refused to uphold its various treaty obligations. The spoils in the 21st-century battles will be natural resources, and underlying those battles will be the familiar thorn of sovereignty. "Back in the old days," says Tom Goldtooth, the national director for the Indigenous Environmental Network, "we used bows and arrows to protect our rights and our resources. That didn't work out so well. Today we use science and the law. They work much better."

Back in the old days, we used bows and arrows to protect our rights and resources. Today we use science and the law.

None of our laws are more deeply anchored to our national origin than those that bind the fate of the Indian nations to the fate of the republic. And none of our Founding Fathers viewed the nation's debt to the Indians with greater clarity than George Washington. "Indians being the prior occupants [of the continent] possess the right to the Soil," he told Congress soon after he was elected president. "To dispossess them . . . would be a gross violation of the fundamental Laws of Nature and of that distributive Justice which is the glory of the nation." In Washington's opinion, the young war-depleted nation was in no condition to provoke wars with the Indians. Furthermore, he warned Congress that no harm could be done to Indian treaties without undermining the American house of democracy.

The country had no sooner pushed west over the Allegheny Mountains than problems began to emerge with the Constitution itself. The simple model of federalism envisioned by the Founders was proving unequal to the task of managing westward migration. Nothing in the Constitution explained how the new federal government and the states were going to share power with the hundreds of sovereign Indian nations within the republic's borders. The Constitution's commerce clause was designed to neutralize the jealousy of states by giving the federal government exclusive legal authority over treaties and commerce with the tribes, but when Georgia thumbed its nose at Cherokee sovereignty in 1802 by demanding that the entire nation be removed from its territory, the invisible fault line in federalism suddenly opened into a chasm.

The Indians found themselves entangled in a fierce jurisdictional battle that they had no part in starting. It was not their fight, but when the smoke and dust finally settled four decades later, the resolution would be paid for in Indian blood. Georgia's scheme was to bring the issue of states' rights to a national crisis point, and it worked. Bewailing the arrogance of "southern tyrants," President John Quincy Adams declared that Georgia's defiance of federal law had put "the Union in the most imminent danger of dissolution. . . . The ship is about to founder." Short of declaring war against Georgia and its sympathetic neighbors, the nation finally turned in desperation to the Supreme Court.

When the concept of Indian sovereignty was put to the test, Chief Justice John Marshall offered up a series of judgments that infuriated Southern states' rights advocates, including his cousin and bitter rival Thomas Jefferson. In three landmark decisions, known as the Marshall Trilogy issued between 1823 and 1832, the court laid the groundwork for all subsequent federal Indian law. In *Johnson v. McIntosh,* Marshall affirmed that under the Constitution, Indian tribes are "domestically dependent nations" entitled to all the privileges of sovereignty with the exception of making treaties with foreign governments. He explained in *Cherokee Nation v. Georgia* and *Worcester v. Georgia* that the federal government and the Indian nations are inextricably bound together as trustee to obligee, a concept now referred to as the federal trust doctrine. He also ruled that treaties are a granting of rights *from* the Indians *to* the federal government, not the other way around, and all rights not granted by the Indians are presumed to be reserved by the Indians. This came to be known as the reserved rights doctrine.

The federal trust doctrine and the reserved rights doctrine placed the government and the tribes in a legally binding partnership, leaving Congress and the courts with a practical problem—guaranteeing tribes that American society would expand across the continent in an orderly and lawful fashion. Inevitably, as disorderly and unlawful expansion became the norm—by common citizens, presidents, state legislators, governors and lawmakers alike—the conflict of interest embedded in federalism gradually eclipsed the rights of the tribes.

For their part, President Andrew Jackson and the state of Georgia scoffed at Marshall's rulings and accelerated their plans to remove all Indians residing in the Southeast to Oklahoma Territory. Thousands of Cherokee, Choctaw, Creek and Chickasaw Indians died in forced marches from their homelands. Eyewitness reports from the "trail of tears" were so horrific that Congress called for an investigation. The inquiry—conducted by Ethan Allen Hitchcock, the grandson of his revolutionary era namesake—revealed a "cold-blooded, cynical disregard for human suffering and the destruction of human life." Hitchcock's final report, along with supporting evidence, was filed with President John Tyler's secretary of war, John C. Spencer. When Congress demanded a copy, Spencer replied with a curt refusal: "The House should not have the report without my heart's blood." No trace of Hitchcock's final report has ever been found.

By 1840 America's first Indian "removal era" was completed, and within a decade a second removal era would begin. Massive land grabs in the West commenced when Congress passed the Kansas-Nebraska Act of 1854, opening treaty-protected Indian lands to white settlement. While the act is most often remembered as a failed attempt to ease rapidly growing tensions between the North and South by giving settlers the right to determine whether to allow slavery in the new territories, it also embodied a brazen disregard by Washington lawmakers of their trust obligations to Western tribes.

Three decades later, the federal government ignored its trust obligations yet again when the 1887 Dawes Act gave the president the authority to partition tribal lands into allotments for individual Indian families. "Surplus" Indian land was opened up to settlement by white homesteaders, and soon 100 million acres of land once protected by treaties had been wrested from Indian control. Euphemistically known as the Allotments Era, this period lasted until 1934, when Franklin Delano Roosevelt and Congress finally put an end to the land grabs. Meanwhile, federal courts began relying on Marshall's century-old legal precedents in a series of controversial decisions that forcefully reminded Washington lawmakers of their binding obligations to the tribes. The decisions also prompted jealous state governments to resume their adversarial relationship with tribes, and to treat the tribes' partner, the federal government, as a heavy-handed interloper.

Surplus land was opened up to white settlement and soon 100 million acres of land once protected by treaties had been wrested from Indian control.

Although many Allotment Era executive orders were eventually ruled illegal by federal courts, the genie was out of the bottle. There was no way to return the land that had been taken to its rightful owners, and besides, the powerless remnants of once great Indian tribes were lucky to survive from one year to the next. Ironically, the turning point for Indians came decades later, courtesy of Richard Nixon.

On July 8, 1970, in the first major speech ever delivered by an American president on behalf of the American Indian, Nixon told Congress that federal Indian policy was a black mark on the nation's character. "The American Indians have been oppressed and brutalized, deprived of their ancestral lands, and denied the opportunity to control their own destiny." Through it all, said Nixon, who credited his high school football coach, a Cherokee, with teaching him lessons on the gridiron that gave him the fortitude to be president, "the story of the Indian is a

record of endurance and survival, of adaptation and creativity in the face of overwhelming obstacles."

In Nixon's view, the paternalism of the federal government had turned into an "evil" that held the Indian down for 150 years. Henceforth, he said, federal Indian policy should "operate on the premise that Indian tribes are permanent, sovereign governmental institutions in this society." With the assistance of Sen. James Abourezk of South Dakota, Nixon's staff set about writing the American Indian Self-Determination and Education Assistance Act, which gave tribes more direct control over federal programs that affected their members. By the time Congress got around to passing the law, in 1975, Nixon had left the White House in disgrace. But for the 1.5 million native citizens of the United States, the Nixon presidency was a great success that heralded an end to their "century-of-long-time-sleeping."

Word of Nixon's initiatives rumbled like summer thunder through the canyon lands and valleys of Indian Country. While the American Indian Movement grabbed national attention by staging a violent siege of the town of Wounded Knee, S.D., in 1973, thousands of young Indian men and women began attending colleges and universities for the first time. According to Carnegie Foundation records, in November 1968 fewer than 500 Indian students were enrolled in schools of higher education. Ten years later, that number had jumped tenfold.

Among the first to benefit from Nixon-era policies was a generation of determined young Indians with names like Bill Yellowtail, Tom Goldtooth and Raymond Cross. "For the first time in living history, Indian tribes began developing legal personalities," says Cross, a Yale-educated Mandan attorney and law school professor who has made two successful trips to the U.S. Supreme Court to argue the merits of Indian sovereignty. "They realized that federal Indian policies had been a disaster for well over a hundred years. The time had come to change all that."

As various tribes slowly developed their political power, young college educated Indians came to view efforts to wrest away their natural resources as extensions of 19th-century assaults on sovereignty and treaty rights. Mineral corporations, federal agencies and state governments—emboldened by 160 years of neglect of the government's trust responsibilities—were accustomed to having their way with Indian Country.

In places like Lodge Grass, Shiprock and Mandaree, long-term neglect of treaty rights had translated into widespread poverty and a 70 percent unemployment rate. In New Town, Yankton and Second Mesa, that neglect meant a proliferation of kidney dialysis clinics and infant mortality rates that would be scandalous in Ghana. In Crow Agency, Lame Deer and Gallup, neglect looked like a whirlpool of dependency on booze and methamphetamines that spat Indian youth out into a night so dark that wet brain, self-inflicted gunshot wounds, cirrhotic livers and the all too familiar jalopy crashes, marked by a blizzard of little white crosses on wind-scoured reservation byways, read like a cure for living. Indians, no less than their counterparts in white society, found themselves prisoners of the pictures in their own heads.

Neglect spat Indian youth out into a night so dark that gunshot wounds and cirrhotic livers read like a cure for living.

Two hundred and thirty-one years after the new United States signed its first treaty with the Delaware Indians, there is too much money on the table, and too many resources in the ground, for either the Indians or the industrialized world to walk away from Indian Country without a fight. There may be occasional celebrations of mutual understanding and reconciliation, but no one is fooling anybody. The contest of wills will be just as fierce as it was in the Alleghenies in the 1790s, in Georgia in the 1820s, and on the Great Plains in the 1850s. "From the beginning, the Europeans' Man versus Nature argument was a contrived dichotomy," says Cross. "The minute you tame nature, you've destroyed the garden you idealized. The question that confronts the dominant society today is 'Now what?' After you destroy Eden, where do you go from here?"

Meanwhile, on a late Sunday evening inside a cabin on Lodge Grass Creek at Yellowtail Ranch, the weighty matters of the world are at bay. Friends and family have gathered around a half moon table in the kitchen for an evening of community fellowship. No radio. No cell phones. Wide-eyed children lie curled like punctuation marks under star quilts in the living room, listening to grown-ups absorbing each other's lives.

Mostly, the grown-ups dream out loud over cherry pie and homemade strawberry ice cream. Gallons of coffee flow from a blue speckled pot on the stove. At peak moments all seven voices soar and collide in clouds of laughter.

Outside, the Milky Way glows overhead as brightly as a Christmas ribbon. The surrounding countryside is held by a silence so pure, so absolute, that individual stars seem to sizzle. Laughter, happy voices and a shriek of disbelief drift into the night where far overhead a jet's turbines pull at the primordial silence with a whisper. From 35,000 feet in the night sky, soaring toward tomorrow near the speed of sound, a transcontinental traveler glances out his window and sees a single light burning in an ocean of darkness. He wonders: Who lives down there? Who are those people? What are their lives like?

Far below, that light marks the spot where the Indians' future meets the Indians' past, where the enduring ethics of self-sufficiency and interdependence, cooperation and decency, community and spirit are held in trust for unborn generations of Crow and Comanche, Pueblo and Cheyenne, Hidatsa and Cherokee—where people who know who they are gather around half moon kitchen tables to make laughter and share grief. Still there after the storms.

PAUL VANDEVELDER is an author and documentary filmmaker based in Oregon. His book *Coyote Warrior: One Man, Three Tribes, and the Trial That Forged a Nation* was nominated for both the Pulitzer Prize and the National Book Award in 2004.

Becoming Us

ALAN EHRENHALT

Of all the maddening complexities that make it hard for the American people to decide what should be done about immigrants, the problem of assimilation may carry the most emotional impact. All those people who look different, speak a different language and eat different food—will they ever blend into American society the way previous immigrant groups have? Or will they be a quasi-alien presence down through the decades of the coming century?

How long does it take for immigrants to assimilate into American society?

One way or another, we have been arguing about this question in America for the past 170 years, since Germans and Irish began arriving in our largest cities in massive numbers. We were an Anglo-Saxon Protestant society: The Irish and many of the Germans were Catholics. Would they be taking orders from the Pope rather than the institutions of American authority? Much of the elite thought so. It turned out to be a ludicrous concern.

Half a century later, the issue was immigration from Italy and from the Pale of Jewish settlement in Russia. The question then was generally not religion per se but the adaptability of the poor from Southern and Eastern Europe to the modern United States. The Jews, Poles and Italians dressed, spoke and behaved so exotically on the streets of New York, Philadelphia and Chicago. How could they represent the future of American society? This wasn't a concern that dwelt mainly on the fringes of American politics. To a remarkable extent, these were the beliefs of the country's best-educated, most affluent and most influential citizens.

The odd thing about these arguments over immigration was that they tended to be self-contradictory. On the one hand, nativists argued that immigrants would never assimilate and would remain aliens in every important way—religion, culture, politics, the fundamental values of Western democracy. On the other hand, it was feared with equal vehemence that these millions of newcomers would intermarry with native-born Americans, dilute the quality of the nation's genetic stock and produce what was referred to frequently as "a mongrel race." This was more than a little crazy. If foreigners couldn't assimilate to Anglo-Saxon culture, why would Anglo-Saxons want to marry them? Still, both of these ideas remained current in national political debate on into the 1920s, and in large part led to the exclusionist immigration bill that was passed by Congress in 1924 and remained in effect for more than 40 years.

Today, at a time when Jews are essentially treated as WASPs when they apply to elite private colleges, and Irish-, Italian-and Polish-Americans have become overwhelmingly middle-class, all of this sounds like the quaint mythology of an unrecognizable time. And to a great extent, it is. But the dilemma of assimilation never really went away, and in the past decade, it has re-emerged as powerfully as ever.

We all know the reason why. The foreign-born population of the United States was less than 10 million when the nation's borders were opened up by law in 1965; today it is nearly 40 million. About a quarter of this immigrant cohort has arrived from Asia; to a great extent, that portion is middle-class and upwardly mobile and has attracted comparatively little controversy. It is the 20 million immigrants from Latin America, a majority from Mexico and many of them in this country illegally, who have returned the question of assimilation to the forefront of public debate.

And it was no less a figure than Harvard University political scientist Samuel Huntington, by no means a proponent of crude racism, who raised the issue most bluntly in his 2004 book *Who Are We: The Challenges to America's National Identity*.

Well aware that the assimilation issue had been a red herring for most of the nation's history, Huntington nevertheless insisted that it was relevant in dealing with Mexican immigrants in the past couple of decades. He offered some provocative numbers: Rates of high-school graduation for the Mexican-born in America were roughly half those of the foreign-born population as a whole. Poverty rates for Mexican immigrants in 1998 were more than double those of any Asian group and considerably higher than the rates for other Hispanic newcomers. Mexicans were much more likely to marry within their own ethnic enclave than any other immigrant population, and more likely to identify emotionally with their country of origin than with their adopted home.

In short, Huntington insisted, the massive Mexican immigration of the 1980s and '90s constituted "a major potential threat to the cultural and possibly political integrity of the United States." Nativists may have cried wolf over and over again in earlier centuries, but now the nation was faced with the genuine prospect of a large alien enclave likely to plague it for decades. In his view, the Mexican influx was simply so large that historical comparisons suggesting more rapid assimilation were irrelevant. Mexicans in America were generating such a large in-group that they had relatively little incentive to venture out of it.

Huntington's analysis was vulnerable to challenge on several counts—and "challenge" may be too mild a word for the response it attracted—but Huntington did perform one valuable service. He refocused interest in the seemingly eternal question of assimilation. How important is it, and how might we begin to measure it?

Four years later, some interesting answers have begun to emerge. They are coming mostly from the work of Jacob Vigdor, a professor of economics at Duke University who has spent the past year developing a statistical index of immigrant assimilation, in collaboration with the Manhattan Institute in New York.

Vigdor believes that we will never understand assimilation as long as we continue to assume that it is a simple, unitary idea: that people either are assimilated or they aren't. He makes the plausible point that there are at least three distinct forms of immigrant assimilation that one might be interested in and want to measure. There is economic assimilation—the pace at which newcomers reach middle-class salary levels and acquire their own homes. There's cultural assimilation—the rate at which they learn English and marry native-born Americans rather than fellow-immigrants. And there is civic assimilation, measured by such things as naturalization and military service.

T he conclusion of Vigdor's study is that each of these brands of assimilation operates on its own schedule and applies to different ethnic groups in strikingly different ways. Asian immigrants are very quick to assimilate economically. They learn English easily, graduate from high school at impressive rates and launch and successfully operate small businesses of their own. On the other hand, they are relatively slow to assimilate culturally, at least according to the criteria that Vigdor uses. They cling to traditional religious practices and look for marriage partners within their own tight-knit immigrant cohort, rather than marrying into other ethnic groups. One's view of Asians as more or less assimilated depends to a great extent on which of these categories one considers most important.

Mexicans are very weak on the index of civic assimilation. They are far less likely to vote than other immigrants, or

even to take out naturalization papers. They maintain political ties to Mexico, just as Huntington noticed, and in many cases return there to live after a period of years in the United States. The numbers on voting and naturalization aren't exactly a surprise: Millions of Mexicans are in this country illegally—they couldn't become citizens or vote even if they wanted to.

But Vigdor argues that the tendency of many new arrivals to tune out from American politics doesn't necessarily imply much about prospects for long-term civic assimilation. The data for Italians who came to America early in the 20th century are actually rather similar to the data for Mexicans now. They were slow to become American citizens and traveled back and forth to Italy on a regular basis. It's been estimated that roughly one-third of those who came here from Italy in the wave of migration a hundred years ago ended up returning for good. But those who remained here did eventually become citizens and vote in numbers roughly comparable to the national average. It just took them a while.

A careful reading of Vigdor's research suggests to me that panic at this point about a permanent enclave of alien foreigners in our midst is about as misguided as it was a century ago, however different the ethnic details might be. What it doesn't suggest is that we ought to throw the borders wide open and welcome another 10 million as soon as they want to move here. Communities that are heavily affected by the most recent immigration have legitimate concerns: schools that can't handle the overflow and inadequate housing stock that invites dangerous living conditions and the flouting of local codes. Long-time residents of any community have a right to be concerned about those things—and not to be derided as racists every time they bring them up.

Panic about a permanent enclave of alien foreigners in our midst is about as misguided as it was a century ago.

This is the moment, if there ever was one, to bring our borders under control and slow down the pace of immigration for a little while. Once we do that, we may be in a position to ponder the implications of Jacob Vigdor's research, and reassure ourselves that, in the long run, the American economy, polity and culture are not going to be destroyed by immigrants from south of the border, any more than they were by immigrants from across the ocean a century ago.

From *Governing*, July 2008, pp. 9–10. Copyright © 2008 by Governing. Reprinted by permission.

Ending the Slavery Blame-Game

Henry Louis Gates, Jr.

Thanks to an unlikely confluence of history and genetics—the fact that he is African-American and president—Barack Obama has a unique opportunity to reshape the debate over one of the most contentious issues of America's racial legacy: reparations, the idea that the descendants of American slaves should receive compensation for their ancestors' unpaid labor and bondage.

There are many thorny issues to resolve before we can arrive at a judicious (if symbolic) gesture to match such a sustained, heinous crime. Perhaps the most vexing is how to parcel out blame to those directly involved in the capture and sale of human beings for immense economic gain.

While we are all familiar with the role played by the United States and the European colonial powers like Britain, France, Holland, Portugal and Spain, there is very little discussion of the role Africans themselves played. And that role, it turns out, was a considerable one, especially for the slave-trading kingdoms of western and central Africa. These included the Akan of the kingdom of Asante in what is now Ghana, the Fon of Dahomey (now Benin), the Mbundu of Ndongo in modern Angola and the Kongo of today's Congo, among several others.

For centuries, Europeans in Africa kept close to their military and trading posts on the coast. Exploration of the interior, home to the bulk of Africans sold into bondage at the height of the slave trade, came only during the colonial conquests, which is why Henry Morton Stanley's pursuit of Dr. David Livingstone in 1871 made for such compelling press: he was going where no (white) man had gone before.

How did slaves make it to these coastal forts? The historians John Thornton and Linda Heywood of Boston University estimate that 90 percent of those shipped to the New World were enslaved by Africans and then sold to European traders. The sad truth is that without complex business partnerships between African elites and European traders and commercial agents, the slave trade to the New World would have been impossible, at least on the scale it occurred.

Advocates of reparations for the descendants of those slaves generally ignore this untidy problem of the significant role that Africans played in the trade, choosing to believe the romanticized version that our ancestors were all kidnapped unawares by evil white men, like Kunta Kinte was in "Roots." The truth, however, is much more complex: slavery was a business, highly organized and lucrative for European buyers and African sellers alike.

The African role in the slave trade was fully understood and openly acknowledged by many African-Americans even before the Civil War. For Frederick Douglass, it was an argument against repatriation schemes for the freed slaves. "The savage chiefs of the western coasts of Africa, who for ages have been accustomed to selling their captives into bondage and pocketing the ready cash for them, will not more readily accept our moral and economical ideas than the slave traders of Maryland and Virginia," he warned. "We are, therefore, less inclined to go to Africa to work against the slave trade than to stay here to work against it."

To be sure, the African role in the slave trade was greatly reduced after 1807, when abolitionists, first in Britain and then, a year later, in the United States, succeeded in banning the importation of slaves. Meanwhile, slaves continued to be bought and sold within the United States, and slavery as an institution would not be abolished until 1865. But the culpability of American plantation owners neither erases nor supplants that of the African slavers. In recent years, some African leaders have become more comfortable discussing this complicated past than African-Americans tend to be.

The reparations debate ignores Africans' role in selling human beings.

In 1999, for instance, President Mathieu Kerekou of Benin astonished an all-black congregation in Baltimore by falling to his knees and begging African-Americans' forgiveness for the "shameful" and "abominable" role Africans played in the trade. Other African leaders, including Jerry Rawlings of Ghana, followed Mr. Kerekou's bold example.

Our new understanding of the scope of African involvement in the slave trade is not historical guesswork. Thanks to the Trans-Atlantic Slave Trade Database, directed by the historian David Eltis of Emory University, we now know the ports from which more than 450,000 of our African ancestors were shipped out to what is now the United States (the database has records of 12.5 million people shipped to all parts of the New World from 1514 to 1866). About 16 percent of United States slaves came from eastern Nigeria, while 24 percent came from the Congo and Angola.

Through the work of Professors Thornton and Heywood, we also know that the victims of the slave trade were predominantly members of as few as 50 ethnic groups. This data, along with the tracing of blacks' ancestry through DNA tests, is giving us a fuller understanding of the identities of both the victims and the facilitators of the African slave trade.

For many African-Americans, these facts can be difficult to accept. Excuses run the gamut, from "Africans didn't know how harsh slavery in America was" and "Slavery in Africa was, by comparison, humane" or, in a bizarre version of "The devil made me do it," "Africans were driven to this only by the unprecedented profits offered by greedy European countries."

But the sad truth is that the conquest and capture of Africans and their sale to Europeans was one of the main sources of foreign exchange for several African kingdoms for a very long time. Slaves were the main export of the kingdom of Kongo; the Asante Empire in Ghana exported slaves and used the profits to import gold. Queen Njinga, the brilliant 17th-century monarch of the Mbundu, waged wars of resistance against the Portuguese but also conquered polities as far as 500 miles inland and sold her captives to the Portuguese. When Njinga converted to Christianity, she sold African traditional religious leaders into slavery, claiming they had violated her new Christian precepts.

Did these Africans know how harsh slavery was in the New World? Actually, many elite Africans visited Europe in that era, and they did so on slave ships following the prevailing winds through the New World. For example, when Antonio Manuel, Kongo's ambassador to the Vatican, went to Europe in 1604, he first stopped in Bahia, Brazil, where he arranged to free a countryman who had been wrongfully enslaved.

African monarchs also sent their children along these same slave routes to be educated in Europe. And there were thousands of former slaves who returned to settle Liberia and Sierra Leone. The Middle Passage, in other words, was sometimes a two-way street. Under these circumstances, it is difficult to claim that Africans were ignorant or innocent.

Given this remarkably messy history, the problem with reparations may not be so much whether they are a good idea or deciding who would get them; the larger question just might be from whom they would be extracted.

So how could President Obama untangle the knot? In David Remnick's new book "The Bridge: The Life and Rise of Barack Obama," one of the president's former students at the University of Chicago comments on Mr. Obama's mixed feelings about the reparations movement: "He told us what he thought about reparations. He agreed entirely with the *theory* of reparations. But in practice he didn't think it was really workable."

About the practicalities, Professor Obama may have been more right than he knew. Fortunately, in President Obama, the child of an African and an American, we finally have a leader who is uniquely positioned to bridge the great reparations divide. He is uniquely placed to publicly attribute responsibility and culpability where they truly belong, to white people and black people, on both sides of the Atlantic, complicit alike in one of the greatest evils in the history of civilization. And reaching that understanding is a vital precursor to any just and lasting agreement on the divisive issue of slavery reparations.

HENRY LOUIS GATES, Jr., a professor at Harvard, is the author of the forthcoming "Faces of America" and "Tradition and the Black Atlantic."

The American Character

Bucking scholarly trends, Simon Schama argues it has a bright future.

LOUIS P. MASUR

With Barack Obama's election, the idea of an American national character is back, and it feels more salient than ever. Time and again during the presidential campaign, Obama told us his story: the mixed-race child of a man from Kenya and a woman from Kansas. He graduated from the Ivy League and was elected a U.S. senator. And then the self-described "mutt" became president. "Only in America," he declared.

Obama's popular narrative, and the way he has told it, promises to revive interest in what scholars term American exceptionalism—the idea that the American story is somehow unique. Attempts to define that quality have led foreigners to these shores, generated countless commentaries, and after World War II helped give rise to an entire academic discipline—American studies. But the topic has been notably out of fashion in the scholarly world. Now, from the well-known historian Simon Schama, we have a new, contrarian view that looks at what's unique in the American character, putting our past in the context of the election of the new president we are just inaugurating.

The discussion of the American character is embedded in the nation's DNA. In the 18th century, J. Hector St. John Crèvecoeur famously asked, "What then is the American, this new man?" He was the product of a place where immigrants escaped their past and melted together into a new race of men, the French-American writer answered. In the 19th century, the French observer Alexis de Tocqueville toured the country and coined the word "individualism" to describe what he encountered. Talking to fellow American historians at century's end, Frederick Jackson Turner identified the frontier as the key element in national development.

In the 20th century, a string of books from history, sociology, and political science furthered the discussion, each seeking to map a part of the American character genome: David Riesman's *The Lonely Crowd* (Yale University Press, 1950); Daniel J. Boorstin's *The Genius of American Politics* (University of Chicago Press, 1953); David Morris Potter's *People of Plenty* (University of Chicago Press, 1954); Louis Hartz's *The Liberal Tradition in America* (Harcourt, Brace, 1955); Michael G. Kammen's *People of Paradox* (Knopf, 1972); Richard Slotkin's

Regeneration Through Violence (Wesleyan University Press, 1973); Christopher Lasch's *The Culture of Narcissism* (Norton, 1979); Robert N. Bellah's *Habits of the Heart* (University of California Press, 1985); Seymour Martin Lipset's *American Exceptionalism* (Norton, 1996); and Robert D. Putnam's *Bowling Alone* (Simon & Schuster, 2000).

Some of those studies probed the dark side of the exceptionalist coin. Instead of assessments of seemingly positive stories like those about the self-made man or the American creed, they identified a wayward gene that manifested itself as pathology, whether racism, violence, or alienation. Such views helped balance more celebratory accounts, but writers who emphasized the underside did not question the exceptionalist paradigm, they reinforced it.

A number of scholars, however, have challenged that notion altogether. Starting in the 1960s, labor and social historians wrote "against exceptionalism" by comparing experiences of the working classes in America and Europe, revealing common interests in the struggle with capitalism. And in the 1980s and 1990s, intellectual historians traced the trans-Atlantic flow of ideas, showing how Americans participated in debates over such topics as the state and social welfare that they neither initiated nor dominated.

More recently, reflecting the transnational, global turn in numerous disciplines, historians have produced an array of sophisticated comparative works that transcend a strictly national framework. Daniel T. Rodgers has given voice to a growing trend in his call for scholars to "re-embed the history of the United States within a world of transnational historical forces." His *Atlantic Crossings: Social Politics in a Progressive Age* (Harvard University Press, 1998) argues that Americans touring Europe encountered ideas and social experiments that they brought back to the United States. With others making a similar argument, exceptionalism as an academic exercise has fallen into decline.

Simon Schama knows transnational history as well as anyone, but he has no interest in abandoning exceptionalism. *The American Future: A History* (published in Britain by the Bodley Head in September and due out from Ecco in the United States in May), stands firmly in the tradition of foreign writers seeking to diagram American distinctiveness and chart the American character. (Schama has simultaneously presented a four-part BBC documentary series of the same title. It aired in Britain last fall and will be issued on DVD and aired on BBC America in the United States on Inauguration Day.)

Born in London in 1945 and educated at Christ's College, University of Cambridge, Schama not only mentions his literary forebears but also relates to them. He compares his first trans-Atlantic crossing, in 1964, for example, to that of Charles Dickens a century before. Because of a storm, Schama's voyage took longer, but both men were shocked by what they first encountered: Dickens despaired over slavery, and Schama over the continued need to struggle for civil rights.

In the book, Schama narrates his travels over the years (many of them during this year's primary season) to such locales as Iowa, Nevada, Texas, and Virginia and sees themes from history refracted in the present. Currently a university professor of art history and history at Columbia University, he identifies four topics that he argues will inform America's future because they have indelibly shaped its past: war, religion, immigration, and abundance.

None of those are new, and they hardly amount to a menu for anything peculiarly American. One could just as easily write about war, religion, immigration, and abundance in France or Russia. But Schama's lyrical writing provides fresh insights, even if his knowledge of American history is scattershot. He devotes pages, for example, to Roger Williams but mentions Billy Graham only in passing. One of his favorite paradigms is to see the United States as split between Hamiltonian and Jeffersonian impulses. The Civil War, he offers, bridged the two paths of cultural politics, a Hamiltonian enterprise—nationalistic and corporate—undertaken for a "supremely Jeffersonian cause: the salvation of democracy." Of course that is to mistake results for origins. Had the Confederacy won, it would have marked the triumph of a very different Jeffersonian vision—an agrarian republic rooted in slavery. For today, Schama finds implications in the war in Iraq: "Hamilton resurrexit."

Jefferson, author of the Virginia Statute for Religious Freedom, is also the unlikely hero of the section on religion. Although spiritual fervor has often divided the nation, religious beliefs are integral to the American desire to create a moral community. What has enabled the nation to survive its paroxysms of undemocratic fanaticism, Schama argues, has been the separation of church and state derived from Jefferson. As a result, Americans are protected from religious coercion, and religious belief flourishes or fades depending only on its capacity to persuade.

"The big American story," Schama realizes, is "the war of toleration against conformity; the war of a faith that commands obedience against a faith that promises liberty." He does not say whether a fundamental change in the American character would occur if the wall between church and state crumbles under, for example, the kind of steady assault it has suffered in recent years. But he does note that the election in 2008, as he was writing, showed signs that "evangelical politics has had its day." In Europe, he says, the state crushes alternative dogmas;

in America, the continuing dialogue between faith and freedom allows for pluralist beliefs.

An even bigger story is the making of Americans, the familiar narrative of America as asylum, melting pot, land of opportunity. Schama, who has a knack for apothegms, puts it this way: "In the Old World you knew your place; in the New World you made it." The language of the self-made can be found everywhere, he points out, whether in the words of Thomas Paine or Abraham Lincoln or Barack Obama.

But not everyone in America is welcome to participate in self-fashioning, Schama goes on. There was ambivalence over immigration present at the founding (for example, Benjamin Franklin denounced German newcomers), and it was never resolved. Immigration promoted liberty and prosperity while simultaneously posing a threat to national purity. The cycles of admission versus restriction have most often been tied to economic conditions. "Every time the American economy hits a reef," observes Schama, "the last on the boat are usually those whom nationalist politicians want to throw from the decks." The 1890s saw the establishment of the Immigration Restriction League, anxious about the influx of Southern and Eastern Europeans. Today an official league may not exist, but immigration officials watch out for groups seen as "undesirable."

Diminishing resources are in tension with a vision of plenty, and the book ends with a discussion of water—irrigation, to be precise. Americans in the West have had to face cycles of devastating drought, yet they continue to cultivate golf courses and lawns, despite the lack of water. Those plowing the future, however, have exhibited another component that often turns up on lists of American identity: inventiveness. In Las Vegas, xerigraphic landscaping—using rocks and native plants that require only drip watering—becomes big business.

And so, according to Schama, Americans face the future equipped with historic tendencies that do not determine, but will certainly shape, their course of action. War can preserve liberty or destroy it. Fervor can unite community or divide it into factions. Being American can mean promoting diversity or trampling it. A faith in boundlessness can inspire creative solutions to resource scarcity or leave us locked in a false optimism that it will all work out OK.

Schama's quartet of characteristics is somewhat idiosyncratic, given the vast literature on American exceptionalism, but they overlap with many of the categories others might choose: for example, nature, frontier, democracy, and individualism. The specific labels matter less than the story of American character, a story by turns inspiring and depressing. Schama is attuned to the tragic side, and he writes powerfully about entering an abandoned house on the plains and standing "inside the dead and broken body of the dream." But the American dream will never die, he concludes, because "it's impossible to think of the United States as a dead end. Americans roused can turn on a dime (check out the waiting list for Smart cars), convert indignation into action and before you know it there's a whole new United States in the neighborhood."

The approach of *The American Future* will no doubt irritate those historians committed to internationalizing the study of American history, but Schama provides an important reminder that Americans continue to sketch the future according to patterns of belief inscribed in their past. The strength of *The American Future* is not history but biography, the way it grounds ideas in the lives of people struggling to make sense of the nation and to transform it.

Schama provides an important reminder that Americans continue to sketch the future according to patterns of belief inscribed in their past.

Schama is at his best writing about Montgomery C. Meigs, the quartermaster general of the Union Army, who described Civil War as "a great and holy war" for American democracy, or about the civil-rights activist Fannie Lou Hamer, who, when asked by Hubert H. Humphrey what she wanted, answered: "Don't you know? The Kingdom of Jesus; that's what I want."

Schama reminds us that, to the extent there is an American identity, it has been forged through words, whether Jefferson's or Hamer's, and images, whether John Gast's 1872 "American Progress" or Dorothea Lange's 1936 "Migrant Mother." Inexplicably, Schama—author of *The Power of Art* (Ecco, 2006) and *Rembrandt's Eyes* (Knopf, 1999) and a former art critic for *The New Yorker* who unpacks paintings and photographs as well as anyone—gives short shrift to visuals in the book. Many art historians view American art as part of the exceptionalist story—exceptionally inferior—and Schama may have fallen victim to that prejudice.

E xceptionalism is above all else the story we choose to tell about ourselves—not some organic, immutable structure. And in telling it, over and over, at times we even make it so. To think about American exceptionalism as a genre of storytelling may revitalize studies of national character without glorifying the concept of nation. What are the stories that people relate about themselves and their nation? How are those stories contested and how do they change over time? How has the American story influenced other narratives and, in turn, been shaped by them?

Exceptionalism is above all else the story we choose to tell about ourselves—not some organic, immutable structure.

Focusing on individual narratives builds upon the call of Thomas Bender, a professor of history at New York University—in the collection he edited, *Rethinking American History in a Global Age* (University of California Press, 2002)—that we "explore those stories of our past, those experiences at scales other than the nation, that have been forgotten, that have been obscured by the emphasis upon the centrality of the nation." At the same time, it reaffirms an observation made by Henry Adams more than a hundred years ago: "Of all historical problems," he wrote, "the nature of a national character is the most difficult and the most important."

That these stories, both local and national, carry great power goes without question. Otherwise, how to explain the continuing faith in the rags-to-riches myth despite a huge increase in inequality? How to explain belief in American democracy when so many people are disenfranchised politically from voting and socially from earning a living wage? How to explain devotion to a providential America when much of the world sees the United States as satanic, not holy?

Barack Obama won the presidency through his words, through the story he tells about himself and the country, a story that resonated with voters and has revived faith in a laudable national character. In his book, writing in September 2008, Schama predicted that the next president of the United States would be "the most compelling storyteller." That was wishful thinking from a distinguished narrative historian who has taught in the United States for nearly three decades. Yet it turned out to be right. America is nothing if it is not a compelling story. New plot lines will emerge, but we've known the central character for a very long time.

LOUIS P. MASUR is director of the American-studies program at Trinity College, in Connecticut, and author of *The Soiling of Old Glory: The Story of a Photograph That Shocked America* (Bloomsbury Press, 2008) and *Runaway Dream: Born to Run and Bruce Springsteen's American Vision* (forthcoming from Bloomsbury in 2009).

Global Warming

Who Loses—and Who Wins?

**Climate change in the next century (and beyond) could be
enormously disruptive, spreading disease and sparking wars.
It could also be a windfall for some people, businesses, and nations.
A guide to how we all might get along in a warming world.**

GREGG EASTERBROOK

Coastal cities inundated, farming regions parched, ocean currents disrupted, tropical diseases spreading, glaciers melting—an artificial greenhouse effect could generate countless tribulations. If Earth's climate changes meaningfully—and the National Academy of Sciences, previously skeptical, said in 2005 that signs of climate change have become significant—there could be broadbased disruption of the global economy unparalleled by any event other than World War II.

Economic change means winners as well as losers. Huge sums will be made and lost if the global climate changes. Everyone wonders what warming might do to the environment—but what might it do to the global distribution of money and power?

Whether mainly natural or mainly artificial, climate change could bring different regions of the world tremendous benefits as well as drastic problems. The world had been mostly warming for thousands of years before the industrial era began, and that warming has been indisputably favorable to the spread of civilization. The trouble is that the world's economic geography is today organized according to a climate that has largely prevailed since the Middle Ages—runaway climate change would force big changes in the physical ordering of society. In the past, small climate changes have had substantial impact on agriculture, trade routes, and the types of products and commodities that sell. Larger climate shifts have catalyzed the rise and fall of whole societies. The Mayan Empire, for instance, did not disappear "mysteriously"; it likely fell into decline owing to decades of drought that ruined its agricultural base and deprived its cities of drinking water. On the other side of the coin, Europe's Medieval Warm Period, which lasted from around 1000 to 1400, was essential to the rise of Spain, France, and England: Those clement centuries allowed the expansion of farm production, population, cities, and universities, which in turn set the stage for the Industrial Revolution. Unless greenhouse-effect theory is completely wrong—and science increasingly supports the idea that it is right—21st-century climate change means that sweeping social and economic changes are in the works.

To date the greenhouse-effect debate has been largely carried out in abstractions—arguments about the distant past (what *do* those 100,000-year-old ice cores in Greenland really tell us about ancient temperatures, anyway?) coupled to computer-model conjecture regarding the 22nd century, with the occasional Hollywood disaster movie thrown in. Soon, both abstraction and postapocalyptic fantasy could be pushed aside by the economic and political realities of a warming world. If the global climate continues changing, many people and nations will find themselves in possession of land and resources of rising value, while others will suffer dire losses—and these winners and losers could start appearing faster than you might imagine. Add artificially triggered climate change to the volatility already initiated by globalization, and the next few decades may see previously unthinkable levels of economic upheaval, in which fortunes are won and lost based as much on the physical climate as on the business climate.

It may sound odd to ask of global warming, What's in it for me? But the question is neither crass nor tongue-in-cheek. The ways in which climate change could skew the world's distribution of wealth should help us appreciate just how profoundly an artificial greenhouse effect might shake our lives. Moreover, some of the lasting effects of climate change are likely to come not so much from the warming itself but from how we react to it: If the world warms appreciably, men and women will not sit by idly, eating bonbons and reading weather reports; there will be instead what economists call "adaptive response," most likely a great deal of it. Some aspects of this response may inflame tensions between those who are winning and those who are losing. How people, the global economy, and the international power structure adapt to climate change may influence how we live for generations. If the world warms, who will win? Who will lose? And what's in it for you?

Land

Real estate might be expected to appreciate steadily in value during the 21st century, given that both the global population and global prosperity are rising. The supply of land is fixed, and if there's a fixed supply of something but a growing demand, appreciation should be automatic. That's unless climate change increases the supply of land by warming currently frosty areas while throwing the amount of *desirable* land into tremendous flux. My hometown of Buffalo, New York, for example, is today so déclassé that some of its stately Beaux-Arts homes, built during the Gilded Age and overlooking a park designed by Frederick Law Olmsted, sell for about the price of one-bedroom condos in Boston or San Francisco. If a warming world makes the area less cold and snowy, Buffalo might become one of the country's desirable addresses.

At the same time, Arizona and Nevada, blazing growth markets today, might become unbearably hot and see their real-estate markets crash. If the oceans rise, Florida's rapid growth could be, well, swamped by an increase in its perilously high groundwater table. Houston could decline, made insufferable by worsened summertime humidity, while the splendid, rustic Laurentide Mountains region north of Montreal, if warmed up a bit, might transmogrify into the new Poconos.

These are just a few of many possible examples. Climate change could upset the applecarts of real-estate values all over the world, with low-latitude properties tanking while high latitudes become the Sun Belt of the mid-21st century.

Local changes in housing demand are only small beer. To consider the big picture, examine a Mercator projection of our planet, and observe how the Earth's landmasses spread from the equator to the poles. Assume global warming is reasonably uniform. (Some computer models suggest that warming will vary widely by region; for the purposes of this article, suffice it to say that all predictions regarding an artificial greenhouse effect are extremely uncertain.) The equatorial and low-latitude areas of the world presumably will become hotter and less desirable as places of habitation, plus less valuable in economic terms; with a few exceptions, these areas are home to developing nations where living standards are already low.

So where is the high-latitude landmass that might grow more valuable in a warming world? By accident of geography, except for Antarctica nearly all such land is in the Northern Hemisphere, whose continents are broad west-to-east. Only a relatively small portion of South America, which narrows as one travels south, is high latitude, and none of Africa or Australia is. (Cape Town is roughly the same distance from the equator as Cape Hatteras; Melbourne is about the same distance from the equator as Manhattan.) More specifically, nearly all the added land-value benefits of a warming world might accrue to Alaska, Canada, Greenland, Russia, and Scandinavia.

This raises the possibility that an artificial greenhouse effect could harm nations that are already hard pressed and benefit nations that are already affluent. If Alaska turned temperate, it would drive conservationists to distraction, but it would also open for development an area more than twice the size of Texas. Rising world temperatures might throw Indonesia, Mexico, Nigeria, and other low-latitude nations into generations of misery, while causing Canada, Greenland, and Scandinavia to experience a rip-roarin' economic boom. Many Greenlanders are already cheering the retreat of glaciers, since this melting stands to make their vast island far more valuable. Last July, *The Wall Street Journal* reported that the growing season in the portion of Greenland open to cultivation is already two weeks longer than it was in the 1970s.

And Russia! For generations poets have bemoaned this realm as cursed by enormous, foreboding, harsh Siberia. What if the region in question were instead enormous, temperate, inviting Siberia? Climate change could place Russia in possession of the largest new region of pristine, exploitable land since the sailing ships of Europe first spied the shores of what would be called North America. The snows of Siberia cover soils that have never been depleted by controlled agriculture. What's more, beneath Siberia's snow may lie geologic formations that hold vast deposits of fossil fuels, as well as mineral resources. When considering ratification of the Kyoto Protocol to regulate greenhouse gases, the Moscow government dragged its feet, though the treaty was worded to offer the Russians extensive favors. Why might this have happened? Perhaps because Russia might be much better off in a warming world: Warming's benefits to Russia could exceed those to all other nations combined.

Of course, it could be argued that politicians seldom give much thought—one way or the other—to actions whose value will become clear only after they leave office, so perhaps Moscow does not have a grand strategy to warm the world for its own good. But a warmer world may be much to Russia's liking, whether it comes by strategy or accident. And how long until high-latitude nations realize global warming might be in their interests? In recent years, Canada has increased its greenhouse-gas output more rapidly than most other rich countries. Maybe this is a result of prosperity and oil-field development—or maybe those wily Canadians have a master plan for their huge expanse of currently uninhabitable land.

Global warming might do more for the North, however, than just opening up new land. Temperatures are rising on average, but *when* are they rising? Daytime? Nighttime? Winter? Summer? One fear about artificially triggered climate change has been that global warming would lead to scorching summer-afternoon highs, which would kill crops and brown out the electric power grid. Instead, so far a good share of the warming—especially in North America—has come in the form of nighttime and winter lows that are less low. Higher lows reduce the harshness of winter in northern climes and moderate the demand for energy. And fewer freezes allow extended growing seasons, boosting farm production. In North America, spring comes ever earlier—in recent years, trees have flowered in Washington, D.C., almost a week earlier on average than a generation ago. People may find this creepy, but earlier springs and milder winters can have economic value to agriculture—and lest we forget, all modern societies, including the United States, are grounded in agriculture.

If a primary impact of an artificially warmed world is to make land in Canada, Greenland, Russia, Scandinavia, and the United States more valuable, this could have three powerful effects on the 21st-century global situation.

First, historically privileged northern societies might not decline geopolitically, as many commentators have predicted. Indeed, the great age of northern power may lie ahead, if Earth's very climate is on the verge of conferring boons to that part of the world. Should it turn out that headlong fossil-fuel combustion by northern nations has set in motion climate change that strengthens the relative world position of those same nations, future essayists will have a field day. But the prospect is serious. By the middle of the 21st century, a new global balance of power may emerge in which Russia and America are once again the world's paired superpowers—only this time during a Warming War instead of a Cold War.

Second, if northern societies find that climate change makes them more wealthy, the quest for world equity could be dealt a huge setback. Despite the popular misconception, globalized economies have been a positive force for increased equity. As the Indian economist Surjit Bhalla has shown, the developing world produced 29 percent of the globe's income in 1950; by 2000 that share had risen to 42 percent, while the developing world's share of population rose at a slower rate. All other things being equal, we might expect continued economic globalization to distribute wealth more widely. But if climate change increases the value of northern land and resources, while leaving nations near the equator hotter and wracked by storms or droughts, all other things would not be equal.

That brings us to the third great concern: If climate change causes developing nations to falter, and social conditions within them deteriorate, many millions of jobless or hungry refugees may come to the borders of the favored North, demanding to be let in. If the very Earth itself turns against poor nations, punishing them with heat and storms, how could the United States morally deny the refugees succor?

Shifts in the relative values of places and resources have often led to war, and it is all too imaginable that climate change will cause nations to envy each other's territory. This envy is likely to run both north-south and updown. North-south? Suppose climate change made Brazil less habitable, while bringing an agreeable mild clime to the vast and fertile Argentinean pampas to Brazil's south. São Paulo is already one of the world's largest cities. Would a desperate, overheated Brazil of the year 2037—its population exploding—hesitate to attack Argentina for cool, inviting land? Now consider the up-down prospect: the desire to leave low-lying areas for altitude. Here's an example: Since its independence, in 1947, Pakistan has kept a hand in the internal affairs of Afghanistan. Today Americans view this issue through the lens of the Taliban and al-Qaeda, but from Islamabad's perspective, the goal has always been to keep Afghanistan available as a place for retreat, should Pakistan lose a war with India. What if the climate warms, rendering much of Pakistan unbearable to its citizens? (Temperatures of 100-plus degrees are already common in the Punjab.) Afghanistan's high plateaus, dry and rocky as they are, might start looking pleasingly temperate as Pakistan warms, and the Afghans might see yet another army headed their way.

A warming climate could cause other landgrabs on a national scale. Today Greenland is a largely self-governing territory of Denmark that the world leaves in peace because no nation covets its shivering expanse. Should the Earth warm, Copenhagen might assert greater jurisdiction over Greenland, or stronger governments might scheme to seize this dwarf continent, which is roughly three times the size of Texas. Today Antarctica is under international administration, and this arrangement is generally accepted because the continent has no value beyond scientific research. If the world warmed for along time—and it would likely take centuries for the Antarctic ice sheet to melt completely—international jockeying to seize or conquer Antarctica might become intense. Some geologists believe large oil deposits are under the Antarctic crust: In earlier epochs, the austral pole was densely vegetated and had conditions suitable for the formation of fossil fuels.

And though I've said to this point that Canada would stand to become more valuable in a warming world, actually, Canada and Nunavut would. For centuries, Europeans drove the indigenous peoples of what is now Canada farther and farther north. In 1993, Canada agreed to grant a degree of independence to the primarily Inuit population of Nunavut, and this large, cold region in the country's northeast has been mainly self-governing since 1999. The Inuit believe they are ensconced in the one place in this hemisphere that the descendants of Europe will never, ever want. This could turn out to be wrong.

For investors, finding attractive land to buy and hold for a warming world is fraught with difficulties, particularly when looking abroad. If considering plots on the pampas, for example, should one negotiate with the current Argentinian owners or the future Brazilian ones? Perhaps a safer route would be the contrarian one, focused on the likelihood of falling land values in places people may leave. If strict carbon-dioxide regulations are enacted, corporations will shop for "offsets," including projects that absorb carbon dioxide from the sky. Growing trees is a potential greenhouse-gas offset, and can be done comparatively cheaply in parts of the developing world, even on land that people may stop wanting. If you jump into the greenhouse-offset business, what you might plant is leucaena, a rapidly growing tree species suited to the tropics that metabolizes carbon dioxide faster than most trees. But you'll want to own the land in order to control the sale of the credits. Consider a possible sequence of events: First, climate change makes parts of the developing world even less habitable than they are today; then, refugees flee these areas; finally, land can be snapped up at Filene's Basement prices—and used to grow leucaena trees.

Water

If Al Gore's movie, *An Inconvenient Truth,* is to be believed, you should start selling coastal real estate now. Gore's film maintains that an artificial greenhouse effect could raise sea levels 20 feet in the near future, flooding Manhattan, San Francisco, and dozens of other cities; Micronesia would simply disappear below the waves. Gore's is the doomsday number, but the scientific consensus is worrisome enough: In 2005, the National Academy of Sciences warned that oceans may rise between four inches and three feet by the year 2100. Four inches may not sound like a lot, but it would imperil parts of coastal Florida and the Carolinas, among other places. A three-foot sea-level rise would flood significant portions of Bangladesh, threaten the national survival of the Netherlands, and damage many coastal cities, while submerging pretty much all of the world's trendy beach destinations to boot. And the Asian Tigers? Shanghai and Hong Kong sit right on the water. Raise the deep a few feet, and these Tiger cities would be abandoned.

The global temperature increase of the last century—about one degree Fahrenheit—was modest and did not cause any dangerous sea-level rise. Sea-level worries turn on the possibility that there is some nonlinear aspect of the climate system, a "tipping point" that could cause the rate of global warming to accelerate markedly. One reason global warming has not happened as fast as expected appears to be that the oceans have absorbed much of the carbon dioxide emitted by human activity. Studies suggest, however, that the ability of the oceans to absorb carbon dioxide may be slowing; as the absorption rate declines, atmospheric buildup will happen faster, and climate change could speed up. At the first sign of an increase in the rate of global warming: Sell, sell, sell your coastal properties. Unload those London and Seattle waterfront holdings. Buy land and real property in Omaha or Ontario.

The Inuit believe they are ensconced in the one place in this hemisphere that the descendants of Europe will never, ever want. This could turn out to be wrong.

An artificial greenhouse effect may also alter ocean currents in unpredictable ways. Already there is some evidence that the arctic currents are changing, while the major North Atlantic current that moves warm water north from the equator may be losing energy. If the North Atlantic current falters, temperatures could fall in Europe even as the world overall warms. Most of Europe lies to the north of Maine yet is temperate because the North Atlantic current carries huge volumes of warm water to the seas off Scotland; that warm water is Europe's weather-maker. Geological studies show that the North Atlantic current has stopped in the past. If this current stops again because of artificial climate change, Europe might take on the climate of present-day Newfoundland. As a result, it might depopulate, while the economic value of everything within its icy expanse declines. The European Union makes approximately the same contribution to the global economy as the United States makes: Significantly falling temperatures in Europe could trigger a worldwide recession.

While staying ready to sell your holdings in Europe, look for purchase opportunities near the waters of the Arctic Circle. In 2005, a Russian research ship became the first surface vessel ever to reach the North Pole without the aid of an icebreaker. If arctic sea ice melts, shipping traffic will begin transiting the North Pole. Andrew Revkin's 2006 book, *The North Pole Was Here,* profiles Pat Broe, who in 1997 bought the isolated far-north port of Churchill, Manitoba, from the Canadian government for $7. Assuming arctic ice continues to melt, the world's

cargo vessels may begin sailing due north to shave thousands of miles off their trips, and the port of Churchill may be bustling. If arctic polar ice disappears and container vessels course the North Pole seas, shipping costs may decline—to the benefit of consumers. Asian manufacturers, especially, should see their costs of shipping to the United States and the European Union fall. At the same time, heavily trafficked southern shipping routes linking East Asia to Europe and to America's East Coast could see less traffic, and port cities along that route—such as Singapore—might decline. Concurrently, good relations with Nunavut could become of interest to the world's corporations.

Oh, and there may be oil under the arctic waters. Who would own that oil? The United States, Russia, Canada, Norway, and Denmark already assert legally complex claims to parts of the North Pole seas—including portions that other nations consider open waters not subject to sovereign control. Today it seems absurd to imagine the governments of the world fighting over the North Pole seas, but in the past many causes of battle have seemed absurd before the artillery fire began. Canada is already conducting naval exercises in the arctic waters, and making no secret of this.

Then again, perhaps ownership of these waters will go in an entirely different direction. The 21st century is likely to see a movement to create private-property rights in the ocean (ocean property rights are the most promising solution to overfishing of the open seas). Private-property rights in the North Pole seas, should they come into existence, might generate a rush to rival the Sooners' settlement of Oklahoma in the late 1800s.

Whatever happens to our oceans, climate change might also cause economic turmoil by affecting freshwater supplies. Today nearly all primary commodities, including petroleum, appear in ample supply. Freshwater is an exception: China is depleting aquifers at an alarming rate in order to produce enough rice to feed itself, while freshwater is scarce in much of the Middle East and parts of Africa. Freshwater depletion is especially worrisome in Egypt, Libya, and several Persian Gulf states. Greenhouse-effect science is so uncertain that researchers have little idea whether a warming world would experience more or less precipitation. If it turns out that rain and snow decline as the world warms, dwindling supplies of drinking water and freshwater for agriculture may be the next resource emergency. For investors this would suggest a cautious view of the booms in China and Dubai, as both places may soon face freshwater-supply problems. (Cost-effective desalinization continues to elude engineers.) On the other hand, where water rights are available in these areas, grab them.

Much of the effect that global warming will have on our water is speculative, so water-related climate change will be a high-risk/high-reward matter for investors and societies alike. The biggest fear is that artificially triggered climate change will shift rainfall away from today's productive breadbasket areas and toward what are now deserts or, worse, toward the oceans. (From the human perspective, all ocean rain represents wasted freshwater.) The reason Malthusian catastrophes have not occurred as humanity has grown is that for most of the last half century, farm yields have increased faster than population. But the global agricultural system is perilously poised on the

A 401(k) for a Warming World

Climate change could have a broad impact on industrial sectors, and thus help or hurt your stock investments and retirement funds. What types of equity might you want to favor or avoid?

Big Pharma. Rising temperatures might extend the range of tropical diseases such as malaria and dengue fever. A 2005 World Health Organization report suggested that global warming may already cause 150,000 deaths annually, mainly by spreading illnesses common to hot nations. If diseases of the poor, low-latitude regions of the world began to reach developed countries, large amounts of capital would flow into the Pharmaceuticals sector as the affluent began to demand protection—so it could prove profitable to be holding pharmaceutical stocks, although exactly which shares to buy would be influenced by laboratory discoveries that are impossible to predict. But consider the social upside: If malaria threatened the United States, this scourge might finally be cured.

Health-Care Service Providers. The contrarian view is that a warming world would, on balance, improve public health in high-latitude areas. Though hot regions in the developing world experience high rates of communicable diseases that scare us, people are still far more likely to die from the cold than from heat—overall death rates in winter are much higher than those in summer. Retirees living in Florida, for instance, have less reason to fear a hot summer than those living in Vermont have to fear a cold winter. If the cold areas of affluent nations became less cold, we would expect longevity to increase. That would be good for society, and also a reason to hold health-care (and pharmaceutical) stocks, since the elderly require far more in the way of hospital services and drugs. The assisted-care industry might also be in for a long bullish run.

Electricity Producers. The World Energy Council has estimated that global demand for electricity will triple by 2050. The lion's share of the increased demand will be in developing nations, but the United States and the European Union nations will need more megawatts too—and that's even assuming increases in energy efficiency. It is all but certain that some form of greenhouse-gas regulation will come to the United States; many Fortune 500 CEOs already assume this. The result will be an electricity sector that's much more technology- and knowledge-sensitive than today's. Lots of brainpower and skill will be required to increase electricity generation and reduce greenhouse-gas emissions at the same time. It's reasonable to guess that power-production firms with a track record of innovation, such as Duke Energy (which pioneered many techniques to improve the efficiency of nuclear-power plants), will be the kind of energy-sector stocks to own. Don't be surprised if nuclear energy, which is nearly greenhouse-gas-free, enjoys a boom in coming decades. General Electric, Westinghouse, and Siemens are some of the leading producers of new "inherently safe" power reactors designed so they can't melt down even if all safety systems are turned off.

"Green" Energy. Renewable-energy industries—such as solar energy and biofuels—might seem like a promising place for 401(k) chips, but bear in mind that no form of green energy is yet cost-competitive with fossil energy, and no one knows which may eventually win in the marketplace. Solar-cell production, for example, is an expanding sector, but nearly all large solar cells for residential and commercial applications are currently sold in California, Japan, or Germany, which heavily subsidize the installation of solar power. Many investors today are racing to ethanol, but wariness seems advisable. Bill Gates has already invested $84 million in a start-up called Pacific Ethanol; venture-capital firms have moved into the ethanol "space." If the smart money is already there, you're too late. Besides, BP and DuPont are now looking past ethanol to bet on butanol, a crop-derived petroleum substitute with superior technical properties.

Agriculture. Should growing seasons and rainfall patterns change quickly, genetic engineering of crop plants might become essential to society's future. DuPont, Monsanto, Syngenta, and other firms that are perfecting genetic improvement of crops—either through gene splicing or via natural crossbreeding aided by genetic analysis—could become even bigger players if there is significant climate change.

The Deus Ex Machina Industry. Be wary of start-ups and venture capitalists who may soon talk up "geoengineering." In theory, it could be possible to cause the seas to absorb more greenhouse gases, if oceans were fertilized with substances that encourage the growth of marine organisms that need carbon dioxide. In theory, the upper atmosphere could be seeded with shiny fleck-sized particles that bounce sunlight back into space, cooling the Earth. In theory, if volcanoes could be made more active, their emissions also would reduce global temperature by blocking some sunlight. (The sole exception to the last two decades of warm years resulted from the 1991 eruption of Mount Pinatubo, in the Philippines, which caused cool weather worldwide.) It's likely that some investors will be tempted by offers of early stakes in geoengineering enterprises. But it's unlikely that any government will ever approve an experiment involving the entire planet.

Want the profile of what seems the perfect large firm of the future? Think General Electric. The company builds nuclear-power reactors and is ready to build extremely efficient coal-fired power plants, which are likely to become more commonplace than nuclear reactors owing to lower cost and less political opposition. George W. Bush talks grandly of Future-Gen, a billion-dollar federal initiative for a prototype coal-fired power plant that emits hardly any greenhouse gases. But the FutureGen crash program doesn't even break ground until 2009. Meanwhile, GE has already completed the engineering work for an advanced coal-fired power plant able to operate with negligible greenhouse-gas emissions. If greenhouse-gas regulations are enacted, GE may be swamped with orders for its new coal-fired generating station. GE has also recently engineered jet engines, power turbines, and diesel locomotives that require less fuel, and hence release less greenhouse gas, than those now in use. The company has also made serious investments in wind turbines, photovoltaic cells, and other zero-emission energy forms. This big, profit-conscious corporation is at the cutting edge of preparation for a greenhouse world—which is likely to keep GE big and profitable.

—Gregg Easterbrook

assumption that growing conditions will continue to be good in the breadbasket areas of the United States, India, China, and South America. If rainfall shifts away from those areas, there could be significant human suffering for many, many years, even if, say, Siberian agriculture eventually replaces lost production elsewhere. By reducing farm yield, rainfall changes could also cause skyrocketing prices for commodity crops, something the global economy has rarely observed in the last 30 years.

Recent studies show that in the last few decades, precipitation in North America is increasingly the result of a few downpours rather than lots of showers. Downpours cause flooding and property damage, while being of less use to agriculture than frequent soft rains. Because the relationship between artificially triggered climate change and rainfall is conjectural, investors presently have no way to avoid buying land in places that someday might be hit with frequent downpours. But this concern surely raises a red flag about investments in India, Bangladesh, and Indonesia, where monsoon rains are already a leading social problem.

Water-related investments might be attractive in another way: for hydropower. Zero-emission hydropower might become a premium energy form if greenhouse gases are strictly regulated. Quebec is the Saudi Arabia of roaring water. Already the hydropower complex around James Bay is one of the world's leading sources of water-generated electricity. For 30 years, environmentalists and some Cree activists opposed plans to construct a grand hydropower complex that essentially would dam all large rivers flowing into the James and Hudson bays. But it's not hard to imagine Canada completing the reengineering of northern Quebec for hydropower, if demand from New England and the Midwest becomes strong enough. Similarly, there is hydropower potential in the Chilean portions of Patagonia. This is a wild and beautiful region little touched by human activity—and an intriguing place to snap up land for hydropower reservoirs.

Adaptation

Last October, the treasury office of the United Kingdom estimated that unless we adapt, global warming could eventually subtract as much as 20 percent of the gross domestic product from the world economy. Needless to say, if that happens, not even the cleverest portfolio will help you. This estimate is worst-case, however, and has many economists skeptical. Optimists think dangerous global warming might be averted at surprisingly low cost (see "Some Convenient Truths," September 2006). Once regulations create a profit incentive for the invention of greenhouse-gas-reducing technology, an outpouring of innovation is likely. Some of those who formulate greenhouse-gas-control ideas will become rich; everyone will benefit from the environmental safeguards the ideas confer.

Enactment of some form of binding greenhouse-gas rules is now essential both to slow the rate of greenhouse-gas accumulation and to create an incentive for inventors, engineers, and businesspeople to devise the ideas that will push society beyond the fossil-fuel age. *The New York Times* recently groused that George W. Bush's fiscal 2007 budget includes only $4.2 billion

for federal research that might cut greenhouse-gas emissions. This is the wrong concern: Progress would be faster if the federal government spent nothing at all on greenhouse-gas-reduction research—but enacted regulations that gave the private sector a significant profit motive to find solutions that work in actual use, as opposed to on paper in government studies. The market has caused the greenhouse-gas problem, and the market is the best hope of solving it. Offering market incentives for the development of greenhouse-gas controls—indeed, encouraging profit making in greenhouse-gas controls—is the most promising path to avoiding the harm that could befall the dispossessed of developing nations as the global climate changes.

Yet if global-warming theory is right, higher global temperatures are already inevitable. Even the most optimistic scenario for reform envisions decades of additional greenhouse-gas accumulation in the atmosphere, and that in turn means a warming world. The warming may be manageable, but it is probably unstoppable in the short term. This suggests that a major investment sector of the near future will be climate-change adaptation. Crops that grow in high temperatures, homes and buildings designed to stay cool during heat waves, vehicles that run on far less fuel, waterfront structures that can resist stronger storms—the list of needed adaptations will be long, and all involve producing, buying, and selling. Environmentalists don't like talk of adaptation, as it implies making our peace with a warmer world. That peace, though, must be made—and the sooner businesses, investors, and entrepreneurs get to work, the better.

Why, ultimately, should nations act to control greenhouse gases, rather than just letting climate turmoil happen and seeing who profits? One reason is that the cost of controls is likely to be much lower than the cost of rebuilding the world. Coastal cities could be abandoned and rebuilt inland, for instance, but improving energy efficiency and reducing greenhouse-gas emissions in order to stave off rising sea levels should be far more cost-effective. Reforms that prevent major economic and social disruption from climate change are likely to be less expensive, across the board, than reacting to the change. The history of antipollution programs shows that it is always cheaper to prevent emissions than to reverse any damage they cause.

For the United States, there's another argument that is particularly keen. The present ordering of the world favors the United States in nearly every respect—political, economic, even natural, considering America's excellent balance of land and resources. Maybe a warming world would favor the United States more; this is certainly possible. But when the global order already places America at No. 1, why would we want to run the risk of climate change that alters that order? Keeping the world economic system and the global balance of power the way they are seems very strongly in the U.S. national interest—and keeping things the way they are requires prevention of significant climate change. That, in the end, is what's in it for us.

GREGG EASTERBROOK is an *Atlantic* contributing editor, a visiting fellow at the Brookings Institution, and the author of *The Progress Paradox* (2003).

Boomer Century

What's going to happen when the most prosperous, best-educated generation in history finally grows up? (And just how special are the baby *boomers*?)

Joshua Zeitz

Just a matter of weeks from now, On December 31, as millions of Americans don party hats and pop champagne corks to usher in the New Year, Kathleen Casey, the Philadelphia-born daughter of a Navy machinist and his wife, will likely find her phone once again ringing off the hook. It happens every decade or so. Journalists and academics and earnest civic leaders, family and friends, all find their way to Casey's doorstep, hoping for just a few minutes of her time, eager to glean a little bit of wisdom about what it all means and where it's all going.

Kathleen Casey, you see, bears the unique distinction of having launched the baby boom.

Born at 12:01 A.M. on January 1, 1946, she was the first of 76 million Americans brought into the world between 1946 and 1964, when, in a sharp reversal of a steady century-long decline, the national birthrate skyrocketed, creating a massive demographic upheaval.

So this year the very first baby *boomer,* the vanguard of that endlessly youthful generation, turns 60. But hers is not like other generations. If its last, unrecorded member was born at 11:59 P.M. on December 31, 1964, he or she will just be turning 41. Certainly this person, the Unknown Boomer, will have encountered very different cultural signposts than did Kathleen Casey (say, Pat Boone vs. the Sex Pistols), but together the two of them bracket a group that, despite its immensity, is strangely unified, and whose influence today defines both the limits and the promise of American life—and will for years to come.

Last summer, 40 years after "(I Can't Get No) Satisfaction" climbed to the top of Billboard's singles chart and earned the Rolling Stones their first gold release in the United States, the Stones launched their 2005 World Tour at Boston's Fenway Park. For tens of thousands of *boomers* who came to see Mick Jagger and Keith Richards perform the greatest hits of yesteryear, age really is just a number.

Their kids might have been mortified to see these graying veterans of the 1960s filling a ballpark for one last great rock V'n roll show. But in many ways, it all makes sense. There is still no more fitting anthem for the baby-boom generation than the Stones' signature hit.

Raised in an era of unprecedented affluence and national omnipotence, but coming of age in a time that perceived more limited resources and diminished American power, the *boomers* have long been defined by a vain search for satisfaction. No matter how much they have, they can't ever seem to get enough. This quest for satisfaction has at times led to nadirs of narcissism and greed. As a generation the *boomers* have always seemed to want it all: cheap energy, consumer plenty, low taxes, loads of government entitlements, ageless beauty, and an ever-rising standard of living. They inherited a nation flush with resources and will bequeath their children a country mired in debt.

But their quest for personal satisfaction has also pushed the boundaries of civic life in radical and unusual directions. In their youth, black and white *boomers* took to the streets to tear down the walls of racial segregation. They strove toward greater equality of opportunity between men and women, made it harder for policymakers to choose war over peace without first convincing a skeptical electorate of its merits, and created a nation that was more accepting of diversity.

For all their faults and all their virtues, they remain exemplars of what Henry Luce called the American Century. The social commentators Neil Howe and William Strauss got it exactly right when they wrote that "from V-J Day forward, whatever age bracket *Boomers* have occupied has been the cultural and spiritual focal point for American society as a whole. Through their childhood, America was child-obsessed; in their youth, youth-obsessed; in their 'yuppie' phase, yuppie-obsessed." Maybe Luce had it wrong. It wasn't the American Century. It was the *Boomer* Century.

Scholars continue to marvel at the phenomenon known as the baby boom. It seemed then, and seems now, to fly in the face of modern demographic and social history. Between 1800 and 1920 the number of children borne by the average American woman fell by more than half, from roughly seven to three. As America transformed itself from a nation of small farmers into an urban, industrial behemoth, increasing numbers of parents no longer needed small armies of children to work the family farm. In this new world of machine and factory, surplus children were a liability. They required much in the way of food, clothing, and shelter but contributed very little in turn to the economic well-being of their families.

The national birthrate, long on the decline, bottomed out in the 1930s. With unemployment running as high as 25 percent, many young Americans, facing an uncertain economic future, decided to put off marriage and parenthood until better days.

When those better days finally arrived in 1940, courtesy of America's swift and total mobilization for war, most commentators expected only a temporary upsurge in births. The editors of Life magazine worried that by 1970 the Soviet Union's population would outstrip that of the United States, Britain, France, and Italy combined. They were taken completely by surprise at the magnitude and duration of what actually followed.

Beginning in 1942 with so-called furlough babies, taking off in May 1946—nine months after V-J Day—and peaking around 1947 or 1948, when an American child was born every eight seconds, the GI generation broke sharply with a century-long demographic trend toward smaller families. The population boom also hit Australia, Canada, and New Zealand, whose economies enjoyed a postwar expansion similar to (though not on scale with) America's, but not Europe, large portions of which lay in ruins. Little wonder, then, that a British visitor traveling in the United States in 1958 observed with something like amazement that "every other young housewife I see is pregnant. "

Though its causes continue to puzzle scholars, the baby boom probably grew from three distinct trends.

First, in the prosperous 1940s and 1950s, thirtyish Americans who had postponed marriage and children during the Great Depression were eager to make up for lost time and start building families. They crowded the field 10 years after they would normally have contributed their share of progeny to the national population.

Second, they were joined by a younger cohort, including many recently demobilized GIs who had come home to find economic prosperity, generous government assistance in the form of housing and educational benefits for veterans, and a general sense of optimism born of conquering global fascism. For these young victors, many still in their early twenties, it made little sense to put off marriage and family. Like their older brothers and sisters, they understood that the years of Depression scarcity and wartime sacrifice were over. Finally, and in a more subtle way, the general euphoria that drove up marriage and birth rates was soon complemented by Cold War-era anxieties over nuclear competition. In an uncertain world, the comforts of home and hearth could provide a salve against atomic angst, just as the stabilizing influence of marriage and parenthood offered a strategic advantage in the nation's struggle against communism.

Noting the dangers posed by the Cold War, two Harvard sociologists informed the Ford Foundation that the "world is like a volcano that breaks out repeatedly. . . . The world approaches this critical period with a grave disruption of the family system. . . . The new age demands a stronger, more resolute and better equipped individual. . . . To produce such persons will demand a reorganization of the present family system and the

building of one that is stronger emotionally and morally." Ultimately, if Americans wanted to do their part in this new global war, they'd settle down, have lots of kids, and raise them to do well in school and well in life.

Even household architecture seemed to reinforce the relationship between Cold War worries and the cult of domesticity in which the baby boom prospered. The standard suburban ranch house favored by many young families in the 1950s was set back from the street and protected by a fence, and it had a low-slung roof and an attached carport, lending it a bit of the appearance of a well-fortified bunker.

Not just homes, but the children who were starting to crawl through them, formed a "defense—an impregnable bulwark" against the horrors of the atomic age, the social commentator Louisa Randall Church argued in 1946. Many Americans seemed to agree, and out of this vague combination of economic optimism and atomic unease, they were fruitful, and they multiplied.

Their children—the *boomers*—were necessarily a heterogeneous lot. America still suffered from deep racial and economic divisions. A country as large as the United States contained a host of distinctive regional folkways. Still, as the cultural critic Annie Gottlieb has observed, for all their differences, the baby *boomers* formed a distinctive "tribe with its roots in time, rather than place or race." By any measure, the America in which they grew up was more abundant, more powerful, and more enraptured with its own glory than ever before. When John F. Kennedy called on his countrymen to "explore the stars, conquer the deserts, eradicate disease, tap the ocean depths, and encourage the arts and commerce," he echoed the optimism that helped forge the new generation's outlook.

Part of this confidence grew out of America's total victory in World War II and the country's scientific and medical achievements, including Jonas Salk's discovery of a polio vaccine in the early 1950s. But most of it was due to the nation's dynamic economy. Between 1940 and 1960 our gross national product doubled; real wages—and real purchasing power—increased by 30 percent; the portion of owner-occupied homes climbed to 61 percent; four-fifths of American families kept at least one car in the driveway; average life expectancy rose by almost 11 percent; most employees of large firms enjoyed such new benefits as private health insurance, paid vacations, and retirement pensions; and the typical American house held seven times more gadgets and goods than in the 1920s. By 1957 the energy of the American economy led U.S. News & World Report to declare that "never had so many people, anywhere, been so well off." When Richard Nixon famously sparred with Nikita Khrushchev at the 1959 American National Exhibition in Moscow and proclaimed the superiority of the American suburban kitchen, with its sleek electric appliances in their myriad styles and models, he articulated a vague but popular sense that America's consumer abundance was a sure sign of its Cold War advantage.

For *boomer* children, this cornucopia translated into billions of dollars' worth of Hula-Hoops, Davy Crockett raccoon skin hats, Hopalong Cassidy six-shooters, bicycles and tricycles,

Slinkys, Silly Putty, and skateboards (and, in California, the shining lure of Disneyland). The writer Joyce Maynard remembered that when the Barbie doll made its debut in 1959, her world changed "like a cloudburst, without preparation. Barbie wasn't just a toy, but a way of living that moved us suddenly from tea parties to dates with Ken at the soda shoppe." Relatively speaking, to grow up a middle-class American kid in the 1950s meant wanting for nothing.

I t also meant television. In just four years, between 1948 and 1952, the number of American households with TV sets jumped from 172,000 to 15.3 million. T. S. Eliot observed that television was "a medium of entertainment which permits millions of people to listen to the same joke at the same time, and yet remain lonesome," but for the millions of children raised on it, the new device offered up endless hours of entertainment in the form of family sitcoms like "The Adventures of Ozzie and Harriet," "Father Knows Best," and "Leave It to Beaver," all of which idealized the carefree, child-centered world of suburban America.

More popular still were the Westerns: "Gunsmoke," "Wyatt Earp," "Bonanza," "The Texan," "Wagon Train," "Cheyenne," "The Rifleman," "The Outcasts," "Wanted: Dead or Alive," "Have Gun, Will Travel." Together, these serial epics captured close to half of America's weekly television audience and, by the end of the decade, constituted 7 of the 11 most popular shows on the small screen. The programs mythologized the rugged individualism and physical strength of the American frontiersman, who tamed both his enemy (the Indian or outlaw standing in for the Soviet menace) and the natural environment. It was a genre well suited for a country confident of its ability to reach the stars, vanquish disease, and collapse the limits of time and space.

Complementing this message of abundance and conquest were new vogues in child rearing and pedagogy rooted in John Dewey's ideas about the merits of progressive education. They entered the mainstream in 1946, when Benjamin Spock published The Common Sense Book of Baby and Child Care. His book instructed the parents of the baby-boom generation to go light on punishment and heavy on reason and persuasion, and to bear in mind that their daughters' and sons' happiness was the paramount objective of child rearing. If Johnny steals someone's toy, don't hit him. Explain that stealing is wrong, and buy him the toy that he coveted. If Suzie misbehaves at the dinner table, don't worry. Table manners are overrated.

Spock was enormously influential. A study conducted in 1961 revealed that two-thirds of new mothers surveyed had read his book. He made permissive or child-centered parenting mandatory for millions of new postwar middle-class families. By the mid-1950s his message was routinely echoed in the pages of Parents magazine and found confirmation in countless sociological studies.

In later years critics would decry the effects of progressive child rearing, some of them crediting it with an entire generation's egotism. The iconoclastic historian Richard Hofstadter worried that America would be overrun by the "overvalued child." Writing of the typical GI generation mother, the novelist Lisa Alther lamented: "If anything had been drummed into

her in years of motherhood, it was that you mustn't squelch the young. It might squelch their precious development. Never mind about your own development."

Hyperbole aside, millions of *boomers* did grow up in prosperous, nurturing homes in which children formed the core of the family. Raised amid plenty, taught to value their needs and satisfy their wants, and imbued with a sense of national greatness and purpose, it would have been odd had they not entered young adulthood with at least some sense of entitlement.

In 1956, noting the connection between postwar vogues in Freudian analysis and progressive child rearing, the literary critic Alfred Kazin was bemused by the national "insistence on individual fulfillment, satisfaction and happiness." Years later the pollster Daniel Yankelovich observed that grown *boomers,* instead of asking themselves, "Will I be able to make a living?," as their parents, raised in the Depression years, often did, were more prone to wonder, "How can I find self-fulfillment?"

N o American generation has been so intensely studied, so widely celebrated, and so roundly condemned as this one. Out of the cacophony of analysis, two standard criticisms—one from the left, the other from the right—stand out.

For contemporary liberals, popular films like The Big Chill and television series like "thirty-something" follow a familiar narrative line in which idealistic, socially committed children of the sixties grow into self-centered, blandly acquisitive adults. In the words of the former sixties activist Todd Gitlin, by the 1980s a generation that once raged against "banality, irrelevance, and all the ugliness which conspire to dwarf or extinguish the human personality" had graduated from "J'accuse to Jacuzzi."

Even when television *boomers* retained their fundamental goodness—think, for instance, of Michael J. Fox's parents, Elise and Steven Keaton, in the popular 1980s sitcom "Family Ties"—they remained painfully conscious of their generation's potential drift toward self-absorption.

To conservatives, on the other hand, the generation embodies the evils of secular liberalism. In Slouching Towards Gomorrah, Robert Bork credits the pampered baby-boom generation with virtually every insidious social trend in recent American history. "The dual forces of radical egalitarianism . . . and radical individualism (the drastic reduction of limits to personal gratification)," explains the book's back cover, have "undermined our culture, our intellect, and our morality."

Of course, traditionalists don't have to look far to make their case. *Boomers* are certainly more tolerant than their parents of looser personal mores. In 1983, 44 percent of them approved of cohabitation outside marriage, 29 percent supported legalizing marijuana, and 37 percent endorsed casual sex. Whereas only a quarter of Americans approved of premarital sex in the 1950s, by the 1970s that figure had climbed to three-quarters.

M ore recently, boomers from left and right have begun weaving a third critique. In an effort of historical revision that comes close to self-flagellation, they have begun to worship their parents' generation. That the "GI Generation" has become "the Greatest Generation" is evident everywhere—in popular television series like "Band of Brothers," in films like Saving Private Ryan, and in official tributes, such as the World War II memorial in Washington, D.C. Offered by the children of G.I. Joe and Rosie the Riveter, these accolades carry an implicit message: Try as we may, we will simply never measure up to our parents' self-sacrificing greatness.

The problem with all these critiques is that they ignore both the creative use to which the generation has sometimes put its terrific sense of entitlement and the continuities between sixties idealism and eighties excess.

In February 1960, when four black college students staged a sit-in at a Woolworth's lunch counter in Greensboro, North Carolina, sparking a national campaign and inaugurating a decade of youth-driven political activism, they were doing nothing so much as demanding access to the same entitlements that other children of the postwar era claimed as their American birthright. A sympathetic advertisement appearing in three Atlanta newspapers in March 1960 hit the nail on the head when it explained "the meaning of the sit-down protests that are sweeping this nation: Today's youth will not sit by submissively, while being denied all of the rights, privileges, and joys of life." Raised on the same television advertisements and political rhetoric as their white peers, young black Americans were determined to get their piece of satisfaction.

In a country where happiness and dignity were so inextricably bound up with the individual's right to enjoy the blessings of the national wealth, this argument resonated. In his "Letter from Birmingham Jail," Martin Luther King, Jr., the father of young baby *boomers* of his own, drove home this point. He spoke of finding your "tongue twisted and your speech stammering as you seek to explain to your six-year-old daughter why she can't go to the public amusement park that has just been advertised on television, and see tears welling up in her eyes when she is told that Funtown is closed to colored children."

The legions of junior high and high school students who heeded his call in Birmingham—who filled the jails, attended the prayer meetings, and drove King himself to embrace more radical tactics and demands—ultimately compelled the nation to confront long-standing inequities that "the Greatest Generation" had been content to ignore.

They were the shock troops of the 1960s rights revolution. Like their white peers, these *boomer* kids had seen an average of 500 hours of television advertisements by the age of 6 and over 300,000 commercials by the age of 21. (King's daughter had clearly seen an ad for Funtown.)

In the aftermath of the Newark riots of 1967, the black poet Amiri Baraka told a state investigatory commission that the "poorest black man in Newark, in America, knows how white people live. We have television sets; we see movies. We see the fantasy and the reality of white America every day." The schism between fantasy and reality could inspire a truly creative tension.

And so it went for other boomers as well. Young black activists influenced women, gays and lesbians, students, welfare recipients, Latinos, and American Indians to appreciate the gap between America's lofty democratic promise and its imperfect reality, and to work to narrow that gap.

By the 1970s *boomer* rights activists forced changes in credit laws, so that married women could have their own credit cards, and pushed for the enactment of Title IX, which broke down gender barriers in education and athletics. In forcing a new liberalization of sex and romance, they insisted on everyone's right to satisfaction and self-realization—not just married couples but also unmarried partners, no matter what their sexual orientation. They played an instrumental role in bringing down a U.S. president, Lyndon Johnson, and in making the Vietnam War increasingly untenable for his successor, Richard Nixon.

In other words, the generation raised on Spock, television, and abundance put its sense of privilege and entitlement to work for the better good. Today most scholars agree that the *boomers* will leave their children and grandchildren a country that's a little more just, a little more humane, and a little more inclusive than the one they inherited from their parents.

These accomplishments notwithstanding, it's small wonder that the generation has accumulated mixed reviews. The radical left is no happier with the *boomers* than is the reactionary right. In their youth they effected so massive an upheaval in politics and culture that they were bound eventually to fall in the public's esteem. Apostles of what Gitlin has called "the voyage to the interior," and what the late historian and social critic Christopher Lasch derided as a "culture of narcissism," they seemed after the 1960s to place an unusually high premium on self-discovery and personal satisfaction.

The generation that had raged against authority, vowing with Bob Dylan, "I ain't gonna work on Maggie's farm no more," was now swinging to Andrea True's refrain "More, more, more. How do you like it, how do you like it?" They bought minivans, microwaves, and self-help books, embraced transcendental meditation, embarked on various diets, visited tanning salons and fat farms, and filled their homes with more durable goods than their prosperous parents could ever have imagined.

Even their politics seemed to change. In 1980 it was an eleventh-hour swing among *boomer* voters that turned Ronald Reagan's razor-thin margin into a landslide victory. In fact, there was always more continuity than the critics liked to admit. Even in 1972, the first year that 18-year-olds were allowed to take part in national elections, fewer than half the eligible new voters bothered to show up at the polls, and just half of those who did cast their lot with the liberal antiwar Democrat George McGovern.

Popular memory notwithstanding, the sixties generation has never been a political monolith. Nor was it uniformly engaged by public issues. Only 20 percent of students who attended college in the late 1960s participated in marches or protests, and far fewer—2 or 3 percent—regarded themselves as activists.

The antiwar movement, which many liberal *boomers* fondly remember as embodying the altruistic, public spirit of the era, was always more self-interested than its veterans might wish to admit. Whereas virtually every able-bodied, draft-eligible man of the GI generation served in the military during World War II, only 10 percent of the 27 million draft-eligible *boomers* were in uniform while America fought the Vietnam War.

The rest, most of them white and middle-class, found creative ways to stay safe. They claimed medical dispensations and student deferments, became schoolteachers or entered defense industries, or married and had children before their local draft boards could sweep them up.

In opposing the war, which many activists did sincerely view as both immoral and unwinnable, protesters betrayed as much selfish entitlement as noble intent. They wanted the United States out of Southeast Asia, but they also wanted to keep themselves out of Southeast Asia. Richard Nixon understood this when he shifted the draft burden away from men in their twenties and back onto 18- and 19-year-olds. Suddenly college campuses quieted down. Why bother to protest once you're safely out of the woods?

In effect, for all their racial, economic, and cultural diversity, if the *boomers* shared anything, it was that perpetual search for satisfaction. In their best moments, and in their worst, they demanded that the country make good on the promises it had handed them in the 1950s. The problem was that when they began to come of age in the 1970s, the bottom fell out on the American economy. Even as they clamored for "more, more, more," what they found was less, less, less. Between the 1960s and 1980s the income of young men just entering the job market declined by 50 percent. This mostly was due to forces beyond anyone's control: Government expenditures for the Vietnam War caused runaway inflation; economic restructuring took a toll on manufacturing; oil shortages in the 1970s drove up energy costs and interest rates. The long slump also came from the gradual erosion of progressive tax policies and growth in entitlements like health insurance.

Ironically, the baby boom was itself a major cause of the nation's economic slide. So many young people seeking jobs drove down wages and accounted for as much as half of the unemployment rate during the 1970s and 1980s. So *boomers* made the necessary adjustments. To maintain a standard of living that reflected their upbringing, they, like their Depression-bred parents, postponed marriage and children. Though women's wages, once adjusted for changing education and skill levels, remained stagnant in the 1970s and 1980s, the proportion of young married women in the work force more than doubled, from roughly 30 percent to 70 percent. Two-earner households helped keep pace with the generation's material expectations, but at the expense of outsourcing Generation X to after-school daycare and sports programs.

Even these adjustments fell short. The generation that couldn't get no satisfaction could hardly be expected to live within its means. In 2002 baby *boomers* spent between 20 percent and 30 percent more money each year than did the average American consumer. In part, this was out of necessity. They had children to feed, houses to furnish, and college tuitions to pay. But the *boomers* have long stretched the limits of sound household economy. According to the economist Robert Samuelson, between 1946 and 2002 consumer debt climbed from 22 percent of household income to 110 percent. In other words, we've become a debtor nation, and the *boomers* have presided over this transition.

Now at the height of their political influence (the 2000 presidential election saw the first-ever race between two baby *boomers,* and the commentators Neil Howe and William Strauss estimate that *boomers* will hold a plurality in Congress until 2015) they are also presiding over the creation of a national debt that their children and grandchildren will be left to pay off in coming years.

In the end the boomers may be less culpable, less praiseworthy, and less remarkable than they, and everyone else, think. Their cohort was so big, arrived so suddenly, and has grown up so closely alongside the modern broadcast media that they have always struck us as standing apart from larger historical forces that drive the normal workings of states and societies. Yet much about this seeming exceptionalism just isn't new.

When the husband-and-wife sociologist team Robert and Helen Lynd visited Muncie, Indiana, in the early 1920s, they found many of the same traits popularly associated with the *boomers* already evident among Jazz Age youth. Their famous, pathbreaking book, Middletown: A Study in Modern American Culture, reported a younger generation in the thrall of movies and music, willing to stretch the limits of romantic and sexual propriety, obsessed with clothes and cosmetics, and eager to stake out shocking new degrees of personal autonomy.

And if the children of the 1950s were technically the first generation raised on Spock, they weren't the first generation raised on the ideas of Spock. By the mid-1950s upward of 75 percent of middle-class men and women were reading advice books that, more often than not, counseled unprecedented attention to the child. Most experts in the 1920s and 1930s had figured out Spock before Spock figured out Spock.

Nor were the *boomers* the first generation to make therapeutic self-discovery a competitive sport. In their parents' youth, in the twenties and thirties, Freud was already all the rage. Popular books of the day included The Psychology of Golf, Psychology of the Poet Shelley, and The Psychology of Selling Life Insurance. Bookstores and mail-order houses peddled new titles like Psychoanalysis by Mail, Psychoanalysis Self-Applied, Ten Thousand Dreams Interpreted, and Sex Problems Solved.

Long before the *boomers* arrived on the scene, Americans were drawn to a new cult of self-improvement that celebrated the mastery of one's deepest impulses and thoughts. In the 1920s millions followed the advice of the French wonder guru, Emile Coué, faithfully repeating the simple catechism "Day by day, in every way, I am getting better and better."

The explosion of self-help literature peaked in 1936 with the publication of Dale Carnegie's How to Win Friends and Influence People.

If the *boomers* weren't entirely original in their loosened sexual standards, emphasis on physical appearance and youth, or search for a therapeutic mind cure, neither were they all that unusual in their resistance to collective sacrifice. It hardly diminishes the decisive effort of the World War II generation to note that civilians traded on the black market, deeply resented rationing and wage and labor controls, and often worked in defense production as much for profit as for patriotism.

A *Boomer* Bookshelf

Given their central role in recent history, baby **boomers** figure prominently in many of the most important and illuminating books about postwar America. Here are 10 volumes that I found of particular interest.—J.Z.

TERRY H. ANDERSON The Movement and the Sixties: Protest in America from Greensboro to Wounded Knee (Oxford, 1995). Anderson, a Vietnam veteran and history professor at Texas A&M University, presents a comprehensive and balanced portrait of **boomer**-generation activism in the 1960s that avoids both the triumphal and condemnatory posturing typical of other works on this subject.

JAMES CARROLL An American Requiem: God, My Father, and the War That Came Between Us (Houghton Mifflin, 1996). Though Carroll, a former priest and antiwar activist, was born in 1943, just barely missing the arbitrary jump-off for the baby boom, his memoir of growing up in the postwar years and coming to political consciousness during the Vietnam War era is a vital contribution to **boomer** literature.

STEVE M. GILLON *Boomer* Nation: The Largest and Richest Generation Ever and How It Changed America (The Free Press, 2004). In this engaging and informative book—written for a popular audience but with a professional's touch—Steve Gillon, of the University of Oklahoma and the History Channel, weaves together several lives to present a sweeping history of an entire generation.

DAVID HALBERSTAM The Children (Random House, 1998). Though almost 800 pages in length, Halberstam's history of the young black men and women who formed the Student Nonviolent Coordinating Committee and other organizations fighting for civil rights in the 1960s provides an exciting and accessible narrative of the **boomer** generation's most committed shock troops for justice.

JAMES T. PATTERSON Grand Expectations: The United States, 1945–1974 (Oxford, 1996) and Restless Giant: The United States from Watergate to Bush v. Gore (Oxford, 2005). A Bancroft Prize winner and professor emeritus at Brown University, Patterson has written the definitive two-volume history of America in the Cold War era. His work is essential for understanding the environment in which the **boomers** were raised and in which they grew to adulthood.

SUSAN FALUDI Backlash: The Undeclared War Against American Women (Crown, 1991) and Stiffed: The Betrayal of the American Man (William Morrow and Co., 1999). A prizewinning journalist and writer, Faludi has written two must-read volumes on the culture and politics of gender in recent American history. Her works are implicitly about the country the **boomers** inherited and made.

RICK ATKINSON The Long Gray Line: The American Journey of West Point's Class of 1966 (Houghton Mifflin, 1999). Atkinson, a Pulitzer Prize-winning journalist, presents a rich and complicated portrait of some of the first **boomers** to graduate from the U.S. Military Academy. As essential as understanding those **boomers** who protested the Vietnam War is appreciating those who fought it.

JONATHAN FRANZEN The Corrections (Farrar, Straus and Giroux, 2001). Most **boomer** literature focuses on the children of the 1960s, ignoring the younger half of the cohort that came of age in the 1970s and 1980s. Franzen's celebrated novel addresses this imbalance and offers a painfully honest glimpse at younger **boomers** approaching middle age.

Even the era's soldiers had mixed reasons for going to war. When The Saturday Evening Post ran a series of articles by American GIs entitled "What I Am Fighting For," readers learned that their sons and brothers were in Europe "for that big house with the bright green roof and the big front lawn," their "nice little roadster," pianos, tennis courts, and "the girl with the large brown eyes and the reddish tinge in her hair, that girl who is away at college right now, preparing herself for her part in the future of America and Christianity."

The same conflation of private and public interests drove home-front advertisers to pitch their wares as a just reward for wartime sacrifice—as in an ad promising that "when our boys come home . . . among the finer things of life they will find ready to enjoy will be Johnston and Murphy shoes. Quality unchanged."

None of this suggests that the **boomers** aren't a distinct category of Americans. If many of the character traits popularly assigned them were in evidence long before they were born—if the **boomers** were, in fact, walking along the arc of history rather than outside it—still, they have, for good and for ill, made a lasting imprint on the nation.

Social commentators have long been inclined to make sense of the world in generational terms. Writing about his travels in the United States in the 1830s, Alexis de Tocqueville argued that "among democratic nations each new generation is a new people." Roughly 100 years later the social scientist Karl Mannheim similarly observed: "Early impressions tend to coalesce into a natural view of the world."

The **boomers**—a generation born into national wealth and power, raised on the promise of their limitless potential and self-worth, reared on television and advertising, enthralled by the wonders of modern science and medicine—are, for all their differences, a most potent emblem of the long American Century.

Even today they remain characteristically unfulfilled. Looking for "more, more, more"—for that "satisfaction" that seems forever to elude them—they will, as they have since 1946, stretch the limits of America's possibilities and its resources.

In 2046 we'll still be appraising their work.

The **boomers,** said one critic, were a distinctive "tribe with its roots in time, rather than place or race." Relatively speaking, to grow up a middle-class American child in the 1950s meant wanting for nothing. A 1961 study revealed that two-thirds of all new mothers surveyed had read Dr. Spock. These students ultimately compelled the nation to confront inequities "the Greatest Generation" hadn't. The antiwar movement was always more self-interested than its veterans might wish to admit. They will continue to do what they have done since 1946—stretch the limits of America's possibilities.

Joshua Zeitz's book Flapper, about an earlier social revolution, will be published by Crown in April.

Test-Your-Knowledge Form

We encourage you to photocopy and use this page as a tool to assess how the articles in *Annual Editions* expand on the information in your textbook. By reflecting on the articles you will gain enhanced text information. You can also access this useful form on a product's book support website at www.mhhe.com/cls

NAME: DATE:

_____

TITLE AND NUMBER OF ARTICLE:

_____

BRIEFLY STATE THE MAIN IDEA OF THIS ARTICLE:

_____

LIST THREE IMPORTANT FACTS THAT THE AUTHOR USES TO SUPPORT THE MAIN IDEA:

_____

WHAT INFORMATION OR IDEAS DISCUSSED IN THIS ARTICLE ARE ALSO DISCUSSED IN YOUR TEXTBOOK OR OTHER READINGS THAT YOU HAVE DONE? LIST THE TEXTBOOK CHAPTERS AND PAGE NUMBERS:

_____

LIST ANY EXAMPLES OF BIAS OR FAULTY REASONING THAT YOU FOUND IN THE ARTICLE:

_____

LIST ANY NEW TERMS/CONCEPTS THAT WERE DISCUSSED IN THE ARTICLE, AND WRITE A SHORT DEFINITION:

We Want Your Advice

ANNUAL EDITIONS revisions depend on two major opinion sources: one is our Academic Advisory Board, listed in the front of this volume, which works with us in scanning the thousands of articles published in the public press each year; the other is you—the person actually using the book. Please help us and the users of the next edition by completing the prepaid article rating form on this page and returning it to us. Thank you for your help!

ANNUAL EDITIONS: United States History, Volume 2, 21/e

ARTICLE RATING FORM

Here is an opportunity for you to have direct input into the next revision of this volume.
We would like you to rate each of the articles listed below, using the following scale:

1. **Excellent: should definitely be retained**
2. **Above average: should probably be retained**
3. **Below average: should probably be deleted**
4. **Poor: should definitely be deleted**

Your ratings will play a vital part in the next revision.
Please mail this prepaid form to us as soon as possible.
Thanks for your help!

RATING	ARTICLE	RATING	ARTICLE
	1. The American Civil War, Emancipation, and Reconstruction on the World Stage		22. Lessons from the Great Crash
	2. How a War of Terror Kept Blacks Oppressed Long after the Civil War Ended		23. When America Sent Her Own Packing
			24. Labor Strikes Back
	3. The Nez Perce Flight for Justice		25. Flight of the Wasp
	4. How the West Was Spun		26. Ike at D-Day
	5. Gifts of the "Robber Barons"		27. Dollar Diplomacy
	6. Lockwood in '84		28. Command Performance
	7. A Day to Remember: December 29, 1890		29. Crisis at Central High
	8. Utopia Derailed		30. Launch of a New World
	9. Where the Other Half Lived		31. Will the Left Ever Learn to Communicate across Generations?
	10. TR's Wild Side		
	11. Joe Hill: 'I Never Died,' Said He		32. King's Complex Legacy
	12. "A Machine of Practical Utility"		33. The Spirit of '78, Stayin' Alive
	13. A Brief History of Fear		34. Soft Power: Reagan the Dove
	14. A Day to Remember: March 25, 1911: Triangle Fire		35. The Tragedy of Bill Clinton
			36. The Rove Presidency
	15. The $5 Day		37. Good Health for America?
	16. To Make the World Safe for Democracy		38. An Empire at Risk
	17. The Democrats' Deadlocked Ballot Brawl of 1924		39. What Do We Owe the Indians?
	18. Between Heaven and Earth: Lindbergh: Technology and Environmentalism		40. Becoming Us
			41. Ending the Slavery Blame-Game
	19. Evolution on Trial		42. The American Character
	20. Remember the Roaring '20s?		43. Global Warming: Who Loses—and Who Wins?
	21. 15 Minutes That Saved America		44. Boomer Century

ABOUT YOU

Name
_____

Date

Are you a teacher? ☐ A student? ☐
Your school's name
_____

Department
_____

Address   City   State   Zip
_____

School telephone #
_____

YOUR COMMENTS ARE IMPORTANT TO US!

Please fill in the following information:
For which course did you use this book?
_____

Did you use a text with this ANNUAL EDITION? ☐ yes ☐ no
What was the title of the text?
_____

What are your general reactions to the Annual Editions concept?
_____

Have you read any pertinent articles recently that you think should be included in the next edition? Explain.
_____

Are there any articles that you feel should be replaced in the next edition? Why?
_____

Are there any World Wide Websites that you feel should be included in the next edition? Please annotate.
_____

May we contact you for editorial input? ☐ yes ☐ no
May we quote your comments? ☐ yes ☐ no

NOTES

NOTES

NOTES

NOTES

NOTES

NOTES